SCOTLAND'S RELATIONS WITH ENGLAND:

A SURVEY TO 1707

SCOTLAND'S RELATIONS WITH ENGLAND:

A SURVEY TO 1707

WILLIAM FERGUSON
Reader in Scottish History, University of Edinburgh

JOHN DONALD PUBLISHERS LTD
EDINBURGH

ISBN 0 85976 022 7

Printed in Great Britain by Morrison & Gibb Ltd, London and Edinburgh

Preface

THIS book has had a complicated history and one that demonstrates, in a rather curious but by no means unprecedented way, the truth of the old Latin adage *habent fata sua libelli*. Initially I intended to cover Anglo-Scottish relations within the context of the United Kingdom—that is, from 1707 to the present day. It soon became evident, however, that a survey of post-union developments would be all but meaningless if robbed of the earlier perspectives, and, attempts to provide these in a brief introduction proving unsatisfactory, there was nothing for it but to abandon the project or else begin at the beginning and try to explain, rather than assume, the earlier history. I was drawn to the second choice because surprisingly little has been written on Anglo-Scottish relations before the eighteenth century, and the existing surveys are old and outmoded. G. W. T. Omond's *Early History of the Scottish Union Question* (1897) is a good sketch and R. S. Rait's *Outline of the Relations between England and Scotland, 500–1707* (1901), though fuller, is little more than that. Both are dated, and both suffer from an approach that is too narrowly political. I therefore chose, reluctantly, the second alternative and have tried to produce a survey up to 1707 that takes a wider view, including, however superficially, social, economic and cultural matters as well as political.

But the first three chapters are mere sketches, designed to emphasise the seminal importance of the Dark Ages and the Middle Ages. These chapters will have achieved my aim if they convey to the reader, however inadequately, the overriding importance of the legacy from the dim and distant past to the theme of Anglo-Scottish relations as a whole. It requires little imagination to see that legacy still at work, helping to condition the present debate on devolution or separatism. Quite simply, if England and Scotland had not become recognisable entities in these early periods then the present debate would be impossible, and whatever tensions racked the United Kingdom today would, inevitably, have to find other means of expression.

Another brief explanation is called for. The book deals in more detail with Scotland, and that for two reasons. First, in general accounts of British history it is the Scottish side of things that usually gets short shrift, and, since more people are familiar with English than with Scottish history, it seemed best to try and redress the balance. Second, relations with England were always of

v

paramount importance to Scotland, but only at intervals did the converse apply. (This, incidentally, is why any account of the relations between the two countries based solely on diplomatic exchanges is bound to be misleading). All in all, therefore, it seems to me that, in discussing the relationship between the two kingdoms and their peoples, greater emphasis on the Scottish side can be justified—up to 1707 at any rate. Thereafter other considerations apply. I hope later to publish a second volume covering the period from the Union of the Parliaments to the present day, and that will certainly, and again I feel justifiably, entail a rather different approach.

Thanks are due to colleagues who in various ways have helped me with this work. Particular thanks must go to Dr. I. B. Cowan of the Scottish History Department in the University of Glasgow who read and made valuable comments on chapters 1 to 9, and to my colleagues in the Scottish History Department in the University of Edinburgh, Dr. J. M. Bannerman and Mr. E. J. Cowan, who gave me the benefit of their expert knowledge with chapters 1 and 2. Veracity and tradition alike require that I should add that the defects are entirely my own.

WILLIAM FERGUSON.

Contents

1

The Making of Two Kingdoms

IN the long history of the relations between England and Scotland the most neglected, but by no means least important, factors are those that were operative long before the two kingdoms came into being or the two nations were formed. Some of these early conditioning factors have in fact had a permanent and continuing influence though long familiarity has tended to hide their significance. One such has been the physical environment, where change, though extensive in the long run, has been delimited by certain obvious facts. Strive as man may, however long and with whatever sophisticated tools he can devise, in this sphere he has to work within the possible. He may alter land-use and the face of the land: over a long period he may deforest, drain bogs, extend arable and latterly, where desired, re-afforestate; and all this demands an infinitude of labour spread over very many generations. But mountain remains mountain and plain remains plain; in historic times no new 'Munros' have appeared and none of the existing ones has disappeared. Thus, the island of Britain's geological history, which has produced two more or less well defined major zones, has been a factor of abiding importance.[1]

The Highland Zone, consisting of the older and harder rocks, is, as its name would suggest, chiefly mountainous and includes not only Scotland but also the North of England, Wales and south-west England—and did so, of course, long before these names existed. The other basic division, the Lowland Zone, composed of plain and gentle hills and having as its centre the chalk plateau of Salisbury Plain, covers the rest of England. From the beginning these two zones have dictated the pattern of human settlement and social evolution. From neolithic times the chalk downs radiating from Salisbury Plain proved more attractive to man, providing as they did an easier environment than the colder and less fertile Highland Zone. The Lowland Zone's relative fertility and the comparative wealth it ensured, coupled with geographical position, has made this zone throughout history more responsive to continental influences; whereas the Highland Zone, on the other hand, has been more open to influences from the northern and western seas. On this last, it is worth stressing that a mere thirteen miles of sea separates the Mull of Kintyre in south-west Scotland from Fair Head, County Antrim, in Northern Ireland. One of the keys to the history of Scotland is implicit in that bald statement of fact.

Apart from the fundamental importance of geological structure and of physical geography, account must also be taken of the subtler influence of 'geographical position'—in this instance the place accorded to the British Isles in the known world. Beyond the British seas the world of antiquity came to an end, and thus in ancient times the British Isles were outliers of cultures that had originated in the continent of Europe. (And here it is worth noting that Ireland because of its easy sea communications with Iberia enjoyed in some respects a more favourable geographical position than Britain, and as a consequence Ireland at times possessed a higher culture.) Britain's geographical position did not alter radically until the great age of discovery and exploration that began in the sixteenth century. Until then the history of Britain reflected varying stresses within the ancient ambience, most notably as a frontier province under the Romans and thereafter as part of the comity of medieval Europe oscillating between northern and latterly west European influences.[2]

But geographical considerations alone cannot explain history. The old academic saw that 'geography is about maps and history is about chaps' has a certain crude force. People and their social customs help to create environment, and in the long run nature itself, within the obvious limits already noted, is often considerably modified. Britain's accessibility has from earliest times led to the mingling of peoples with widely differing cultures, and these early peoples are of more than antiquarian interest. In brief, their coming together produced not a mere sum of constituent parts but new entities, a process that has been repeated time and again. Thus in early Britain various neolithic groups followed by successive waves of Celtic-speaking Iron Age peoples met and ultimately coalesced. Later incomers were thrown into the melting pot—notably Gaels from Ireland, Anglo-Saxons and Jutes from the Low German coast, Norsemen and Danes, Normans and Flemings, and in still later times more peaceful and less trumpeted, but none the less substantial and important groups, such as the Huguenots or the Jews. No racialist doctrine, sung in whatever siren strains, can survive the hard facts of the British experience. Whatever the criteria employed, Britain is a racialist's nightmare; its people are a mongrel-mixture, and in the nature of things must always have been so.

But nations are not based on anything as hypothetical as race or on attributes as flexible as speech. Many ethnic groups and many languages have in their time flourished in Britain only to disappear, absorbed into new groupings. None the less, they all helped to shape the problems, and in ways that often baffle explanation have left durable marks. Teleological determinism, however, should be avoided. In the end it was politics that fashioned separate nationalities, however unpalatable that fact may be to modern social scientific determinism. Today the curious delusion exists in some quarters that politics is a modern invention, unthinkable in the absence of Whigs and Tories or Conservatives and Socialists. It is a feeble notion, no sooner examined than refuted. The essential, though sparsely documented, truth is that 'power politics' played a leading role in the creation of the kingdoms of England and Scotland. Here, indeed, is yet another basic fact in the long history of Anglo-Scottish relations: out of the confused tribal struggles of the Dark Ages there emerged in Britain not one but two kingdoms which had to accommodate themselves within the one island, a small island by present day standards but large in medieval reckoning. And the effects of the emergence of two kingdoms are felt to this day, not only in terms of vague national characteristics but in the more palpable spheres of law, politics and administration.

How did it come about? At the time of the Roman conquest, from 43 A.D. onwards, there seems to have been no wide divergence of race or speech in Britain. Over the greater part of the island dialects of P-Celtic, or Brittonic, were spoken by a number of tribes who jostled, through war and alliances, to extend their sway. At this stage society was in the tribal phase and the concept of nationality had still to make its appearance. The Romans brought new forces to bear, and by the close of the Roman dominion in the early fifth century a very different state of affairs existed. The northern part of the island, known to the Romans as Caledonia (roughly the modern Scottish Highlands) was never conquered and only at best contained. But the Antonine Wall between Forth and Clyde proved an ineffective barrier against the Caledonians, and Hadrian's Wall between the Solway and the English Tyne was latterly the main, though increasingly insecure, frontier of the Roman province of Britain. Roman cultural influences, therefore, operated most strongly in the Lowland Zone of Britain, stopping short at the bounds of the Highland Zone. Thus the vexed question of Roman survivals, of minor import in Britain as a whole, scarcely arises in Scotland at all.

There was no sudden collapse of Roman power in Britain, but rather a gradual withering away. The internal weaknesses of the empire were evident long before 407 when Constantine took the legions over to Gaul in an effort to shore up its defences and at the same time extend his own sphere of influence. Pretenders, in fact, have a long history in Britain—from Clodius Albinus in 196 who tried to use Britain as a base in his vain effort to attain supreme power, to Carausius, who acted similarly in 288, and the Spaniard Magnus Maximus in 383.

The last named illustrates the involved history of late Roman Britain, for, as 'Macsen Wledig', he has his place in Welsh folk-lore. He figures, not improbably, in some of the early Welsh genealogies and, more revealingly still, in the medieval story 'The Dream of Macsen Wledig'.[3] For, paradoxical though it may seem, as a consequence of the decline of Roman strength and the exposure of the province to barbarian attacks, the culture of the Highland Zone through the influx of refugees became for a brief space markedly more Roman. Perhaps as early as the late fourth century, sub-kingdoms of British *foederati* were being supported by the Roman administration in North Wales and southern Scotland.[4] A curious consequence is that the earliest Welsh heroic verse relates to what is now southern Scotland. In it the sixth century poet Taliesin commemorated the deeds of his lord Urien of Rheged (roughly modern Galloway), while in the *Gododdin* (the ancient Votadini of Lothian) his contemporary Aneirin elegised a brave but unavailing attempt by the Britons of Caereidyn or Eidyn, most likely Edinburgh,[5] to retake from the Angles Catraeth, now Catterick in York-shire. The remarkable survival of the work of the early Welsh bards, it has been reasonably conjectured, is probably due to the fact that the old Celtic oral tradition had continued to flourish in North Britain unimpeded by Roman cultural influences.[6] However this may be, the chiefs, regarding themselves first as the allies and latterly as the heirs of Rome, aped Roman usages. And as many Romano-Britons were pushed into the Highland Zone by the Germanic invaders Romano-British culture for a brief spell maintained a feeble existence.

In a broader view events in Britain bore some analogy to what was happening elsewhere in the wreck of the western empire, but they led to different outcomes. On the continent the barbarians were making inroads, at first destroying but later trying to adapt Roman institutions to their own use. Britain differs from the continent in that Romano-British culture was not strong enough to survive the shock. This added to the complexity of the situation, and in the British archipelago change was more lengthy and tortuous than historians of the romantic nineteenth century Germanist school could possibly envisage.

Little is really known of North Britain in the fifth and early sixth centuries, and not until the second half of the sixth century does a clearer picture begin to come into focus. Two British kingdoms then existed in south-west Scotland —Strathclyde, with its capital at Dumbarton, and Rheged covering Galloway and Cumberland, both speaking Cumbric, a P-Celtic congener of Old Welsh.[7] These two British kingdoms were often at feud, however, and largely because of this in the early seventh century they were being hard-pressed by the Angles of Northumbria, Germanic invaders closely related to the Saxons but speaking a different dialect of Anglo-Saxon. Barred from expanding southwards by the Mercians, the Angles were forced to look to the north and west, and at its greatest extent the Anglian kingdom of Bernicia covered south-eastern Scotland as far as the Firth of Forth. Attempts by the Angles to expand beyond the Forth ended in defeat by the Picts at Nechtansmere in 685, and in the next two centuries Anglian power slowly declined as, torn by internal dissensions, Northumbria was latterly shaken by Scandinavian assaults.

The decline of Northumbria is a matter of the very first importance, for it put an end to the possibility that the entire island of Britain might have been consolidated as an English kingdom. Nevertheless the Angles have left a prominent mark on later Scotland. They lived on in Lothian and in the eighth century were entrenched on the Solway, penetrating as far north as Ayrshire. The Viking onslaught, however, enabled the Strathclyde Britons to recover ground lost in this quarter, though even so an appreciable Anglian element remained in parts of the south-west.[8] All in all, the Angles probably settled north of Tweed in greater numbers than some authorities nowadays would allow. In the past Scottish history was looked at very much through Lowland eyes, and as a result the numbers and influence of the Angles tended to be exaggerated. Recently more interest has been shown in the Celtic components of early Scotland, and the tendency is now to sweep the Angles aside as little more than minor irritants. The truth would seem to be that, though forming only a small part of the stock from which the Scottish nation was to evolve, the Angles made substantial contributions to it. The chief effect of these was that in time a development of their tongue was to be spoken throughout

Lowland Scotland, from the Solway to the North East plain, and that later again this facilitated the spread of modern English throughout Scotland. There can be no avoiding the conclusion that the presence of the Angles, and their detribalised descendants, as a native constituent element of the Scottish nation that later came into existence was of crucial importance to that nation's subsequent history. Many similarities can be pointed out between Ireland and Scotland; but here from earliest times we find a crucial difference. The English language, in short, is just as native to Scotland as is Gaelic.

North of Tay the struggle for supremacy was waged mainly between the Picts and the Scots, the latter Gaelic-speaking incomers from Ireland. The Picts have for centuries excited and defied the curiosity of scholars. In a humorous passage in one of his novels Sir Walter Scott all too faithfully summarised what was for long the state of knowledge on this subject.

' "There was once a people called the Piks—"
"More properly Picts," interrupted the baronet.
"I say the Pikar, Pihar, Piochtar, Pioghter, or
Peughtar", vociferated Oldbuck: "they spoke a Gothic dialect—".
"Genuine Celtic", asseverated the knight.
"Gothic! Gothic! I'll go to death upon it!" counterasseverated
the squire.'[9]

And so the controversy raged on, hopeless of conclusion. But where the champions invoked by Scott's obstinate disputants, the learned eighteenth century pundits John Pinkerton and George Chalmers, failed to pierce the darkness, modern scholarship has cast some light. The Picts are now held to have been a confederation of older Brittonic stocks (earlier lumped together as Caledonians by the Roman historians) who spoke a brand of P-Celtic that seems to have been more akin to Gaulish than to Welsh.[10] They also seem to have absorbed an earlier non-aryan people whose language they retained for inscriptional purposes. But since little or nothing of either language has survived nothing is known of events as seen through Pictish eyes; as a consequence, the Picts got a bad press and have long been saddled with a hob-goblin image. Yet far from being degenerate and uncultured savages the Picts were an artistic, virile and formidable people who in the eighth century looked as if they would emerge triumphant from the struggle for supremacy in North Britain. Had they done so, little would have been heard of the Scots and still less of Scotland —except insofar as these terms related to Ireland. But what a Pictish North Britain might have become there is no way of telling, for even the name that the Picts applied to themselves is unknown.

As it was, the decision was close. In 737 the Pictish King Angus MacFergus (an Anglicised rendering of a Gaelicised version of his name) defeated the Scots and reduced the Britons; and when he died in 761 Angus was virtual master of Dalriada (the original kingdom of the Scots) and of Strathclyde.

The Picts may have been cheated of their prize by the sudden onslaught of the Vikings in the early ninth century. The undermining of their position by

Scandinavian attacks may have enabled Kenneth MacAlpin, king of the Scots, successfully to assert a claim to the throne of Pictavia, though the peculiar Pictish custom of reckoning descent through the mother may have justified Kenneth's claim. The details have perished, and all that is certainly known is that about the middle of the ninth century (844–850) Kenneth MacAlpin managed to unite the two kingdoms. There has never, however, been any doubt about the significance of this achievement, which was the decisive factor in the making of Scotland. The Scandinavians continued to disrupt and harass but did not succeed in building a compact durable state; their chief effect was to weaken the Britons and Angles who, most exposed to their assaults, did not have strong inland redoubts to enable them to make effective resistance. By the eleventh century mastery of the north clearly lay with the Scoto-Pictish monarchy of Alba, for though the Scandinavians still held wide possessions these were scattered round the northern and western coasts from Shetland to Man.

By the eleventh century the linguistic map of North Britain had changed radically, and indeed was long to continue in a state of flux. Gaelic, a Q-Celtic language introduced by the Scots, a small tribe of incomers from Northern Ireland in the late fifth century, is held to be an earlier form of Celtic than Brittonic. And, contrary to modern preconceptions, in the Dark Ages Gaelic was a thrusting aggressive language which in time displaced the P-Celtic tongues in Scotland. After the union of the kingdoms of the Scots and Picts in the mid-ninth century the Pictish language rapidly went down before Gaelic—a process that had probably begun even before the union. The Brittonic of Strathclyde also seems to have been declining by the eleventh century, and certainly by that time Gaelic was spoken in Galloway and English in other parts of the south-west. By the eleventh century the three main languages spoken in Scotland were Gaelic, Norse and English; Cumbric, a cognate of Welsh, was in decline and restricted to dwindling parts of Strathclyde. Of these different tongues Gaelic, the most widely spoken, was solidly entrenched north of the River Tay (the ancient Alba, also by then known as Scotia, that was to become the traditional Highlands of Scotland) and in the west. Norse was spoken in the Northern Isles and parts of the far north, such as Caithness, and in the Hebrides where it co-existed with Gaelic. English was based mainly on Lothian but was shortly to enter an expansive phase largely because it became the language of commerce and hence of the burghs.

The ease with which these linguistic changes occurred was due to several causes. The peoples struggling for supremacy or survival in Dark Age North Britain were all roughly at a similar stage of development. All were organised along tribal lines and shared similar attitudes and characteristics, an indication of which appears in their passion for genealogy, which was not, as some imagine, a peculiarly Celtic fixation. The leading Anglo-Saxon dynasties, for example, also had elaborate genealogies: here, the Mercian dynasty was of unique eminence, spanning 'the gulf between the English peoples of historic times and their continental ancestors';[11] and the West Saxons claimed a lineage from Cerdic (possibly a Welsh name) that was only slightly less imposing.[12] Indeed, as the name Cerdic would suggest, intermarriage was far from uncommon and, as in the case of the Picts and Scots, could play an important historical role. The Angles of Bernicia, too, did not so much displace the Britons as impose their rule and eventually their language on them, and the English kingdom of Northumbria as a whole retained many Celtic features in its law and administration.[13]

The advent of Christianity was another powerful unifying force, particularly in Scotland where it was introduced largely through the agency of the so-called Celtic or Columban Church. The work of the Irish Columba, who settled on the island of Iona in 563 and subsequently founded a monastery there, has in the past been misinterpreted or exaggerated. Protestant historians of an earlier apologetical school regarded the Celtic Church as 'protestant', and indeed some even saw it as proto-presbyterian. Roman catholic and episcopalian writers riposted by discounting Columba's labours and awarding the palm to Ninian, whose episcopal orders were not in doubt and who in any event was earlier than Columba, having possibly founded, circa 400 A.D., a church at Whithorn in Galloway. Truer perspectives remove these misconceptions without diminishing the importance of either Ninian or Columba.[14] Ninian seems to have been part of the process whereby the Romano-British Church penetrated into North Britain, only for it to falter with the collapse of Roman imperium, leaving the way open for other missionaries. Columba was one of those, perhaps the most important, through whose labours Scots, Picts and Angles were Christianised.

The so-called 'Celtic Church' was in some respects idiosyncratic. It is hard to describe or to define accurately and has, accordingly, had many labels attached to it. In its widest application the term 'Celtic Church' is quite a good one, in that early ecclesiastical organisation in Ireland, Scotland and Wales showed strong similarities. But in the present context the church to which Columba belonged, and which is sometimes called after him, is perhaps best referred to as the *Scottish* Church, bearing in mind that Scottish then meant Irish. This is no semantic quibble but a fact of the first importance, for the Columbans were to play a remarkable part in making possible the emergence of a Scottish nation as opposed to an Irish tribe transplanted to North Britain. In the context of North Britain the early importance of this church was that it furnished the Scots of Dalriada with a powerful political and cultural weapon which helped to undermine and latterly destroy the native culture of the Picts. In all probability it was the advent of Irish Christianity that forced the Picts into the cultural sphere of the Scots of Dalriada, with all the momentous consequences that flowed therefrom.

The evolution of the church in Ireland, however, was complex, and reproduced in Scotland what were later to be regarded as deviations from the accepted norm of Latin Christendom. Diocesan episcopacy of the kind evolving on the continent (and particularly in Italy where the idea of a strong central government survived the fall of the Western Empire) did not fit well into the tribal societies of the Celtic west. Instead, in Ireland tribal bishops were adopted, only to be overshadowed from the late sixth century onwards by the rise of monasticism. But Irish monasticism also had its peculiar features. It did not attempt to withdraw from the world, as did Benedictine monasticism, but was from the beginning deeply imbedded in society, and all this in spite of the anchoritism so frequently displayed by individual monks. Irish monasticism strongly reflected the realities of Irish society, the most outstanding of which was stress on kinship. Thus monasteries were founded and presided over by abbots who, like Columba, were presbyters and not bishops; and such monasteries came to be regarded as family property, over which the old tribal bishops, who continued to be recognised, had no administrative authority. The early Irish Church came to appear ill organised and chaotic; but it worked. Indeed, it made possible the great missionary ventures undertaken by the Irish not just in the British Isles but on the continent as well. This was the loose-jointed but workable system that was introduced into Scotland by Columba and his followers; and in Scotland the church long continued on the Irish model.[15]

Formerly it was the fashion to describe this church as isolated from the mainstream of European developments and backward-looking. This is pure inversion of fact. Throughout the seventh century Irishmen (then referred to as Scots) were in close touch with the continent, and indeed Irishmen founded some of the most famous of continental religious houses. The Christian culture of Ireland was honoured throughout Latin Christendom, and its creed was, and remained, orthodox. The real trouble arose over ritual. The Celtic or Scottish Church clung to its traditional customs at a time when most parts of Western Christendom were undergoing rapid change, and in particular it retained an old mode of reckoning the date of Easter. Problems of another kind were posed by the emergence of larger and more complicated political units which challenged a church saturated in the values of a tribal society. On these grounds conflict was likely; it followed hard on the introduction of Christianity to the heathen English, a work that was undertaken by the Scottish Church in the north and by the Roman in the south.

The clash came to a head in Northumbria. The synod of Whitby was summoned by King Oswiu in 663 or 664 to resolve the problem of the dating of Easter, which was, of course, of vital importance to devout Christians. The synod decided in favour of the Romans, but the results of this decision can all too easily be misinterpreted. It was, in a sense, a great turning point, as a consequence of which the Romans triumphed throughout England. As a result of Whitby the cultural influence of the Scots over Northumbria rapidly waned, but no overnight transformations followed in Scotland, even though, in time, the Celtic Churches fell into line. The Picts accepted Whitby in 711, the Scots of Dalriada in 716, the British Church in Strathclyde in 768, and at various later dates so did the church in Ireland. These were important developments, but it is even more important to realise that such acceptance did not imply uniformity of polity. It cannot be sufficiently stressed that really effective organisation along Roman lines was not achieved in Scotland as a whole until half a millennium after the Synod of Whitby. And to stretch cause and effect over five centuries is hardly a credible exercise.

After 664, and after 716, the church in Scotland continued in its old way, and in the context of the Europe of that time this was not surprising. Not, for example, until the end of the eleventh century was the church in Spain forced to abandon its old Gothic ritual, and only gradually thereafter was it reduced to the obedience of Rome. The Scottish church, therefore, however peculiar it may have appeared to English eyes, was far from unique in its strong sense of regional individualism. Like its counterpart in Ireland it fitted well into existing society, and it exercised an active and beneficial, if poorly documented, ministry.

Moulded by these political, linguistic and ecclesiastical developments, by the end of the tenth century the kingdom of Scotland (in the precise sense, the old Scoto-Pictish monarchy north of Tay) was well established and indeed expanding. Strathclyde retained a fitful independence until it was finally absorbed in 1034. The tenacity and durability of this remarkable fossil is one of the most mysterious and intriguing features of Dark Age history. The Strathclyde Britons resembled the Finns of modern times, constantly threatened by more powerful neighbours, often occupied, but in the end successfully parrying the threat by brilliantly opportunist diplomacy and shrewd alliances of convenience. Their flank was turned at last when in 945 Edmund of England leased all 'Cumbraland' to Malcolm I of Alba;[16] and in 1018 on the death of Owen, the last native king of the Strathclyde Britons, Malcolm II of Alba was able to set his grandson Duncan on the throne of Strathclyde. On Duncan's succession as king of Scots in 1034 he brought in Strathclyde; and by the mid-twelfth century Strathclyde and Cumbria were little more than memories.[17] In the south-east as well expansion was the keynote. A victory over the Northumbrians at Carham in 1018 confirmed the grip of the Scots on Lothian, which had already been ceded to them in 971 by Edgar of England, and this predominantly English-speaking area received an appreciable Gaelic-speaking element.

By the mid-eleventh century, therefore, the kingdom of Scotland, in the modern sense of the term, was emerging as one of the main products of the struggle for supremacy in Dark Age Britain. The Norse threat had been contained, though in many areas Norse power had still to be reduced; and the major problem confronting Scotland was that of its relationship with the larger, richer, and more powerful kingdom of England that had been formed by processes similar to those that had created Scotland.

The history of Dark Age England is, relatively speaking, much better documented than that of Scotland. Thanks mainly to the *Anglo-Saxon Chronicle* (or *Chronicles*) and Bede's great *Ecclesiastical History*, the main outlines of Anglo-Saxon England are widely known; so details of the evolution of a united kingdom need not be recited here.[18] The issue again turned on a struggle for supremacy. In the seventh century Northumbria made a bold bid for the mastery until checked by the Picts and the rising power of the Mercians. For nearly two centuries thereafter the main contest lay between Mercia and Wessex with at first the odds apparently favouring the Midlanders. But the death of the great King Offa in 796 marked the zenith of Mercian power; and under Egbert Wessex, aided by a good geographical position and for its time a remarkably effective system of administration, began to outstrip its rivals. The shock of the Danish onslaught in the ninth century weakened Wessex's main rivals (Northumbria, Mercia and East Anglia), and the strongest resistance to the Danes came from Wessex under Alfred. It was the West Saxon dynasty that successfully undertook the long and difficult task of recovering the lost English territories; and Alfred's grandson, Athelstan, had by 927 every right to style himself king of England even though a Scandinavian element remained to be absorbed right up until the Norman Conquest. In spite of the reign of the Danish King Cnut (1016–1035) Anglo-Saxon England had too marked an individuality to become a permanent part of a somewhat loose-knit Scandinavian empire. The old West Saxon line was restored in the person of Edward the Confessor, by the end of whose reign the Scandinavian element had become relatively insignificant.

All in all, the conclusion is plain: broadly similar though the long process of English unification was to the making of Scotland, there is a clear and significant contrast—the people of the kingdom of England were much more homogeneous in language and in customs than were those of early Scotland.

The problem of the relationship between the two kingdoms then began to crystallise. With the consolidation of England, and the confining of the Cymri to Wales, one of the chief recurrent problems of the later kings of Anglo-Saxon England, including the great Cnut, though hardly at that stage a critical one, was that of the frontier with Scotland. At this time, and for long enough thereafter, it is best to think in terms of a frontier zone with no definite border. The real problem, indeed, is that no natural borders divide Britain, and in the north there were in fact several possible frontier zones. The line of the Antonine Wall on the wasp-waist of Scotland between the Firths of Clyde and Forth suggested one, and that of Hadrian's Wall from the Solway to the English Tyne another. The eventual frontier was the outcome of yet another lengthy struggle. Cumbria, for long a no-man's land, was latterly in the possession of the Scots, while Northumberland was also an object of Scottish ambition; and England never lost sight of the fact that Lothian had once been part of an English-speaking kingdom. During MacBeth's reign (1040–57) the Scottish grip on Cumbria south of Solway weakened, and it grew steadily more insecure in spite of strenuous efforts at recovery by Malcolm III (1058–93).

The frontier, in fact, long remained shifting and undefined. The building of Newcastle by William the Conqueror in 1080 seems to suggest that he favoured the line of Hadrian's Wall; but the recovery of Carlisle was left to William Rufus, and even after that was accomplished in 1092 nothing like a proper march was established. Not until the erection of Norham Castle by Henry I in 1121 and the fortification of Carlisle in the following year did it seem likely that the frontier zone might turn on the Solway–Tweed line. Significantly, a charter of the Scots King David I of c. 1124 granting the lands of Annandale to Robert Bruce posited a boundary at the Solway, and this line was confirmed in 1157. What came to be regarded as the historic frontier, then, only began to take shape in the twelfth century; and for long thereafter it remained fluid, a frontier zone rather than a march, with strenuous efforts being made to shift it north-wards by the English and southwards by the Scots.

The frontier, however, was not the only problem in the relations between the two kingdoms; an equally vexed question concerned the status of Scotland *vis a vis* England. In the tenth century the growing power of England was allegedly acknowledged in acts of submission by Scots and Welsh kings. In 926, for example, Constantine king of Scots submitted to Athelstan; in 945 Edmund of England granted Cumbria to Malcolm I 'on condition that he be his helper both on sea and land'; and in 971 Lothian was ceded to the king of Scots after he paid 'homage' to Edgar.[19] The exact meaning of these acknowledgments was later to be the subject of keen debate. Were they acts of feudal dependence or not? If so, then it could be argued that Scotland was a fief of England; but in fact these incidents, even if authentic, reveal little about the relationship between the two kingdoms. Indeed, the most significant thing about them is that they are only recorded in English sources, the most explicit of which are post-Conquest and apt to present them as acts of feudal subjection.

The problem of the relationship between the two kingdoms must obviously have been affected by their social systems and institutional structures. But here difficulty is piled upon difficulty. Even in the much better documented case of England there are gaps in the evidence, and at the moment pre-conquest conditions are matters of controversy.[20] It is clear, though, that, as among the Germanic peoples generally, folk-right played an important part in the early history of the Anglo-Saxons and that much of their customary law was never reduced to writing. The later written codes were compiled to meet novel situations—as, for example, the acceptance of Christianity and the need to give the church a standing at law, or to accommodate the changes implicit in the rise of lordship. Still, the early dooms or codes reveal much, in particular that kinship was all-pervading and the kinless man an anomaly. But society was not, as some seem to believe, petrified in a hypothetical 'heroic age', and from Alfred's time the rights and responsibilities of the kin were being territorialised—i.e. transferred to territorial units of administration such as shires and hundreds. The rise of lordship, too, meant that in late Anglo-Saxon England the lordless man had become the anomaly. In spite of these developments, however, the entire legacy of folk-law was not obliterated, and it has been claimed for the Anglo-Saxons that they fashioned the characteristic institutions of medieval England.

But whether late Anglo-Saxon England was evolving feudal tenure is keenly debated. The great legal historian, F. W. Maitland, saw some grounds for favouring such a view, but until recently it has found few supporters. The prevailing opinion came to be that, 'The device of the fee the Saxons had not, nor up to the date of the Norman Conquest is there any sign that they were on the way to acquiring it'.[21] On the other hand it has recently been argued that a new form of tenure, loan-land, could constitute a fief; but for this the evidence is slight, the arguments sometimes strained and the conclusions somewhat forced.[22] The latest writer on the subject, R. A. Brown, judiciously concludes that the hall-marks of feudalism (the knight, the fief and the castle) were all absent from Anglo-Saxon England and that they were introduced at the Norman Conquest.[23] But there is much to be said for the general proposition that many features of Anglo-Saxon England (such as the development of something like manorialism) resembled continental conditions and that this resemblance increased in the reign of Edward the Confessor when Frenchmen were given high positions in England. The Confessor's reign, in fact, in some ways resembled the later peaceful Norman penetration of Scotland, and as a result the Conquest was not quite the violent break with the Anglo-Saxon past it has traditionally been represented to be.

Nowhere was this continuity more apparent than in the concept of kingship. The early English concept of kingship was tribal, the king being chosen from a restricted blood-group, the *cynecynn*, which was analogous to the Gaelic *derbfine*. With the advent of Christianity arose the idea of kingship by divine appointment, strikingly instanced by Alfred the Great's revision of the West Saxon genealogy in which Woden lost the status of a god and piously, if improbably, the line of Cerdic was pushed back to Adam. By the early eleventh century, too, it was being asserted that 'A Christian king is Christ's deputy among Christian people', and that none durst lift his hand against the Lord's anointed.[24] Under these influences it looked for a time as if primogeniture might prevail; but it was certainly not followed as an inviolable rule though from Alfred's death the kings of the English (Cnut and his sons excepted) were drawn exclusively from Alfred's descendants. The early Norman kings followed the same lax customs.

Changing social values were also reflected in Old English writings, which constitute one of the earliest and richest of West European national literatures. In Germany the old heroic tradition collapsed, but in England it survived side by side with a growing Latin Christian culture. 'Beowulf', the oldest extant poem in any Teutonic tongue, probably dates from the eighth century, though parts of the surviving fragment may be older. In all likelihood oral tradition long carried on a considerable body of heroic poetry of this kind that has since been lost; and at the same time England became famous for its Latin studies. That so much, relatively speaking, is known of Anglo-Saxon England is due to the survival of some of its literature, notably, the *Anglo-Saxon Chronicle* and Bede's great *Ecclesiastical History*. The historic significance of such a culture has been subtly diagnosed: 'There is a double way of escape for young nations from their outgrown fables and mythologies. They start with enormous, monstrous, and inhuman beliefs and stories. Either they may work their way out of them, by gradual rejection of the grosser ingredients, to something more or less positive and rational; or else they may take up the myths and transmute them into poetry'.[25] It was the truly remarkable achievement of the Old English to do both; and the importance of their cultural achievement is that, in spite of the Norman Conquest, it contributed to a continuous tradition.

The lack of comparable sources accounts for much of the obscurity of early Scottish history, for the evidence that has come down from the time before the reign of David I (1124–53) is fragmentary and hard to synthesise. 'Celtic Scotland' is little more than a vague short-hand expression, which may none the less denote essential if hazily understood realities. For one thing, though the peoples of Scotland were of mixed origins, by the eleventh century Gaelic was the most widely spoken language in the country, as the place-name evidence demonstrates.[26] Under the dynasty of Kenneth, whose lineage stretched back to Fergus Mor who had led the Scots from Ireland, it was the customs, legends and traditions as well as the language of the Gaels that held the early kingdom together and so contributed powerfully to the making of a nation. Nor can the cultural achievement of the Gaels be ignored, for they too produced an early vernacular literature of remarkable power and versatility.[27] It has to be noted, however, that it derived mainly from Ireland and that the Scottish contribution seems to have been slight.

The great problem in the study of early Scottish history is that of continuity. It is curious, for example, that by the eleventh century the term *Scotia*, which previously had denoted Ireland, was being applied to Scotland; but of the social and political organisation of this kingdom of diverse origins little is known for sure. Much that once passed for knowledge is now recognised to be based on myth, fragile place-name evidence, or else over-bold analogy with early Celtic Ireland. Thus, to speak of Celtic law with reference to Scotland is to beg innumerable questions since no codes of Scottish provenance similar to the Anglo-Saxon dooms have survived. The details of early law in Scotland are therefore unknown, though it has been stated that some 'fragments of Celtic law survived, sufficient to indicate that there was in operation in Scotland a Gaelic system of law up to the reign of Malcolm Canmore'.[28] The Brehon law of Ireland must indeed have had some application in early medieval Scotland, for the judex or deemster survived the transition to feudalism.[29] But the evidence, legal and other, is too scanty to yield a convincing detailed account of society and government in Celtic Scotland. An elaborate attempt to provide such an account was made by the nineteenth century scholar W. F. Skene, but it was patchy at best and is now ripe for supersession.[30]

Scotland seems to have been divided into provinces which apparently corresponded to the Anglo-Saxon earldoms, and shires and thanes were introduced in some parts, though exactly when and denoting precisely what has yet to be determined.[31] But hazy and beset with difficulties though the matter is, a strong general impression is conveyed that Celtic Scotland and Anglo-Saxon England do not seem to have been so very differently ordered. The chief points of difference were of stages of development. As an instance of this, kindred in Scotland continued to be stressed while its importance was clearly diminishing in England. Thus the *notitiae* in the twelfth century *Book of Deer* contain some suggestive references to clans, but again the meagreness of the evidence prevents a clear picture from emerging. Then, too, though the late Anglo-Saxon monarchy had obvious enough weaknesses it possessed strengths that were denied to monarchy in contemporary Scotland. There particularism, due to some extent to the difficult geography of the country, was more marked, and some parts, notably Galloway and Lothian, long retained their customary laws. In 1305 Edward I decided to supersede the laws of the Bretts (i.e. Britons) and Scots; but, in fact, long before Edward's sledge-hammer blows law and administration in Scotland were being remoulded on English and Anglo-Norman models. It is also important to remember that Norse influence was still strong not only in the Northern Isles but also in the Hebrides and on the West Coast; and, indeed, of the surviving literature of the early period the Norse sagas reveal as much as any other source. Gaelic Scotland's historiography seems to have relied on oral tradition, much of which became garbled; but this may well be a false impression arising from loss of records. In sum, the best approach to the history of early Scotland is that of the sympathetic agnostic—willing to believe but inhibited by lack of proof.

Dimly as we discern the outlines of Celtic Scotland, already in the eleventh century it is clear that forces were at work which were in time to revolutionise it. One point epitomises the great changes that took place: whereas in the early Middle Ages the term Scots with reference to language meant Gaelic, by the close of the Middle Ages it meant a dialect of English. The main causes of this fundamental transition are known—and yet in many respects the whole process remains mysterious and uncharted.[32] The growing influence of England was clearly a factor of considerable weight but that alone cannot provide a sufficient explanation. It may well be that the most important causes of this transformation are to be found within Scotland itself, and to a large degree in changing views on the succession to the kingship.

Under the old system of succession any male descendant of a king down to the fourth generation might succeed, and, since the aim was to prevent minorities and so ensure firm government, this led to the selection of collaterals rather than direct descendants. The better to achieve this aim of strong government, tanistry, or the nomination of a successor in the life-time of a king, was also practised. 'Derbfine succession' and tanistry, however, tended to promote blood-feuds and brought to violent ends many scions of the stock of Kenneth; but in spite of such obvious drawbacks, the old rules were hallowed by custom and defended by interested parties intent on preserving their prospects. The matter goes deeper, for the derbfine system may not have been confined to kingship but probably governed general rights in property. Thus any break with the system of succession to the crown could be seen as an attack on the existing social structure and bitterly resisted as such.

It is not easy, however, to date the beginnings of the tensions that gradually arose over this question. Malcolm II, possibly in an attempt to restrict the succession to his own direct line, may have twisted the rules in favour of his grandson Duncan. The whole matter is doubtful, for it seems to have been a hard case. The succession had broken down and only descent through a female, Malcolm's daughter, who had married Crinan abbot of Dunkeld, could initiate a new royal derbfine, which is usually referred to as the House of Atholl. The right of Crinan's son did not go unchallenged; MacBeth, mormaer of Moray, believed that his own claim, also derived from a female, was at least as good as that of Duncan, whom he killed and replaced in 1040. Sadly, all the poetry in the world cannot redeem bad history. Shakespeare's MacBeth, through no fault of the bard's, is a travesty of historical truth, for the real life MacBeth (1040–57) was acceptable to most of his subjects and appears to have ruled vigorously and well. His death in battle against Malcolm, son of Duncan, was yet one more illustration of the grisly aspects of the old rules of succession. These had worked well enough in the tribal phase, but in a larger and more complex society they simply fomented disorders. The most significant feature of the overthrow of MacBeth, however, was that it owed much to English intervention.

Malcolm III, known as Canmore, and his successors of the House of Atholl continued to interpret the rules to suit themselves and in so doing provoked an understandable opposition which historians (those slavish worshippers of success) have persisted in dismissing as 'typical Celtic anarchy'. In point of fact, the pretenders who troubled the reigns of Malcolm III and his successors were not mere brawling ruffians, as the historians of the dominant nineteenth century Germanist school, such as Hill Burton,[33] liked to imply. They were mostly members of the rival House of Moray, claiming descent from MacBeth's stepson Lulach, who were determined to preserve their customary rights and were rendered desperate by the knowledge that after three generations their claims must lapse.

These dynastic squabbles helped on the first deviation from the Celtic past. And to that same end Malcolm's second marriage to Margaret, sister of Edgar Atheling, may also have contributed. Other forces were at the same time encouraging the introduction of new ways, and perhaps the most notable of these was a shift in the centre of gravity of the kingdom away from its ancient heartland Alba towards the south. This move could be doubly justified in terms of foreign relations: firstly, as a necessary safeguard against English encroachment; and secondly, as an indispensable pre-condition for the expansion of Scotland. At the same time it is noticeable that whilst Canmore and his descendants were often at odds with the kings of England they freely availed themselves of English aid to strengthen their position in Scotland. The importance of English influence appeared in the upheavals that followed Malcolm III's death in 1093, when the traditionalists seized their opportunity and accepted as king Malcolm's anglophobe brother Donald Bane, who promptly drove out the English favourites.

Then followed yet another example of the dangers of derbfine succession. In 1094 Malcolm's son by his first marriage, Duncan, with the help of some Anglo-Normans overthrew Donald Bane; but Donald recovered and killed Duncan, whose progeny, however, later furnished a fresh crop of pretenders to trouble the descendants of Malcolm and Margaret. The latter triumphed in 1097 when Donald was finally overthrown by Edgar, the fourth son of Malcolm and Margaret, who had managed to enlist the aid of William Rufus. Rufus exacted the full price for his help, and, though Edgar's seal bore the grandiloquent title 'Basileus Scotorum', King Edgar was forced to hold Scotland as a fief from the king of England.[34] By an odd coincidence both Edgar and his successor, his next brother Alexander I, died childless and Alexander was succeeded by his younger brother David. This curious succession created a rather puzzling situation, for the break with established custom was not absolutely clear and the old rules could be said to have been applied. But for all that, it seems likely that the rule of primogeniture was supplanting derbfine succession. The first incontrovertible instance of primogeniture, however, was the succession of David I's grandson (who was a minor at that!) as Malcolm IV in 1153. In passing it is worth repeating that the English rule of succession was also loose and not unlike the traditional Scottish system; but the transition to the feudal principle of strict primogeniture took longer to accomplish in England and was not fully established until after the accession of Edward I in 1272. Indeed it was settled by an ordinance of Edward I in April 1290, most providentially on the eve of the Great Cause of Scotland.

To sum up the stage reached by the close of the Dark Ages and the early

Middle Ages: by the end of the eleventh century the two kingdoms of England and Scotland had been firmly established; each was the product of the Dark Ages, retaining, though in different degrees, elements of tribalism; and each was about to undergo gradual metamorphosis brought about by the introduction of new concepts of government.

2

The Feudal Kingdoms: Attraction and Repulsion

THROUGHOUT the twelfth and thirteenth centuries it looked as if the two kingdoms of England and Scotland were coming to have certain important features in common. Much of Lowland Scotland became increasingly anglicised; feudalisation created many similarities; the first attempts at constructing a uniform system of law, the king's law, drew heavily on Anglo-Norman practice; and the two national churches ceased to diverge so noticeably in structure. In the broad sense, all this is undoubtedly so. Yet it can be misleadingly interpreted, for much of Scotland long remained relatively unaffected by the new ways and there is nothing to warrant the conclusion that the two kingdoms were insensibly drawing together and that an organic unity of the whole of Britain was likely to ensue.

Tensions within Scotland itself, rather than the much exaggerated influence of Margaret, contributed to the anglicisation of southern Scotland. Initially, the spread of the English language sprang from developments within Scotland; it was not imposed by pressure from without. The crucial points to remember are that the English language already had a substantial base in Scotland from which to expand and that the pressure from England was secondary. With the centre of government coming to be fixed on the region of the Forth, at first at Dunfermline and only latterly at Edinburgh, and with the growth of commerce on the east coast and the rise of sea-ports, it was not in the least strange that south of Forth, with the exception of Galloway, the English tongue should gradually have ousted the Gaelic. The efficient cause of this cultural revolution was probably the determination of the line of Canmore to engross the succession to the crown. Their claim was not, as has been suggested, a defective one;[1] to make it good, however, they had to trample on the claims of others. But to advance such an explanation is in no way to minimise the extent or the importance of the changes ushered in by the line of Canmore. Their policy of 'innovation at the behest of the crown', whatever the precise motives underlying it, undoubtedly led not only to a transition from tribal kingship to feudal kingship but also created a state, however rudimentary, in place of a loose unity of semi-autonomous regions.[2]

Feudalisation became one of the means whereby the Canmore dynasty strengthened its hold on Scotland; but the introduction of feudalism was not so much a deliberate and consistent policy as a gradual and somewhat haphazard process. Just possibly the trend may have begun in the reigns of Edgar and Alexander I, but for this the evidence is meagre and the conclusions that can be drawn from it vague. If David I did not initiate the policy, under him it certainly gathered momentum. In the reigns of David and his successor, Malcolm IV, prominent features were 'the penetration of Anglo-French barons and knights into Scotland, the spread of the monastic order and the growth of royal government'.[3] Whatever the precise motivation underlying them these prominent features were to become crucial developments. Initially perhaps for personal reasons rather than as state policy, David I brought into Scotland many Anglo-French, who were mainly of Norman origin, from his lands in Northampton-shire. These lands formed part of the great Honour of Huntingdon which David acquired through marriage and which was to bring the kings of Scots into a direct and at times vexatious relationship with the kings of England. The incoming of the Normans, however, was spread over the better part of a century, lasting to 1219, and long before this process ended Scotland was being transformed. By the time of Malcolm IV (1153–65) most of the country south of Forth, Galloway again excepted, was feudalised, and a beginning had been made in the setting up of great feudal lordships in the Highlands and the north.[4]

But here a salutary note of caution has been sounded by the latest writer on the subject, who judiciously sums up: 'In the making of feudal Scotland much was achieved by David I, but it is important to realise that his achievements were made without wholesale expropriation of native landowners, without intensive settlement by Anglo-French landholders throughout the whole kingdom, and without significant diminution of the resources of the king'.[5] Every qualification in that well-considered judgment carries weight.

In both England and Scotland, in fact, feudal concepts were adapted to meet the native situation; there was no blind acceptance of some standard feudal pattern. Indeed, no such archetypal feudal pattern existed; and so in each kingdom the 'feudal system', to use much later terminology, evolved gradually, at its own pace, and not altogether out of harmony with native custom. But it is important to recognise that in the early stages of English and Scottish feudalism their similarities outweighed their differences. It thus happened that a man could hold a fief in England and a fief in Scotland without serious problems arising. In the end, however, the two systems diverged in some important respects, and their divergences were to give rise to fundamental legal and social differences between the two realms.

But, to return to the matter in hand, what did feudalisation entail? New forms of land tenure were introduced which were in the long run, in legal theory at any rate, to apply throughout the whole kingdom, though no such end was in view when they first appeared. In addition to the grant of military fiefs to Anglo-Normans and Bretons and Flemings, castles were built at key-points, and sheriffs were introduced to act as the king's factotums in the new administrative units—sheriffdoms—that were being created. Burghs were either founded or chartered, trade increased, and the church too was over-hauled. The diocesan system was improved and extended;[6] smaller units, which in time became parishes, the basic units of the church, gradually appeared through the exertions of individual patrons;[7] and the introduction of monastic orders in time quickened not only the spiritual but also the economic life of the country. At the same time the royal household developed on Anglo-Norman lines. Royal charters increased in number, and from them has been pieced together the main outline of the changes that were wrought by the descendants of Margaret and Malcolm Canmore. But it needs to be stressed yet again that to call this process a 'peaceful Norman Conquest' is to obscure its true nature. As we have seen, some native Scots, those who felt their rights threatened in one respect or another, resisted change; but most of the old aristocracy played an essential part in the transformation of Scotland. Spread as it was over several generations, no one thought in terms of transformation; but that was the net result.

Here too it is important to realise that although the descendants of Canmore and Margaret became increasingly 'Normanised' ('Frenchified' might be more accurate) they did not entirely reject the Celtic past. How could they, since, whatever the precise rules of succession that were followed, descent was what counted? There was a symbolic reminder of this at the inauguration of young Alexander III in 1249, which was carried out with traditional ceremony at Scone. The boy king was seated on the *lia fail*, the sacred Stone of Destiny, and, after being consecrated by the Bishop of St. Andrews and after feudal homages had been made, a Highland sennachie read in Gaelic the royal genealogy. The bard traced Alexander's lineage back to Malcolm Canmore and Kenneth MacAlpin, beyond Kenneth to the founder of the line Fergus Mór MacErc, before plunging boldly through myth and legend to the eponymous Iber Scot. Alexander's inauguration, thus, unwittingly perhaps, symbolised the moulding together of the old and the new: the ancient Gael and the Anglo-Norman.

Equally revealing is the fact that most of the Normans, with their ever-open eye for the main chance, married into old Scottish families, and it was just such politic unions that raised to prominence the Bruces, the Balliols and the Comyns. 'Norman Conquest', therefore, is an oversimplified misnomer for a complex reciprocal process. As a result of that process the royal house and much of the old nobility acquired a veneer of French (and not just Norman) culture. But in a remarkably short time the Normans in Scotland became Scots. All these terms —Scots, English, Norman, or French—acquire special meanings in this context, failure to recognise which has led to serious misunderstanding. In the twelfth century they referred to culture groups; but by the middle of the thirteenth century 'Scots' was the accepted generic term for all the subjects of the kingdom of Scotland. It was the fusing of such diverse but compatible elements that produced the distinctive society of medieval Scotland, evidence of which can be seen not only in the political institutions but also in the material culture of the country. This merging is symbolised, for example, in the fine mini-Gothic of the cathedral of Dunkeld which was later to rise at no great distance from the ancient *regalis civitas* of the kings of Scots where Alexander III's inauguration took place.

The address of the royal charters also epitomised this mixed society and its evolution. From the reign of David I to that of William the Lion (1165–1214) the following style was used: 'rex Scottorum episcopis abbatibus comitibus baronibus justiciis vicecomitibus ceterisque probis hominibus tocius terre sue Francis Scottis et Galwahensibus clericis et laicis salutem. . . .' The seminal changes of the twelfth century are summarised in this standard form in which the king of Scots addressed his 'probi homines', French, English, Scots and Gallovidian alike. But by the 1180s the king of Scots was simply addressing himself to his faithful subjects without reference to ethnic origin or language. (Incidentally, the racial address fades away in England, whence it had originally been borrowed, at almost exactly the same time.) In other words, by the end of the twelfth century the first phase of an important transition had been completed. The old tribal connotation of 'Scots' was expanded to cover all the inhabitants of the kingdom of Scotland. A new and more cohesive Scotland lay under firm royal government; indeed, devotion to the king was to provide another nucleus from which Scottish nationality was to develop. All the forces that moulded the Scottish nation were fused in the person of the king: he was at once the representative of an ancient line, the head of the greatest kindred of all, and also (though for its full expression this still lay in the future) *ultimus dominus* or feudal overlord. The kings of Scots were sustained, therefore, not just by feudal ties, but also by claims of greater antiquity rooted in blood and tradition. A telling example of this is found in the fact that the last king of Scots to be crowned at Scone, Charles II in January 1651, also had his genealogy recited. Indeed, in 1651 the only really novel additions to the ancient ceremony were the covenants and the interminable Calvinist sermons, and the only omission the absence of the sacred stone.

For Scotland the thirteenth century was a period of consolidation and steady progress. By the end of the preceding century Argyll had been firmly secured, seriously weakening the power of the Norse and paving the way for the lucky victory scored over Haakon IV of Norway at Largs in 1263. The cession of sovereignty over Man and the Hebrides to Scotland by the Treaty of Perth in 1266 left the Norse with only Orkney and Shetland (not handed over to Scotland until 1468–9, and then in the peculiar form of a pledge for a marriage dowry).[8] The other great territorial question, that of the frontier with England, had already been settled, in all seeming, by the Treaty of York in 1237, which turned on the relinquishment by Alexander II of all claim to the northern English counties. In pursuance of this forward policy David I had tried to wrest an advantage from the civil war that broke out in England on the death of Henry I. David won recognition for his son's claim to be Earl of Northumberland, but Henry II, who finally emerged victorious from the civil war, later went back on his word and wrested the lost northern territory from the youthful Malcolm IV in 1157. Victorian moralising would here be out of place; for to gain his advantage David I had not exactly kept his pledge to Henry I that he would support Henry's heiress, Matilda.

It should be stressed, however, that in the normal run of things the relations between England and Scotland were good, and the more so as the two royal houses were closely connected by marriage. All the same, English kings were apt to claim suzerainty over Scotland, and it was not always possible for Scottish kings to evade the issue. By the Treaty of Falaise in 1174 the rash William I of Scotland was forced to acknowledge his captor Henry II as his overlord 'for Scotland and for all his other lands'.[9] In that same treaty an effort was also made to settle the longstanding question of control over the church in Scotland.

The church in Scotland had grown in a seemingly odd way, and by the twelfth century it still appeared ill-defined and in some respects anomalous. Its diocesan organisation, though improving, was not as firm as was, for example, the case in England; and, most important of all, the church in Scotland did not rank as a province and thus had no metropolitan or archbishop to exercise overall juris-diction. On the strength of its old association with Whithorn the province of York claimed metropolitan authority in Scotland, and certain bishops of Glasgow in the eleventh century, who were probably titulars, were suffragans of York. For long enough in this difficult situation the Scots were able to play off one English province against the other, but at the Council of Windsor in 1072, York was recognised to have metropolitan authority north of Humber including Scotland. The Scots, though, were no party to this agreement and continued to refuse to acknowledge York's authority in spite of frequent papal commands to do so. Thus, in 1119 Pope Calixtus II ordered the Scottish bishops to obey their metropolitan, the Archbishop of York; but with the backing of their kings the Scottish bishops disregarded all such papal injunctions and threats.

In keeping with this tradition the submission made in the Treaty of Falaise in 1174 was vague and equivocal—'the church of England shall have that right in the church of Scotland which by right she ought to have'. Luckily for the Scots, York and Canterbury at this point resumed their quarrel, and on appeal to Rome (where Henry II's interference in church matters, which had led to the murder of Archbishop Becket in 1170, was not appreciated) interim judgment went in favour of the Scottish bishops. In 1176 Pope Alexander III forbade the Archbishop of York to exercise metropolitan power over the Scottish bishops until he had proved his right to do so at the Roman curia. The Scottish church was strengthened by the support of such a powerful ally, though for a time its victory was jeopardised by a bitter investiture dispute that arose between King William and the papacy. After this was finally composed, in 1192 the church in Scotland was recognised as a special daughter ('filia specialis') of the Holy See.

For the Scots, this fortunate outcome did not altogether end English pre-tensions, and the lack of a metropolitan long continued to be a source of weakness. As a result the church in Scotland, keen to ensure its independence, came to form one of the most powerful and consistent supports of Scottish nationalism. The word 'nationalism' is here used deliberately, for the influence of the bishops and clergy far transcended the, to them, crucial question of ecclesiastical independence.

In the secular sphere the Treaty of Falaise was no more successful, for Henry II's successor Richard, the lion-hearted but impecunious, in 1189 quit-claimed William from vassalage in return for a money payment. But two could play at the game of word-juggling and the English claim to overlordship over Scotland was not entirely given up by the rather cryptic terms of the Treaty of Canterbury. That claim, too, continued to be nourished by the fact that Scottish kings still rendered homage for the Honour of Huntingdon and other lands they held in England, an act of homage that English kings could interpret as covering, if only by implication, the kingdom of Scotland as well.[10] But over the greater part of the thirteenth century chronic dissension in England, in the reigns of John and Henry III, prevented the issue from becoming critical. Again the kings of Scots tried, with scant success, to wrest a profit from England's troubles, and in 1209 and 1212 King John seems to have promised the northern counties to William the Lion's son Alexander; but any rights thus acquired were given up in 1237. Such incidents were really the small change of politics—essentially opportunist and not basic. The same can be said of Pope Gregory IX's curiously imprecise instructions to Alexander II in 1235 to render homage to Henry III. So, too, with Henry III's later intervention in the affairs of Scotland in the minority of Alexander III, which was designed not so much to further English claims to overlordship as to protect the interests of his daughter and her husband, the boy King of Scots. Nor should too much be read into the fencing that took place over Alexander III's homage to Henry III in 1251 or again to Edward I in 1278. Edward was simply stating a claim for the record, as the modern phrase would have it, and he took in apparent good part Alexander's denial that he owed homage to the English king for his kingdom of Scotland.

All in all, the two kingdoms were at peace and seemed to be drawing closer together. Scottish institutions increasingly reflected English influence. Many great men held lands in both kingdoms. The anglicisation of Lowland Scotland was steadily advancing. English policy towards Scotland was friendly, and not entirely because of tensions in England during the Barons' War. England had to subdue Wales and Ireland, and had at the same time to fend off the encroachments of the French king in Gascony. Peace with Scotland was thus a keystone of English policy, and only a serious misreading of history can represent England and Scotland as inveterate enemies before the end of the thirteenth century. In 1286 no one could have foreseen that the two countries stood on the brink of almost three centuries of intermittent but bitter and wasteful warfare. Indeed, as the foremost authority on these matters has pointed out, 'It was remarkable how little feeling of crisis seems to have arisen after the death of Alexander III'.[11]

The ill feeling that arose was mainly the consequence of Edward I's maladroit policies.

English historians, rarely as objective as they would fain appear, are prone to whitewash Edward I; and Scottish historians, who tend to suffer from chauvinism, cast Edward as a villain of darkest hue. It may be that both sides would gain better perspectives, and truth have a more sporting chance, if Edward were condemned not for his supposed moral lapses but for his real offence—political ineptitude. That Edward should have taken a keen interest in the Scottish question was natural, and that he should have striven to secure maximum advantage for England was equally natural. The real criticism of Edward is not that he involved himself in the problem but that fairer dealing and less masterful methods on his part would almost certainly have yielded better results. But this possibility his overbearing nature ruled out. As Keith Feiling has noted: 'In fifty years humanity revenged itself on the disproportions in Edward's policy. Only a block of sandstone in the Abbey remained of his Scottish imperialism.'[12] That is a just and penetrating judgment. And whether regarded from the standpoint of Scottish or English interests, or both taken together, the outcome of the dispute over the succession to the crown of Scotland was just about the worst possible, an outcome from which the policies pursued by Edward I cannot be divorced. Certainly, he was right to think that Alexander's premature and accidental death opened up great opportunities for both England and Scotland. But the prospects of a peaceful future for the two kingdoms were dashed by Edward's blind opportunism and obstinacy. True statesmanship would have dictated a very different approach, and that such statesmanship was not alien to 'medieval thinking' (a favourite English plea in bar) the Treaty of Canterbury of 1189 bears silent witness.

The failure of the line of Canmore is the key to the entire problem. Not for the first, or by any means the last, time dynastic considerations were to play a crucial role in Anglo-Scottish relations; and in this, as in later instances, the problem was implicit for some considerable time before the point of crisis was reached.

As early as 1284, on the death of Alexander III's last surviving son, Alexander, the king's granddaughter, the infant Margaret of Norway, was recognised as the successor to the throne of Scotland, and following King Alexander's death in 1286 she was so accepted. By the Treaty of Salisbury of November 1289 (negotiated by Edward I, King Eric of Norway and representatives of the Scottish Guardians) it was agreed that Margaret should be taken from Norway to England and then, if good order prevailed, to her own realm of Scotland; and it was further stipulated that she was to be free of marriage contract. This last point touched on the thorniest question of all—to whom might the Maid of Norway convey Scotland through marriage and subsequent progeny? Edward I had secretly given some thought to this problem and taken steps to solve it in his own interests. Shortly after the Treaty of Salisbury was concluded, the English king suggested that the best solution was a marriage between Margaret and his son, Edward of Caernarvon. An obvious objection—that the children were within the forbidden degree of blood relationship—was soon disposed of, Edward having already applied for and obtained a papal dispensation. The Scottish Guardians seem to have been a little taken aback at the ease with which this obstacle had been overcome but recognised that such a marriage might prove beneficial.

The Guardians expressed themselves well content with the proposal, and by the Treaty of Birgham of July 1290 the marriage was arranged. From that point onwards the pressure was on the Scots, gentle at first but persistent. Thus, in the Treaty of Birgham the Scottish negotiators flatly refused to compromise the laws and liberties of Scotland, which were to be safeguarded against all eventualities. Edward in the end accepted these points, but put forward counter-provisos saving his own undefined rights over Scotland. It was a time for diplomacy, however, and he did not press matters. True, he demanded that the castles and fortified places in Scotland should be surrendered into his keeping, but on the Scots refusing he did not make an issue of it. Edward was satisfied with the marriage treaty, which, in spite of its safeguards for the independence of Scotland, would likely promote a peaceful union of the two kingdoms—or at least a relationship between them that would have reduced the independence of Scotland to nominal proportions.

The death of Margaret, which occurred in Orkney late in 1290, ruined these prospects and opened up a new and more perplexing situation. The direct line of Canmore was extinguished and there were, ultimately, thirteen claimants to the throne of Scotland. There seemed to be the possibility of an armed contest, and under cover of a rather cryptic invitation from the Balliol faction Edward I again intervened. Had he been content to play the rôle of honest broker the profit would still have been his, but Edward could not resist the temptation to resurrect the old claim to overlordship. On this subject has been lavished much ink and no little gall. The best verdict on the earlier submissions on which Edward relied so much is that, 'Feudal agreements were like twentieth century international treaties: they were valid so long as they could be enforced'.[13] But Edward took a legalistic view of politics, studiously ignoring unwelcome realities unknown to the law books. Such a reality was the community of the realm of Scotland, which was made up of the great lords, the prelates and freeholders. The community of the realm protested against Edward's claim to overlordship; Edward thrust the protest aside as being 'to no purpose' and may have felt justified in so doing by the acceptance of his claim by the principal competitors. There then followed the protracted adjudication[14] known as 'the Great Cause', as a result of which Edward in November 1292 awarded the crown of Scotland to John Balliol, the Lord of Galloway. It was a right judgment. By feudal rules Balliol had the best claim, and there is no substance in the old Scots fable that Edward chose the most spineless competitor in order to ensure for himself an easy exercise of suzerainty. After all, Balliol's chief rival, Robert Bruce, had also already accepted Edward as overlord, and this being so it cost Edward nothing to make an impartial award. Edward indeed rejected the plea put forward by some of the claimants, including latterly Bruce, that Scotland was partible. No doubt in doing so the English king was consulting his own interests, hoping to confirm primogeniture as the rule of succession to kingdoms; but Edward was an enigmatic character and seems according to his lights to have tried to act at this point fairly, and even with some degree of respect, towards Scotland.

Edward's intentions may have been admirable, but his acts were rash and ill-considered, and none more so than his treatment of King John. Balliol was hectored and bullied by his lord paramount, while at the same time Edward— a great stickler for forms—was defying his own overlord for Gascony, the French king. The comedy has been ingeniously played down by English historians, but no amount of quibbling can quite snuff it out. Indeed it was Edward's quarrel with the king of France that led to violence in Scotland. Since 1296 there had been recurrent rumours of strife in Scotland, but in point of fact the peace of Scotland was not seriously disturbed until Edward's demands for levies against the French king forced John Balliol to refuse. The Scots nobles would have none of it and made it plain to Balliol that if he acquiesced, then his newly awarded crown was at hazard. Balliol was not quite the 'Toom Tabard' of Scottish legend but was probably well limned by a contemporary chronicler who, with reference to the Scots, described King John as 'quasi agnus inter lupos'.[15] Already humiliated by Edward over legal pleas, he was forced by the Scots nobles to defy his masterful overlord and make a treaty with France in October 1295. For Edward, to defy was natural; but to be defied was unthinkable. His answer was short, sharp and decisive. In 1296 he sacked Berwick, invaded Scotland, routed the Scots at Dunbar and deposed Balliol, at the same time making it clear that he had no further use for puppet kings. As a token of this he removed the enthronement stone of Scone (or possibly a crude substitute that had been planted in its place) and put it in Westminster Abbey; and he also took south many of the records of the kingdom. Balliol submitted to his fate, was imprisoned for three years in England and spent the rest of his life exiled in his ancestral domain of Bailleul in France. The Scottish nobles and freeholders also gave up, swore fealty to Edward in the so-called Ragman Rolls, and were admitted to his peace.

It seemed as if Edward I had triumphed. Further resistance to him seemed impossible. A few powerful Scottish nobles who held lands in both England and Scotland saw in peace the only answer to their dilemma; and the continuance of the quarrel between the Balliols and the Bruces further weakened the Scots. How, then, could England and its vigorous king be resisted? Edward, of all people, should have had an inkling of the answer. He should have remembered his old adversary de Montfort, and, above all, the source from which Earl Simon drew much of his support. The commons of Scotland as little relished high-handed government as had the bachelors of England of the preceding generation, and Edward's high-powered administration soon became unpopular. Deserted by their natural leaders, the lesser men made shift for themselves. Headed by Sir Andrew de Moray in the north and by William Wallace in the south, they rose against the English and scored a notable victory at Stirling Bridge in September 1297. Again Edward reacted vigorously to the challenge. Using what were to become the deadly standard tactics of the English in the later Middle Ages (skilful utilisation of longbowmen and heavy cavalry), he defeated Wallace at Falkirk in July 1298. Wallace's authority was destroyed, though he himself was not captured and executed in London until 1305.

None the less, the abortive rising of 1297–8 in the end swung the issue against England. A long and bitter guerilla war ensued which lasted with few real intermissions until 1328. The purpose and the composition of the forces opposed to the English invaders and their collaborators varied over these years; but the fact of resistance did not. Wallace (who soon captured the popular imagination and became the national hero of Scotland, rather like William Tell, though with more flesh and blood to him than the apocryphal hero of the Swiss Confederation) had fought throughout for 'the illustrious King John'. King John's cause did not disappear after 1296 and until 1304 it was the Comyns, relatives and allies of the Balliols, who were the main resisters, impeded by the jealousy of the janus-like Bruces. Finally in 1306 an effort was made to patch up the differences between those two powerful factions, only to result in the murder

of the Red Comyn in a church at Dumfries by young Robert Bruce, the grandson
of the competitor. Bruce had had a checkered career, as often as not serving
Edward in the hope of acquiring the vassal crown of Scotland. Edward's growing
suspicion of Bruce's shifty ways, culminating in the sacrilegious slaying of
Comyn, ended Bruce's career of duplicity and forced him to pursue a consistent
policy that bristled with danger and hardship.

Shabby as the beginning of the enterprise was, and feeble as were his
resources at the outset, Robert Bruce improved in adversity. In March 1306
he was enthroned with scant ceremony at Scone, only to be defeated in June
at Methven and forced to flee his 'kingdom'. But he had the luck of the brave.
While hurrying north (filled with righteous, and justified, indignation) to deal
with 'King Hob', this ungrateful upstart who had met nothing but kindness at
his hands, the old king, arguably the greatest of the Plantagenets, fell ill and
died at Burgh-on-Sands in July 1307. The folly of his son and successor,
Edward II, ensured that the English grip on Scotland could not be maintained.
Bruce went from strength to strength, reducing Lorn and Buchan, until by 1314
only a few strongholds in Scotland were held by the English. The attempt to
relieve the chief of these, Stirling Castle, led to Bruce's unexpected victory at
Bannockburn on 24 June 1314.

Edward II, obstinate as well as weak, refused to accept the implications of
this shattering defeat, chief of which was that 'Bannockburn proved the most
important single factor in ensuring the ultimate independence of Scotland and
saving her from the fate of Ireland'.[16] Indeed, for a time it looked as if
Bannockburn might save Ireland too from her fate; for not only did Bruce
devastate the north of England but he also encouraged his brother Edward's
furious invasion of the sister island. Some of the native Irish had been following
the struggle in Scotland with great interest and after Bannockburn actually
invited Edward Bruce to accept the crown of Ireland.[17] The strain on England's
resources was great, the more so as the country was weakened by internal
dissensions caused by Edward II's feeble rule; and in 1323 a thirteen years'
truce was made with Scotland. But for years Robert Bruce was unable to win
international recognition as king of Scots, owing to Edward II's obstinacy, the
hostility of the papacy, and indifferent support from the king of France. Not
until 1328, two years after the deposition and subsequent murder of Edward II,
was peace made by the Treaty of Edinburgh–Northampton under the terms of
which the independence of Scotland was fully recognised and provision made
for a peaceful future by the marriage of David, Bruce's heir, and Joan, daughter
of Edward II.[18] It was a wise peace, which, if kept, would have gone a long way
to solve the problem of Anglo-Scottish relations.

But it was not just the heroism of Robert I and his famous captains or the
folly of Edward II that secured the independence of Scotland. Something very
like national feeling existed in Scotland by 1286. Though inchoate and as
yet relatively untested, national feeling reacted strongly against Edward I's
assumption of power and inspired much of the resistance to him. English
historians on the whole reject this interpretation but manage to do so only by
disregarding the evidence. Thus Freeman, a prominent nineteenth-century

historian, held that there was no real Scottish nation in Edward I's time and that there was little community of feeling among the Scots, the Galwegians, the Normans and the English of Lothian. His anachronistic sociology led him to the absurd conclusion that 'The Scots who resisted Edward were the English of Lothian'.[19] According to Freeman the Highlanders leagued with the English out of hatred for their Saxon countrymen. Illogically, but of set purpose, Freeman concludes his revealing essay: 'I do not regret that Scotland won her independence. I cannot regret the formation of a nation, a nation essentially of English blood and speech . . . An Englishman born north of the Tweed should deem himself as little bound to malign Edward as an Englishman born north of the Thames deems himself bound to malign Ecgherht'.[20] 'An Englishman born north of Tweed' is an interesting and revealing concept. The whole philosophy is Germanist; but somehow we are required to believe that anglicisation, as distinct from germanisation or russification, is free from moral taint.

In his own vivid eye-witness style J. R. Green, Freeman's pupil, elaborated the master's tale; and the great English medievalist Tout borrowed the very language as well as the concepts of Freeman and Green. Tout summed up for them all, piling blunder upon blunder: 'Bruce's difficulties were not so much with the English as with the Scots. It was no small task to unite the English of the Lothians, the Welsh of the south-west, the Norsemen of the extreme north, and the Celts of the hills into a single nation'.[21] Various recensions by the same hand did nothing to improve these vague anachronistic generalisations; as when, elsewhere, Tout wrote that 'The violent policy of Edward was gradually welding together the sturdy Anglian peasant of the Lothians, the Anglicised Gael of the north-east, and the half-Anglicised Briton of the south-west, into a real vigorous national unity'.[22]

It need hardly be pointed out that by the time of Edward I Britons and Angles had long since gone the way of all flesh, or that the 'Celts of the hills' and 'Anglicised Gaels' never were on land or sea. Yet the legend persists, as legends will that serve national prejudices, and even such a distinguished historian as Sir Maurice Powicke could not altogether free himself from its influence, as is glaringly obvious in his treatment of Edward I and Scotland.[23] Professor Barrow's brilliant and scholarly study of Robert Bruce and his times should, if anything can, finally demolish this peculiarly English Victorian Gothic version of early medieval Scotland—at least as far as serious history is concerned.[24]

It was not Green's 'stout-hearted Northumbrians' of Lothian, or Tout's 'sturdy Anglian peasants', who liberated Scotland. Indeed, the comparative inaction of the people of Lothian during the First War of Independence has to be explained, as it can be readily enough: Lothian was the easiest part of Scotland for the English to penetrate and hold, and its terrain was not well adapted for a guerilla resistance. The question does not, as Germanist historians imagine, turn on the supposed inveterate hostility between Gaelic-speaking and English-speaking Scots, for which in the Middle Ages there is no real evidence.[25] The divisions of the Scots in the War of Independence were bitter, but they were factious and not racial (except in the precise sense that blood-feud is racial). In the end a sense of community, ably supported by Bruce's skilful appeals to self-interest, prevailed. And behind all this can easily be detected another factor at work—the most neglected and perhaps the most important of all.

The plea of the community of the realm in 1291 (which English historians usually follow Edward I in sweeping aside as of no account) and the splendid rhetoric of the Declaration of Arbroath in 1320 are not isolated phenomena. They represent something new and vital that was to condition the relations between England and Scotland for centuries to come. They are the related products of a burgeoning nationalism that was intensified but not created by the struggle with Edward I. This was not a peculiarly Scottish development, for the rise of national feeling was then evident elsewhere in Western Europe, and most notably in England itself.

For the vindication of this sense of nationality Scotland had to pay a high price. But only those who believe that the past never lived and that the material needs of the moment are alone of consequence can suppose that failure to vindicate the nationhood of Scotland would have cost less. Even such a sensitive historian as H. A. L. Fisher could fall into this trap. 'But,' he writes, 'to the critic who asks what use Scotland made of the independence so bravely won, so triumphantly secured on the field of Bannockburn, the answer is less reassuring. The history of medieval Scotland is a tangle of savage broils and convulsions.'[26]

The judgment is far too sweeping. The history of medieval Scotland was not simply a welter of anarchy and blood. And there is, of course, another side to the question. English activity in Scotland in the later Middle Ages was not designed to promote a higher civilisation; on the contrary, it was purely destructive. But speculation is pointless. The facts must be taken as they are; and, paradoxical as it may seem, the independence of Scotland was probably also in the best interests of England. For it is extremely doubtful if, faced with long wars with France and the need to hold down Ireland and Wales, England could have absorbed, or subdued, a resentful Scotland.

3

The Later Middle Ages: the Long Siege

THE Treaty of Edinburgh, which ended the First Scottish War of Independence, did not end Scotland's peril, for that treaty was generally detested in England as derogatory to the country's honour and dangerous to her security; so, not unnaturally, Edward III, who as a minor had had no real hand in the making of 'the Shameful Peace', grasped the first opportunity to break it.[1] The opportunity soon came, hastened on by the coincidence in time of several important developments.

The resumption of a forward policy in Scotland was made possible by the death of Robert I in 1329, by the confusions caused by the minority of his infant son David II, and not least by young Edward's seizure of power in England. Of Edward's influence on this matter it has been well said: 'Not only was Edward III conscious of his rights, and perhaps acquisitive of rights that he did not possess, but he was prepared to fight for them, and fighting successfully, he fired the warlike enthusiasm of his people'.[2] A *casus belli* was provided by the 'Disinherited' (the Scots nobles who had been forfeited for supporting the English cause), but not, as formerly imagined, a *casus foederis*, since the problem of the Disinherited was not dealt with in the treaty.[3] Edward III was lucky to find in their natural leader, Edward Balliol, the son of King John, an able lieutenant, the unexpected success of whose expedition into Scotland whetted the English king's interest. Nor was it merely a matter of hurt pride and desire for revenge with Edward III. Scotland, in spite of many years of devastating warfare, was still an attractive prize: her share in the lucrative wool trade remained considerable, nearly 5,500 sacks of wool being exported annually mainly through Berwick; and all too clearly the richest part of Scotland, the southern counties, was precisely 'the area which England could most easily conquer'.[4] It was also important to Edward III's foreign policy to reduce Scotland and so nullify the Franco-Scottish Treaty of Corbeil of 1326. The Scottish question had in fact become entangled in a wider web of relationships, at the centre of which was declining English strength in Gascony. True, the French threat to Gascony could not be disposed of in Scotland, but the reduction of Scotland would undoubtedly weaken the position of the French king.

On all these grounds Edward III's concern with Scotland was understandable, and, from his point of view, justifiable.

The weakness of the Scots, who were deprived of the services of Robert I and his experienced captains, was exposed when at Dupplin Moor in Fife in August 1332 Balliol routed a much larger but feebly-led Scottish army. This was a vastly different outcome from young Edward III's abortive campaign of 1327 against Bruce's veterans, the Earl of Moray and Douglas, that is so brilliantly described by Froissart, and possibly Edward was picqued by the contrast. Dupplin made a brilliant start to Edward Balliol's enterprise, and on the strength of it he was crowned at Scone as Edward, King of Scots. Balliol, however, was well aware that this was not exactly the game that the English king had in mind, and in an effort to make the best deal possible the new king of Scots issued letters patent at Roxburgh in which he acknowledged Edward III as his overlord and offered to cede to the English crown in perpetuity much of southern Scotland, including the coveted town of Berwick. Edward III would have liked to go further and assert direct overlordship over Scotland, but at this point he was deterred by the reluctance of his parliament to reopen the Scottish question in such a vexed form.[5] The way was finally cleared for direct English intervention in December 1332 when, as the result of a treacherous surprise at Annan, 'the swelling bubble of Balliol's fortunes had been pricked and Balliol himself was a fugitive in England'.[6]

In the work of reconquest Edward III openly helped Balliol, justifying this course on the specious plea that the Scots were preparing to invade England; but in reality the aggressive moves were made mainly by Edward. Soon Berwick was closely besieged, and the Scottish obsession with their most important sea-port led them to fight the wrong kind of war. In an attempt to raise the siege they offered battle instead of adopting the guerilla tactics so successfully employed by Robert I. The odds told heavily against them; at Halidon Hill in July 1333 the Scottish spearmen were mown down by the English archers and the rout completed by the cavalry—a variant of the same deadly tactics Edward I had used, and which were shortly to win the English even more stunning victories in France.

Indicative of the fierce hatred that now characterised Anglo-Scottish relations, no quarter was given. Halidon looked like a final victory and if properly followed up perhaps it might have been; but, and again this was curiously prophetic of the coming French wars, victory was not properly exploited. In particular Edward III erred in leaving the task of reoccupying Scotland to Balliol. Balliol fighting for the restoration of his inheritance had wrung a grudging measure of sympathy from many Scots, but Balliol as the acknowledged lackey of Edward III had little appeal. Then, too, Balliol's confiscations, and above all his cession of the eight southern counties of Scotland to England, alienated the Scots. The ceded territories (the three Lothian counties, and the shires of Berwick, Rox-burgh, Selkirk, Peebles and Dumfries) constituted one of the richest areas in the kingdom, and, perhaps just as significantly, they formed a very large part of English-speaking Scotland. Community of speech, though, did nothing to sweeten the ruthless harrying of these lands by the English in 1334–5, and the Scots, English-speaking and Gaelic-speaking alike, reverted to the tried guerilla tactics of Robert Bruce. In 1334 resistance stiffened as the young David was dispatched to France for safety, and his heir, Robert the Steward, son of Robert I's daughter Marjorie, successfully organised a national resistance in Scotland. Balliol steadily lost ground and in September 1334 was finally driven out, becoming thereafter a mere figurehead, which, had his affair been handled more intelligently, he might never have become. Edward III then repeatedly invaded Scotland but, in spite of massive efforts, failed to overcome the evasive tactics adopted by the main leader of the Scots, Sir Andrew Moray. It was not possible to reduce Scotland as North Wales had been reduced, by massive strength meticulously deployed, for the Scots, unlike the Welsh, had room in which to manoeuvre, and if they wished to decline battle they could not be forced to it. By 1336 Edward III recognised that his victories had not enabled him to subdue the country; and again this was a preview in miniature of the greater venture towards which his thoughts were turning.

The French war had many causes, and Edward's precise aims cannot now be determined; he probably began the war in an opportunist frame of mind, not committed to any one objective but keen to secure any possible advantage. He could not have envisaged a Hundred Years' War, a term of art supplied by nineteenth-century hindsight, but inevitably his claim to the throne of France led to a prolonged struggle.[7] The crucial matter was the rising power of the French monarchy, which had long been encroaching on the Plantagenet possessions in France and which as recently as 1324, in the Little War of St. Sardos, had led to conflict. Then in 1326 the Capetian line had failed and a colourable claim to the throne of France had been put forward on behalf of young Edward III. It was not strongly urged, and Philip VI, the first of the Valois line, took advantage of England's weakness to put further pressure on Gascony. In 1337 Edward III determined to bring the matter to an issue, and the impasse in Scotland may have helped him to make up his mind. After all, any threat from Scotland could be checked, for the English still had strong garrisons in the ceded territories; on the other hand, if France could be overcome the problem of Scotland might easily be settled. The invasion of France also held out much greater prospects of spoil than had Scotland, and in the so-called wars of chivalry spoil was a paramount consideration.

Yet Edward may have miscalculated. Scotland was near exhaustion and con temporary opinion there hailed the French war as an unlooked for deliverance, for the Scots had their problems too—a timely reminder that in war the discomfiture of one belligerent does not necessarily imply the triumph of the other. Thus the chronicler Bower records a widespread feeling that the outbreak of the Anglo-French struggle in 1338 spared Scotland from effective English occupation —'for if the king of England had continued his warfare in Scotland, he would have gained possession of the whole land, without difficulty, as far as it is humanly possible to judge'.[8]

As it was, the French wars by no means ended English designs on Scotland. Edward III, a flexible opportunist, well knew how to take advantage of the unexpected chance; and in 1346, the year of his great victory at Crécy, he had just such a windfall when the young David II, intent on helping the French by an invasion of northern England, was defeated and captured at Neville's Cross.

The relations between captive and captor have mystified historians ever since. His contemporaries apparently did not see David Bruce in the same light as later historians, who, with two notable exceptions, dismiss him as a degenerate renegade.[9] In fact, the least part of the puzzle is David's character. He seems to have been self-centred, courageous and able, and but for the obscurity of his later dealings with Edward III he would probably have been tagged by historians as promising but luckless. The question is: did David II fall in with a scheme whereby Edward or one of his sons was to be recognised as heir-presumptive of Scotland? It is not easy to produce a convincing answer to that question.

David was not always a free agent, and the proposals he brought to the notice of the pope in 1350 cannot be taken too literally; they represent Edward III's views and say nothing of David's attitude to them. To aid the ploy, the aging and childless Edward Balliol was in 1356 made to surrender his empty title, and the claim to overlordship was relegated to the background while Edward III tried to reach an agreement with the king of Scots. David, Edward's brother-in-law be it remembered, was, like Balliol, childless; and furthermore David hated his nephew and heir-at-law, Robert the Steward, whom he blamed for the disaster of Neville's Cross and the long years in captivity. After Neville's Cross the Steward had governed Scotland, adequately if not well, but had used the needs of the French ally as an excuse to defer ransoming his king, who was not liberated until 1357. For England it was a time of glowing visions following the Black Prince's victory at Poitiers in 1356, which yielded an even more valuable captive, King John of France. The Scots king's ransom was high, 100,000 marks spread over ten annual instalments, and most historians have concluded that it was a poor bargain for his country. Certainly, David does not seem always to have accounted for the moneys raised to pay the ransom and a good deal remained in his own coffers. From this background came a curious, and still in some respects baffling, crisis. In January 1363 three of the greatest nobles—the Steward, the Earl of Douglas, and the Earl of March—banded against the king, but for what purpose is not clear. Ostensibly they protested against David's spendthrift ways, but the real motives probably went deeper. The rebellion probably resulted from David's efforts to curb the nobles; and a subsidiary aim might have been to prevent the king's second marriage, which would threaten the expectations of the Stewarts. Whatever its precise cause and whatever its exact object, the point is that the rebellion was suppressed *before* David submitted to parliament certain proposals for the future of the kingdom. It has too often been assumed that the rebellion was a rejection of these terms; but this can hardly have been the case, for only after the rebellion had been put down did David II proceed to have talks with Edward III in an attempt to decide amicably the future relationship of the two kingdoms.

It was proposed, precisely in what circumstances is still not clear, that Edward III or his eldest son should be recognised as David's heir-presumptive, thus excluding the Steward. Professor Nicholson suggests that David was toying with Edward, but if so the Scottish king's audacity was a tribute to his nerve rather than his intelligence.[10] Edward was vainglorious enough without having his ambitions fanned in this dangerous fashion. In any event, the Scottish parliament decisively rejected the plan—just what, in Professor Nicholson's view, David wanted. Edward then prepared to invade Scotland but was prevented by a crisis in France, and when in 1369 the burden of King David's ransom was lightened it was again because of the situation in France and apparently had no reference to the abortive talks of 1363–4. And so matters stood when David died in 1371.

What is to be made of this puzzling reign? It seems evident that far from being feckless and degenerate, as the old story has it, David II was in fact a vigorous and capable ruler. He seems to have diagnosed correctly the country's ills and curbed the over-mighty subjects whom some historians nowadays dismiss as illusory but whose disorderly ways are well documented. David was also shrewd and businesslike, if something less than honest, and he profited from the ransom to become the wealthiest ruler of medieval Scotland. The real question about David Bruce, however, abides. Was he willing to barter his father's hard-won kingdom for his own ends? Or was he simply deceiving Edward III? To answer that 'at his death he left his kingdom as free and independent as it had been at his accession'[11] rather begs the further question: was this because of David's acts or in spite of them? An excellent case had been put for David II; but perhaps the best verdict at the moment would be a cautious 'not proven'.

Whatever the heart of David II's mystery, one of the main reasons for the survival of Scotland as an independent kingdom was England's unhappy legacy from Edward III's French wars. Eventually it became clear that, in spite of startling initial success, England was over-matched in manpower and resources. Thus, the terms of the advantageous peace of Brétigny of 1360 could not be realised. Edward III, too, suffered from premature senility, and his eldest and ablest son, Edward the Black Prince, predeceased him, leaving as heir to the throne the young Richard of Bordeaux. Deprived of experienced leadership, the war of 1369–89 went badly for England and in the course of it most of Edward III's gains in France were lost. That war also cost England most of her gains in Scotland, for the Scots seized the opportunity to recover some of their lost southern territory, such as Lochmaben in 1384. So hard pressed was England latterly that Richard II concluded that the only solution lay in peace with France —a wise policy but one whose unpopularity increased his domestic problems. Thus, throughout Richard's troubled reign from 1377 to 1399 Scotland, though subjected to a devastating retaliatory raid in 1385, was not seriously threatened; indeed, Richard's aim was a durable peace. The usurpation of Henry of Boling-broke in 1399 did not greatly alter the state of play. Each side could damage without vanquishing its enemy, and each was weakened by internal developments derived from, or aggravated by, the vicious cycle of hostilities that had begun in 1296.

The wars had equally obvious ill effects on Scotland, notably in the cheapening of the crown and the weakening of the central administration. Robert I could be regarded as the leader of a baronial faction who had fought his way to the throne, and what he had done others, like Edward Balliol, could try. Well aware of the danger, Robert Bruce had been forced to build up a strong party whose interests, he hoped, would be tied to his dynasty by lavish grants of forfeited lands and powerful private jurisdictions. In the short term this policy had the effect of increasing the dangers posed by the Disinherited; and in the long run, in spite of Robert I's caution, it helped to create the problem of over-mighty subjects. Most prominent of these, the Douglases, already substantial land-owners in the south-west before the First War of Independence, received great accretions of strength until by the end of the fourteenth century they rivalled in power the greatest of the old nobility, including their relations, the royal Stewarts themselves. When in 1371 Robert the Steward at last succeeded to the crown, he first had to buy off a claim advanced by the Earl of Douglas, who held that by virtue of his Comyn descent he had a better right than either Bruces or Stewarts.

The aged Robert II (1371–90) may also have made the tenure of his successors even shakier by his matrimonial ventures. His first wife was within the forbidden degree of consanguinity, the marriage was not legitimised until 1347, and from it the royal line derived—though not without awkward questions hovering over its legitimacy. About the second marriage there was no such doubt, and its offspring posed, however passively, a latent threat to the early kings of the Stewart dynasty.[12] The threat may not always have been so latent, for the claims of the descendants of Robert II and Euphemia Ross may just possibly have contributed to the murder of James I in 1437. A more vexing problem, however, stemmed from the fact that in addition to thirteen children born in wedlock, Robert II had at least eight bastard sons, and the nobility of Scotland looked destined to be saturated with prolific Stewarts.

The problem was compounded by the fact that the earliest Stewart kings were not strong enough to hold down their over-mighty subjects, some of the un-ruliest of whom were 'sib to the king'. The Borders became scenes of anarchy, ostensibly because of bad relations with England but too often, as in the case of the victory of the Douglases over the Percies at Otterburn in 1388, because of the ambitions of the marcher lords of both kingdoms. In the Highlands too the administration had virtually collapsed as the great feudal lordships that had maintained order in the thirteenth century disintegrated in the deadly rivalries thrown up by the War of Independence. The wars that began in 1296, in fact, played a critical rôle in the evolution of Highland society. As elsewhere, the victorious partisans of Bruce were rewarded with the best lands, and one of them, Angus Og of Isla, made the fortunes of the MacDonalds. Angus's son, who treated with Edward Balliol but like many others cleverly switched in time to be on the winning side, possessed more territories in the Hebrides and on the western seaboard than had belonged to the old Norse kingdom of the Isles. By 1354 John of Isla had assumed the proud title of *Dominus Insularum* or Lord of the Isles, and it was soon officially confirmed.[13] Though checked in a hard fight at Harlaw in 1411 over the acquisition of the earldom of Ross, in 1424 this prize too finally fell to the Lord of the Isles who thereafter affected regal status. Indeed, one of the most significant consequences of the English wars was the resurgence of Gaelic Scotland and the way in which the Lordship of the Isles gave it political as well as cultural expression.

All this was symptomatic of a wider malaise whereby by the end of the fourteenth century whole regions of Scotland were falling under the sway of over-mighty subjects armed with extensive private jurisdictions, a development that the regents who acted for the feeble Robert III (1390–1406) were unable to prevent. That such a process took place is certain. But it poses problems of interpretation. A drift towards anarchy may not be the whole story, though centuries of slanting have given it the ring of authenticity. The turmoils of the fifteenth century seemed to confirm the debilitating effects of bastard feudalism and to put the seal on this interpretation. But of late this view has been called in question.[14] The time-honoured strife between crown and baronage, it is argued, may simply be an illusion based on faulty analysis. The new approach offers some interesting insights but tends to rely on theory rather than on demonstrations from the sources. Undoubtedly, in some respects the old view needs to be modified, but the new cannot as yet be said to have superseded it.

England was equally troubled, but in a rather different way; there disorders arose from armed contests for the crown. It has been well said that, 'In the long run, descent from Edward III was to be more than dangerous; it was to become practically equivalent to a sentence of death (unless you happened to descend by one particular branch)'.[15] Henry IV justified his usurpation in 1399 by a vague parade of titles: the cock-and-bull story that his ancestor Edmund Crouchback was the elder of Henry III's sons and had been passed over in favour of Edward I; by conquest, which was palpably true but dangerous doctrine; and by acclamation. Whatever its precise rights, under a strong king like Henry V the house of Lancaster seemed safe enough; his triumphant reassertion of English power in France saw to that. But Henry V died young, leaving as heir to the dual-monarchy (created, on parchment at least, by the Treaty of Troyes of 1420) a mere babe, who as Henry VI was to prove incapable of ruling. Further dynastic troubles followed the decline of the English cause in France, a decline that dated from Joan of Arc's triumphant intervention at Orléans in 1429 and culminated in the loss of the last English possession, save Calais, in 1453.

The disaster in France ushered in a period of chronic conflict and serious disorders, for which present day specialists in fifteenth century English history tend to adopt a naïvely apologetic tone. The period, they hasten to explain, was not as bad as it has been painted; the battles were intermittent and conducted in amateurish fashion; and the superb administration of the kingdom ground on in spite of temporary dislocations. Our historians are at pains to disavow the title, and even most of the uglier realities, of the 'Wars of the Roses'. Thus, according to J. R. Lander, 'In the fifteenth century disorders were certainly less in England than in its poorer neighbour Scotland. Seen against events in the northern kingdom—two kings assassinated within twenty years and the interminable blood feuds of the Black and the Red Douglases, the Crichtons and the Livingstones—the Wars of the Roses seem less ferocious'.[16] The logic of this statement would be highly suspect even if its facts were right, which they are not. In the entire Middle Ages only two Scottish kings were murdered—James I in 1437 and his grandson James III in 1488; and indeed from the time of Duncan II, who was killed in 1094, two is the grand tally of assassinated Scottish monarchs, if one excepts, as one well may, Mary Stewart and her equally unlucky grandson Charles I. If, therefore, the effusion of royal blood is the criterion of lawlessness, then the facts declare heavily in favour of Scotland, the more so perhaps as Dr. Lander's other remarks are equally inept. In truth, England in the fifteenth century was notorious for regicide: 'They have a way in England,' wrote Jean Juvénal des Ursins in 1444, 'of not thinking twice about changing their kings when it seems convenient, to kill them or evilly bring about their death.'[17] What the Gallic moralist would have made of the murderous strife between the rival dynasts from 1455 to 1487, and even beyond the battle of Stoke, can perhaps be imagined.

But the criterion implicit in Dr. Lander's assertion is false and could be seriously misleading. Scotland and England, like most of the nations of the west in the late Middle Ages, were racked by the problem of government, by the contest between the crown and the over-mighty subject that was thrown up by the rise of bastard feudalism. France too was torn by dynastic strife, which again was fomented by the interminable wars, and Louis XI only narrowly defeated the ambitious Dukes of Burgundy, who used the archaic concept of the 'grand fief' to cloak their designs. Perhaps the trouble, so far as the study of English history is concerned, is that, as Sayles and Richardson have stated, the spirit of Bishop Stubbs still broods over the medieval scene.[18] It may well be, too, that a kindred spirit now hovers north of Tweed, finding in baronial licence the seeds of government by consent.

So far as Anglo-Scottish relations are concerned, the consequences of these distractions are clear enough, however problematical they might be in other contexts. In the late fourteenth century and throughout the fifteenth the weakness of Scotland time and again offered England opportunities that she was unable to exploit properly; and equally Scotland was unable to wrest any real advantage from England's troubles. So, in a sense, the contest became rather unreal, dominated by tactics without strategic aim, and it is hard to dissent from the view that it all adds up to a 'tedious and repetitive story'.[19] But two dangers lurk in this almost impeccable judgment: it ignores the fears felt by people at the time, and it tends to foster the romantic steel-bonnet image of Anglo-Scottish relations, over-stressing the rôle of the unruly Borderers. In reality there were some interesting developments that do not always support the stereotyped view of ages of savage raid and counter-raid when 'Between Scotland and England lay memories of Bannockburn, of naked prisoners and black, ruined farms, and all the breadth of a Border for ever under the shadow of war'.[20] Such a view draws more heavily on folk-lore than on record; to redress the balance, a brief review of the main trends is needed, and not of political developments alone.

If he had been left free to decide, Henry IV would probably have opted for continuing Richard's policy of détente, but he was forced into confrontation with Scotland largely because of the animosity shown towards him by the Scottish governor or regent, the Duke of Albany, and by the accommodating treachery of the Earl of March. Once committed, Henry then took his claim to overlordship seriously and certainly went to considerable trouble to document it.[21] But his invasion of Scotland in 1400 was a half-hearted and, comparatively speaking, oddly gentle affair, suggesting that Henry's real hope was for peace with Scotland. In truth, he had troubles enough nearer home and was kept too busy defending his usurped crown to do much about implementing his ambitions in Scotland. Faced by the formidable alliance of the Welsh rebel, Owen Glendower, the Percies, the Mortimers and even the Earl of Douglas (who had been captured by the Percies following the Scottish defeat at Homildon Hill in 1402), Henry had no time for grandiose foreign ventures. Glendower tried hard to enlist the aid of the Scots. He made an appeal to pan-Celticism, using the prophecies of Merlin and petitioning the help of Irish chiefs and of Robert III of Scotland by virtue of an alleged common descent from Brutus. But even in an age addicted to legendary genealogy such moonshine availed him nothing. He and his allies were defeated at Shrewsbury in 1403; but the conspiracy continued, throwing up in 1405 the 'preposterous Treaty of Partition, whereby Wales and the Marches were to go to Glendower, the northern half of England to the Percys, and the southern half to Mortimer'.[22] Henry finally triumphed, and in 1406 he had the further good fortune to capture young James of Scotland whom his father had been sending to France, ostensibly for education but in reality to ensure his safety. This curious and important incident raises a large question mark over the new-look medieval Scottish history: if Scotland were as stable and law-abiding as some would have it, why should Robert III have sent his heir on such a long and dangerous journey?

Possession of the young king of Scots gave the Lancastrians a powerful weapon, and James was even taken on Henry V's French wars in an effort to stop the Scots from helping the French king. He was not ransomed until 1424, partly because of English reluctance to give up such a useful hostage and partly because of the lukewarmness with which his uncle, the Regent Albany, conducted negotiations. An absentee king suited Albany and his successor, his son Murdoch, well enough, all the more so perhaps as they must have known something of James' imperious temper, which was in such marked contrast to his father's feeble nature. James I of Scotland (1406–37) has recently been described as 'an angry man in a hurry',[23] a debatable verdict. However regarded (and posthumous psycho-analysis has been hard at work on him of late), he was the ablest and most interesting of the Stewarts. Like Henry V, he had a determination to rule and a passion for government, but unlike Henry he was no adventurer. James' situation was too desperate for such indulgence; instead, he correctly diagnosed his country's ills and resolutely applied himself to a cure. A man of intellect and a gifted poet, he wisely confined his sense of chivalry to verse; though orthodox and bitterly hostile to heresy, order was his god, to secure which he was prepared to go to any lengths. Henry V could afford to follow a policy of conciliation at home and adventure abroad, thus cleverly harnessing up for his own ends the fierce energies of the English nobility; but no such course was open to James I whose fight, primarily against his own kin, could only be won or lost in Scotland. To this overriding need even the struggle with England had to yield precedence, and not until his last year of life did he wage tepid warfare against the 'auld enemy' with a poorly conducted siege of Roxburgh. On the domestic front, as well as producing results, James' drastic and unscrupulous methods raised problems. One such led to his assassination at Perth in February 1437; but it is worth noting that, though James' harsh methods must have made him many enemies, the assassins were drawn from a small band and did not receive any appreciable countenance or support. Instead they were executed with a ferocity that has few parallels in the history of any medieval country.

In the long and troubled minority of James I's son government degenerated into factious brawling and it looked as if James I's efforts at peace-keeping had been in vain. But when he came of age James II was to prove himself as able and unscrupulous as his father, and more successful. In the struggle with the Black Douglases it was James who took the initiative, spurred on by greed as well as apprehension. The power of the Douglas kin was excessive and could be seen as a challenge to the crown, potential if not overt; the Douglas lands were wide and their revenues capable of filling the king's depleted treasure chest; and a grisly episode of his minority may have pointed the way forward for James—the Black Dinner of 1440 when the young Earl of Douglas and his brother were summarily executed. The example may not have been lost on James II, whose decade of personal rule was taken up with the struggle with the Douglases and its aftermath. Again it needs to be stressed that that struggle was largely of the king's own making. In 1452 James of the Fiery Face (as he was called on account of a birthmark) in a fit of temper murdered the Earl of Douglas and managed to ride out the ensuing storm. Early in 1453 an uneasy peace was patched up, but in 1455, taking advantage of the disturbed condition of England, James struck again. It may have been a matter of getting his blow in first, or he may simply have seized an opportunity. Whatever his exact reason, James II destroyed the Black Douglases in a few weeks of vigorous campaigning. Of the great name of Douglas only a cadet branch, the Red Douglases, escaped through a politic alliance with the king; and in time they too were to become thorns in the flesh of the kings of Scots. But James II was evidently not just swayed by greed or ill-temper; he saw where the real evil lay. After the fall of the Black Douglas he tried to curtail the system of heritable jurisdictions that had made the emergence of the over-mighty subject all too possible; but the system was too powerful and the sinister interests it spawned were long to trouble James II's successors.[24]

In the few years remaining to him after the overthrow of the Douglases, James II concentrated his energies against England, nominally in support of the hard-pressed Lancastrians, but in reality following purely Scottish interests. In August 1460, however, while supervising the siege of Roxburgh Castle (apart from Berwick, the last of Edward III's gains in Scotland to be held by the English), James was accidentally killed by the bursting of a cannon. The misfortunes of the Stewarts seemed to be endless, and the dreary sequence of a long and troubled minority repeated itself. An able king such as James II must have profited from the uneasy early years of the Yorkist dynasty. The opportunity was certainly there, for after the Lancastrian defeat at Towton in March 1461, Margaret of Anjou, Henry VI's wife and the mainspring of the cause, fled to Scotland and ceded Berwick in return for aid. The Scots, however, were too divided to profit from this promising situation. They failed to follow their true interests and give consistent help to the Lancastrians, largely because the queen-mother, Mary of Gueldres, schemed on behalf of her Burgundian kinsman, who was the ally of the Yorkist King Edward IV. And so the chance was frittered away.

Edward IV in the meantime discovered that he could profitably revive the old gambit of making use of dissident elements in Scotland, and he found in the forfeited and exiled Earl of Douglas a useful tool. The pact made by Douglas, the Lord of the Isles and Edward IV was reminiscent of the treaty between Glendower, Northumberland and Mortimer, and was almost as preposterous. At Ardtornish in Morvern in 1462 these parties agreed to divide the realm of Scotland; the MacDonalds and Black Douglases were to partition the country north of Forth and hold it under the overlordship of Edward IV, while in addition Douglas was to regain his old possessions in southern Scotland but again as the vassal of the English king. Nothing came of the project except a lasting distrust between the Stewart kings and the Lords of the Isles.

For much of James III's reign Anglo-Scottish relations were bedevilled by such intrigues. In 1482 Edward IV concluded yet another treaty aimed at securing him the overlordship of Scotland, this time with the help of James III's disaffected brother, the Duke of Albany. Albany, who acknowledged Edward IV as his overlord and in return was recognised as king of Scots, for his part undertook to break the Auld Alliance with France and to hand over to England Berwick, Lochmaben, Liddesdale, Eskdale and Annandale. This was a much more serious threat than the bizarre treaty of Ardtornish of 1462; not only was Albany's league with Edward IV more realistic but also James III had estranged his nobles and Scottish powers of resistance were at a low ebb. Scotland was spared this trial by the death of Edward IV and the desperate shifts of his brother, the Duke of Gloucester. Gloucester, who succeeded as Richard III, was beset by troubles, needed peace with Scotland, and ultimately made good terms. But the retaking of Berwick by the English in 1482 (it remained English thereafter) for long seriously impeded the prospects of lasting peace between the two kingdoms. The loss of Berwick was a blow to the security of Scotland, and plans for its recovery owed little to romantic irredentism. But that there was an inclination for peace was proved by the failure of an expedition into Scotland in July 1484 by Albany and Douglas, since that failure resulted largely from the withholding of substantial English aid.

James III is said to have supported Henry Tudor in his successful bid for a throne, but the tradition rests on poor authority and their good relations are more easily explained.[25] In the early years of his reign Henry VII was too cautious to put at needless hazard the crown so luckily picked up at Bosworth Field in August 1485, and James III, embroiled with his nobles, had no interest in foreign adventures. Instead he inclined increasingly towards a policy of peace with England, a policy that alarmed his chief opponents, the Border lords, who saw that a lasting peace would seriously reduce their power. In fact, James III seems to have reached the shrewd, if premature, conclusion that the Auld Alliance no longer served Scottish interests and that a durable peace with England had much to commend it. The peace treaties he negotiated with Richard III in 1484 and Henry VII in 1486 were masterly and show that James was able as well as shrewd. His policy was not popular, however, and speeded on fresh conflicts with some of the nobles, headed by the great Border family of Home. In his final unsuccessful struggle with his rebellious nobles, James III tried vainly to enlist the support of Henry VII, and this the rebels knew and resented. The policy of rapprochement, therefore, perished with James III, who was mysteriously slain after the battle of Sauchieburn in 1488.

The new regime in Scotland was belligerently anti-English and relations between the two countries soon deteriorated. Possibly, this was a mistake on the part of James IV (1488–1513), who was treated with every indulgence by Henry VII. James, vigorous and able as well as cultured, broke the Lordship of the Isles in 1493 and was well on the way to reducing the Gaelic north-west to order, and had he confined his attentions to the better government of Scotland all the indications are that he would have done well. But he was impetuous and in 1495–6 he could not resist the opportunity of harassing England by backing the 'Yorkist' pretender, Perkin Warbeck. Their joint invasion of the north of England, however, was feeble and something of a comedy; they fell out and in July 1497 Warbeck left Scotland in a Breton ship hired by James that bore the not inappropriate name of 'The Cuckoo'.[26] After another abortive raid a truce was made in 1497 between England and Scotland, which was to be cemented into a treaty of perpetual peace in 1502 and sealed a year later by James IV's marriage to Henry VII's eldest daughter Margaret—the so-called 'Marriage of the Thistle and the Rose', which was to have such momentous consequences. The treaty was a genuine démarche and was hedged in by stringent safeguards, including papal interdict against whichever party should repudiate it. That the peace policy was seriously intended seems clear, and Henry in particular was at great pains to repel objections to it. He silenced those who objected that the marriage might lead to a Scottish king of England should the Tudor line fail by observing that, just as in the case of the Norman conquest, 'the greater would draw the lesser'.

By 1503, then, it looked as if the age-old enmity between England and Scotland had at last worked itself out, and such a dénouement would have accorded well with new realities in international relations. By the opening of the sixteenth century France was bidding fair to become the dominant power in Europe, and the Auld Alliance was becoming for Scotland more dangerous than beneficial as France began to treat her junior partner as a mere lackey, a fact that was noted and resented by some Scottish notables in the early sixteenth century. Tensions over the Auld Alliance also helped to revive English interest in Scotland, and the Tudor monarchs, most particularly Henry VIII, aimed at weaning or cajoling Scotland from the orbit of France. If he had been as good a diplomat as his father, Henry VIII might well have pulled off such a coup, for after 1503 James IV vacillated and showed a marked reluctance to go to war with England to favour France. But, all the same, at that time there were still serious snags to the policy of Anglo-Scottish détente. James, who was intelligent enough to see the advantages of peace with England, was also alive to the disadvantages. He was a complex character, a romantic whose dream of a great crusade against the Turk was encouraged by Louis XII but not by Henry VIII; and a realist who desired a voice in the councils of Europe and recognised that becoming the client of Henry VIII was certain to frustrate that ambition. And so in 1512, succumbing to the subtle diplomacy of France, James, reluctantly, renewed the Auld Alliance and went to war with England. In 1513 he invaded England only to meet defeat and death at Flodden, where the heavy Scottish losses increased unease with the French Alliance. A period of slow, uncertain and spasmodic rapprochement between England and Scotland was resumed.

So far we have been tracing the course of international relations, with brief glances at their domestic repercussions; but to consider these alone would give a most misleading impression of Anglo-Scottish relations in general. Certainly, the bitterness engendered by the conflict that began in 1296 was great and enduring, but in some respects the two countries were by no means poles apart. Their laws and constitutions were originally very similar, though by the end of the Middle Ages they were evolving in different ways. Thus, for example, the Scottish parliament remained unicameral,[27] the three estates deliberating in one chamber, unlike the English parliament which divided into two houses. In powers, however, they did not greatly differ, for fifteenth-century English parliaments were almost as weak and as much subject to manipulation as were their Scottish counterparts. The really striking differences came in Elizabethan times, when the English parliament boldly began to claim for itself a say in the nation's affairs, while at the same time the Scottish parliament was being fettered by the monarchy. As for the laws, in medieval Scotland canon law made a greater contribution than was possible in England because of the early pre-dominance and rigidity of the English common law and the power of the common lawyers. Then in the sixteenth and seventeenth centuries Scots law benefited from the Reception, another massive wave of Roman influence, this time from the civil law; but again the English common law was too strong and too conservative to admit such alien intrusions. Each country, then, by the end of the Middle Ages had built up a political and administrative system which, in spite of marked points of resemblance, was individual and unique, with that of Scotland more reminiscent of continental practice.

England was the more populous and wealthier country, but in neither respect was the disparity as great as it was subsequently to become. The absence of social statistics, however, here forces argument to give way to speculation. Thus, efforts based on tax records to calculate the population of medieval England are laboured and not altogether convincing. Working on the poll tax returns of 1377, R. A. Pelham concluded that the total population must have been 1,361,478;[28] but another investigator's figure of 2,232,373 has been criticised as far too low.[29] Be that as it may, there is evidence of considerable but unquanti-fiable decline in the course of the fourteenth century, attributable to some extent to the Black Death. As to distribution, throughout this period the North of England was sparsely populated, with few towns or villages; and the bulk of the English population, which outside London was nowhere densely con-centrated or highly urbanised, lived in the Midlands and South-east. Vague and unsatisfactory as these results are, they have at least an authentic ring about them, which is more than can be said for attempts that have been made to work out the population of medieval Scotland. These can only be described as illusory, based as they are on absurd extrapolations of the supposed English figures. Lord Cooper, using this highly suspect method and further assuming (though with what warrant is not clear) that the Scottish population must have been one fifth of the English, concludes that in 1300 the total population of Scotland was about 400,000, so concurring with E. M. Barron's outright guess.[30] Further, in considering the distribution of this national population Cooper clearly errs in assigning far too great a share to the West Lowlands and conceding far too little to the Highlands and Islands.

Whatever the exact populations of the two countries in the Middle Ages, and however these were distributed, there can be no doubt that country-folk far outnumbered towns-folk, that agriculture was the main provider, and that in both countries agrarian life was dominated by some blend or other of seignorial administration and feudal tenures. Thus serfdom was a common feature, but in Scotland, where pastoral activities tended to preponderate, it was not so important in the agrarian structure and did not long survive the disruptive effects of the Wars of Independence. By the end of the fourteenth century serfdom had vanished in Scotland, whereas in England it lingered on until Elizabethan times. Some of the marks of servility, however, long remained active in Scottish agriculture, notably labour services and other dues owed by tenants to lords.

The precise agrarian structure in either England or Scotland is difficult to determine. In truth, to speak of agrarian structure in such a broad context is virtually meaningless; and in general it is really impossible to dogmatise about medieval agrarian history where so much depended upon differences of terrain, climate, law and custom. One obvious common feature, however, was that in both countries in the Middle Ages some variant of open-field cultivation was followed. England, too, with its greater acreage of easily worked arable was a better grain-producing country, and this to a large extent determined social structure. The champion country of the English Midlands, the rich country of the three-field system which made fallowing possible, was heavily manorialised, with vill and manor tending to coincide. In the North of England manors were more diffuse, a two-field system was used, and, as in Scotland, greater emphasis was put on pastoral activities.

There was indeed a marked similarity between northern England and southern Scotland. Each was mainly pastoral, specialising in sheep, and each used the system of bovates and carucates as areas of measurement in place of the hides and virgates of the manorialised Midlands. But in Scotland as a whole the extent of workable arable was slight, and because of this there evolved a primitive infield-outfield system. The best arable, or infield, was under constant crop and to effect rough drainage it was worked by ridge cultivation; often associated with this was the curious run-rig layout whereby holdings consisted of intermixed rigs. Much the greater part of the land, however, was given over to rough pasture in the form of outfield or common, parts of the outfield being used for temporary cropping. Variants of the system (if, indeed, that is the right term for it) were to be found in every part of Scotland where in the Middle Ages no vast economic gulf stretched between Highlands and Lowlands. Some fairly heavily assessed lands then lay in the north, but taking the Highland area as a whole probably the main difference from the Lowlands resulted from the absence of monastic houses in the Highlands, for the monks, particularly the Cistercians, were skilled farmers and adept at converting wastes into prosperous estates. Not only were the monks of Melrose and Kelso, for example, great sheep-masters who did much to build up the wool trade in the Borders, but in addition they were excellent arable farmers and enlightened landlords. Indeed, our main knowledge of medieval farming in Scotland—and to a lesser extent in England too—is drawn from monastic estates, largely because of their continuity of administration and well-kept records.[31] Of lay estates relatively little is known, and any tendency to equate them with ecclesiastical lands has no warrant. But, on the whole, lay farming seems to have been less productive, characterised, as in medieval Europe generally, by a low seed/yield ratio, which meant that too much of the limited workable arable had to be given over to seed corn.[32]

Adherence to primitive scourge-cropping methods led to the gradual exhaustion of marginal land and to a very serious recession in the later Middle Ages. The rise of a highly developed woollen cloth industry offered England a way out, but in Scotland no such profitable staple industry arose. Scotland continued to be a primary producer and her trade was mainly in wool, wool-fells, skins, hides and fish—all useful commodities but all available elsewhere. Since Scotland traded mainly with the Low Countries and the Baltic her busiest ports were in the east, such as Leith, Dundee and Aberdeen. But trade was of modest proportions and in the late Middle Ages the economy of Scotland stagnated, a sure index of this being the dramatic fall in the value of Scottish currency. Until about 1360 Scottish and English money stood at the same value, but thereafter Scottish currency steadily depreciated. By 1390 the Scots pound was worth only 10s. 0d. English, by 1456 it had dropped to 6s. 8d., and by 1560 it was down to 4s. 0d. The fact that this steady decline was attributable in part to chronic wars with England, resulting in disrupted trade and devastations, must have given a considerable economic motive to those who favoured a policy of Anglo-Scottish rapprochement. And further to justify such a policy, growing cultural similarities between the two countries could also be invoked.

Between northern England and southern Scotland, particularly on the eastern march, a foreign traveller would have noticed little fundamental difference; and certainly not in speech, for long before the close of the Middle Ages the English language was firmly established in southern Scotland. There Gaelic had long since been displaced, except possibly in the remoter areas of Galloway and Carrick where it retained a feeble existence, probably dying out in the sixteenth century. The problem of the survival of Gaelic in the south-west is intensified by the fact that no fragment of it has survived; Galloway Gaelic is, in fact, a philologist's artefact, reconstructed on place-name evidence and analogies culled from northern Ireland and Kintyre. The problem of Galloway, however, cannot obscure the fact that English, known as Scots, was the tongue of Lowland Scotland; and it is also important to remember that Scots was spoken not only south of Tay but in the north-east as well.[33] By the end of the fourteenth century it had replaced French as the language of the upper classes and was beginning to vie with Latin for first place as the official language. Gradually it came into general use in written documents, though Latin was retained for certain legal purposes, notably the Register of the Great Seal. Parliament used Scots after 1417, and to the terse qualities of the vernacular was largely due what Francis Bacon later called 'the admirable brevity' of the old Scots statutes.

Further, the brand of English spoken in the contiguous parts of the two kingdoms must have been very similar. In spite of claims sometimes advanced for Middle Scots as a distinct language in its own right, in the Middle Ages the real distinction was between northern and southern dialects of English. To be sure, Scottish literature had a sharp flavour of its own; but that is another matter. The striking point is that, ironical as it may seem, the great literature of medieval Scotland was produced in English. It was in English, not in Gaelic, that the epic struggle for independence was celebrated, first in Barbour's chivalrous epic 'The Brus' and latterly in the virulent 'Wallace' of the anglophobe Blind Harry, who wrote bitterly of

> Our auld enemys of Saxony's blud
> That unto Scotland never sall do gud.

Blind Harry's uncouth but forceful strain summed up popular prejudice in Scotland and helped to sustain it for centuries to come. Laurence Minot's war ballads in praise of Edward III's exploits did as much for England:

> Skottes out of Berwik and of Abirdene,
> At the Bannok burn war ye to kene;
> Thare slogh ye many sakles, als it was sene,
> And now has king Edward wroken it, I wene.[34]

Anglophobia, however, was a comparatively minor strand in the Scottish tradition, and the work of the late medieval makars—Henryson, Dunbar, Gavin Douglas and Sir David Lindsay—enriched English poetry. Indeed, without the Scottish contribution late medieval English literature would be sorely reduced, both in volume and in quality.[35]

Nowhere perhaps are the strong resemblances and marked differences more clearly brought out than in the ballads. The international folk-art of balladry was practised all over Europe, and ballads were common in both late medieval Scotland and England, particularly England north of Trent.[36] Often the same themes were covered, but on the whole the Scottish versions, with their hard realism and dramatic impact, are usually superior. This judgment can easily be put to the test by comparing the Scottish 'Otterburn' with the English 'Chevy-Chace'—and more revealingly still by comparing the chilling 'Twa Corbies' with its sentimental English analogue, 'The Three Ravens'. In the English version a dead knight's lady dies of grief, his hounds and hawks pine, and the entire piece drips of saccharine sentimentality. Not so its Scots analogue—

> As I was walking all alane
> I heard twa corbies making a mane;
> The tane unto the t'other say,
> 'Where sall we gang and dine today?'

'—In behint yon auld fail dyke,
I wot there lies a new-slain Knight;
And naebody kens that he lies there,
But his hawk, his hound, and lady fair.'

'His hound is to the hunting gane,
His hawk to fetch the wild-fowl hame,
His lady's ta'en another mate,
So we may make our dinner sweet.'

'Ye'll sit on his white-hause bane
And I'll pick out his bonny blue een:
Wi'ae lock o' his gowden hair
We'll theek our nest when it grows bare.'

'Many a one for him makes mane,
But nane sall ken where he is gane;
O'er his white banes, when they are bare,
The wind sall blaw for evermair.'[37]

However 'un-English' these stark sentiments may appear, there can be no doubt about the language, which is pure English and nothing else. So too is the language of the makars, traipsed out though it is with Latin and French borrowings.

There was, then, a cultural differentiation between Lowland Scotland and England, but the difference was of degree and not of kind. In many ways—social and economic as well as cultural—northern England had more in common with southern Scotland than it had with England south of Trent. Such a statement would not have been relished by the medieval inhabitants of either Alnwick or Coldstream, or Carlisle or Dumfries: but it was so, and had it not been so the course of Anglo-Scottish relations would have been rougher than it was, approximating perhaps to the hopeless Anglo-Irish imbroglio.

Ireland, indeed, cannot altogether be excluded from the reckoning, for the north and west of Scotland long remained linked to Gaelic Ireland through a common language and, to some extent, a common culture. It has been claimed that spoken Scottish and Irish Gaelic were substantially identical 'until at least the tenth century, and in most respects the thirteenth' and that thereafter until the seventeenth century the literary language of both Celtic Ireland and Celtic Scotland was a late and increasingly archaic form of Common Gaelic.[38] Thus, all through the Middle Ages Ireland and the Highlands formed a single cultural province, with frequent contacts and interchanges. The famous MacMhuirich bardic family, for instance, which flourished from the thirteenth to the eighteenth centuries, derived from an exiled Irish poet who settled in Scotland; and Scottish bards also frequently repaired to the famous Irish bardic schools. Less peaceful but just as historically significant contacts were maintained by the Hebridean gallowglass mercenaries who figured so prominently in the history of late medieval Ireland.[39] So close indeed were the affinities of Scottish and Irish Gaeldom that among Lowland Scots the language of the Highlands came to be called Irish, a term which, by extension, was sometimes made to refer to those who spoke it.

We have, then, a curious, and in some ways baffling, dichotomy in medieval Scotland, with the English-speaking part drawing heavily on English sources, notwithstanding bitter political animosities,[40] and the Gaelic-speaking north and west continuing to be strongly influenced by, and in turn exerting an influence on, Gaelic Ireland. That dichotomy has frequently been attributed to racial antagonism and usually portrayed as part of an imaginary epic struggle between Celt and Saxon. This age old struggle, beloved especially of nineteenth-century historians, has little foundation in fact. The differences between Highland and Lowland Scot in the end ran deep; but they were linguistic mainly, and the growing gulf between the two sections of the Scottish nation was caused chiefly by the weakening of government in the north and west. The Highlanders came to be regarded as barbarians and were frequently described as 'wild Scots' by the chroniclers in unflattering contrast to the 'domesticated Scots'.[41] The fourteenth-century English versifier, Laurence Minot, also noted the distinction, which may indeed have been of English origin:

> A litell fro that forsaid toune
> Halydon hill that is the name,
> Thare was crakked many a crowne
> Of wild Scottes and alls of tame.[42]

But in social organisation the Highlanders did not greatly differ from their Lowland countrymen: both north and south of the Highland Line the bonds of kinship were strong, and there was little to choose between Highland clans and powerful Lowland kinship groups like the Douglases. Nor, in spite of such dramatic incidents as the famous clan duel at Perth in 1396, was turbulence confined to the Highlands. Language was the main divisive influence, and it is significant that after the forfeiture of the Lordship of the Isles in 1493 the Stewart kings tried to suppress Gaelic in the belief that it fostered barbarism and fomented disorder. Whether they were justified in this ill-opinion or not (and it must be remembered that the old Gaelic tradition was a martial one), it seems clear that difficulties of communication, geographical as well as linguistic, did more than anything else to create discord between Highlanders and Lowlanders. This was most obviously true of the West Highlands and Islands; but elsewhere in the Gaelic-speaking parts contacts were established and bilingualism must have been a common phenomenon, as some of the strange surnames of the marchlands of Argyll, Perthshire and Aberdeenshire would suggest.

To sum up, in spite of linguistic and cultural differentiation between Highlanders and Lowlanders, they saw themselves as belonging to one nation. This appears most powerfully in an anonymous Gaelic poem that was addressed to the Earl of Argyll on the eve of Flodden in 1513. Argyll is eulogised as the champion of the Scots against the English, and the poem proves that the term

'Saxons' referred to the English and not to the Lowland Scots. Familiarity with the situation in Ireland also emerges in the following lines:

Against Saxons, I say to you,
lest they rule our country too;
fight roughly, like the Irish Gael,
we will have no English pale.[43]

In spite of this sense of national identity, however, the cultural gap was actually widening at the close of the Middle Ages. Education could do little to bridge the gap between the two cultures of medieval Scotland; but with medieval education, as with agriculture, there is more to surmise than to recount. The old tradition—exemplified in England by the work of A. F. Leach[44]—was to accept every reference to a school as evidence of continued existence, but this method is now regarded as highly suspect, and particularly so with reference to Scotland. Indeed, as we have been recently reminded, we have little concrete knowledge of schooling in medieval Scotland, mainly because the extant records are too sparse, too fragmented, and too laconic to support anything like a systematic account.[45] The case of England is a little better, but still open to too much conjecture.[46] It can be said, however, that under the influence of the church educational provisions in both countries were similar. Each country had its cathedral schools, grammar schools and song-schools, which, since the aim was simply to train clerks, catered for a very small section of the population. But by the end of the Middle Ages the number of literate laymen was growing, and this forced on many changes: in Scotland, Latin, for example, began to lose its monopoly, many of the song-schools becoming in reality vernacular schools; and in general it is evident that by the early sixteenth century there was a growing discontent with an archaic system that aimed solely at an output of clerks. The church, too, was already losing some of its influence over education, and this again was perhaps particularly true of Scotland where the appropriation of parish revenues had reached absurd proportions which must have adversely affected many schools. If poor 'Sir John Latinless', the parish priest, was left to starve, it seems unlikely that adequate provision could have been made for the dominie. Yet more and more people were clamouring for education. King's College was founded at Aberdeen in 1495 to increase the number of literate laymen; and a year later the Scottish parliament passed an act ordaining that all freeholders, burgesses and men of substance 'should put their eldest sons and heirs to the schools from their being eight or nine years of age, and to remain at the grammar schools till they be competently founded and have perfect Latin'.[47] There is no reason to regard the act of 1496 as an absolute dead-letter, except in the West Highlands and Islands, which long remained a challenge to both sheriff and dominie. Similar trends in England are equally apparent and fortified by stronger evidence; there scholasticism became the great target of abuse, and criticism of it hardened when in 1510 Dean Colet founded St. Paul's School on the new humanist model.

The renaissance came late to England and Scotland it barely touched,[48] a difference that was to have profound effects on the cultural attitudes and relations of the two countries. It meant that humanism never really struck root in Scotland, where the old speculative scholastic tradition continued to flourish in universities and schools alike. After the Reformation the trivium and quadrivium were deployed for the defence of new orthodoxies, and, in spite of later efforts at reform by Andrew Melville, survived with little fundamental change. Indeed, until the early eighteenth century Scottish education was largely a more vigorous development of the medieval system. The three Scottish universities—St. Andrews founded in 1411–12, Glasgow in 1450–1, and King's College, Aberdeen, in 1494–5—not only taught the old subjects in much the same old way, but their organisation and ethos remained medieval.[49] They continued to cater for the poor scholar, regardless of social rank, and their aims remained utilitarian and practical. In England, Oxford and Cambridge had also begun in this tradition and were also slow to absorb humanist teachings; but the triumph of the collegiate system in the sixteenth century led to élitist values and to an increasing emphasis on classical and literary studies. The difference can be simply but effectively illustrated: Scotland produced no figure comparable to John Milton, whose puritanism had perforce to co-exist as well as it could with renaissance ideals. Yet in one important respect Scotland did not escape the repercussions of the more disruptive aspects of humanism. The critical approach to Scripture pioneered by Lorenzo Valla and advanced by Erasmus, Reuchlin and the German humanists exposed the sorry state of Biblical knowledge and helped, however unwittingly, to undermine the authority of the church. And to question the church and its authority was to question an entire civilisation, with momentous effects in most walks of life.

It has long been something of a truism that the late Middle Ages were times of rapid and cumulative change in many fields (social, economic and cultural), and that, even when treated as a vague postulate, the simple medieval stratification of society no longer corresponded with the facts. The church question was central to the entire issue, for the church was in many of its aspects simply the greatest of medieval corporations. It was the very core of a waning civilisation; and since the church question was, among other things, to play a crucial part in determining the relations between England and Scotland it is necessary to examine the main trend of ecclesiastical affairs.

The salient fact to emerge is that the church itself had changed; by the end of the fifteenth century it was far removed from the ecclesiastical ideals, and even in reality the structure, of the early Middle Ages. This is one of the great stumbling-blocks in studying the late medieval and early Reformation period. Some historians, Roman catholic mainly but also some Anglican, will persist in regarding the church as a static concept—universal, timeless, changeless. Of the church invisible this may be a tenable article of faith, but of the church visible it can only be described as an illusion. In both England and Scotland the church at the end of the fifteenth century was in many vital respects not what it had been two centuries earlier. A common factor of considerable consequence was that the power and prestige of the papacy had declined during the Great Schism and had never fully recovered; and of this the states of western Christendom took full advantage. In England the claims of the papacy were countered by the three Praemunire Statutes, the effects of which have been variously assessed; but the papal registers themselves bear witness to the loss of papal power over the English church. The struggle for control in Scotland was complicated when in 1472 the bishop of St. Andrews was made an archbishop and granted by the pope metropolitan powers over the church in Scotland. Earlier such a development would have given general satisfaction in Scotland, but the emergence of a metropolitan in 1472 was a curious business and little to the liking of the king or the suffragan bishops whose vested interests seemed thereby to be threatened. Indeed the first Archbishop of St. Andrews, Patrick Graham, who had, in conditions of great secrecy, bought his promotion at the Roman Curia, was so harassed and badgered that he became mentally unbalanced and had to be replaced. But the change took root, and if metro-political status did little to infuse zeal, at least it made the church more national by affirming that three dioceses—Galloway, the Isles, and Orkney—which formerly, nominally at least, were subject to other metropolitans, were now subject to the metropolitan of *ecclesia scoticana*. On the other hand, as a sop to western particularism, in 1492 Glasgow also became an archdiocese.

But even more significant than changes in relationship between crown and papacy was the ingrained anti-clericalism and anti-papalism of the vast majority of the English people, both of which were manifest long before the Reformation. What is not so generally recognised is that the same was true of Scotland, obscured possibly by the fact that in Scotland nothing analogous to Lollardism arose. In Scotland heresy was not the problem that it was in England, possibly because the church was still valued as a bulwark against English pretensions. There is, in fact, little real evidence of heresy in fifteenth-century Scotland, and no more than half a dozen heretics at most were executed.

Of far more importance than heresy as a disruptive force was the question of the church's wealth, which in Scotland became a matter of consuming interest to many acquisitive parties, from the crown down. The greater part of the church's lavish endowments had been donated in the twelfth and thirteenth centuries; and it has been reckoned that at their maximum extent kirk-lands accounted for almost half the valuation of the kingdom. Little wonder, then, that James I is alleged to have lamented that his pious ancestor David I was but 'ane soir sanct for the crown'. The church, indeed, was dangerously over-endowed, and this led to corrupt practices. Since it was virtually impossible for a handful of ecclesiastics to control such vast estates, laymen were brought in to administer them and often large tracts of land were leased out; as early as the twelfth century feus were granted, alienating lands for annual money-rents, and in addition ordinary leasing of kirk-lands was common enough to lead to a thirteenth-century statute curbing the letting or renting of church-lands.[50] The records of most of the monastic houses show that such regulations went unheeded, and from a trickle in the thirteenth century alienations came to the flood in the early sixteenth century. Powerful noble families, eager to offset the agricultural depression and the disastrous decline in the value of Scots money, steadily infiltrated the higher positions in the church in order to alienate, dilapidate, and even in some cases simply loot, in favour of their kin. All this went on in spite of prohibitions by provincial councils and papal bulls. The truth is that by the late fifteenth century churchmen were no longer masters in their own house; and indeed many of the most prominent ecclesiastics were no more than thinly disguised laymen, with mistresses and illegitimate children to provide for.

In this profitable game of milking the church the crown led the way. Throughout western Europe the monarchy was usually able to turn to advantage the problem of the church's place in the developing national state, and the practices this led to were not peculiar to Scotland. England and France had secured favourable terms from the papacy long before the papal indult of 1487 allowed the Scottish crown virtually to control appointments to higher benefices. As a consequence of the Pragmatic Sanction of Bourges of 1438 and the Concordat of Bologna of 1516, the Gallican church was laicised and looted, and by the mid-sixteenth century, like the Scottish church, it was corrupt and prostrate. Corruption of this kind was not unknown in England, but there it was not allowed to get out of hand and the English church managed to preserve the greater part of its patrimony.[51] In Scotland by contrast the church was, to use a later expression, 'tulchanised' by royal and noble wreckers and exploiters.[52] The crown could tap the revenues of the church in several ways. James IV used the highest benefices to provide for his bastard sons, one of whom, Alexander Stewart (a favourite pupil of Erasmus), became Archbishop of St. Andrews at the age of eleven and died eight years later fighting valiantly at Flodden. The same king used the church to support and reward his servants and favourites; it was not a new practice but James vastly extended its scope. And James V, using the leverage of his uncle Henry's frightening example, was able to divert a great part of the church's revenues into the royal coffers. Undoubtedly, this whole process of alienation and secularisation by kings, nobles and lairds was made easier by the failure of the church's spiritual ministry, which was in itself largely the consequence of appropriation of parish revenues to bishoprics and monastic foundations. Nowhere else in western Christendom was appropriation carried to such heights, and it has been calculated that in Scotland on the eve of the Reformation 86% of the parish revenues had been diverted in this way.[53]

All these factors—new international alignments, social and economic change, and cultural developments—were caught up in the labyrinthine ecclesiastical struggle that followed Luther's stand against indulgences in 1517. The question for Scotland came to be: conservatism and France and the papacy, or radical change and a rapprochement with England. The decision was not, as so many seem to imagine, fore-ordained. For long enough it looked as if Scotland would remain catholic. Only after complicated shifts and struggles was a decision reached, and that decision was by no means as conclusive as some would have liked. The first half of the sixteenth century was, therefore, a period of change, of conflicting aims and great uncertainty, punctuated by tentative shifts of direction and violent reactions. That England was in much the same case made Anglo-Scottish relations extremely complex.

4

Uncertain Balance, 1513–60

THE sixteenth century, in the popular mind irrevocably identified with the Reformation, was to prove of vital importance in Anglo-Scottish relations. Not every development in that century of pell-mell change, however, can rightly be ascribed to religious causes; yet religion is still commonly stressed as the prime agent of change in the relations between the two countries, even though there were unmistakable signs of a possible *renversement des alliances* before the Reformation movement began.

By the early sixteenth century the old axioms on which foreign policy rested were beginning to be queried, mainly because the international order was in flux and both England and Scotland were caught up in the uncertainties of the new situation. As we have seen, Scotland's medieval foreign policy mainly pivoted on Anglo-French hostility; the resulting Auld Alliance was largely self-contained, though occasionally entangled in a wider mesh of relationships. But by the end of the fifteenth century some Scots were beginning to doubt the wisdom or the utility of this policy. France had become the strongest power in Western Europe and was using the Auld Alliance to further its expansionist schemes, which were inaugurated by Charles VIII's invasion of Italy in 1494. Many Scots saw Flodden as the bitter fruit of satellite status and likely to be repeated as Hapsburg and Valois struggled for supremacy. The great danger was that each of the antagonists sought the good will of England, and in order to attain it was prepared to sacrifice Scotland. The new European alignments, therefore, gave the Anglo-Scottish problem a fresh urgency, and this largely explains the gyrations of English policy towards Scotland. These ranged from efforts at rapprochement to berserker attempts at subjugation or annihilation.

A weakened England, fearful of being attacked through Scotland or Ireland, could not ignore the struggle between France and the Empire. England was forced 'to join in the play and try to manipulate their rivalry in a manner that would secure her own safety and her own interests'.[1] Both geographical and strategical considerations made it impossible for England to stand aloof from the contest. The British Isles held a key strategic position, control of which could well give victory to one side or the other. And, quite apart from the struggles of Hapsburg and Valois, the British Isles, from being Europe's off-shore islands, were now placed in the centre of the new *mappa mundi* that was being created

51

by the great geographical discoveries of the time and the consequent shift of emphasis away from the Mediterranean to the Atlantic. The security of England thus became a pressing problem, and because of this English policy within the British Isles became markedly, and at times ferociously, aggressive. In sum, to meet the larger external threat the English grip on Wales and Ireland had to be strengthened and a settlement of some sort reached with Scotland.

In this great new world of diplomacy and intrigue the importance of Scotland was enhanced; but Scotland itself remained little more than a pawn in the game. Anglo-French concord meant giving England a virtual free hand in Scotland, while Anglo-French hostility led to quarrels over Scotland as a sphere of influence. Scotland's subordinate position was further emphasised by the weakness caused by long royal minorities, slack government and baronial turbulence. Exposed to subversion from both England and France, by the mid-sixteenth century Scotland seemed destined to share the fate of many of the smaller states of Western Europe and be absorbed by one or other of the great powers—either the Auld Enemy or the Auld Ally. But, as often happens in such cases, the supposed cadaver was not content to be anatomized and retained enough vitality to upset the best laid schemes.

The changed climate became obvious in 1514. Not only did England and France then make peace without bothering to consult the Scots, but they also tried to settle Scottish domestic issues. The Duke of Albany, who had been nominated governor by the Scottish council in a bid to check the Anglophile tendencies of the queen mother and also to suppress aristocratic factionalism, was forbidden to travel from France to take up his appointment. On the English side Henry VIII, eager to protect the rights of his sister and her sons (while naturally not unmindful of his own) openly styled himself 'Protector of Scotland' and acted as though he, and not Albany, had been invested with the governorship.

But the pro-English faction that already existed in Scotland, headed by Margaret Tudor and her second husband, the Earl of Angus, soon became unpopular and had to defer to a pro-French party led by Archbishop James Beaton of Glasgow and the Earl of Arran, head of the ambitious House of Hamilton. The conflict was far from simple and turned not just on distrust of England but also on the bitter jealousy harboured for each other by Red Douglases, Hamiltons, and Humes. Much to Henry VIII's chagrin, Albany, a royal Stewart and third in succession to the throne, prevailed.[2] Though born and reared in France and thus to all intents and purposes a Frenchman, Albany (son of James III's troublesome brother) was strongly attached to Scotland and did his best to forward her interests.[3] It may be that in so doing he served his own cause, for not only was he close to the throne but also, in order to persuade him to accept the regency, the council agreed to restore to him his father's titles and possessions. Strongly Francophile, Albany believed in the French alliance and, indeed, for most Scots this was still the obvious refuge in the aftermath of Flodden. The old league was therefore renewed in 1517 by the Treaty of Rouen which also contained provisions for a marriage alliance between James V and the French royal house. The governor, however, was not a mere agent of France, as Henry VIII and Wolsey made out, as their cats-paws in Scotland dutifully maintained, and as Anglophile historians have been content to repeat.[4] The evidence suggests that in spite of enormous difficulties and serious handicaps, Albany, disregarding his own interests, acted honourably throughout and not without achieving a degree of success.

Flodden was not for Scotland quite the crushing disaster tradition has made it, and when Albany first arrived in May 1515 he found the Scots ready to defend themselves in spite of being deserted by France. Indeed, his first problem was to force the unruly Borderers to keep the peace that had just been agreed and in which, belatedly, Scotland had been included. But the fighting spirit of the Scots was gradually eroded by chronic internal feuding. Divisions were fomented by the English government, while the supercilious treatment accorded to Scotland by France lowered faith in the Auld Alliance.

On English activity, most of it crude and some of it criminal, there is a plethora of evidence, the mere recitation of which would serve little purpose. In July-August 1515, for example, Angus and the English Warden of the West Marches, Lord Dacre, plotted to carry the queen and the young princes (James V had a younger brother, Alexander, who died later in that same year) to England, where uncle Henry would watch over their, and no doubt his own, interests. Foiled in this, Angus and Margaret fled at the end of September to take shelter with Dacre. Henry then considered invading Scotland but finally decided that intrigue would better serve his purpose. Dacre was instructed to begin a campaign of subversion, at the height of which he could boast of four hundred Scotsmen in his pay, though whether they all earned their wages seems open to doubt. Next, in 1524 the English government made repeated efforts to lure Archbishop Beaton to England where he was to be treacherously seized and imprisoned; but Beaton, well aware of the danger, refused to incur it. Henry was later to sanction even more villainous designs, including murder, to advance his Scottish schemes. But he made a poor Machiavellian, his lack of finesse betraying him at every turn.

Scarcely less mischievous for Scotland were the machinations of France. Having, as he thought, secured peace with England and restored internal order, Albany sailed for France in June 1517 in order to see to his affairs there and to consult with Francis I. He intended to return to Scotland within a few months but was frustrated by the tortuous demands of French policy. Francis I was eager to enlist Henry VIII as an ally, and Henry demanded that Albany should not return to Scotland. Two developments wrecked the fine scheme. Charles V had already got at Henry and nothing came of the famous meeting between Henry and Francis at the Field of the Cloth of Gold in June 1520; and the Scottish council, exasperated by the disorder prevailing in Scotland, repeatedly demanded the governor's return, and in the end threatened to terminate his regency and to negotiate with Henry VIII. Alarmed by all this, Francis allowed Albany to return to Scotland in November 1521. Albany was further fortified by the good will of Pope Leo X, who issued a bull threatening to excommunicate any Scots who resisted the governor.

Albany needed all the support he could get. On his return to Scotland he found his work largely undone. The country was again riven with internal disputes, and the English faction was growing in strength. But in the event Henry VIII's furious blustering alienated most of the Scots, and the country as a whole put its trust in Albany and the French alliance. There were some dissident voices, one of which, that of Lord Forbes, could not have been more explicit. He stood up in the estates and denounced the French connection, claiming that, 'For the love of France the realm of Scotland suffers great pain as daily appears'; the pains were dolefully itemised in order to point the conclusion that, 'If we would keep amity with the realm of England we were out of all these dangers'.[5] This was not yet the majority opinion among the nobles; but, even so, Albany found that though the nobles were willing to defend the Border they showed no enthusiasm for crossing it. And so the campaigns of 1522 and 1523 turned out to be fiascos.

At this point a note of caution needs to be sounded. Albany's failure, which was by no means as complete as is sometimes made out, was not necessarily the result of growing English influence in Scotland. There has been a tendency to regard the ultimate union of England and Scotland as something natural and pre-ordained; but to endorse such crude determinism smothers the real issues. Anti-French feeling certainly existed in Scotland but it was not new—the old allies had never loved each other and had always agreed best at a distance. Again, Albany's administration was not French and so did not rouse the well-known xenophobia of the Scots. The belief that France was using Scotland as a pawn was certainly gaining ground but any resentment this raised was checked by Henry VIII's mad activities; and checked too must have been the feeling that continual conflict with England was contrary to the best interests of Scotland, a view skilfully advanced in the schoolman John Major's *History of Greater Britain* (1521).[6] This notion, for which a good case could be put, could hardly survive the wild tramplings of Henry VIII.

Indeed, it was a very complex and uncertain situation that existed between Scotland and England in the first half of the sixteenth century. For one thing, as a result of the marriage of the Thistle and the Rose, the Stewarts had great expectations. The Tudor stock was sickly and for much of the sixteenth century only one life seemed to stand in the way of a possible Stewart succession to the English throne[7]—though that succession was never as certain as hindsight would imply. All the same, this consideration had an inhibiting effect and does something to account for a certain air of Micawberism among the royal Stewarts of the sixteenth century. But a more immediate and potent reason for Albany's lack of success in 1522-3 lay in the fact that the Scots had failed to keep abreast of developments in the art of warfare, a defect that had already been exposed at Flodden and was to be even more evident later at Solway Moss and Pinkie. Where other countries had long used competent professional troops, Scotland in her poverty clung to the antiquated feudal host; her armies lacked experience, were amateurish and ill-equipped, and their leaders, devoid of strategical or tactical skill, quarrelled and intrigued without respite. England also lagged behind continental practice and had no standing army; but England at need hired foreign professionals, particularly specialists such as gunners, and her armies were usually well equipped. Against such odds, even an experienced general like

Albany and his small force of French professionals could do little. Indeed, for the Scots the worst and most dangerous outcome of the botched campaign of 1523 was the exposure of their poor fighting qualities to the French. Disgusted by it all, Albany left Scotland for good in May 1524, much poorer than when he had first arrived, thanks to the insatiable rapacity of the Scottish nobles.

The withdrawal of Albany led to a fresh struggle between Angus and Arran. For a time Angus triumphed. Again Henry VIII seemed to command the situation; but again it slipped through his fingers, for his support of Angus ended any prospect of winning his nephew's confidence. James V grew up hating the Douglases and everything that they stood for, including friendship with England, and when in 1528 he managed to free himself from Angus and began his personal rule Scotland veered again towards France. The time seemed propitious. After his defeat at Pavia in 1525 Francis I, eager to be on good terms with both England and Scotland, held out as bait the fulfilment of the marriage contract contained in the Treaty of Rouen. The policy was too complex to endure; not only was Henry VIII mercurial but his Reformation also contributed its quota of discord. In the event the possibility of an entente between England and Scotland was shattered by the ecclesiastical policies of Henry VIII, by the fears of encirclement to which they gave rise, and by Henry's barbarous diplomacy.

The disruptive influence of religion at this time is an important point that badly needs stressing. It has been said that, in improving Anglo-Scottish relations, 'In the whole period down to 1603 religion probably did more than anything else to foster the consciousness of common aims and a common destiny'.[8] This is probably true of the period after 1560, but it has little real application to the first half of the sixteenth century. Reformed doctrines were slow to take root in Scotland, and John Knox's testimony in his highly partisan *History of the Reformation*, which assigns all to religious fervour and divine providence, finds little support in the record. Until the 1540s heresy does not seem to have been much of a problem, and even thereafter religion played a less dominant role in the history of Scotland than is commonly supposed. The Reformation struggle was largely the product of secular politics, and, in spite of hallowed tradition, this was as true of Scotland as it was of England.[9] When freed from the glare of hindsight and no longer refracted to justify confessional bias, the contemporary evidence is clear on this essential point.

On no subject has hindsight been so productive of myth, and it is difficult, perhaps impossible, in brief space to make any kind of sense of this involved period of Anglo-Scottish history, which, inevitably, is known as the period of the Reformation. Rather than make a jumbled, tendentious and anachronistic 'analysis' of the kind now so fashionable, it is better to pay close attention to the facts of the case, and not least to chronology. Our latter day metahistorians see little to choose between Albany and Mary of Lorraine, Edward VI or Elizabeth; to them events are forever severed from causes, which are always deep, woolly and highly theoretical. But the events, and their timing, cannot be thus blindly ignored, for the situation evolved rapidly and not according to any obvious or pre-determined pattern. The Reformation in England, for example, far from being a simple unity was complex and moved uncertainly through many different phases. Granted, all the conditions precedent for some kind of reformation existed. The church was at a low ebb, corrupt and inefficient; a growing class of literate laymen resented clerical privilege and were covetous of clerical wealth; a residue of post-Wycliffite Lollardy still battened on age-old, endemic anti-clericalism; the papacy had never really recovered from the Great Schism and the demand for conciliar government; and a new and potent factor was the rise of the printing press which made widely and readily available new views, new doctrines, and, perhaps most potent of all, vernacular renderings of Scripture. Thus William Tyndale's translation of the New Testament, printed in 1526, found ready sale; and by 1530 reformed doctrines were appearing in England where Cambridge and London became noted centres of Lutheran influence.[10]

Yet it took more than all this to produce a Reformation in the religion of the state. As long as Henry VIII was content to be *Defender of the Faith* the way of the reformers was hard and their prospects decidedly gloomy. Cardinal Wolsey's great concern was to maintain papal supremacy, for it was from his legatine status that his own unique authority largely derived. It was Henry VIII's need for a male heir, and his decision to divorce Catherine of Aragon, that acted as a catalyst. The Pope, prisoner of Catherine's uncle the Emperor Charles V, dared not grant the English king's far from unprecedented request, and step by step papal authority was renounced by king in parliament.

At the outset of the revolution Wolsey fell and the conquest of the church was engineered by Thomas Cromwell, who made use of the erastian views earlier advocated in Marsilio of Padua's *Defensor Pacis*. Cromwell, a good administrator unhampered by principle, seized the opportunity not only to subjugate the church to the crown in parliament but also to curtail feudal liberties and to remodel the administration of the kingdom. It was he who stage-managed the early acts of the Reformation drama in England, the so-called (and not necessarily miscalled) Henrician phase of non-Roman catholicism governed by caesaro-papistry, for Henry himself was perfectly capable of deciding the broad lines of policy, leaving the able and indefatigable Cromwell to manage the details. By 1534 the papal power had been renounced and the ancient conflict of jurisdictions settled in favour of the state, the king being acknowledged as supreme head of the visible church, which was shorn of its former power and much of its wealth. And all this had been achieved with astonishing ease, mainly because the papacy was not popular and the church, already national in many ways,[11] caved in without a fight, especially as doctrine was preserved virtually unchanged.

The Reformation Parliament in England has a unique record of achievement, and no other parliament has produced such a volume of radical legislation the consequences of which have endured for ages. Yet in some quarters it is fashionable to regard the Henrician Reformation as inferior in scope or quality to Lutheran, Calvinist or later Anglican models. Such misconceived criticisms probably arise from the fact that the Henrician position did not long survive the death of its author; but its early demise was due mainly to the strife of parties contending for power in the state. It is important to recognise that in the 1530s the Henrician Reformation appeared to most Englishmen as a natural, logical, and satisfying development. It was not so very far removed from the Emperor's own solution; then, too, at the end of the century Henry IV tried to unite France on Henrician principles; and it is, therefore, not surprising that Henricianism should have had a fleeting appeal in Scotland. Pressed in 1535 to follow his uncle's example and grow rich from the spoil of the church, James V seems to have given the matter some thought; he was deterred by his understandable distrust of Henry and also by the fact that the pope, appalled at such a prospect, had already conceded much of the revenues of the Scottish church to the crown.

The problem of Anglo-Scottish relations became acute once more in 1536 when one of the keystones of Henry VIII's policy, a good understanding with France, collapsed. Scotland then became an object of overriding interest to the great powers, and for a brief space the provision of a bride for James V was one of the leading issues of European diplomacy with England, France, and the Empire competing for the honour. In spite of Henry's threats and blandishments, James chose the French princess Madeleine, and so by implication the Auld Alliance and the old church. This was the result of prudent calculation as well as sentiment. Henry had been ruthless in his endeavours to make Scotland a satellite state; on several occasions he had seriously considered kidnapping James, who was not taken in by his uncle's false good humour. In short, the danger apprehended from England was real and immediate, and James had little choice but to turn to France for support. But the delicate Madeleine died within a year, and shortly thereafter James married another French princess, Mary of Lorraine or Guise, a splendid woman of remarkable ability whom the much-widowed Henry coveted for himself. James' general policy, however, was not just shaped by matrimonial and diplomatic considerations, but also by his need for ready money. His penury resulted from several causes: from his father's lavish expenditure, from maladministration and peculation during the minority when successive factions plundered the revenues, and also from the spiralling inflation of the times. A good dowry was essential; and so too was a continuing subvention from the church. By 1532 the church was contributing £10,000 a year to the crown, supposedly to establish and maintain the College of Justice; but later this was commuted for £72,000 in eight instalments spread over four years plus £1,400 a year in perpetuity; all, needless to say, in Scots pounds. The moral was plain—the Scottish crown could tap the wealth of the unreformed church and saw no reason to incur the risks, internal and external, that a reformation would involve. Reformation, for one thing, would weaken the alliance with France and tend to drive Scotland into the dangerous embrace of England. Thus, though he was well aware of the corruptions of the church and frequently warned churchmen to mend their ways, in religious matters profitable inactivity was the policy of James V.[12]

James V's policies in both kirk and state, then, were defensible; but mainly because of his failure to discipline without alienating the ambitious nobles his policies failed. It is rather too facile to condemn James for the harshness of his attempts to reduce to order the lawless Highland and Border areas. Few countries have been cursed by such selfish and treacherous nobles as Scotland, to keep whom in any semblance of order necessarily involved rough work and a hard hand. In the interests of the country as a whole it was work that had to be done, and in particular the treacherous Douglases had to be put down again. Recently blander views of the Scottish constitution, and particularly the part played by the nobles, have found favour: the constitution, it is held, was 'discrete' and not centralised, and the nobles were really striving for a strong but limited monarchy. But this, it is to be feared, is to take George Buchanan's influential *De Jure Regni apud Scotos* all too literally.[13] What James' critics should really condemn is his failure. Not his severity but his incompetence was his undoing. The truculent Border clans were a menace, and it would have been well for both kingdoms if they could have been curbed. James' trouble was that he could not complete what he had well begun; and in his hour of need, which also happened to be his country's, the unruly Borderers took their revenge. Nowadays, when Border history is again being treated in the romantic spirit of Sir Walter Scott,[14] this is not popular doctrine; but it is sustained by hard fact.

Meanwhile, Henry VIII continued to work on James, trying to persuade him that his true interest lay in renouncing the French alliance and keeping peace with England. Finally, in the absence of his chief adviser, Cardinal David Beaton, who was the great champion of the French alliance, James weakly agreed to meet Henry at York in September 1541. His council strongly advised him against placing his person at the mercy of his uncle, whose lack of moral scruple was notorious, and wisely James did not keep tryst. Henry, who to keep the rendezvous had for the first time in his life crossed the Trent, was beside himself. War was the inevitable outcome of Henry's wrath, the more certain since Cromwell, who had always pleaded for a pacific policy towards Scotland, had fallen in 1540.

In this situation James had no luck with his allies. He had agreed to join a holy alliance of France and Austria against heretical England; but even in such a sacred cause the Most Christian King and the Holy Roman Emperor could not co-operate and each was soon competing for the alliance of Henry VIII. And so, not for the first time, Scotland, deserted by its allies and rent by internal dissensions, was left alone to confront England. In this crisis James found his staunchest supporters among the clergy, but their support was vitiated by their growing unpopularity. The increase of anti-clerical feeling, however, cannot be taken to denote the presence of a powerful protestant party. The nucleus of a reform party did exist; but it was regarded, and rightly, as a pro-English faction, dependent on English support and English money. Far more dangerous to the crown was the attitude of the nobles, who cared nothing about religion but feared that James intended to mount a sustained attack on their order. To prevent this the bulk of the nobles wished Henry's threats to continue, since in such a menacing climate James could hardly lash out at his over-mighty subjects. Well aware of the situation, and knowing that Scotland's allies would make no move, Henry VIII took aggressive action, and in support of his cause re-asserted the old English claim to suzerainty. Both sides botched their campaigns; but James V was mortified by the discovery that his army could not be relied upon, and he did not long survive the news of its disgraceful rout at Solway Moss in November 1542. On 14 December he died, leaving as his heiress a daughter Mary, who was then barely a week old. Confusion again ensued over the regency; but after a fortnight of wrangle and compromise Arran became regent, in name at least.

Thus ended what a great English historian once called, somewhat exaggeratedly, 'the mournful procession of the five Jameses'.[15] That melancholy procession ended, fittingly enough, by ushering in yet one more of those long minorities that had proved to be the curse of late medieval Scotland and the source of so many of the misfortunes of the house of Stewart. It is noteworthy, though, that in spite of the confusions and disorders which such minorities brought, the heir to the throne was never set aside or murdered, as had happened not infrequently in England. Minorities, in fact, were general sources of tribulation, as Tudor England itself was soon to discover.

But in the opening months of 1543 all this lay in the future as England's fortunes soared. The death of James V seemed once more to portend the triumph of Henry VIII, for whom, apparently, 'the year 1286 was come again'.[16] Henry's plan for a diplomatic marriage between the infant Queen of Scots and his son Edward must have seemed all the more feasible in view of the internal dissensions that had again broken out in Scotland.

The plan was lauded in a curious letter written in 1542 to Henry by John Elder, a Scots clerk who, on the strength of being born in Caithness, described himself as a 'Redshank' or Highlander. According to Elder, Scotland was longing to throw off the hated French and popish yoke. Furthermore, the Highlanders would league with England, wishing to profit from Henry's largesse just as the Irish chiefs had done. In short Henry should emulate Edward IV and pit Gael against Lowlander. This, one of Elder's brighter suggestions, derived some force from James V's recent harsh treatment of the Highlanders and Islanders which encouraged the efforts being made by Donald Dubh to restore the Lordship of the Isles. Before his venture collapsed in 1545, Donald, grandson of the last Lord of the Isles, was actually to acknowledge the sovereignty of Henry VIII. The letter, which mixed sense and grovelling nonsense, was intended to introduce a map of Scotland drawn up by Elder in which all places of importance were pin-pointed.[17] Elder and his works are of little importance. He seems to have been a forerunner of the Vicar of Bray, becoming a devout catholic again under Mary Tudor and tutor to Darnley. But he has a certain significance as an early specimen of what was later to be an awesome phenomenon—the Scot on the make in England whose passport to fame and fortune was bitter denigration of Scotland, the Scots and all things Scottish.

Undoubtedly, something of this spirit was abroad in the Scotland of the 1540s; and certainly there existed a considerable and growing fifth-column which took Henry's pay but which, to his annoyance, rarely carried out his orders. This fifth-column was heavily reinforced by the captives taken at Solway Moss, many of whom were released after giving assurances that they would faithfully serve King Henry. They became notorious under a variety of labels but were most commonly referred to by their English paymasters as the 'Assured Scots', the name by which they have become known in history.

With the weak regent, the Earl of Arran, who stood next in the succession, Henry made easy headway, especially as he was able to use the arch-schemer Angus, who was one of the Assured Scots. To co-ordinate the activities of the pro-English elements Sir Ralph Sadler, who was reputed to be an expert on Scottish affairs, was early in 1543 sent up to Edinburgh where he soon found the Assured Scots to be a rapacious and shoddy lot—large of speech, ever ready to exact money and favours, but remarkably slow to make good their promises. In fact, as Sadler soon discovered, the great nobles, however treacherous (and the baseness of some knew no bounds), were unable to go against national opinion which was strong for independence and thus still inclined to the Auld Alliance.[18] Such was the case even of Angus, a traitor of many years' standing, whose own vassals were prepared to defy him once his designs had become clear. As Sadler later reported, 'the whole realm murmureth that they had rather die than break their old leagues with France'.[19] A recent study confirms Sadler in every detail, showing how unsubstantial and unreliable the pro-English party was, and how it bent and broke under the savage blows of the crude English diplomacy of the time.[20] The impossible Henry, however, still has champions among English historians. Thus Hester Chapman dismisses the Scots as unruly and fit only for colonisation by a higher power, a typical example of imperialist historiography in the age of post-imperial frustration.[21]

In fact, Henry's dealings with Scotland, never very sophisticated, became at this point incredibly stupid as well as brutal. Compared to Henry VIII, Edward I almost appears as a model of enlightened statesmanship. To that model Henry at first deferred. Like Edward he hoped to arrange a marriage treaty that would bind the two kingdoms together, and like Edward he seemed to achieve his object. On 1 July 1543 two treaties were concluded at Greenwich, one of which provided for an alliance between England and Scotland, and the other for a marriage between Prince Edward and the infant Mary of Scotland. Like its obvious precedent, the treaty of Birgham of 1290, the treaty of Greenwich contained clauses preserving the identity and sovereignty of Scotland, and the infant Mary was to remain in Scotland unmarried until ten years had passed from the conclusion of the treaty. This last clause was probably the result of the patient and highly skilled diplomacy of Mary of Lorraine. How this wonderful woman, alone in a strange and violently disordered country, managed to outwit Henry and his agents makes a remarkable story,[22] and one that has been too long overlooked because of the fixation so many historians have shown for the melodramatic aspects of her daughter's subsequent career. Mary of Lorraine was an outstanding woman—courageous, cool and intelligent, with the true Gallic levity that laughs at odds but at the same time realistically assesses them. Henry in his decay was no match for such an opponent.

Mary of Lorraine agreed with Sadler on point after point; but all the time she was steadily, with French help, building up a faction headed by the Archbishop of St. Andrews, Cardinal David Beaton, nephew of the late Archbishop James Beaton; and the Cardinal's party, unlike Henry's Assured Scots, was both willing and able to act. In the event Henry VIII was completely outmanoeuvred by the subtle Frenchwoman and the crafty prelate. The crisis came over the reception accorded to the treaties. The treaties were not popular in Scotland and their cool reception angered Henry, who was also incensed at not having the infant Mary placed in his 'safe-keeping'. Henry had tried to win over Arran, before whom all sorts of tempting bait was dangled. Thus, if Arran stood true to King Henry the young Elizabeth might be married to his son, so opening up glowing prospects for the near-royal house of Hamilton; and if the worst came to the worst and Henry had to subdue Scotland by force of arms a compliant Arran might reign as a sub-king north of Forth. Arran was tempted; but already the bizarre Hamilton destiny was at work—to win the head of that house was to lose the game. Within a week of the Regent Arran's ratifying the treaty he had tamely surrendered to the strong party built up by the cardinal, which, urged on by its French paymasters, had no intention of respecting either of the compacts of Greenwich

Henry VIII went berserk and resolved to read the Scots a bitter lesson, one that seemed all the more necessary as England once more stood on the brink of war with France. On 10 April 1544 the Earl of Hertford was accordingly instructed to ravage Scotland where he was to 'put all to fire and sword, burn Edinburgh town, so rased and defaced when you have sacked and gotten what you can of it, as there may remain forever a perpetual memory of the vengeance of God lightened upon them for their falsehood and disloyalty'.[23] Hertford doubted the wisdom of such orders, but his mild protests were brushed aside; and though Henry VIII's last campaigns against Scotland are usually jocularly dismissed with the Protector Somerset's under the nickname of 'the Rough Wooing', they were in fact the most savage and devastating of the numerous English invasions of Scotland. In the course of them many of the leading towns of Scotland were sacked and burned, and so were the chief border abbeys and many churches. English policy was simply to pulverise Scotland, to beat her either into acquiescence or out of existence, and Hertford's campaigns resemble nothing so much as Nazi total warfare—'blitzkrieg', reign of terror, extermination of all resisters, the encouragement of collaborators, and so on.

The all-out policy, however, failed; and, more, its mad excesses even managed to antagonise many of the Assured Scots. Angus, for example, infuriated at the wanton destruction of his own property and with his patriotism resurrected by the grant of a substantial pension from the Scottish government, switched sides and inflicted a sharp defeat on the English at Ancrum in February 1545. Not a great battle but important in its results, Ancrum stiffened the resistance in Scotland and, powerfully assisted by massive counter-bribery by the French interest, led to the disintegration of the English party.[24] A second devastating raid by Hertford in the autumn of 1545 failed to retrieve the situation for England. Only the handful of dedicated religious reformers continued to support Henry VIII, and, frustrated by the pig-headedness of their popish and laodicean countrymen on the make, the godly party then turned to assassination. George Wishart was not only a zealous preacher of the Word but also an English agent and as such probably involved in Henry's plot to murder his arch-enemy, Beaton. On the failure of the plot, Wishart was taken and condemned for heresy, bravely meeting a martyr's death at St. Andrews under the very eyes of the gloating cardinal, if tradition is to be believed.

Beaton's triumph was short-lived. On 29 May 1546, just two months after Wishart's execution, the cardinal was surprised and done to death in his castle of St. Andrews. The assassins belonged to the small pro-English reforming faction, though the murder itself bore the hallmarks of a personal feud between Beaton and the powerful Fife family of Leslie. History, or tradition, views the cardinal's end in another light, mainly because of the prominence given to it in the remarkable account of these times written by one who, while not active in the deed, became closely associated with the murderers. While Wishart had evangelised in East Lothian he had had for body-guard a renegade young priest who had become inflamed by reforming views. The execution of Wishart confirmed the acolyte in his new faith and at the same time filled him with a burning hatred of the cardinal and all 'rotten stinkand papists'. In the spring of 1547 John Knox's zeal led him to enter the beleaguered castle of St. Andrews, there to act as chaplain to its godly garrison. It was the one rash act in a lifetime of politic calculation, and a lapse that was soon paid for. Before the expected English aid was forthcoming a French force took the castle, and, while the noble prisoners were warded in France as political figures of consequence, Knox was sent with the lesser 'Castilians' to the galleys. All this acquires significance in Knox's vehement *History* as the prelude to the great Reformation drama; it makes rather more sense as simply one more grisly episode in the long-drawn-out duel between Scotland and France on the one side and England on the other. But, in a rather different sense from that insinuated by Knox, it did mark the beginning of a fresh phase in that age-old struggle.

New men, making what they could of old schemes, now occupied the stage, for Henry VIII had died in January 1547 and his rival Francis I survived him only a few months. The struggle in Scotland intensified as the English Protector Somerset (the former Hertford) strove to impose a protestant (more properly, English) solution on the Anglo-Scottish problem and was as vigorously opposed by the powerful Guise faction in France. At first Somerset, who became obsessed with the problem of Scotland, tried peaceful means, but the Scots remembered him as Hertford and put no trust in his fair words. Only force could implement the treaty of Greenwich; but in spite of Somerset's resounding victory at Pinkie in September 1547, and in spite of the occupation of strong points and the setting up of a 'pale' on the Irish model, the English cause in Scotland foundered. In vain did Somerset again appeal for union between Scots and English, who should merge 'under the old indifferent name of Britons' in one empire of Great Britain which would be able to defy the powers of Europe. The ruin and devastation of Somerset's late campaigns made a mockery of his rhetoric, and the Scots again turned to France for salvation. In July 1548 a Franco-Scottish treaty was negotiated at Haddington, in which a marriage was arranged between young Mary of Scotland and the dauphin, and in which care was again taken to insert the usual safeguards for the liberties and independence of Scotland. In that same summer of 1548 Mary and two of her bastard half-brothers were safely convoyed to France. Meantime, French forces continued to aid the Scots and the English hold on Scotland was loosened, so that 'by the autumn of 1549 both the Queen of Scots and her realm had slipped out of England's weakening grasp'.[25] A catholic rising in the West Country and a peasants' revolt headed by Robert Ket in East Anglia completed Somerset's discomfiture. The autocratic 'good

Protector' could not survive such blatant failures and was overthrown, leaving the way open for his successor, the Earl of Warwick (later created Duke of Northumberland), to make the ignominious treaty of Boulogne of March 1550 whereby the French recovered that town and the remaining English troops were withdrawn from Scotland. 'The Rough Wooing' had come to an end, having apparently secured the exact opposite of what it had been intended to achieve.

The 'British Problem', as the nineteenth-century English historian Sir John Seeley dubbed it, seemed as far from solution as ever. In the turmoil of the minority of Edward VI, England, divided and weak, was faced with the dismal choice of becoming the lackey of either France or Spain. But England's weakness did not end Scotland's peril; the treaty of Boulogne threatened Scotland from a new quarter—from the old ally itself. Henry II of France assured the Scottish Privy Council that he acted out of pure altruism, but to his ambassador in Constantinople he explained his real motive. At the end of March 1550 he wrote to his ambassador at the Porte in the following terms: 'En faisant ladite paix [i.e. the treaty of Boulogne], j'ai pacifié le royaume d'Escosse, que je tiens et possède avec tel commandement et obéissance que j'ay en France, auxquels deux royaumes j'en ay joint et uny un autre, qui est L'Angleterre, dont par une paix perpetuelle, union, alliance et confédération, je puis disposer, comme de moimesme, du roy, et des sujets et de ses facultez: de sorte que les dits trois royaumes ensemble se peuvent maintenant estimer une mesme monarchie'.[26] Henry II believed that he had solved the British Problem by reducing Scotland to a mere appanage of France and England to a state of clientage.[27] The marriage treaty with the Scots and the presence of French troops in Scotland would secure that kingdom, while stirring up trouble in Ireland would add to England's weakness and so prevent her from resisting French dictation. It was a classical demonstration of the ambivalent nature of the British Problem. Scotland, Ireland and, rarely, Wales, could be used as springboards for an attack on England; English retaliation could be provoked in this way, but English aggression in Scotland evidently offered no solution, as the long record of Anglo-Scottish hostility from the time of Edward I onwards clearly showed. How, then, could the problem be solved?

England's exhaustion and France's arrogance combined to provide the answer; but not without a large measure of chance. The long wars had emptied the English treasury and dissipated the loot wrested from the church; as a consequence, the later Tudors did not have the wherewithal to wage aggressive wars. Protector Northumberland's need for support led to an entente with Henry II, and until Mary Tudor's accession in 1553 England was little more than a satellite of France. As part of the price of French support England had not only to waive the treaty of Greenwich but also had to contract Edward VI to Henry II's daughter, Elizabeth of Valois. Thus Henry II's plans to reduce the British Isles to his obedience seemed to progress well; through his eldest son's marriage to Mary Stewart Scotland would be secured, while his daughter's progeny might yet rule in England. And should all else fail he had an ace up his sleeve—Mary Stewart's claim to the English throne. Never had England's fortunes seemed so low as in that miserable decade 1548–1558. Divided in religion (for Northumberland's protestantism was too extreme for the bulk of the nation), and impotent on the international scene, the question for England was really one of survival. The triumph of France seemed imminent, but Henry II fumbled his opportunity. On Edward VI's death Northumberland's wild attempt to keep out Mary Tudor staved off a French invasion, since to prevent Mary's accession was Henry's aim and if Northumberland could do it for him so much the better. Within a fortnight, however, by her own courage and with popular acclaim, Mary Tudor ruled England; and in spite of strenuous opposition she swung her realm into the catholic imperial camp.

Mary's aim was to restore the old faith in England, and to achieve it she realised that she needed the support of a powerful consort and heirs of her body to ensure continuity of policy. On the need to perpetuate the dynasty most of her subjects agreed, for the bloody dynastic disputes of the fifteenth century were still vividly remembered. And yet the marriage with Philip of Spain was strongly opposed by all shades of opinion, religious as well as political, in England. The opposition, indeed, was nationalist, reflecting the bitter frustrations felt in England, and was actually headed by the chief of the catholic party, the chancellor, Bishop Stephen Gardiner. Englishmen now knew what it was to fear for their country's independence, and when applied to themselves showed little relish for their old ploy against Scotland, let the terms in which it was couched be never so fair. There was now poignant force in the question put by a doubting Thomas of a Scot to an Englishman in 1543: 'If your lad were a lass and our lass were a lad . . . could you be content that our lad should marry your lass and so be King of England?'[28]

A Spaniard as 'king of England' proved just as distasteful. But in spite of opposition, and a rebellion headed by Sir Thomas Wyatt that came uncomfortably close to success, the Spanish marriage, with all its dangers, was celebrated in July 1554. The customary guarantees were given for England's continued independence, but to alarmed patriots it looked as if their country were to be swept into the Hapsburg maw to become a northern Naples or Milan. No doubt such fears were exaggerated; but in the context of the times they were not absurd, and, more than the catholic reaction and the burning of nearly 300 protestants, these fears robbed Mary of her initial popularity. Philip, in English eyes the traditional villain of the piece, throughout acted circumspectly and urged caution; the 'dull fanatic' of protestant myth and legend was a politician of considerable ability who knew how to keep popes and priests in their places. He was interested in England as an important political pawn and tried to moderate the Marian persecution, realising as he did that the burnings seriously jeopardised his chances of political success. In spite of all his efforts he failed to overcome English prejudices, parliament refusing to grant him the crown matrimonial. But parliament did not control foreign policy, and to serve Hapsburg interests England in June 1557 was dragged reluctantly into war with France (and so also with Scotland), the only consequence of which was the loss of Calais.

English disgust with the Spanish connection was then complete. Such was the gloomy situation when Mary Tudor died in November 1558, childless, unpopular, and neglected by her cold, calculating husband. There are few more pathetic figures in history than 'Bloody Mary', and fewer still who have been so consistently libelled by posterity. Her failure, as woman and as ruler, was complete; but her brief and stormy reign had lasting significance. It identified protestantism with the security of England and gave catholicism a treasonable aura that it was to take centuries to dispel. And Mary's reign inevitably shaped her sister's course.

Meanwhile, the French were having trouble in Scotland. They tried to edge the weak but limpet-like Arran from the regency but found the right leverage hard to obtain. Since in reality the queen-mother and her French officials ran the country, an issue was not made of it; but Mary Tudor's impending marriage to Philip of Spain made this arrangement too precarious, for Spanish gold might easily buy a faction in Scotland. In 1554, therefore, Arran was replaced as regent by Mary of Lorraine and solaced with hereditary rights to the French duchy of Chatelherault. The truth is that Scotland was as essential to the Guises as England was to Philip; their kinswoman, Mary, Queen of Scots, was destined to be queen of France, and she had besides a claim to the throne of England which, if Mary Tudor died childless, would have a special appeal to good catholics who could see in Anne Boleyn's daughter, Elizabeth, only a bastard upstart.

It need not thereby be concluded that religion was a paramount consideration with Mary Stewart and her uncles. To them it could be a potent political weapon. Mary Tudor was a stumbling block, and against her other weapons had to be used. But when Mary Tudor was no more, the religious approach came into its own, since not otherwise could Elizabeth's title be impugned. Besides, religion in itself was rapidly becoming a force in the politics of the age, not just in England or Scotland but in France and the Netherlands as well. For all these reasons the French hold on Scotland had to be strengthened, and, in addition to garrisoning the main strong points with French troops, Mary of Lorraine after she became regent set up a French administration headed by the Most Christian King's ambassador D'Oysel, who enjoyed the title of Lieutenant-general in Scotland. Mary of Lorraine, in fact, anticipated the measures later successfully employed in Scotland by Oliver Cromwell. No great discernment was needed to diagnose the country's ills or prescribe cures. The regent and her French advisers were appalled by the rickety administrative structure they found in Scotland. Never too strong, the administration had virtually collapsed as a consequence of English aggression since 1542. Mary of Lorraine tried to build up in Scotland a replica of the authoritarian system that was developing in France.

But to set up an administration on French lines run by Frenchmen, however necessary or desirable, was to tempt the fates. Such a policy had the inevitable drawback of antagonising many of the Scots nobles, some of whom soon began to refer not to 'the auld alliance' but to 'the auld tyranny'. Nothing could reconcile them to strong government, and the regent's plan for taxation to provide royal troops (something on the lines of a miniature *maison militaire*) led to open opposition. To rifle the revenues rather than contribute to them was the sum and substance of Scottish aristocratic fiscal theory. Yet what alternative was there for Mary of Lorraine? Control of Scotland was essential to the French, but, as the English had already learnt, to control Scotland was not easy. No reliance could be placed in Scottish noble factions, whose leaders could slide with brazen effrontery from one paymaster to the next. And to hold Scotland by force was no answer either, as the English had also learnt from costly experience.

Given the daunting nature of the task, Mary of Lorraine succeeded remarkably well and in more propitious circumstances would probably have succeeded completely. Pinning her hopes on good governance, she tried to make her regime acceptable by ruling justly and tolerantly, and to the end she remained a popular figure—except, of course, in the pages of the partisan Knox. She was a catholic but no bigot, and to begin with would not allow religious persecution; indeed, some of the refugees from the Marian reaction in England found shelter in Mary of Lorraine's Scotland, among them such notable preachers as Knox and Willock. The Scottish regent at this point actually struck an accommodation with the protestants, whose support made possible the setting up of a vigorous French administration in Scotland. She also wished to avoid over-dependence on the national church, which she well knew was corrupt and highly unpopular. Besides, Archbishop Hamilton, who headed the hierarchy at this point, put the interests of his own family first, and the ambitions of the Hamiltons did not coincide with the regent's plans. Mary of Lorraine had two clear purposes— to preserve her daughter's inheritance and to augment the power of her own family of Guise. And to further these ends she was prepared to contract odd alliances.

The accommodation with the reform party, however, could not last. In December 1557 the first Band or Covenant was drawn up to further the reformed cause, but it had only five signatories, chief of whom were the Earls of Argyll, Glencairn and Morton.[29] The death of Mary Tudor, which occurred shortly afterwards, and the accession of Elizabeth encouraged the reformers in Scotland, who, hopeful once more of English aid, went over to the offensive. Elizabeth, weak though her position was, would be likely to grant such aid, for Henry II of France was already flaunting Mary Stewart's claim to the English throne, and it was mere policy on England's part to stir up trouble in Scotland.[30] Mary of Lorraine then had no choice but to look to the church for support, though she was well aware of the problems that such an alliance must bring. At a time when reformation was becoming a key issue in Europe the church in Scotland actually degenerated. For example, much of the kirk's vast patrimony was secularised in a spate of alienations that came to the flood in the 1550s as bishops, abbots and commendators enriched themselves and their families. Clearly, the nobles had a vested interest either in maintaining the church in its corrupt state or in overthrowing it; but they had no interest in catholic reform, which, if it succeeded, might restore respect and popularity to the church, and which might, in time, also restore its lost patrimony. The economic incentive for the nobles to adopt the new anti-popish godliness was as marked as it was obvious. This, and not some fantastic version of the discredited Tawney-Weber thesis, is what put fire and purpose into the reformed camp in Scotland in the late 1550s. Further, the extortions of the parish priests—most of whom were miserably poor and could not otherwise make a living—had soured the lower orders, very few of whom, however, could be described as doctrinal protestants.

Nothing, then, could be more calculated to precipitate a protestant rebellion than a serious attempt to reform the church, and in the last decade of its existence such an attempt was made. It was the old story—too little and too late. In 1549 a council of the church had vaguely considered the problems, and three years later another provincial council made some feeble efforts at reform from within. The most interesting product of this attempt at conservative reform was Archbishop Hamilton's *Catechism*, which made some notable concessions to protestant opinion.[31] But catholic reform proved to be a chimera. Neither crown nor nobility could be brought to support the necessary measures; and, indeed, the very prelates who presided over the reforming councils were luke-warm. One example epitomises their dilemma. Archbishop John Hamilton had become abbot of Paisley at the age of twelve; yet in 1553, one year after the publication of his *Catechism*, when he resigned the abbacy (pluralities also being recognised as abuses) he did so in favour of a nephew who was only ten years of age. Reformers of this sort could hardly hope to find favour in the eyes of the 'raskill multitude', whose inveterate anti-clericalism, stimulated not only by the preaching of the protestant reformers but also by such propaganda as the *Gude and Godlie Ballads*, was coming to the boil.

There was a long anti-clerical tradition in Scots literature, and many scathing attacks on priests and priestcraft are to be found in, for example, the works of Dunbar and Sir David Lindsay—and notably in the latter's *Ane Satyre of the Thrie Estaitis*. The brothers Wedderburn popularised such sentiments in *The Gude and Godlie Ballads*, which consisted of vigorous jingles such as 'Hay Trix, Tryme go Trix' whose opening line, 'The Paip that Pagane full of pryde', marks its tone. Thus,

> The Bischop wald nocht wed ane wyfe,
> The Abbot not persew ane,
> Thinkand it was ane lustie lyfe,
> Ilk day to haif ane new ane,
> In everie place, ane uncouth face,
> His lust to satisfie.

In addition to such stinging satires there were ballads which, in homely strains, sang of the saving grace of Christ crucified; and this oral tradition probably did more to undermine the church than the exertions of reformed theologians and preachers. There is, indeed, much to be said for the view that, 'It was the play, the ballad, and the popular song which were doing the real mischief to the established system, and were preparing the ground for the coming revolution'.[32]

From 1558 onwards the church was seriously alarmed by increasing outbursts of anti-clericalism and by the progress made by the protestants. The Guises, plagued with similar problems in France, determined on a root and branch policy of extirpating heresy in all the French dominions. Henry II's motto, 'Un roi, Une loi, Une foi', was enjoined by the Edict of Compiègne of 24 July 1557, which imposed the death penalty on heretics. A similar policy for Scotland was recommended to the unwilling Mary of Lorraine, who strove to the end to reach a compromise settlement. In the meantime every effort was to be made to purify the church, and the provincial council of 1559 passed many statutes which, if implemented, would have ended the scandals of juvenile prelates, grasping commendators, and ignorant priests.[33] Many such took the hint and promptly threw in their lots with the protestants, swelling the ranks of the self-styled 'Lords of the Congregation'.[34]

To say the least of it, many who 'contended for Christ's evangel', as Knox defined the cause, were not unmindful of the profits they hoped to reap from a protestant victory. As a contemporary source states: 'all kirkmennis goodis and geir were spoulzeit and reft fra thame, in everie place quhair the samyne culd be apprehendit; for everie man for the maist pairt that culd get any thing pertenying to any kirkmen, thocht the same as wele won geir'.[35] Were there, then, no true 'professors'? Indeed there were; but they were few in number and their presence merely added to the confusion. John Knox stood for a definite version of the reformed faith, one that was inspired by the Geneva of John Calvin.[36] It was a radical faith and a fighting faith, which was fast becoming a potent force in the new Europe that was emerging from the dynastic and religious quarrels of the sixteenth century. In principle theocratic, at this stage it was flexible and ready to adapt to political realities: if it could gain the countenance of the state, well and good; but if not, then Calvinism, in practice if not in original theory, was ready, unlike Lutheranism, to challenge existing principalities and powers. In spite of being forced to ally with feudal reaction— as happened in both Scotland and France—Calvinism, again unlike Lutheranism, had a strong levelling content and in the long run acted as a powerful social solvent. And it differed again from Lutheranism in its international appeal. Appealing to the professors of all nations, Calvinism created new loyalties and new concepts of patriotism. The Calvinist aim was to create a worldwide communion of believers, whose great task it was to restore the church to apostolic purity.[37] Thus, in the end, Knox (who was not himself a great theorist) cannot be classed as a Scottish, English or British patriot—though his occasional utterances at different phases of his career would seem to give him a right to each and every one of these labels. Knox was a pupil of that 'maist perfect school of Christ', Calvin's Geneva; his cause was nothing less than the triumph of God's law; and his task was to labour for it in whatever vineyard he happened to be called. Throughout western Europe the Calvinists, not yet known by that name, were gathering strength. The Lords of the Congregation who rebelled against the regent of Scotland in 1559 were not as a body of this party, though they knew how to make use of its slogans, just as they knew how to encourage popular anti-clericalism but to restrain social revolutionary tendencies.

Those curiously mixed motives and diverse purposes were all exemplified in the event and did much to give the Reformation in Scotland its peculiar character. Fears for the continued independence of the kingdom were brought to a head by the marriage of young Mary and the dauphin in April 1558. Whether the Scots knew of the secret documents in which Mary signed away the sovereignty of the kingdom is debatable; but the worst was suspected. Certainly the French attitude was well known and that was 'that the sovereignty of Scotland had, quite simply, been transferred to the French royal house'.[38] Events, however, conspired to undermine the position of Mary of Lorraine, and the gathering opposition to her regime was strengthened by the death of Mary Tudor in November 1558. By March 1559 the reformers had broken with the Regent, who then reluctantly adopted the policy of repression long advocated by France. In April peace was made at Cateau-Cambrésis between France and Scotland on the one hand and England on the other, but not without awkward queries remaining about Mary Stewart's claim to the English throne. Even before this, some of the reforming party in Scotland were putting out feelers for English support and as early as January 1559, Maitland of Lethington, a late defector from the regent's side, was in touch with Elizabeth's secretary of state, William Cecil. Cecil fostered the move but without making any specific commitment, since he evidently felt that the party of reform in Scotland was weak and unpromising. Later, in July, he became more encouraging, assuring the confederate lords that 'the best felicity that Scotland can have is either to continue in a perpetual peace with the Kingdom of England or to be made one monarchy with England, as they both make but one isle, divided from the rest of the world'.[39] This merely echoed the views of Cecil's old master Somerset and in itself gave the Scottish plotters little comfort; many of them, indeed, fearing that English aid was not to be had, disbanded themselves and quietly went home.

The situation was saved from degenerating into a round of pointless diplomatic exchanges by the blunt Knox who in April 1559 wrote from Dieppe a remarkable letter to Cecil. The main purpose of that letter, permission to travel through England on his way to Scotland, was refused; but in other ways Knox scored heavily. He reminded Cecil of his recent apostasy under Bloody Mary (characterised as his 'most horrible defection from the treuth'), which could only be rightly interpreted as God sparing Cecil for some mighty work. The opportunity for redemption had come and if Cecil failed to take it he would rightly burn in hell.[40] This was not an isolated outburst but typical of Knox, whose correspondence with Cecil sharply brings out the various forces at work. In the beginning Cecil, like his mistress, was playing an elaborate game of diplomatic bluff, the object of which was to discomfit France by secretly encouraging a rebellion in Scotland while taking care not to become actively involved. Knox saw that this was too clever by half and would not do; Knox, in deadly earnest, as usual, had no use for finesse and was convinced that God's purpose required more positive support.

There was more to Knox's view than religious exaltation and blind fanaticism. The unsubtle and untheoretical reformer was right in his appraisal of the situation, for the simple reason that he was first and foremost a realist. He minced no words, warning Cecil that if exhortation was all he had to offer then he was simply wasting time. Knox, no gullible fanatic, had few illusions about the Lords of the Congregation. He knew that their party was weak and that though their anti-French stance was popular their pro-English bias was not. He also knew that most of them were contending not so much for religious truth as for personal gain. All this he set before Cecil in the plainest of plain words: material aid and money were needed, otherwise the rebel leaders would each one shift for himself with most succumbing to French promises and French gold; and where then would be the cause of the evangel or the prospect of an Anglo-Scottish entente? In his hard uncompromising way, the great reformer concluded: 'Therefore, in the bowels of Christ Jesus I require you Sir, to make plain answer what they may lippen to [i.e. rely upon] and when it will be ready'.[41]

And so, step by faltering step, Cecil was drawn in, only with difficulty managing to justify involvement to the even more hesitant Elizabeth, who had no use for rebels and especially such as owned a prophet like the author of the notorious *First Blast of the Trumpet against the Monstrous Regiment of Women*. The English queen's dislike of Knox was real and proved an impediment to the rebel cause in Scotland, which an insufficiently apologetic letter from the reformer did nothing to remove.[42]

In May 1559 the flashpoint came in Scotland. Largely as a result of Knox's fiery preaching, anti-clerical riots broke out at Perth; but the hard core of the rebellion was provided by the Lords of the Congregation headed by the prior of St. Andrews, the Lord James Stewart, the young queen's bastard half-brother. The most inexplicable feature of this whole complicated business was the passivity of the Scottish people as a whole. They played remarkably little part in the Reformation-Rebellion; they seem to have disliked the French without being enamoured of the English, and for the most part they seem to have been indifferent to the fate of the old church and ignorant of the tenets of the new. Nothing else can explain the halting course of events. The Reformation in Scotland began as a feudal reaction against an attempt to set up a strong government shored up by a foreign power and a corrupt church. Cecil hoped that the protestant party would be able to act as a brake on the regent, weaken the French hold on Scotland, and thus ensure England's northern frontier. As an earnest of good faith and to hold the reformers together, Elizabeth embarked on one of her matrimonial gambits and flirted with Arran, Chatelherault's eldest son, in this way detaching the powerful Hamilton interest from the regent. When the rebels entered Edinburgh in triumph at the end of June 1559, it looked as if Cecil's cautious policy would succeed. But again the element of chance supervened. In July Henry II's death brought the Guises to supreme power in France, and, more than ever determined to preserve their niece's inheritance, they hurried reinforcements to Scotland. But even before they arrived it had become obvious that the rebels had little real support, a fact of which the leaders were well aware. An accommodation with the regent was attempted but broke down, the rebels were obliged to fall back on Stirling, and in a letter to Lord Errol, Lord James and the other leaders admitted 'that our force is to small to resist thair tyrannie'.[43] The inferiority was in quality not in numbers, and the troops of the Congregation made a very poor showing against the regent's French professionals.

Cecil's ploy was in danger of coming unstuck, as Knox told him in no uncertain terms. And so in August that veteran intriguer, Sir Ralph Sadler, was again dispatched to Scotland carrying with him £3,000 for the succour of the rebels.

In October the rebels again occupied Edinburgh and the regent was declared deposed; for a time there was a prospect that her daughter might also suffer the same fate to make way either for Arran or Lord James, one of whom was to rule as an English puppet-king. But again the rebels talked big and did little. Mary of Lorraine laughed at her so-called deposition, and, in spite of failing health, she never lost heart. Firmly entrenched in Leith and ably supported by D'Oysel it looked for a time as if she would triumph, as indeed she might have done had it not been for Knox's formidable epistolary style. The exasperated reformer again rudely shattered Cecil's complacent diplomatic day-dreaming when on 29 October he wrote to Sir James Croft, Comptroller of the Household, informing him that the covert aid that England had so far given was insufficient, and concluding: 'In few words, sir, if you join not with us in open assistance we will both repent when the remedy shall be more difficult'.[44]

Unless the regent's strongly fortified base at Leith, which secured communications with France, could be reduced the Congregation had little hope. Here the omens were not good. In November an assault on Leith ended in disastrous failure, and D'Oysel, going over to the offensive, easily scattered the rebels whose makeshift levies lost heart and melted away. Substantial help from England became imperative for the rebels but remained difficult to procure, as Maitland, toiling away in London, found to his dismay. But in the last month of 1559 an unforeseen conjunction of events began to work on the English government. The regent expected a relief expedition from France which would have confirmed her hold on Scotland; but the fleet was dispersed by foul weather. D'Oysel's success, however, meant that England could not rely altogether on the winds of Heaven, and the English government was alarmed into taking a calculated risk. In January 1560 an English fleet under Admiral Winter arrived in the Forth to cut the regent's vital lines of communication with France. To the indignant French all sorts of frivolous excuses were given for this highhanded behaviour.[45] Winter's fleet, however, was only partly successful. It relieved the pressure on the rebels but could not take Leith, which was the key to the whole situation. While the French held Leith their hold on Scotland could not be broken; but to take Leith further help from England was needed. Finally, Knox's blunt hectoring and Lethington's suave diplomacy did the trick. On 22 February 1560 the Treaty of Berwick was concluded between the English government and the rebel lords in Scotland, whereby the latter, recognised as a provisional government with Chatelherault as heir-apparent to the crown, were to receive aid from England.

The treaty had also been helped on by secret intelligence from France. By this time Elizabeth and Cecil knew that the power of the Guises was being undermined, and that a situation closely analogous to that which obtained in Scotland was rapidly evolving in France. There too the Huguenots were ready to challenge the civil power, and there too the distinction was well known between Huguenots 'of religion' and Huguenots 'of state'. Many of the great feudatories of France (including the Bourbon princes) were jealous of the ambitious Guise family and were also, under the cloak of religion, preparing to combat them in arms. The storm broke with the Tumult of Amboise on 16 and

17 March 1560, which may be said to have begun the long and destructive Wars of Religion that were to paralyse France.

England's moment had come and dared not be missed. On 28 March Lord Grey led a small English force into Scotland in an attempt to invest the regent's stronghold at Leith. It has become traditional for historians to over-dramatise this whole development and exaggerate its long-term significance. For example, great stress is laid on the fact that for the first time an English army was welcomed in Scotland. But what needs to be emphasised is that it was welcomed, and none too cordially at that, only by a hard-pressed faction. Grey himself complained bitterly of that very faction's lack of co-operation: he found the Congregation's forces sullen and useless, and he too failed to take Leith: he even had trouble getting help for his sick and wounded, and when he tried to hire Scots soldiers to fill his depleted ranks he found to his surprise and chagrin that recruits could not be had, even though he was offering good money. The conclusion seems plain. The old enmity between English and Scots did not, could not, vanish overnight. Indeed, this odd and inconclusive series of scuffles was really brought to an end by events in France.

The first result of the French Wars of Religion was the loss of French dominion over Scotland. The Guises were unable to send adequate supplies and reinforcements to the Regent; but for the crisis in France itself, these would have been made available to D'Oysel and would almost certainly have overcome the rebels and their English allies. Instead, the Guises used the hostilities in Scotland as an excuse for raising troops for service in France.[46] The better to cope with the growing domestic crisis, they also began negotiations with England to settle the Scottish question. These talks were speeded up by the death of Mary of Lorraine on 11 June 1560, and on 6 July the Treaty of Edinburgh was concluded, under the terms of which both English and French troops were to withdraw from Scotland and some vague concessions were made to the Scottish protestants. In the name of Mary and Francis II a parliament was to be held in Scotland, which was not, however, to deal with religious issues.

This was certainly a very curious situation, and one that was far removed from the simple stereotype of reformation as a triumph of God's will that protestant piety was later to require. It is impossible to avoid the conclusion that chance played a large part in bringing about the Reformation in Scotland and in drawing to a close the long centuries of baneful Anglo-Scottish hostility. Remarkably little was settled by the mid-summer of 1560: if fortune had smiled on the Guises, as they confidently expected it would, they might later have ignored the Treaty of Edinburgh and, supreme in France, succeeded in re-occupying Scotland. The full consequences of that would have been incalculable; but certainly it would have driven a formidable wedge between England and Scotland. In Scotland the reformed faith might never have taken root, again with far-reaching if unimaginable consequences. But one may conjecture that in such circumstances in Scotland, as in Ireland, catholicism would have reinforced nationalism, making union with protestant England either unthinkable or, if forced, unendurable.

In the event, the Lords of the Congregation, little thanks to their own efforts and to their considerable surprise, carried the day. Rightly, if for all the wrong reasons, this has been recognised as a great, if somewhat fortuitous, turning point in the history of Scotland. But no snap verdict is applicable here; for the Reformation in Scotland, more than in most countries, was marked from the beginning by uncertainty and divergent purposes, and in the long run these cardinal facts conditioned not only the future of Scotland but also her relations with England.

5

The English Great Cause, 1560–1603

IN the historian's reckoning certain years are apt to loom larger than life, and so it has proved with 1560 which has come to be regarded as something of an *annus mirabilis* in the history of Scotland. In the history of Great Britain too it has acquired some significance, for like 1707 it has been invested with talismanic power and indeed these years are often worked into a causal relationship. To 1560 is assigned the beginning of the better understanding between England and Scotland that was in time, in this interpretation, to lead to the incorporating union of the two kingdoms. Thus A. G. Dickens, casting aside for a moment the caution that normally characterises his work, in dealing with the period after 1560 speaks of 'the steady convergence of the two countries, which continued its triumphal march through history past the milestones of 1603, 1643 and 1707'.[1]

Hindsight seems to provide some justification for such a view. But neither hindsight nor foresight could light the way for contemporaries; and to the few who cherished such an ideal solution to the 'British Problem' the triumphal march must have seemed a perfect maze of false starts and blind alleys. Yet again we are reminded that the high theoretical approach to history, with its contempt for mere facts, too easily makes nonsense of actual trends and too readily raises assumptions into dogmas. Far from being profound, such an approach is hopelessly superficial, sweeping airily aside as it does all mystery and uncertainty.

Rather, it is clear that from 1560 until 1603 the conditions that shaped the relations of the two countries remained uncertain and until almost the end of Elizabeth's long reign were capable of yielding various results. This was most notably true of the question of the succession to the throne of England, and it was precisely this complex question that dominated Anglo-Scottish relations.[2] On this issue Mary Stewart came to grief, but her son's more politic attitude confirmed the re-alignment of foreign policy that had been forced upon the weak Scottish regents after 1567—Moray, Lennox, Mar and Morton—who badly needed English support against the Marian party. As a consequence Scotland became a satellite of England and James a pensioner of Elizabeth, albeit an ungrateful and untrustworthy one. In 1603 the new relationship was formalised by the Union of the Crowns, but, it is worth stressing, mainly because James VI of Scotland had outlived his serious rivals.

Nor did protestantism form as powerful a bond between the two countries as it had promised to do at the time of the Reformation-Rebellion in Scotland. This growing divergence in matters of religion, however, is another subject that is far too complex to lend itself to facile *ex-post-facto* explanations, though, needless to say, these abound. The crucial point is that in the sixteenth century too much stress should not be laid on the church question as a divisive force between the two kingdoms. Rather, ecclesiastical problems caused serious dissensions in both countries, and the matter cannot be represented as a head-on collision between English and Scottish views. It is indeed positively misleading to identify presbyterianism with Scotland and episcopacy with England, so overlooking the vital point that in Elizabeth's reign a powerful puritan movement arose in England while at the same time in Scotland a fierce conflict began between presbyterians and supporters of episcopacy. In the late sixteenth century, then, it was by no means obvious that in the long run presbytery was to triumph in Scotland and episcopacy to weather the storm in England.

On the religious side the first complications arose from some peculiar developments in Scotland following the Treaty of Edinburgh. In 1560 little was settled except the overthrow of *ecclesia scoticana*, accomplished by a sweeping act of parliament on 24 August which renounced papal authority and, on pain of heavy penalties, forbade catholic worship. The rejection of papal claims caused little trouble, for the papacy had shown scant interest in the ecclesiastical struggle in Scotland and had long been ill regarded there. But papal claims are not the sum and substance of catholicism, and harsh penal laws were needed against the numerous Scots who clung to the mass and the old rites. Only slowly was the bulk of the catholic population dragooned out of its faith, and, in the years immediately following the Reformation of the religion of the state, catholics were particularly numerous in the Highlands and Islands, the North-East and the Borders. The legality of this legislation, however, was open to question since the consideration of religion by the parliament of 1560 had been expressly forbidden by the Treaty of Edinburgh. The conventional answer is that the will of the nation prevailed. According to this theory the small barons or freeholders, who could not hitherto be coaxed or bullied into attending parliaments, turned up to safeguard protestantism.[3] Little evidence is adduced to substantiate this theory, and it seems equally likely that the barons attended to pick up what crumbs they could of the plunder of the church. The Reformation in Scotland, then, was carried out in defiance of lawful authority, and not surprisingly Mary, Queen of Scots refused to ratify these acts, which were not accepted as fully legal until 1567. But in practice they were applied, and their dubious legality was the least awkward and least puzzling feature of the Scottish Reformation. Far more troublesome was its general untidiness.

The reformers were obviously caught unprepared by their victory, but the hard facts of the situation could not be burked; if the old faith were to be rejected, then another must first take its place. The Confession of Faith accepted by the parliament on 17 August is, however, a puzzling document.[4] The work of Knox and the other leading preachers, it was hastily got up for the occasion and seems to have been something of a stop-gap. Written in pithy Scots and composed in rhetorical Old Testament style, it is a forceful piece of work and notably free from the arid hair-splitting of later confessions; but as a statement of the doctrines of the reformed Church of Scotland it was vague. Well aware of this, its authors, following the practice of the earliest reformers, showed the open-mindedness of the uncertain by dispatching copies to the leading reformed theologians of Europe, and in their Preface expressed their willingness to amend the Confession whenever the critics could justify their strictures from Holy Writ.[5] In its general lay-out the Scots Confession followed the Augsburg Confession; its main arguments were drawn from Scripture eked out by appeals to the basic symbols of the Catholic Church—the Apostolic, Nicene and Athanasian creeds. The result was a 'sempill Confession' with little pretension to intellectual distinction; nonetheless its authors felt it to be inspired by the Holy Ghost.[6] Later commentators have found it hard to categorise, and it is usually regarded as a mixture of Lutheran, Calvinist and Anglican elements. In a sense, this is correct enough, in that such an eclectic approach was a common feature of the earliest stages of the Reformation in most countries. But at a deeper level the Scots Confession clearly belonged to the Calvinist camp, even though justification and predestination were not rigorously defined.

The essential Calvinism of the Scots Confession is evident in its treatment of the sacrament of the Lord's Supper in which transubstantiation and the supposed Zwinglian commemorative interpretation were both roundly condemned. The high rhetorical vein of the argument does seem to verge on the Lutheran doctrine of consubstantiation but in reality does not. In the Scots Confession there is indeed a strong emphasis on mystic action but operative in the faith of the true communicant and not in the elements as such, a doctrine that was to become a hallmark of Scottish Calvinism; and it is also surely significant that the communion itself was to be carried out according to the Order of Geneva.[7] At the same time, it is interesting to note that the Calvinism of the Scottish reformers was not so clearly expressed as that used in the formulation of the Thirty-Eight Articles of 1563 which were finally ratified in 1571 as the famous Thirty-Nine Articles of the Church of England. To regard Calvinism as peculiarly Scottish is thus another grave, if common, error.

The great point of divergence between the two national churches came later over polity and the vexed question of the relationship between church and state. In Elizabeth the English reformers had again found a 'godly prince', whereas in the crucial opening stages of the Reformation in Scotland the godly prince was conspicuously absent in more senses than one. The young queen was a Roman catholic as well as an absentee; but even if a godly prince had materialised in the shape of either Arran or the Lord James Stewart (notions with which the reformers had toyed) the English solution, indeterminate as that then was, would hardly have worked in Scotland. Both in practice and in theory the authority of the crown in England was much stronger than it was in Scotland where too many sinister interests stood in the way of the evolution of an Anglican-style polity. Knox, for one, was thoroughly aware of the difficulties and tried to shape his course accordingly. He had already broken with Calvin's political theory, boldly positing the right of subjects to oppose ungodly rulers, and something of this appears, muted but menacing, in the Confession of 1560. Article eleven clearly asserts the doctrines of spiritual independence and the Headship of Christ, who is described as 'the onelie head of his Kirk' and 'our Soveraine and supreme Governour'. Clearly, the doctrinal reformers had no use for Caesaro-papistry however qualified. The seed of much future strife, and marked divergence from England, thus lay in these fundamental, and quite explicit, passages of the Scots Confession of 1560.

On a more practical plane, the higher benefices in Scotland were not open to the reformed church, for the existing incumbents, few of whom were committed papalists, remained in legal possession and could not have been forcibly dispossessed without endangering the reformed cause. For example, to have deprived Archbishop John Hamilton would have been to alienate his powerful kin, and this might have had disastrous consequences for the Reformation.[8] The traditional protestant view that ecclesiastical corruption ceased after the Reformation is therefore at odds with the facts, for the old rotten structure stood.[9] Indeed after 1560, alarmed by the uncertainty of the times, the old clergy continued to feu or otherwise dispose of kirklands; and long after 1567 the titulars continued to enjoy kirk revenues and to despoil the church. This is an important topic that has never received anything like the attention it deserves. The massive transfer of church lands and revenues, before and after the Reformation, initiated the greatest economic and social developments in Scottish history prior to the coming of the Industrial and Agrarian Revolutions. New classes of men, feuars, acquired substance and the appetite for power; and the poor commons suffered as kindly tenants had their customary rights eroded by secularising lords and commendators. But of all this our economic historians, bewitched by such outmoded theoretical models as 'religion and the rise of capitalism', seem virtually unaware.[10]

The plundering of the church also helped to give rise to a radical ecclesiastical movement, whose social ideals were clearly stated in the two Books of Discipline. In the First Book of Discipline of 1560 the germ of class antagonism appears in an attack on the lay appropriators: 'Some gentlemen are now as cruel over their tenants as ever were the Papists, requiring of them whatsoever before they paid to the Church; so that the Papistical tyranny shall only be changed in the tyranny of the lord or laird'.[11] And in 1571 one of the most fearless and outspoken of the ministers, David Ferguson of Dunfermline, preaching to the General Assembly before the Regent Lennox and many of the nobility, inveighed against the iniquitous system that starved the clergy to fatten a rapacious nobility and its corrupt dependents: 'For this day Christ is spulzeit among us, while that which ought to maintain the ministry of the kirk and the poor is given to profane men, flatterers in courts, and hirelings. The poor, in the mean time, oppressed with hunger, the kirks and temples decaying for lack of ministers and upholding, and the schools utterly neglected and overseen'.[12]

Yet some authors, such as H. R. Trevor-Roper and his following, can explain Scottish ecclesiastical radicalism only in terms of crackbrained fanaticism. Perhaps sometime they should descend from their airy theoretical heights to dart a glance at the evidence. They would then surely find a significant contrast between English and Scottish experiences during the Reformation. The rape of the Church of England was mainly the work of the crown, and, as Christopher Hill has demonstrated, this was an inhibiting factor of some weight which prevented the church from being reduced to a mere ruin.[13] It was far otherwise in Scotland.

In Scotland, in marked contrast to England, the early government of the reformed church was a muddle partly because of political circumstances and partly because of the confused thinking of the reformers, though nothing, apparently, can dispose of the folk-belief that Knox and his brethren set up a presbyterian church in Scotland.[14] They certainly condemned prelacy but said little either for or against episcopacy. Their chief concern, indeed, was practical, to restore an active preaching ministry, and to this end the office of superintendent was introduced. It was not novel, for the concept of the superintendent as 'godly bishop' had already been advocated by both continental and English reformers.[15] But it does not follow that the Scottish superintendents should be equated with these examples. They are best defined on the terms in which they were conceived in Scotland; the Scottish superintendents were not consecrated and did not constitute a superior order in the spiritual ministry, were censurable by their fellow ministers and held accountable to the General Assembly. The Scottish superintendents, then, were not simply the bishops 'done into Latin': they may or may not have been intended as temporary expedients, for the key passage in the First Book of Discipline, that superintendents were 'most expedient for this time', is notoriously ambiguous.[16] The evidence is too weak to decide the point; but, on balance, it looks as if the superintendents were intended as temporary expedients who might have become permanent features if the difficulties occasioned by Mary's reign had not supervened.

It is not even known what proposals about church government were put before the parliament of 1560, and there are grounds for believing that the Book of Discipline was only completed some months later. At any rate the Reformation parliament made no effort to provide for the government of the reformed kirk, which was left pretty much to its own devices and starved of finance. The seal was set on this indifference when in January 1561 parliament rejected the First Book of Discipline, many of the nobles sneeringly dismissing that remarkable document as mere 'devout imaginations'.

The First Book of Discipline had little to say about church government but went into considerable details about endowment. It emphasised the social witness of the new kirk, outlining a national system of education that would cover every parish and cater for the educational needs of all classes in the community right up to university level; it also stressed the claims of the poor; and the reformers evidently hoped that their ambitious social programme would be financed from the patrimony of the old church, so much of which was by then in the hands of the Lords of the Congregation. The First Book of Discipline proposed that the ministers, the dominies and the poor should be provided for from the teinds (anglicé tithes), while the universities and the superintendents were to be financed from the bishops' temporalities. It was indeed a 'devout imagination' to expect feudal magnates, however pious, meekly to hand over their hard-won spoil. Creed vied with greed and lost hands down. And from this much flowed. Stormed Knox in his *History*: 'Everything that repugned to their corrupt affections was called in their mockage "devout imaginations". The cause we have before declared: some were licentious; some had greedily gripped to the possessions of the Kirk; and others thought they would not lack their part of Christ's coat, yea, and that before that ever he was hanged, as by the preachers they were oft rebuked . . . There was none within the realm more unmerciful to the poor ministers than were they which had greatest rents of the churches'.[17]

In the upshot, all that the reformed church could secure at this time were Thirds of Benefices; and, as Knox predicted might happen, sometimes dishonest manipulation of the Thirds reduced the sums provided for the ministers to meagre doles.[18] Here, then, is another important point that helped to shape the future: the sacrilegious greed of the landed proprietors was not forgotten, and the bitter memory of it further stimulated the formation of a radical party within the kirk, a party whose aims could ultimately only be realised by control not only of the church but of the state as well. It need hardly be added that the story that the noble thieves were simply regaining lands foolishly lavished by their superstitious ancestors on the kirk malignant is mere silly rationalisation; the nobility and baronage of Scotland had changed out of all recognition since the twelfth and thirteenth centuries, and few indeed could claim to be legatees of the original donors. It was rank theft and well known to be such. That knowledge also helped to shape future events, and not just the policies of the covenanters but also those pursued by James VI and I and even, surprising as it may sound, by Charles I.

Such polity as did emerge, if polity is the right word for it, was a *pis aller*, some elements of which could later be identified with episcopacy and others (such as the General Assembly, kirk sessions and the eldership) could easily be integrated into a conciliar, or presbyterian, form of government. At any rate, it seems clear that the gulf that is supposed to lie between John Knox and Andrew Melville is largely illusory.[19] Knox, after all, had helped to set up a non-episcopal polity at Frankfurt in 1556;[20] and both Knox and Melville saw that the crucial problem facing the reformed kirk of Scotland was that of endowment. But Knox and the earlier reformers, unlike Melville and his followers, had no dread of what was later to be abominated as erastianism. On the contrary they were eager for parliamentary approval, and intent on securing for the church all the recognition and support that statutes could provide. To describe the first generation of reformers as anti-erastian (and it is a common enough error) is a bit wide of the mark. The terrors of erastianism did not become self-evident until a party in the church fared ill at the hands of the state; but as long as the state gave some countenance to the kirkmen the comforting doctrine of 'the godly magistracy' was invoked, and it was only when parliament refused the demands of the more radical reformers like Melville that the rift between church and state really began to open up. As we have seen, tension had arisen as early as 1561; but open strife did not begin until the 1570s.

To ask why the Scottish reformers did not follow the way of England, then, is obviously a non-question. The Elizabethan church settlement was such a protracted, complex and uncertain process that it could have afforded no real guide to the early reformers in Scotland, quite apart from the fact that the religious and political situations in the two countries were markedly different. Besides, Knox was already disenchanted with 'Anglicanism', his disenchantment having recently been reinforced by the quarrels at Frankfurt. He condemned the second Edwardine Prayer Book as stained with popery; and, just as obviously, Elizabeth and Archbishop Parker feared that Knox was really intent on civil, if not social, revolution. Wrote Parker, 'God save us from such a visitation as Knox has attempted in Scotland; the people to be orderers of things!'[21] Elizabeth was well aware that there were Englishmen like Christopher Goodman who thought as Knox thought and who had no time for half measures. But she had to move cautiously, for to have shifted too rapidly into the protestant camp might have induced Philip of Spain to make common cause with France. At the same time the moderate reformers in England could not be left dangling indefinitely, any more than the crown could allow the party of Geneva its head. Well aware of the dangers that beset her, and personally free from deep religious convictions, Elizabeth was determined to avoid rash moves and to control events by consummate if deceitful diplomacy. Possibly her own ideal would have been a simple reversion to Henricianism; but in practice this was clearly impossible.[22] It was not just in foreign affairs that Elizabeth gave early demonstrations of her cool mastery of diplomacy.

Apart from Edmund Bonner, bishop of London, the Marian bishops put up a very feeble resistance and were cleverly outflanked at every turn. Providence, too, seemed from the outset to favour the new regime. The archbishop of Canterbury died only a few hours after Mary Tudor, and this gave Elizabeth a great advantage. Her first primate exactly met her needs: Matthew Parker was a scholar, a convinced believer in moderate reform, and, steeped in the tradition of Cranmer, was unwilling to countenance the radical demands that were being put forward by the Marian exiles who had sat at the feet of 'the pope of Geneva'. A decisive break with Rome and Roman usages was not to lead to subjection to other foreign influences and doctrines; the structure and the polity of the Church of England were to stand, and a protestant faith was not to sweep away every vestige of catholic piety. Parker, in short, was a stout upholder of what could already be vaguely defined as the 'Anglican' position—to use his own term, he believed in 'mediocrity', an avoidance of extremes whether Roman or reformed. This was the position which in his quiet but effective way he was determined to consolidate. It was also the queen's view, and, highly suspicious of the Marian exiles, she turned naturally to the stay-at-home, down-to-earth Parker.

The details of the Elizabethan church settlement are well known:[23] how Elizabeth prevaricated until peace was made at Cateau-Cambrésis; how thereafter the pace of reform quickened; how an Act of Supremacy undid Mary Tudor's work and vested supreme power over the church in the crown; and how the basic changes were completed by an Act of Uniformity to enforce acceptance of the new regime in church and state. The most striking contrast with Scotland is that the Elizabethan settlement firmly grasped the problem of sovereignty and began by defining the polity and the state connection. This fundamental approach conferred many benefits. The English church, like that of Scotland, was troubled by corruption, spoliation and feeble parochial administration;[24] but in England these blemishes, though troublesome, were kept within reasonable limits mainly because of the closeness of the concordat established between church and state. The Marian bishops who refused to conform (all, that is, except Kitchin of Llandaff) were deprived and had to make way for reformed bishops—again a fundamental point of difference between Scotland and England. Elizabeth, too, cleverly removed the stigma of caesaro-papistry by insisting upon being regarded as Supreme Governor rather than Supreme Head of the Church of England. In addition, the parliament was now a factor to be reckoned with, and parliament obliquely defined the terms of the royal supremacy, which could only be exercised through a body of ecclesiastical commissioners.[25]

Important though the questions of polity were, however, answers to them did not entirely solve the ecclesiastical problem. The Marian exiles returned from the Continent too late to affect the crucial opening stages of the settlement, but were still eager to ensure that the revision of the faith would bring it into line with Genevan orthodoxy. Foiled in the ecclesiastical forum by the mild but, when occasion required it, firm Parker, the radicals, fully appreciating the enhanced powers of parliament, turned with unerring instinct to the House of Commons. There was much to argue about, for few reformers were content either with the second Edwardine Prayer Book or the Articles of Religion of 1553. Their replacement, the Thirty-Eight (later Thirty-Nine) Articles, worked up by Parker and accepted by Convocation in 1563, were a compromise built largely on the Articles of 1553 but accepting Calvinist views on predestination and the sacrament of the Lord's Supper.[26] Some had thought fleetingly of modelling the revised Articles on the Augsburg Confession,[27] which was as unrealistic as Cecil's advice to the Scots to follow the example of Denmark. The ill effects of simply copying the Augsburg Confession would have been twofold—to deepen the strife with the Genevan party and at the same time, by rejecting Cranmer's work, destroy the very basis of Anglicanism. The resulting Thirty-Nine Articles did not please everybody—in which respect at least they have had through the ages a remarkably consistent history—and were not sanctioned by parliament until 1571. But in the age of religious strife in which they were drawn up, the Thirty-Nine Articles furnished useful weapons both of defence and offence. By firm denunciation of papal claims and Romish doctrines the Articles answered the theologians of Trent, and by adopting some of the tenets of Geneva they established the *bona fides* of the English church in the protestant world. On the other hand, to have attempted to adopt Lutheran doctrines at this point would have been folly, for Lutheranism had become inward-looking and riven by fierce disputes. One may well suspect that the Thirty-Nine Articles of the Church of England owed not a little to the needs of foreign policy, and that they were, in the fullest sense of the term, Elizabethan. In fact, it was not then possible to separate religion from foreign and domestic policy.

Nowhere was this more apparent than in the question of the succession to the throne, which was a vexed subject from the very first day of Elizabeth's reign.[28]

Indeed it was the most persistent problem that dogged the Tudors, worse even than financial stringency. It had exercised Henry VIII and had dictated most of his policies. Indeed, the possible failure of his line was the great fear of Henry's life and one that he tried to settle in his will, a baffling document that was to cause much controversy. In 1558 Elizabeth was the last survivor of the direct line of Henry VIII, and if she were to die without leaving heirs a very serious situation would arise. Dark memories of York and Lancaster still haunted the mind of mid-sixteenth-century England, which was made even more apprehensive by the menacing situation in which England stood in that age of ruthless expansionism and bitter religious strife. The fact that Mary Stewart (though excluded by the will of Henry VIII) was nearest of blood, and that she was not only a Roman catholic but closely tied to France could conjure up nightmare visions. It was Mary's tragedy that she epitomised the very dangers that were most widely feared in England. Nor from the very outset was there any doubt about this, for her claim was used by France to exert pressure on England, and indeed continued to be so used in spite of the provisions of the treaties of Edinburgh and Cateau-Cambrésis. From Mary's pretensions Elizabeth wrung a dividend by forcing oblique support from Philip II of Spain; to counteract the designs of France, Philip supported a rival claimant, Lady Catherine Grey, who traced her descent from Mary Tudor, the younger daughter of Henry VII. Other possibles seemed to be in the running—notably the Earl of Huntingdon (who was descended from Edward IV), and Henry, Lord Darnley (a Lennox Stewart and through his mother descended from the second marriage of Margaret Tudor). But in reality they were never much more than pawns in the game, though they played it assiduously. From 1558 onwards there was something like an English 'Great Cause' in anticipation, with much complicated intrigue, pamphleteering and canvassing of learned legal opinion.

As far as strict descent was concerned Mary Stewart undoubtedly had the best claim, the more so as, unlike Elizabeth, she was one of the few descendants of Henry VII whose claim could not be impugned on the score of legitimacy. The strength of Mary's claim was well appreciated in Scotland, and in fact her brief but stormy personal reign from her return as a young widow in August 1561 was throughout conditioned, not, as is so popularly supposed, by the religious question but by the problem of the English succession. Though Mary insisted on remaining a Roman catholic (partly out of conviction but also partly because her catholicism could be a weapon in the succession struggle) she made no attempt to undo the Reformation in Scotland.

Indeed, one of Mary's first acts was to join enthusiastically in a campaign which broke the leading catholic noble in Scotland, the Earl of Huntly, who virtually ruled the north-east Lowlands and was a great, if unloved, power in the Highlands. The campaign of autumn 1562 that culminated in the triumph of the queen's forces at Corrichie and the death of Huntly turned not on religious considerations but on the old thorny question of the maintenance of royal authority. Mary, in short, at first co-operated wholeheartedly with the regime established by the reformers which was headed by her half-brother the Lord James, or as he became in 1562 the Earl of Moray. And, significantly, one of the motives of the

Corrichie campaign was to prise the lands of Moray from the grasp of the Gordons. In spite of the fulminations of Knox, then, Mary was not intent upon overthrowing the reformed faith and reimposing popery. Nor, in spite of the misleading light cast on her reign by Knox, did Mary from the first lack support or popularity. Guided by the advice of her Guise relations, her aim was directed throughout at the English succession; and so initially she worked with Moray and his friends, on the understanding that they would do everything in their power to advance her claim. Since they were already strong for the English interest and in good standing with Elizabeth, and since they could expect to profit from the success of Mary's claim, it was the logical policy all round.

Moray, prompted and supported by the far-seeing Maitland of Lethington, threw himself energetically into the project. Writing to Cecil on 6 August 1561, Moray contended that Mary's claim was the best according to 'the law of all nations' and suggested a bargain—if Elizabeth would recognise Mary's right of succession Mary in return would drop her immediate claim, no longer regard Elizabeth as an usurper, and refrain from pressing her suit as heir presumptive during Elizabeth's lifetime.[29] The wily Maitland was dispatched to London to argue the case before Elizabeth, and in particular to assure her that Mary was ready to accept the compromise. Maitland also argued that the will of Henry VII, which did not exclude the issue of Margaret Tudor and James IV, should take precedence over the will of Henry VIII, the authenticity of which was doubtful in any case. The arguments were all in vain. Cecil disliked the prospect of Mary Stewart succeeding to the throne of England, and a handle was given to his opposition by Mary's failure to ratify the Treaty of Edinburgh. Mary's attitude, though, was reasonable enough: for her to renounce her claim without adequate guarantees for the future would have been foolish, and neither Moray nor Maitland advised this course. On the other hand, for Elizabeth to acknowledge Mary as her heir-presumptive would have been dangerous; in Elizabeth's own words, compliance would have set 'my winding sheet before my eye'.[30] In an age that believed in political assassination, and practised it on all sorts of pious pretexts, Elizabeth was right to leave the question open. But almost certainly she herself regarded Mary Stewart's claim as best and showed no inveterate hostility to it, perhaps because she disliked Lady Catherine Grey whom she treated harshly.[31] Cunning diplomatist and mistress of all the histrionic arts though she was, Elizabeth seems to have been sincere in her desire to safeguard Mary's right. For one thing, she must have realised that, failing issue of her own, the Tudor blood could best continue in the Stewart line; and, quite apart from the crying need for diplomatic flirtations, none of which had any real prospect of getting as far as the altar, Elizabeth possibly feared that like her sister Mary she would be 'but a barren stock', in which case marriage would merely further complicate an already involved problem. It is equally likely, as has been recently suggested, that in the man's world of the sixteenth century marriage would have led inevitably to diminution of her own power[32]—a shrewd assessment to which the history of Mary Stewart was soon to give point.

In practice, however, Mary Stewart's claim suffered from serious weaknesses: as an alien she was debarred by English law; Henry VIII's will, if its validity was accepted, told against her; and above all her religion and French connections ensured determined opposition from convinced protestants. From the English protestant point of view the Suffolk claim, in the person of Lady Catherine Grey, was much to be preferred. Nor could Mary Stewart at the outset counterbalance the antagonism with English catholic support which at this time plumped for the Lennox claim and looked to Henry, Lord Darnley, who was English by birth and upbringing and a catholic. And so from the outset there was very strong opposition to Mary both inside and outside parliament. Thus, 'Gorboduc', a play by Sackville and Norton, was a thinly veiled attack on Mary's title and made free use of the Scottophobia that was still endemic in England. The campaign against Mary intensified in October 1562 when Elizabeth had a serious attack of smallpox and her death seemed likely. The Privy Council then tried to settle the succession but failed to reach agreement, the protestant majority wavering between Catherine Grey and the Earl of Huntingdon, thus enabling the catholic minority to stave off a decision. The following year parliament insisted on discussing the succession, much to Elizabeth's displeasure, but in spite of strong anti-Marian propaganda the matter was still left unresolved.

Alarmed by all this, the Scottish government again sent Maitland south to urge Mary's case. Moray and Maitland were getting into difficulties over the question of Mary's marriage. Like Elizabeth, Mary Stewart was the last of her line and it was important to her, to Scotland, and even to England, that she should re-marry and beget heirs. But such a natural step as marriage was surrounded by difficulties, not the least of which was that care had to be taken to secure Elizabeth's prior consent. And to secure Elizabeth's consent to anything was labour of Sisyphus. Then, too, if Mary were to marry a foreign prince, such as Spain's Don Carlos, this could easily impair Anglo-Scottish relations. For a time it had seemed as if the ever-ready Arran, who was no longer of use to Elizabeth as a prospective husband, might acquire Mary's hand, so committing her to the reformed cause and the mercurial Hamiltons to the House of Stewart; but Mary showed no interest in a marriage of such very limited convenience to a man who was already obviously hovering on the brink of madness. Elizabeth with cool effrontery then brought forward her own bold wooer, Robert Dudley (later created Earl of Leicester), whom scandal accused of the providential death of his wife Amy Robsart in September 1560 the better to press his suit with Elizabeth. It is essential to remember that at this point Elizabeth Tudor and not Mary Stewart was regarded as the royal wanton. Understandably, Mary contemptuously spurned Elizabeth's 'horse keeper', and relations between the two women rapidly deteriorated. Moray and Lethington could make nothing of Elizabeth, and gradually Mary lost faith in her half-brother's policies and began to work out moves of her own. And here she deserves every sympathy. Moray's policies sounded fine, but in the face of Elizabeth's intransigence they were so much hot air. The intelligent Lethington was only too well aware of the problem, for he had pushed Mary's case vigorously, in and out of season, but without result. Elizabeth does not seem to have had any conscious design in this, but was simply playing her usual game of wasting time and staving off decisions.

The upshot was Mary's marriage to her cousin Darnley, which was celebrated by catholic rites in Edinburgh on 29 July 1565. The origin of this match remains obscure and mysterious, not least because Elizabeth 'could hardly have done more to ease the way to the Darnley marriage, short of openly pressing for it'.[33] Elizabeth had known since 1562 that the Earl of Lennox, Darnley's father, was eager for such a match, and in June 1563 she herself supported the project in order to undermine the negotiations with Don Carlos. She then grew suspicious of the Darnley suit, back-pedalled on it, but finally allowed Darnley to go to Scotland, with, as the near inevitable result, his marriage to Mary. There is mystery too about Mary's motives; for her it may well have been an affair of the heart, but it was certainly also deliberate policy. Had Mary, Queen of Scots resembled her mother in more than appearance, the Darnley marriage might have turned out a master stroke; but Mary was a poor politician, and from this false move her troubles inexorably followed. For her the main benefits of the Darnley marriage were that it united the Stewart claims to the English succession, and thereafter little was heard of the Lennox title; and it transferred to Mary the still very considerable support of the catholic faction in England. But in practice the drawbacks outweighed the advantages. The Darnley marriage led to a breech with the moderate reformers headed by Moray, and though in the Chase-about-Raid Mary put her opponents to flight the damage remained. She had lost the middle ground and could not thereafter regain it. The marriage, in fact, stiffened the opposition of the more extreme protestants in both Scotland and England. Elizabeth, too, with matchless duplicity, pretended to be outraged by the marriage; and all in all the English puritans had some cause for believing that the moment had come to settle the question of the succession on their terms.

At this point Maitland went to desperate lengths to urge Mary's case. On 3 January 1566 he wrote to Cecil a long tendentious letter on the subject, in which he hinted that the English claim to dominion over Scotland might after all be valid, and that, though he did not dare avow it in public, he would not object if Cecil saw fit to make use of it.[34] The purpose, of course, was twofold: to restrain Mary, who as a vassal of the English crown would have to take orders from London, and to remove from her path the objection that she was an alien. But Cecil, who was as long in the tooth as Maitland, remained hostile to Mary and, having no wish to revive the old quarrel with Scotland, wisely steered clear of this Machiavellian ploy. As it was, the year 1566 was critical. The claim of Lady Catherine Grey was vigorously pushed in the House of Commons, partly because the puritans feared for the security of the protestant religion but partly also because the House was determined to win a larger voice in the making of policy. On either score the interference of parliament was anathema to Elizabeth, and she refused to give way; to name a successor, whether Catherine Grey or Mary Stewart, would be, again in her own graphic words, 'to dig her grave before she was dead'.[35] So the question remained open. But, if anything, Mary's claim appeared to be strengthened by the birth of her son on 19 June 1566, even though James was baptised by the Roman rite.

Already, however, some extraordinary changes of fortune were taking place, with great issues depending not on vague sociological forces but on the career of a young woman caught up in a difficult, and perhaps impossible, situation. Politics, not sociology, explain the downfall of Mary, Queen of Scots. But the many puzzling aspects of her brief personal rule cannot be gone into here, and a bare outline must suffice. She was young and inexperienced but scarcely the hapless victim of wicked men and cruel circumstances that her defenders have depicted.[36] There was, rather, a masculine streak in Mary's nature, revealed in a boldness and resilience seldom found in women and rarely enough in men. Like Elizabeth she was determined to rule as well as reign, but, unlike Elizabeth, she lacked the cool calculation that alone could make this possible. Yet she refused to be a passive agent. It is important to remember that 'the Daughter of Debate', as Elizabeth dubbed her, helped to make her own destiny through her head-strong policies. She was indeed surrounded by wicked men—the turbulent, ruth-less Scottish nobles who, aided by the English government, had repeatedly in the past half-century brought their country to the verge of destruction. Moray's pious speech could not disguise the fact that he was of their number or that he was driven by the same primitive lusts and vaulting ambitions. Mary knew all that and took the risks in her stride. She flattered herself that she, a *politique*, could outwit these savage survivals from the feudal past. And here the fall of Huntly might well have played a significant rôle: it may have led Mary to believe that adroit policies could bring down in ruin even the greatest noble house, but it may also have led the other magnates to reflect that what was meted out to Huntly might well be their own fate if Mary secured a firm grip on her kingdom. And to secure such a grip undoubtedly was Mary's aim. It is essential to remem-ber that in the months following the Chase-about-Raid she governed the country, and that she was actively building up an interest to enable her to perpetuate her rule. Not only was this a threat to the feudal nobility of Scotland but it would inevitably have entailed foreign support and so have jeopardised the continuance of good relations with England. The whole future of Anglo-Scottish relations therefore turned upon the success or failure of Mary's policy.

The marriage with Darnley brought all these latent issues to a head. It occasioned the eclipse of Moray and his faction; and it made the protestants in Scotland fear that Mary was intent upon overthrowing their religion, suspicions that remained even though Mary went out of her way to dispel them. The real flaw, however, proved to be Darnley, whose head the marriage turned. Younger and even less experienced than Mary, his vanity and his ambitions knew no bounds. He desired the crown matrimonial, but his idiotic conduct soon alienated Mary and she refused to grant it. King Henry (to give Darnley his courtesy title) then began to intrigue with the disaffected protestant lords—if they would secure him the crown matrimonial, he would undertake to see that Moray and the other refugees of the Chase-about-Raid were restored. The bargain was sealed in the blood of David Riccio, Mary's secretary, whom the jealous Darnley suspected of being her lover. Riccio, who was also falsely believed to be a papal agent, was brutally murdered at Holyrood on 9 March 1566, almost literally in the presence of the queen who was then pregnant.

Mary showed both courage and a certain ruthless astuteness in the desperate weeks that followed. Though she now hated Darnley, whose connivance at the murder was no secret, she needed to make use of him, at least until after the birth of her child. So she managed to detach her husband from the other conspirators, who then marked him down as a dangerous double-dealer who knew enough to destroy them all.[37] The birth of Prince James on 19 June 1566 probably confirmed his father's fate. Nor can there be much doubt about Mary's complicity. Ever since her sinister conference with Moray's adherents and other leading nobles at Craigmillar near Edinburgh in November 1566 she knew that a violent end was intended for Darnley; but the details of his death at Kirk-o'-Field in Edinburgh on 10 February 1567 remain enveloped in mystery. The blowing up of the house was certainly the work of the Earl of Bothwell, who had been notoriously close to the queen for some time, and public opinion was justified in pointing to him as the murderer, in spite of shoals of red-herrings that recent commentators have dragged and re-dragged over the murky scene. That the Earl of Morton, and innumerable others, would as cheerfully have dispatched King Henry does not answer the case against Bothwell, nor yet dispose of the likelihood of Mary's complicity.

In any event, it was not the murder of Darnley that ruined Mary. Few mourned that luckless popinjay, apart from his own kin and such a strong Lennox man as George Buchanan, who was later to be the most virulent of the queen's accusers. Her accusers could make much of the circumstantial evidence; as, for example, that within a few days of Darnley's murder the court tailor was hard at work refashioning his finery to fit Bothwell, who was acquitted after a farcical trial. Shortly thereafter Mary's diminishing credibility was completely destroyed by her alleged abduction, ravishment and marriage by the protestant rite to the masterful Bothwell. Sympathetic biographers have astonishingly little difficulty in explaining away such a curious sequence of events; to contemporaries matters appeared in a very different light, and Mary had to pay the price for her reckless folly. Public opinion, hitherto on the whole favourable, swung violently against her, and even the catholic powers and the pope himself joined in the chorus of condemnation.[38] But resilient and optimistic as ever, Mary hoped with the support of the Hamiltons to beat down all opposition. The Hamiltons were too slow in rallying to her aid, and, outfronted at Carberry on 15 June 1567, she was forced to part with her murderous husband and to abdicate in favour of her infant son, James, for whom Moray was to act as regent. In one way Elizabeth welcomed these events but in another sincerely deplored them; it was good that Mary should be pinioned but bad that a crowned head should be so treated by rascally subjects. Elizabeth, therefore, tried to have Mary restored on terms that would ensure her subservience to England; but Moray's intransigence foiled the attempt.

'The Good Regent' had evidently no intention of relinquishing power, and had, in all probability, high hopes of his own; if the infant James were to die, Moray, bastard though he was, might have prospects. As for Mary, her captivity in Scotland was simply a death sentence with an indefinite respite. But the daughter of debate was not yet finished. Charming some of her jailer's family and enlisting their aid, she escaped from Lochleven on 2 May 1568 and, supported by the Hamiltons, made a courageous bid to restore herself. Moray's iron nerve damned the enterprise. And, of course, the help of the Hamiltons, whether merely promised or given, was the surest prescription for failure. Mary's forces were defeated at Langside near Glasgow on 13 May 1568, and she herself fled to England for aid and refuge.

As far as the succession was concerned Mary now had no prospect of being countenanced by Elizabeth, but, buoyant as ever, she hoped that the English queen would help to restore her. This Elizabeth could not do. Moray would not have it; and also the puritan outcry in England against popish Mary touched new heights. After the Bothwell marriage Lady Catherine Grey's stock soared to such an extent that Leicester, a shrewd opportunist, deserted Mary for the Suffolk side. But that cause was soon shattered by the death of Lady Catherine whose issue by the Earl of Hertford Elizabeth had already bastardised. The remaining Suffolk claimants were of poor calibre and never seriously considered. There is thus surely supreme irony in the fact that if Mary Stewart could have contented herself a little longer with the fabian policies of Moray and Maitland her position in 1568 would have been virtually unassailable. Instead, captive and besmirched by a commission of inquiry which carefully refrained from pronouncing her either guilty or innocent, she could no longer figure as an official candidate.[39] True, all was not lost of the Stewart claim, for the Regent Moray worked closely with the English government, hoping that the infant James would be recognised as Elizabeth's successor. But that also proved to be a long and difficult row to hoe. James like his mother was alien in English eyes, and his future seemed almost as uncertain as hers. Uncertain, too, seemed the future of his kingdom, which after Moray's assassination in January 1570 was rent by a fierce civil war between the king's men and the followers of Mary, chief among the queen's men being 'Chameleon' Maitland. Thus Elizabeth, aided by events, was able to continue her career of endless prevarication. Yet, paradoxically, the main problem was still Mary Stewart. Her catholicism, so lightly borne in Scotland, furnished her in England, close prisoner though she was, with a powerful political lever. She became the great hope of the English catholics with whom she was linked as early as the Northern Rebellion of 1569, and far from ending with the harsh suppression of the rebellion English catholic support for Mary increased after the pope formally excommunicated Elizabeth in 1570. No wonder the Queen of Scots had for her motto, 'in my end is my beginning'! But her game was now a deadly one—not just to be recognised as Elizabeth's heir but to dispatch her as an illegitimate usurper.

The fall of Mary, then, did not solve the problem of Anglo-Scottish relations. The principal issue between the two kingdoms remained the succession question, which subsumed religious complications and international threats. The catholic interest, galvanised by the activities of the missionary priests, became an even greater menace in England, and the government was forced to take strong measures against recusancy. From this situation, embittered by the growing threat from Spain, Mary's doom ultimately stemmed. After the discovery of the Ridolfi Plot in 1571 the English puritans bayed for blood and Elizabeth was hard driven to protect Mary from a violent end. The hysteria mounted again after the Massacre of St. Bartholomew in August 1572, and yet again after the assassination of William the Silent in July 1584. In the meantime Mary had schemed with French help for her restoration in Scotland; and this her son knew and resented. As James put it to Leicester in December 1586, when his mother's life was at stake: 'how fonde and inconstant I were if I shude preferre my mother to the title let all men judge'.[40] In the circumstances James' attitude was not as callous as his mother's champions like to make it appear. Nor was Mary as innocent as the claims of biography would imply. Certainly, Secretary Walsingham more or less superintended the Babington Plot whereby Mary agreed to Elizabeth's assassination, but that hardly lessens Mary's guilt. Walsingham deliberately embarked on Mary's destruction; but the fact remains that she accommodatingly destroyed herself. The evidence of her complicity, though denied like the Casket Letters in 1568, was irrefutable; and when in October 1586 the queen of Scots was tried, in spite of her refusal to recognise the court she was found guilty and condemned to death.

Elaborate play-acting all round attended Mary to the block, and, needless to say, she upstaged all the other actors, though they had their moments too. Elizabeth gave the crowning performance of her career. Having failed in an attempt to instigate the jailers to murder Mary, Elizabeth hummed and hawed: she would sign the death-warrant, she would not; she wept and wailed but signed it at last, again to hesitate and agonise; and finally she had the warrant served without her knowledge! She then raged and stormed at the base underlings who had dared shed royal blood, and Tudor blood at that. She even committed her secretary William Davison to the Tower. Much of Elizabeth's bravura performance was for the benefit of King James (and, one might add, most of her subsequent biographers). As for that promising *jeune premier*, the king of Scots, he ably responded to such a lead. He would obey the indignant clamours in Scotland, avenge his martyred mother and vindicate national honour; but instead he took to heart a message from Walsingham which pointed out that only friendly neutrality towards England could safeguard his ambitions for the English throne. Walsingham's was a sure calculation, for by the Treaty of Berwick of 1586 James had become an English pensioner; and, besides, his fear of being supplanted by his mother was well known to the English government. James, then, fumed and postured, but the treaty survived both the execution of Mary and the coming of the Armada.

Indeed a certain community of perplexity bound James to Elizabeth. To each, Mary Stewart while she lived had been a threat; but in addition each faced similar troubles in church and state. In England the puritan campaign for thorough reform of the church had begun with the Vestments Controversy which raged between 1563 and 1567. So serious was the strife that the establishment and English protestantism 'could never again pretend to be entirely at peace'.[41] Many of the bishops were out of sympathy with the queen and Archbishop Parker, and some of the leading politicians, notably Leicester and Burghley, sided with the more moderate puritans. Puritanism also had powerful support in the House of Commons, thus welding together demands for reform of the church and, by implication, the state. Enraged by their defeat over the vestments, the puritans continued to agitate against many aspects of English worship and to complain bitterly about the retention of many pre-Reformation practices, such as the use of the sign of the cross and kneeling at communion, which were stigmatised as hall-marks of popery. Soon too they were railing bitterly against the discipline imposed by the ecclesiastical courts, for, contrary to popular superstition, censure was not a peculiarity of Scottish presbyterianism but was exercised by every national church,[42] (whether Calvinist, Lutheran, Anglican or Roman), and, indeed, was the one part of the medieval tradition that was carried over holus-bolus into the post-reformation period. The curiosity is that the English puritans while objecting to the discipline of the established church pined for a system that was even more rigorous. Finally, despairing of further reformation under the legal establishment they appealed to Theodore Béza, Calvin's successor at Geneva, who had lost faith in the protestant common-front advocated by his predecessor and instead urged that reformed churches should accept not only the theology of Geneva but also its polity. To Calvin episcopacy had been a thing indifferent, though personally he had no high regard for it as a system of church government; but to Béza episcopacy savoured of popery and he was soon scornfully referring to England as a minor Babylon. However, Béza did not altogether despair of English episcopacy and retained a hope that by infiltration and steady pressure the episcopate might still be made to incline towards Geneva.

The puritan movement was concentrated heavily in the Midlands and South-East of England, with its nerve centres in London and Cambridge. Over much of the north catholicism was still strong, and this, combined with the fact that the reformation was slow to take root on the Scottish Borders, gave much cause for alarm. The English puritan movement, then, was not initially nation wide. Its main support came from the burgesses of the larger towns, and from the gentry who saw in it a means of attaining prestige in the countryside at the expense of the bishops while at the same time enhancing their own power in parliament. Today there seems to be a marked tendency to exaggerate the strength and importance of Elizabethan protestant dissidence, attributing to it many of the qualities associated with seventeenth-century puritanism, and in the process the power of the establishment is correspondingly diminished. But in fact few of the Elizabethan bishops went far along the puritan road; and over large tracts of the country the Anglican *via media* was quietly accepted and struck root.

The real troubles followed Parker's death in 1575; but even before this the puritan movement, which was not homogeneous or well organised, had found a leader in Thomas Cartwright, who roundly denounced episcopacy as unscriptural. The hard core of the movement soon adopted presbyterian tenets, which were first clearly expounded in 1574 by Walter Travers. Parker's successor was not the man to cope with such a challenge, for Edmund Grindal sympathised with the puritans, and, as well as this, though honest and well intentioned, he proved a feeble archbishop and had to be suspended. A really determined stand against the presbyterians, who were attempting to set up their discipline within the establishment, did not come until after Grindal's death in 1583, when John Whitgift, already well known for his hostility to Cartwright and his ideas, succeeded to the primacy. Under Whitgift a rigorous reaction began which ended in the shattering of the presbyterian caucus but, significantly, failed to eradicate puritanism, which thereafter tended to exist as an umbrella protest movement within the established church. Only latterly did a minority of puritans show separatist and sectarian tendencies.

All this may seem a far cry from Anglo-Scottish relations. But it is not. The essential point is that at the same time a comparable struggle was being waged in Scotland but with far other results. And these differences were to condition very heavily the future relations of the two kingdoms. Developments in Scotland stemmed from the fact that the muddled expediency that had characterised the opening stages of the Reformation in Scotland could not be maintained indefinitely. Mary's deposition in 1567 ended the period of uncertainty for the reformed church and the basic acts of 1560 were at last ratified. In any event, the church badly needed to be reorganised; but here was the rub—reorganised in what way and by whose means? Could the episcopate, now that the higher benefices were open to the reformed ministry, be revived? Could the Anglican *via media* be followed? Or was the party of Geneva at last to triumph? Those who had control of the government plumped for the Anglican model; the successive short-lived regents from Moray to Morton were dependent on political support from England and tried hard to fashion an Anglican-style polity in Scotland, though no attempt was made to introduce Anglican worship. But there were other, and possibly more pressing reasons, for 'conformity with England'.[43] It held out financial benefits not only to the state but to the statesmen. Thus Morton was particularly eager to implement an anglicising policy, partly for its political dividends but also because 'tulchan' bishops, mere creatures of the state, could continue to siphon off the revenues of the church for the behoof of the statesmen. Such a programme of pious racketeering had few attractions except for the government. It left untouched the problems arising from the church's lack of endowment and meant that the great social visions of the First Book of Discipline would never be anything more substantial than 'devout imaginations'. The provision of parish schools, for example, had made no real headway, and the relief of the poor was a growing problem. Generally, as a consequence of the policies adopted by the regents, in many parts of Scotland the kirk existed on paper only.[44]

So desperate was the situation of the church that Knox, ailing and alarmed by the civil war, gave an extremely qualified and reluctant blessing to Morton's programme, which was accepted by the Concordat of Leith in 1572;[45] but at the same time Knox's sympathies obviously lay elsewhere.[46] He was in close touch with, and approved of, the advanced puritanism of London which was already verging on presbyterianism; his friend Christopher Goodman was a link between the Calvinist parties in both kingdoms; and also prominent among the early London presbyterians was Knox's former neophyte, Anne Locke.[47] Clearly, the radical reforming temper that existed among the Scottish Calvinists would not take kindly to Morton's rapacity, and this doomed any real prospect of a smooth passage for the revived episcopacy. Indeed, but for the fact that Morton was irrevocably committed to protestantism the outcry would have been greater, for by the early '70s the bogey of the Counter-Reformation was uppermost in protestant minds.

The rise of the presbyterian movement in Scotland has been ascribed to various causes. The old view that it was introduced by Knox and his fellow reformers in 1560 has long been exploded, though, as we have seen, many of the characteristics of presbyterianism can be detected in the work of the early reformers. But presbyterianism as a coherent system evolved slowly. Some authorities regard it as a direct borrowing from England, and certainly English influences played a considerable part in the rise of the presbyterian movement in Scotland.[48] To ascribe all to English influence, however, is to take an unduly narrow view of matters. Alternatively, it used to be the fashion to attribute the rise of Scottish presbyterianism solely to the influence of Andrew Melville; but, gifted though Melville was, this view grossly exaggerates his powers. The truth would seem to be that from 1560 onwards there had existed in Scotland a hard core of Calvinists who, like Knox, chafed at the bit of expediency throughout Mary's reign and whose hopes were raised by her deposition. But the state gave them no countenance and gradually the radicals coalesced into a party, a party that eagerly accepted Béza's ideas on polity. It is a remarkable and highly significant fact that at Geneva in 1571 there sat at Béza's feet, eagerly absorbing his doctrines, the three founding fathers of presbyterianism in Britain—the Englishmen Cartwright and Travers, and the Scot Melville.[49] Cartwright and Travers clearly fitted into an existing English puritan movement, whose doctrines they clarified and whose programme they shaped; and in a less obvious way the same is true of Andrew Melville.[50] His link with Béza and the nerve centre of international Calvinism was closer than that maintained by Cartwright. Béza, indeed, concerned himself more with the Scottish than with the English church question; he gave the Scottish puritans firmer directives than those he sent to their English counterparts, and in a roundabout way his advice to the Scots came to exercise an influence on the English presbyterians.[51] Partly this was because Béza's hard logical line made a greater appeal to the Scots, and partly it was because he still entertained some faint hope of good from the episcopate in England, whereas he had nothing but disgust for the corrupt mockery projected by Morton in Scotland.

When Melville returned to Scotland in 1574 his Genevan doctrines found many sympathisers who were willing and eager to fall in with the new hard-line puritanism. How otherwise could a young man in his early twenties have pushed through a virtual revolution in a few brief years? Melville's programme had an added appeal—not only was it ideologically and theologically satisfying but its implementation would have solved the economic problems of the church and enabled it to realise its social witness. This was why the Second Book of Discipline, which incorporated the ideas of Béza and Melville, was enthusiastically adopted by the General Assembly in 1578 but resolutely rejected by the state.

So far as polity and endowment were concerned the Second Book of Discipline was as clear, logical and explicit as the abortive First Book had been muddled.[52] It roundly condemned episcopacy as unscriptural and asserted the parity of ministers, equating episcopé and ministry; it demanded a conciliar form of government with a graded system of courts (though strangely the word 'presby-tery' was not used); it grappled with the problem of sovereignty and sought to resolve politico-ecclesiastical conflict by claiming that the church was supreme in the spiritual sphere. This so-called 'Hildebrandinism' is frequently misrepre-sented. The Second Book of Discipline did not aim at theocracy, but rather postulated the 'two kingdoms' theory of separate but co-ordinate jurisdictions; and finally, with characteristic starkness, it sought to solve the problem of endowment by asserting that the entire patrimony of the old church belonged as of right to the new!

The political instability of Scotland at this time gave the Melvillians a chance to implement their programme. Faction undermined the overbearing Morton, but presbyterian satisfaction at this soon turned to dismay when the young king became infatuated with his father's Frenchified cousin, Esmé Stewart, Sieur d'Aubigny, who engineered the final fall of the regent.[53] James had little reason to love the Douglases, and in spite of efforts by Elizabeth to save Morton, the deposed regent was executed in June 1581. But the reaction against d'Aubigny (or the Duke of Lennox as he had become) was swift and powerful. Elizabeth feared his catholic associations, and this alarm was shared to the full by the Melvillians. In vain James attempted to allay these fears by the King's Confession of 1581, which consisted largely of fierce denunciations of Rome. The extreme protestant group, headed by Mar and Gowrie, kidnapped the king, and the General Assembly seized the opportunity to push forward the work of organising presbyteries. But by one of the sudden reversals of fortune that characterised Scottish politics at this time, James escaped and by the so-called 'Black Acts' of May 1584 undid the presbyterian revolution. Yet the reaction was not complete. Though the leading presbyterian ministers, including Melville, had to flee to England, their cause continued to be upheld; and from that point onwards, in spite of frequent attempts at compromise, the battle between episcopacy and presbytery was fairly joined.

Thereafter episcopacy in Scotland sought its main support in state authority, and already the youthful British Solomon probably had among his ever-growing stock of wise saws and modern instances the cry of 'No bishop, no king'. Episcopacy certainly won a large measure of popular support in the conservative and backward north; but in central and southern Scotland it was faced by a consistent opposition which included most of the ministers, a few nobles, many lairds, and an increasingly large number of burghers and tenant farmers. It is pointless to try to explain this movement on the worn-out theme of 'religion and the rise of capitalism'. The strength of Calvinism as an ideology furnishes the major explanation; but it was also reinforced by the decay of feudalism and the decline of kinship, processes that had already begun in Scotland south of Tay before the end of the sixteenth century. And underlying these ecclesiastical tensions was a strong craving for representative and constitutional government. Far from reaching their peak in 1559–60, these forces were only openly unleashed in the 1580s and did not culminate until the 1640s. Herein lay one of the chief differences with England, where presbyterianism never succeeded in becoming a popular or mass movement.

The special strength of Scottish presbyterianism lay in the fact that it embraced the idea of one national church and fiercely rejected the notions of Brownists and other millenarian separatists. There was to be, as Knox had put it, 'but ane face of a kirk in Scotland', and the national church was to be uniform in doctrine and in worship. Here Scottish episcopalians and presbyterians were at one; their differences really arose from the vexed question of the relationship between church and state. The episcopalians accepted royal authority over the church, though they were far from accepting the degree of erastianism that obtained in Lutheran lands. The presbyterians, however, proposed to work through constitutional channels and rejected royal control. They did not overtly challenge the monarchy or the existing social hierarchy, though clearly their programme posed long-term threats to each. Scottish presbyterianism was, in fact, a revolutionary movement whose strongest weapon was its respectability. Already can be discerned the outlines of the brilliant paradox that made such a deadly weapon of the National Covenant of 1638, and which a few years later raised an army in the king's name to fight against royal pretensions. The presbyterian revolution was to be achieved by purely legal and constitutional means. The dangers it posed to the status quo were well understood at the time. In 1590 the astute Elizabeth gave James a warning that he really did not need: 'ther is risen, bothe in your realme and myne, a sect of perilous consequence, suche as wold have no kings but a presbitrye . . . Yea, looke we wel unto them'.[54]

Yet though Elizabeth shared James' horror of presbytery it remained the fact that, so far as Scotland and its problems were concerned, 'In this maze of faction and intrigue the Presbyterian kirk was England's able ally'.[55] The defeat of the Armada had not ended the threat from Spain; and James, intent as ever on strengthening his claim to the English throne, had embarked on some dangerous intrigues with the Scots catholics, some of whom pinned their hope on Spanish help. The Spaniards toyed with the notion of landing troops in Scotland, and early in 1589 news of the plot came into Elizabeth's hands. She warned James, and he apparently did nothing about it, largely because he was annoyed with Elizabeth, who was mean about his pension and too apt to interfere in Scottish affairs. In retaliation, Elizabeth supported the extreme protestant faction in Scotland, then headed, for purposes of his own, by James' mad-cap cousin, Francis Stewart, Earl of Bothwell. James was again suspected of cavorting with popery, and in 1592 the presbyterians took advantage of the king's weak situation to force him to establish their system. It has been questioned whether the Golden Act of 1592 'established' presbyterianism, but the criticism is over-refined, turning largely on disputes about dictionary definitions. The reality can hardly be disputed; the clear and unambiguous terms of the act undoubtedly set up a presbyterian polity in which bishops were to have no part.[56] But the measure did not go as far as the Melvillians would have liked, in that the right to summon General Assemblies lay with the king. James, a cunning politician, posed as the champion of Calvinism, and actually continued to make capital out of the act of 1592. But all along he hated the measure and was determined to undo it. He was impeded, however, by the affair of the Spanish Blanks that came to light early in 1593, a matter that was wildly exaggerated and was probably a plot 'born of the brain of a dreaming and impractical priest'.[57] It placed James in a dilemma. The protestant hue and cry was up; yet he was unwilling to take a hard line with the catholic earls of the North-East, since he felt that he needed them as a counterweight to the presbyterian party and still hoped to make use of their continental connections to further his English ambitions. James, in fact, wanted to use every faction and not get shackled to any of them.

Thus Scottish politics in the 1590s appeared to be a mad whirligig, compared to which the Marian maze of thirty years earlier seemed almost simple. In each period the complicating factor was the same. The clue that solves the mystery is that everything had reference to the Stewart claim to the throne of England. The great difference between the two periods of complex intrigue is largely that in guile and prevarication James, unlike his mother, proved a match for Elizabeth. Neither Elizabeth nor James cared a straw about principles; each was concerned only with results; and each was far-seeing and devious, carefully avoiding rash moves. Their correspondence thus makes rich reading, full as it is of muffled threats, sly hints and false bonhomie.[58] With consistency such bright minds had evidently little to do. Thus Elizabeth could speed on a puritan programme in Scotland while busy suppressing a very similar one in England; and James, with staggering effrontery, was even more adept at this Machiavellian game. He posed as the sympathiser, even at times as the champion of such diverse groups as catholics, puritans, and episcopalians. The catholics he impressed by his mild and tolerant attitude; and, in addition, the apostasy of his queen, Anne of Denmark, seemed to hint, but falsely, at Romeward leanings on the king's part. At the same time he was widely regarded as the great intellectual champion of Calvinism; as a universal genius, tutored by the awesome Buchanan, naturally James took theology in his stride. Further, in 1591–2 he interceded with the English authorities on behalf of puritans caught in the toils of Star Chamber.[59] The puritans thereafter became the main English supporters of the Stewart claim, and they eagerly awaited the coming of a presbyterian king. At the same time James took care secretly to assure the English bishops that his succession would not impair the establishment, and that he was busy undermining the presbyterians in Scotland. That ploy was well advanced by 1603, for in 1597 James, on the plea that the church needed to be represented in parliament, had introduced 'parliamentary' bishops, round whom in time a full system of episcopal government was to be built up.

By 1600 the strain of the long years of uncertainty about the succession began to tell on James. He had tried every trick he knew to get Elizabeth to name him as her heir, and he had failed. Yet, in many respects, he had enjoyed a measure of success. Elizabeth was forced to keep in with him if only because, unlike his mother, he had shown such a marked talent for mischievous plotting. Besides, by the end of the century credible alternatives to James were hard to come by, and though the Spanish Infanta cut some sort of a figure it was mainly in diplomatic circles. James, in fact, had played such a cunning rôle that he appeared to the pope himself to be a better bet than the far-fetched official catholic candidates. At the same time, James clearly recognised that international opinion did not count for everything. He knew that the long wars of religion had, for the time being at any rate, worked themselves out, and that the death of Elizabeth would not lead to any grave international crisis of the kind that would have been inevitable in the 1580s. This the growing weakness of Spain and the slow convalescence of France more or less guaranteed. In the last decade of his long quest James realised that it was really English opinion that counted, and this he eagerly courted. But, unlike most modern historians, he was far from certain of the outcome. Indeed, so nervous and impatient did he become that he made what might easily have proved to be a disastrous blunder.

Suspicious of the Cecils, he threw himself into the arms of Essex, and by 1598 the earl was virtually King James' agent at the court of Elizabeth. The king of Scots undoubtedly became implicated in Essex's treason, which was designed to seize the reins of government in England and then to acknowledge James' title. Indeed, but for chronic lack of funds, James would probably have invaded the north of England in support of the earl. For once the alleged benefits of poverty were demonstrated, for Essex was easily crushed and had James been openly in the venture his prospects of the succession must have been badly damaged. As it was, Elizabeth knew of his complicity and took care to let him know that she knew[60]—and yet, significantly, she did not make it public, a striking application of her motto, *Video et taceo*. In short, in spite of her apparent inconsistency, Elizabeth throughout the whole succession dispute was probably consistent. She obviously accepted the Stewart claim as the most valid and, from every point of view, the most expedient; so in spite of her personal and political objections to openly acknowledging it, she did everything she could to protect it.

Sir Robert Cecil understood and approved of the queen's attitude to the succession, and had never really been hostile to James. His bitter quarrel with Essex had been about power, and after the earl's fall in 1601 Cecil had no difficulty in forming a close liaison with James whose main champion in England he became.[61] As Elizabeth's end obviously drew near, James, well advised by Cecil, ceased to torment and embarrass the queen, who responded by hinting rather than stating that James should be her successor. So at last in March 1603 James, to adopt his own words, was to change from 'the wild unruly colt' that was Scotland to 'St. George's towardly riding horse';[62] and, of course, not to ride the metaphor to death as James would have done had he made a full tally of his gains, at the same time he acquired the kingdom of Ireland. All in all it was a goodly inheritance, and one that had been well worth striving for over the long years of tantalising uncertainty. And the British Solomon was not short of ideas on how best to develop his inheritance.

A more honest and upright man might easily have lost out on the English Great Cause, but the scheming James was just right for such a situation. The so-called Union of the Crowns of 1603 was to play a large part in the evolution of modern Britain, but it is well to remember that important results are not always obtained by admirable means. The Union of the Crowns owed much to the patient, devious Elizabeth, and as much to the unprepossessing, and at times ridiculous but essentially astute, James.

6

Regal Union and New Tensions: 1603–39

THE nature of the union of 1603 is rarely closely examined and as a result is frequently misunderstood or misrepresented. It is imperative, therefore, to define the precise meaning of the Union of the Crowns. The term itself is ambiguous and something of a misnomer, for the accession of James VI of Scotland as James I of England, by virtue of his descent (unspecified in the official proclamation) from Henry VII, did not in any organic sense unite the two crowns far less the two realms. Until his death in 1625 James Stewart remained James VI, King of Scots, even though on 25 July 1603 he was anointed and crowned in Westminster Abbey as 'James the First, King of England, Scotland, France, and Ireland'.[1] Indeed, strenuous efforts by James to unite the realms of England and Scotland failed, and their general laws and administration remained separate and distinct, as did their crowns and the rules of succession thereto.

All this retains its validity in spite of the fact that James assumed the style of King of Great Britain, which became accepted diplomatic usage.[2] The term 'Great Britain', to distinguish the island of Britain from the Little Britain of the continent, Brittany, had long been current and was sufficiently widely known to be used by Cervantes in 1604.[3] But, as was wittily said at the time, James' self-bestowed title (which was a second thought, for he had toyed with the notion of calling himself emperor) made the British Solomon a king without a kingdom, thus possibly attracting the attention of the author of Don Quixote. There is, however, no great mystery about the perplexities raised by King James' title. The answer lies in the simple fact that the union of 1603 was purely dynastic, a vindication of the feudal doctrine of primogeniture and no different in essence from similar unions that had done so much to shape the political map of Renascence Europe. In law, and in constitutional theory, the Union of the Crowns was strictly limited to the two kingdoms sharing one monarch and one dynasty. And luck, as much as anything, had dictated this outcome, for an English-born heir to the Tudor inheritance would have been a practical debar to James' succession. Nevertheless, the long term implications of the dynastic union were to be profound. Limited though it was in itself, the fortuitous dynastic union was in time to create conditions that were to reduce the independence of Scotland almost to the level of a legal fiction.

One school of thought tends to elide all difficulties by regarding the dynastic union as merely a stage, and a none-too-significant one at that, in an inevitable progress towards complete union. According to this view a common language and a common protestantism, reinforced by the war-weariness induced by generations of unprofitable strife, had at long last provided the basis for a peaceful union of the peoples of England and Scotland.[4] There is some force in these contentions, but the overall conclusion needs to be qualified. Too much is assumed, and too much is conjectured on hindsight. Cultural assimilation was, in fact, a more protracted process than this theory would suggest, and it is doubtful if it had reached significant proportions before the eighteenth century. Cultural assimilation was the consequence of union rather than the cause of it.

Certainly in the fifteenth and sixteenth centuries the Scots tongue, a congener of Northern English, was steadily spreading in Scotland and the Gaelic-speaking area was slowly contracting. But the Scots language had its own cultural connotations, and these did not perish at the Reformation. In this period, too, the decline of Gaelic was relative and far from catastrophic. The old Celtic tongue of Scotland still reigned supreme in the Highlands and Islands, and though it had pretty well disappeared in Galloway it was still spoken in Kintyre, the Clyde islands, parts of Dunbartonshire and Stirlingshire and the uplands of Angus, Mar and Moray. In all probability, in the opening decades of the seventeenth century Gaelic was still the language of just under half the people of Scotland—a point that can hardly be regarded as of no consequence. The really significant linguistic development at the end of the sixteenth century was not so much that Gaelic was losing ground but that Scots, as a literary language, was beginning to be assimilated to the English of the south. In this process protestantism, with its emphasis on Scripture in the vernacular, played a very important rôle. The English Bible (whether in the Geneva or the King James version) helped to end the old Scots literary tradition by creating a marked divergence between the spoken dialects of Scots and a new literary language which became saturated with the rhythms and usages of the Authorised Version. There is no need to elaborate a point that is so patently clear in seventeenth-century Scottish writings. Open at random any edition of the letters of the well-known Scottish presbyterian minister Samuel Rutherford and the influence of the English Bible is startlingly, and indeed sometimes ludicrously, revealed.

Even before the English Bible had done its work, the Scots language was moving towards English—possibly as a consequence of the rise of printing—and this change was noted by the famous English antiquarians, Harrison and Camden. Wrote William Harrison in 1587: 'The Scottish [not, it is worth pointing out, 'Scotch'] english hath beene much broader and less pleasant in utterance than ours, because that nation hath not till of late indevored to bring the same to any perfect order, and yet it was such in maner, as Englishmen themselves did speak for the most part beyond Trent, whither any great amendment of our language had not as then extended itselfe. Howbeit in our time the Scottish language endevoreth to come neere, if not altogether to match our toong in finenesse of phrase, and copie [i.e. copiousness] of words'. Harrison goes on to say that the 'wild Scots' or 'redshanks' (i.e. Highlanders) 'speake good Irish which they call Gachtlet'.[5] William Camden took the matter a stage further, arguing that the English-speaking Scots were of Anglo-Saxon race—an extremely dubious theory which, as we have already observed, has bedevilled much subsequent English writing on Scotland and the Scots. Says Camden: 'For certainly it is that the greatest and best parts, the East and South of Scotland, which call themselves the Lawland-men, speake the English tongue varied only in *Dialect*, as descended from the English-Saxons: and the old *Scottish*, which is the verie *Irish*, is ussd only by them of the West, called the *Hechtland-men*, who call the other as the Welsh call us *Sassons*, *Saxons*, both in respect of language and originall . . .'.[6]

The linguistic situation in Scotland in the early seventeenth century, then, was more involved than is commonly realised. Scottish Gaelic, far from degenerating, was in fact entering its period of greatest vitality. The breaking of the last ties between Irish and Scottish Gaeldom by the Jacobean settlement of Ireland led to a loosening of the Old Irish bardic influence, thus stimulating a vigorous development of vernacular Scottish Gaelic. And so, far from being in its death throes at the end of the sixteenth century, Scottish Gaelic really stood on the threshold of its most vigorous period of literary life. To assume, therefore, that linguistic differences between England and Scotland were extinguished after the Reformation is to ignore contemporary realities and to indulge in anachronism. It is also to reject much of the history of Scotland in the seventeenth century.

Indeed, in many ways the linguistic situation was becoming more complex. At long last a received version of English was beginning to predominate in England, and literary Scots was increasingly influenced by it;[7] but Scottish Gaelic was also coming into its own, and this was a fact of very considerable social and political as well as cultural significance. The view, then, that a common language and culture were virtually dictating union between England and Scotland has to be received with caution. In truth, when tested by the facts of the situation it is demonstrably false.

Why, if circumstances were so propitious, was no closer bond established after 1603? If there is any substance to the theory of natural gravitation, then logically a complete union should have followed James' accession to the throne of England. It did not—though not for want of trying. King James himself believed that such a union was not only desirable but practicable, and again and again, in his obstinate pedantic way, he strove to achieve it. After 1603 there was a flood of royally inspired propaganda—poems, tracts and treatises—advocating complete union. From the Scottish side Sir Thomas Craig, a distinguished lawyer, in 1605 composed a lengthy treatise, *De Unione Regnorum Britanniae Tractatus*, which though not published until 1909 seems to have circulated widely in manuscript;[8] and from the English side Sir Francis Bacon spoke and wrote eloquently on the same theme. But Craig and Bacon, lawyers both and servants of the crown, did not argue out of conviction only but also to please their master. And as much is true of the authors of nearly all of the pro-union literature of the period, which was designed to flatter James and win his favour. James' conceit revelled in flattery, and these works can in no sense be accepted as representative of public opinion in the two kingdoms.

Other writings of the time strike a more authentic note. The well-known 'Satire against Scotland', written in 1617 and attributed to Sir Anthony Weldon, accords better with the known facts than do the juristic arguments of Craig and Bacon or the panegyrics of the poetasters. Weldon's 'Satire' belongs to a familiar enough genre and speaks for itself: Scotland the satirist finds 'too guid for those that inhabit it, and too bad for others to be at the charge of conquering it.[9] The ayre might be wholesome, but for the stinking people that inhabit it . . . Thair beastis be generallie small (women excepted), of which sort thair ar no greater in the world'.[10] And so it goes on, ranting away in a silly but highly self-revelatory vein, now fortunately confined to certain professors in England's most venerable seats of learning. Not that Englishmen have ever had a monopoly of scurrility, for through the ages the Scots have retorted in kind and particularly wounding was the glee with which they fastened on the French medieval legend that English people had tails. Such virulent anti-English libels continued to be produced after 1603, to the annoyance of James, who in 1609 had an act passed against them threatening with dire penalties the authors of 'pasquillis, libellis, rymis, Cockalanis, comedies and sicklyk occasionis whereby they slander maligne and revile the estait and countrey of England and divers his majesties honorable Counsallors, magistratis and worthie subjectis of that his majesties kingdome'.[11] As Firth demonstrated long ago, the slanging match in the early seventeenth century was certainly not one-sided;[12] and, nonsensical as these satires and lampoons must now appear to any rational person, they confirm that, even after the Union of the Crowns, Scots and English loved each other not.

James, pedantic bumbler though he was, was aware of these problems and sought to solve them by a closer union. James VI and I is an enigma: learned, opinionated, vulgar and uncouth, he was susceptible to flattery; weak, and conscious of his weakness, he strove to be masterful and merely succeeded in being capricious. But though in some ways a ridiculous posturer, in others he was shrewd and far-seeing, and he could become obsessed with great ideals.[13] Besides, his theory of divine right monarchy virtually required the complete unification of the two kingdoms: such was God's will, and James as the representative of God on earth had to implement it. Difficulties that stood in the way he refused to consider, though Cecil for one itemised them and warned that the time was not ripe for a complete union. Undeterred, in his first address to the English parliament in March 1603, a sensible speech marred by some bombast, James outlined his aims: 'What God hath conjoined let no man separate. I am the husband and all the whole isle is my lawful wife; I am the head and it is my body; I am the shepherd and it is my flock. I hope therefore that no man will think that I, a Christian King under the Gospel, should be a polygamist and husband to two wives; that I being the head should have a divided or monstrous body or that being the shepherd to so fair a flock should have my flock parted in two'.[14] James envisaged a unitary kingdom of Great Britain, an aim he summed up to the Speaker in 1604: 'his wish above all things was, at his death, to leave one worship to God; one kingdom entirely governed; one uniformity in laws'.[15] He even at one point considered making Archbishop Bancroft primate of all Britain.

The House of Commons, unimpressed either by James' good sense or by his antique rhetoric and very likely annoyed by his patronising tone, refused to give statutory sanction to his desire to adopt the style of King of Great Britain and was offended when in November 1604 he assumed the title by proclamation. The rebuff merely confirmed James' belief in the necessity of complete union, even though it was becoming ominously clear that the project had little real support in either country. Finally the two parliaments were cajoled into taking the matter into consideration. Bacon argued the case cogently in the House of Commons: religion, he thought, would be no problem; the parliaments might be induced to merge; but to his legal mind the two systems of law presented a difficulty.

Bacon found the idea of a fusion of laws attractive, as did some other lawyers (most notably civilians like John Hayward and John Cowell who hoped that the civil law could form a bridge between the two systems and be a means of mutual reformation);[16] but Bacon's pragmatic mind saw the difficulties and in the end recommended that the public law of the United Kingdom should be the same but that each country should retain its system of private law—exactly the solution that was adopted a century later. The difficulty was that the two systems of law were rapidly diverging, with Scots law beginning to be shaped by free use of Roman principles whereas English common law had become rigid and conservative. The English solicitor-general believed that the two systems were not fundamentally different and that they could be fairly easily assimilated, but the main weight of legal opinion in each country thought otherwise. The differences in the two systems were, in fact, more fundamental than the champions of union made out, and particularly so respecting matters that were then of first importance—the laws relating to rights in land and property. In Scotland, for example, nothing analogous to English freehold had developed and any attempted assimilation of Scots and English law in this sphere would have led to appalling problems, the political connotations of which could have been explosive. In the end no real effort was made to fuse the laws of England and Scotland. From the purely theoretical juristic standpoint fusion looked feasible, but from the practical point of view it was impossible. Each system had created property and prescriptive rights that could not be reconciled.

Cecil warned King James that his grand design was premature and unworkable. Bacon also pleaded for a gradualist approach, but his advice, like Cecil's, went unheeded. Nonetheless, they were proved right. The House of Commons, on the whole, was not enamoured of the project. The Commons wished no new fangled 'emperor' in the place of the kings of England, and the common lawyers, a powerful voice in parliament, virtually reiterated the famous plea of 'nolumus leges Angliae mutari'. It was generally alleged that the benefits of incorporation would lie with the Scots at the expense of the mere English. The Scots, for their part, do not seem to have thought much about the proposed union at all and appeared to be little more than interested spectators. Nonetheless, it is perhaps significant that the king told the English parliament at the beginning of his project that 'if Scotland should refuse, he would compell their assents, having a stronger party there than the opposite party of the mutineers'.[17] Evidently there was strong if covert opposition to union in the Scottish parliament; in particular the stated intention of unifying the two national churches was resented in Scotland as simply a means of imposing Anglicanism. But finally in June 1604 the two parliaments passed lukewarm acts nominating commissioners to treat for union, and those unfortunates were apparently to achieve the impossible—a complete union that would still preserve all the laws, honours, dignities, offices and liberties of each kingdom! In his final speech James rebuked the Commons for clouding over his grand vision: 'There [i.e. in Scotland] all things warranted that came from me. Here all things suspected . . . He merits to be buried in the bottom of the sea that shall but think of separation, where God hath made such a Union'.[18]

The English and Scottish commissioners met at Westminster in October 1604, deliberated for some weeks with no great enthusiasm, and finally in December a more complete union was recommended; but since the report was drawn up by two of the king's servants who had strenuously pressed the royal case (Bacon and Sir Thomas Hamilton) it may well be that it reflected the king's wishes rather than the convictions of the majority of the commissioners. Nonetheless, the Instrument of Union proposed virtual free trade and the abrogation of all hostile laws (with the Borders to be converted into the Middle Shires); it also recommended that the *post-nati* (i.e. all subjects in both countries born after the death of Elizabeth) should by common law be entitled to the privileges of subjects in both countries, while the *ante-nati* (who were not such a pressing problem, since death in time would remove them) were to have the same rights conferred by statute but were not to be eligible for office except in their native land. These proposals fell short of what James had originally intended, but, disquieted by his difficulties with the House of Commons, he was no longer keen on immediate parliamentary union. Truncated as the articles were, however, the problem of pushing them through the two legislatures remained formidable. They were to have been debated by the English parliament that was summoned for 5 November 1605, but the furore raised by the Gunpowder Plot diverted attention to other matters.

James, though, refused to let the matter rest, and from his speech to parliament in 1606 it seems that he was still hopeful that in time a complete union could be attained. His plea was to 'let it be as Wales was, and as all the Heptarchy was, united to England, as the principal; and let all at last be compounded and united into one kingdom. And since the crown, the sceptre, and justice, and law, and all is resident and reposed here, there can be no fear to this nation, but that they shall ever continue continual friends; and shall ever acknowledge one Church and one king, and be joined in a perpetual marriage, for the peace and prosperity of both nations, and for the honour of their King'.[19]

In spite of the fact that the unified kingdom of Great Britain envisaged by James was to be simply an enlarged England, the articles were furiously assailed in 1606 in the English parliament. There was a storm of opposition in the Commons where the trading interests inveighed bitterly against free trade, and the case for economic union (not particularly strong at that time) perished in a maelstrom of prejudice in which the Scots were eclectically damned as beggars, thieves and murderers. The proposals on naturalisation were also fiercely, and scurrilously, opposed. In vain Bacon tried to placate the House, pointing out that without naturalisation and reciprocal benefits the union was unlikely to endure and illustrating his point by numerous examples drawn from ancient and modern history of unions foundering through injustice.[20] He was supported by the great common lawyer Sir Edward Coke, but even the unwonted alliance of Coke and Bacon could not move the House. The fact was that the Commons no longer trusted the king, resenting particularly his failure to deal with grievances on wardship, purveyance and other matters; and besides the question of naturalisation was a thorny one. Dynastic unions were unpredictable and might have curious consequences. For example, if Philip and Mary had had a son, would it have been necessary to naturalise Spaniards and Sicilians? Such reciprocal naturalisation had been a consequence of the brief Franco-Scottish union, and this complication too was raised. Prejudiced though these arguments were, they went to the very heart of the problem, which was that dynastic unions could no longer automatically settle national issues. The negotiations really perished on this impasse, though James stubbornly refused to give in.

In August 1607 he got the rigged Scottish parliament to accept the proposed articles; but the estates managed to smuggle in a proviso that their assent was conditional on that of the English parliament.[21] The English opposition made much of this proviso, alleging that all was to be given to the Scots but that they would concede nothing in return. As a wrecking device, therefore, the House of Commons, influenced by Sir Edwin Sandys, took up James' original scheme and demanded a complete incorporating union under English law. This demand for 'a perfect union' was advanced safe in the knowledge that it was unacceptable to the Scots, who feared that their country would be treated as 'a conquered and slavish province to be governed by a Viceroy or Deputy' on the Irish model.[22] Bacon weakly riposted that complete incorporation would take ages to accomplish, and the project really fizzled out. All that was saved was the repeal of the hostile laws, which, as James scornfully remarked, was a pointless concession since the dynastic union had effectively suspended them. And, indeed, the Middle Shires as a concept never really took root; the two kingdoms remained distinct, and the old turbulent spirit of the Borderers did not evaporate overnight but was still, though a waning force, detectably at work in the last years of the Protectorate.

Clearly, the whole attempt at union had been premature and had foundered because the two nations were still poles apart (socially, economically and institutionally) and still animated by the ill-will born of centuries of bitter antagonism. Indeed, it fell out just as the French ambassador had predicted—'The little sympathy between the two nations, the differences of their laws, the jealousy of their privileges, the regard of the succession, are the reasons they will never . . . join with another, as the King wishes'.[23]

But one matter James was determined to rescue from the shipwreck of his grand design—naturalisation. As we have seen, the question was a most difficult one; but it was crucial to the success of the regal union and James was right to insist on a solution. After all, the Scots had to give up much as a result of the dynastic union; to deprive them of all benefits would be dangerous, and to continue to treat them as aliens in England made little sense. Anyway, the problem of their status was not altogether new, for even before the Union of the Crowns the legal position of Scots in England was ill-defined. Under the common law they were treated as aliens and could not inherit or hold land; but on criminal charges they were sometimes denied the privileges usually conceded to foreigners,[24] possibly because it was held that, unlike the general run of foreigners, they had no language difficulties to impede the administration of justice. One possible solution lay in denization, which belonged to the prerogative rights of the crown and which had frequently been used from the fifteenth century to grant rights to Scots domiciled in England;[25] but the rights so conferred were limited, and at best denization would have been a clumsy and troublesome device. Thus, when recourse to parliament had obviously failed James determined to use the power of the crown, but deviously, by recourse to the judiciary. And so a collusive action was raised in the King's Bench to determine the position of the *post-nati*.

A piece of ground in Shoreditch was purchased in the name of Robert Calvin, an infant described as being born in Edinburgh on 5 November 1606. The object was to determine whether or not he, as a post-natus, had the right to sue, and accordingly an action of *novel disseisin* was brought in his name against two persons who were alleged to have occupied and refused to give up his tenement; at the same time, to make full discussion of the issue certain, a suit was raised in Chancery for the recovery of papers relating to the ownership of the property. The case was heard in Exchequer Chamber before the Lord Chancellor and a full bench of judges. Known as Calvin's Case* (more accurately, the Case of the Post-Nati) it was settled in 1608 in favour of the plaintiff, the overwhelming majority of the judges concurring with the Lord Chancellor Ellesmere's view that 'all the post-nati in Scotland, are in reason, and by common lawe of England, naturall-borne subjects within the allegiance of the king of England; and inhabled to purchase and have free-hould and inheritance of lands in England; and to bring reall actions for the same in England'.[26] The grounds on which the case was settled really derived from medieval precedents, drawn largely from the Plantagenet dominion in France, and the effective *ratio decidendi* was simply that the king's subjects owed him allegiance and that he in turn owed them protection. The conflict was really between parliament and the king, with the common lawyers for once wholeheartedly in favour of James. Thus, no one supported Calvin's case more trenchantly than Coke, who throughout recognised the importance of the Case of the Post-Nati, which he termed 'the shortest in syllables and the longest in substance'.[27] Later commentators have confirmed

---

* There is some mystery about the identity of the plaintiff. He is held to have been Robert Colville, a grandson of Lord Colville of Culross—Calvin or Colvin being an alternative rendering of Colville. That the plaintiff was indeed Lord Colville's grandson is attested by *R.P.C.* VIII (1607–10), 557–8; the difficulty is that 'Lord Colville's oy' (grandson) there referred to was named James, not Robert, and was born in 1604 (*Scots Peerage*, II, 557–8). His father, the Master of Colville, was called Robert, and possibly this may have led to confusion. Oy, however, could signify nephew (*Scottish National Dictionary*, VI, 465); but no known nephew fits the bill.

the soundness of Coke's views on this matter. Holdsworth summed up admirably when he noted that the decision in the Case of the Post-Nati gave 'a uniform status for natural born subjects, not only in England and Scotland, but also in the many lands which, in the succeeding centuries, were added to the king's dominions'.[28]

So far we have been discussing the nature of the Union of the Crowns and concluded that, in constitutional terms, it was purely dynastic. This is by no means to deny it any significance, but simply to point out that its real importance lay not so much in constitutional forms as in political realities. It deprived Scotland of a foreign policy and subordinated her interests to those of England (as it turned out, neither happily nor profitably), while for England it strengthened her security by at last firmly locking the northern postern. And so it was too in the domestic sphere, where English interests tended to predominate in Scotland, particularly in the ordering of the church. But here it is essential to note that all this was done by royal prerogative, and that English laws and statutes were of no effect in Scotland. It was the king of England, acting as king of Scots, who imposed anglophile policies on his other kingdom, and not the English nation acting in its corporate capacity. The distinction, a valid one, was well understood at the time, and indeed played a powerful role in politics. Growing opposition to divine right monarchy brought the two countries into the same arena if only because what happened in one was of crucial importance to the other. Had 'Thorough' succeeded in Scotland and Ireland, as Strafford desired,[29] then the hope of attaining responsible government in England would have been correspondingly diminished. And this too came to be well appreciated at the time.

It has not been so clearly appreciated since, and one reason for this is that King James' achievement in Scotland has recently been so exaggerated as to throw the whole interpretation of early seventeenth-century British history out of perspective. Recent historians have on the whole followed James in believing that in Scotland his policies had succeeded. James is nothing if not quotable, and the terms in which he crowed to the English parliament in 1607 have been repeatedly cited as conclusive testimony: 'This I must say for Scotland, and may truly vaunt it; here I sit and govern it with my pen; I write and it is done; and by a Clerk of the Council I govern Scotland now,—which others could not do by the sword'.[30] The vaunt had a certain validity, but nonetheless it considerably exaggerated the real situation. Most of James' new-found authority was due to favourable circumstances, principally accord with England and succession to its throne. Had he been born a century earlier he would in all likelihood have joined the mournful procession of the Jameses. The real point, however, is whether James was wise to boast about his autocratic rule in Scotland to an increasingly suspicious English parliament. Many in England feared the spread of absolutism on the continent, which was equated with the Counter-Reformation, and James' reliance on favourites and rough dealing with an admittedly ill-defined constitution raised alarms for the preservation of constitutional government. True, the problem had begun to emerge under Elizabeth, but it was undoubtedly intensified by the new king's preoccupation with divine right theories.[31] That he was, or claimed to be, absolute in Scotland provided no comfort for those who wished to maintain the Tudor system or those who, invoking medieval precedents, desired to establish responsible government. As early as 1610 the problem arose when parliament tried to resort to the medieval device of impeachment in order to check arbitrary acts of the king's servants. The attempt failed; but as government by muddle, corruption and monopoly continued (to favour courtiers, like Buckingham, and unpopular foreign and domestic policies) the House of Commons persevered and by 1621 impeachment was successfully revived.[32] To contemporaries, then, it appeared that in England a constitutional conflict had begun, whereas in Scotland the prerogative was apparently sweeping all before it.

But was this really the case? Had James, as he boasted, established absolute government in Scotland? The answer would seem to be—not to the extent that he believed and that some recent historians have accepted. Certainly, as James put it, 'he knew the stomach of that people', and in his dealings with his ancient kingdom he undoubtedly succeeded better than with his new subjects in the south, the workings of whose digestions were clearly beyond him. James, however, did not so much fashion a new polity in Scotland as find the means successfully to operate the old. He tried hard to curb feudalism and inculcate a sense of order, but in this laudable endeavour he enjoyed only limited success. His system really rested on recognition of one crucial fact—that the gravest political problem in Scotland had been, and potentially still was, its strong and grasping nobility, which was always on the lookout for a rich ploy or a rewarding master and not in the least fussy about where the desired largesse came from. James simply became the lavish but astute purse-master. In the last analysis his system in Scotland depended not so much on acceptance of the cult of divine right monarchy as on judicious grants of old kirklands to the nobles. It was, in fact, a system of 'management'.

And so we are brought back again to the central issue of the fate of ecclesiastical property. An Act of Annexation of 1587 had sought to enrich the crown by claiming for it all the old kirklands except such as had been legally disponed to laymen.[33] As well as easing the chronic insolvency of the crown, this was intended as a riposte to the Melvillians, who claimed that the entire patrimony of the pre-Reformation church belonged as of right to the church reformed. The act of 1587 did not unduly alarm the nobles, who had no reason to favour this aspect of the presbyterian programme, and in practice James found it expedient to lavish ecclesiastical properties on the nobles, while later, in 1606, to strengthen his revived episcopate, he restored the episcopal lands to the bishops. In other words, the disposition of the old kirklands was crucial to James' system, for he was intelligent enough to see that a façade of absolutism could only be maintained by bribing the nobles with charters of erection on former ecclesiastical property. In this way he built up a strong party of kingsmen.[34]

By thus placating the nobility, and by skilful use of the bishops and a new class of professional administrators drawn mainly from the lairds and burgesses, James gained control over the main organs of government—parliament, Privy Council and church. The Scottish parliament, unlike the English, was unicameral, a fact which, when properly manipulated, solved the problem of the relationship between executive and legislature. Indeed, in the heyday of James' system it was hard to say where one ended and the other began. The Council, whose members were nominated by the crown without reference to parliament, had an extremely wide range of powers, and in addition members of the Council played a leading role in parliament. The crown's grip on parliament was completed by skilful rigging of the vital Committee of the Articles. The device of the Articles was not new. The committee had evolved in the late Middle Ages, when parliaments were ill-attended, and its original purpose was to ensure a quorum in order to pass the necessary legislation. But in time the Articles came virtually to engross the work of parliament. Clearly, if James could secure the Articles then parliament would come under his close control. Everything depended on how this all-important committee was chosen: at one time the separate estates had elected their representatives; but James, not without precedent, hit upon a cunning means of rigging the Articles in favour of the crown. The bishops chose eight nobles, who returned the compliment, and together these sixteen representatives of the first and second estates chose eight burgesses and eight shire commissioners. The bishops, as mere pawns of the crown, naturally elected eight nobles who were strong for the royal interest, and in this vein the so-called election would continue. The Articles ended up consisting of crown nominees, and naturally in a parliament so dominated there was very little debate or discussion. Rarely can management have been pushed so far, and when this system was at its height the Scottish parliament really became a rubber-stamp for decisions reached elsewhere.[35] James' system, in fact, was simply a practical application of a well-attested version of his famous saying; 'No bishops, no king, no nobility'.[36]

In James' reign, therefore, and most notably after 1603 when his position was immeasurably strengthened by his accession to the throne of England, Scotland became aware of a new phenomenon—a stable central government that could make its power felt, not intermittently but regularly, a government that could launch and in a measure implement long-term policies rather than live frantically from day-to-day appeasing and balancing rival interests, hoping for the best and dreading, often with sufficient cause, the worst. Such as it was, James' triumph rested not on new constitutional theories, or on social change forcing on the collapse of feudalism and so ending baronial turbulence, but on clever manipulation of existing circumstances. It depended completely on the alliance between crown, nobility and bishops. While this alliance endured, opposition could be beaten down; but if the alliance were to break so would the system. And even before James' death in 1625 the system was creaking. By then the prestige of the Council was dwindling, and there were fresh outbreaks of disorder in the Highlands and even on the supposedly pacified Borders.[37] In the upshot, what James left his luckless successor in Scotland was little more than a dangerous illusion of absolute government. The real problem, however, was that such a system had to be paid for, and once the ecclesiastical property had been used up no comparable source of bribery emerged. Management without the wherewithal cannot function efficiently; it was left to Charles I to discover that management based on threats to expropriate the managers cannot function at all.

There was another flaw in James' system—the regime of the bishops—though to some this represents the high peak of his achievement in Scotland. Even before 1603 he was actively undermining the presbyterians, and by 1612 he had broken the Melvillians and had succeeded in reimposing a full diocesan episcopacy. But the limitation of his power is clear from the fact that he did not suppress the presbyteries, which was certainly not due to any affection for them or any desire to set up an ecumenical polity. The mixed polity that it is now fashionable to praise was the result of prudence, and may indeed have been a grave error. For the retention of the presbyteries, even though they were dominated by the bishops, brought the ministers together periodically and enabled the die-hards of the presbyterian party to confer and cabal, whereas, deprived of the presbyteries they might, like their English counterparts, have become mere shadows of a shade. Another mistake arose from the king's dream of uniting, or at least forcing into close conformity, the two national churches. Thus from 1614 onwards he embarked on a policy of liturgical innovation in Scotland which at first was resented even by the bishops, who were still at one with the presbyterians on doctrine and worship. Not that a 'liturgy' was then anathema to Scottish Calvinists; but the purpose behind these proposals roused nationalist resentment. When James outlined his Five Articles he was amazed by the opposition they met and angrily threatened that his English doctors would instruct the Scottish bishops. Whereupon William Cowper, Bishop of Galloway, revealingly exclaimed: 'God make us wise and faithfull, and keepe us from their usurption over us'.[38]

The Five Articles of Perth, of which the observance of holy days and kneeling at communion were the most unpopular, continued to be bitterly opposed; and again the opposition had to be beaten down by a mixture of guile and force before the Articles were accepted by a packed and skilfully managed General Assembly at Perth in 1618 and narrowly squeezed through a rigged parliament in 1621. Quite apart from the fact that they flew in the face of Calvinist orthodoxy, now well driven home by generations of rigorous indoctrination, these moves were resented as an attempt to pave the way for Anglican domination of the Church of Scotland. The Five Articles never won general acceptance and, particularly in the south, were steadily resisted. So charged indeed was the atmosphere that James was forced to defer another favourite project, namely the imposition of the Anglican Prayer Book on Scotland.

All in all, 'it may be seriously questioned whether the king at his death in 1625 left a Church at peace, or whether by the raising of these issues and an opposition determined to thwart them, James did not undermine the structure of episcopal organisation which he had so laboriously erected'.[39] Furthermore, by rejecting puritan claims at the Hampton Court conference in 1604, and by his acceptance of the canons of the same year and steady support for the episcopal regime in England, James had strengthened the existing bonds between the puritans in both kingdoms; for the observance of holy days and kneeling at communion were just as detested by English puritans as they were by Scottish presbyterians. Clearly, to promote such an alliance was not part of James' intention, but it grew naturally as a reaction to his policies, and was indeed to prove one of the most important consequences of the Union of the Crowns. In spite of the strains and stresses that ultimately disrupted the puritan alliance, it has to this day left an indelible mark on the Church of Scotland in the shape of the Westminster Standards.

The opposition to divine right monarchy in England, or at any rate to Charles I's conception of it, sprang from many sources. The economic policy of the crown alienated many vested interests and irritated public feeling: monopolies were generally detested; industrialists and merchants desired free trade; and archaic feudal dues annoyed the new gentry, who were also infuriated by the government's attempts to regulate enclosure. Parliament, drawn mainly from the propertied classes, became the obvious vehicle of protest, and the protests finally covered not only the fiscal expedients adopted by an impoverished crown but also unpopular religious and foreign policies.[40] Wars were increasingly expensive to wage; and adding to the natural reluctance of parliament to vote higher supplies was general detestation of a foreign policy that seemed at best lukewarm to the protestant interest and at worst pro-catholic. Laud's Arminianism, and his furious assault on the puritans, seemed to smack of crypto-popery: and, besides, his attempt to solve the economic problems of the Church of England forged an alliance between the men of property and the puritans. Equally crucial was the character of Charles I himself—at bottom honourable and well-intentioned, but unrealistic, devious and obstinate.

This is not to regard the Civil War as inevitable (an all too common snare) or to espouse any one of the numerous explanations that have been advanced to explain it. American historians, conscious of the importance of constitutional themes to their own history, still apparently hanker after S. R. Gardiner's interpretations; but British students of the period, on the whole, have been more concerned to explore the social background to the Civil War. In the wake of Gardiner's magisterial work few periods in British history have been so minutely investigated as the Jacobean and the Caroline; but a major difficulty is that, in spite of intensive research, the new way has still to produce a grand synthesis.[41] All that can be done here is to pick out what seem to be the most important points relevant to Anglo-Scottish relations. The limitation does little to reduce the difficulties, for, neither in England nor in Scotland (nor in Ireland either for that matter) were the issues simple and capable of being explained in terms of single causes. Thus, to dismiss this whole complex and sometimes chaotic period in terms of the 'Puritan Revolution' in England or the 'Reign of King Covenant' in Scotland would be idle; equally so would be any attempt to explain all by reciting the National Covenant followed by the Grand Remonstrance; or by speculating as to whether gentry and lairds were rising or falling. Only if the inevitability of the Civil War is accepted can any one theory of causation command respect, let alone acceptance. But contemporaries themselves were bewildered by events, and many altered course (like Wentworth, Hyde, Falkland or Montrose), either blinded by new convictions, just snatching at the opportunities of the moment, or else simply buffeted by circumstances beyond their control. Then, too, the resort to arms seems to have been unpremeditated and confused, and on the whole the idea of inevitability has little to recommend it.

Hindsight is best discarded, and as one authority puts it: 'in 1640 the one thing quite out of the question was a civil war'.[42]

What has to be explained is the failure of a system of government, and underlying that the serious divisions that had arisen in the governing class. The Levellers and other chiliastic visionaries burgeoned, in all their fascinating diversity, as a consequence of the Great Civil War; but they neither caused it nor began it. The 'Troubles', as is well known even if none too well understood by many, began with the collapse of 'Thorough' in Scotland. Developments north of Tweed, however, remain to most English and American historians as veiled and mysterious as they were to Clarendon, and on the whole English and American scholars opt too readily for the easy solution that 'Scotch matters' were too trivial or too wild and woolly to warrant their serious consideration. Thus, Professor Roots' otherwise admirable volume is disfigured by its feeble treatment of Scottish affairs—a defect that is highlighted rather than concealed by the disparaging tone that he adopts. Though Professor Trevor-Roper seems to be aware of the difficulty his contributions are not in the least helpful; they really constitute a mish-mash of elementary points, none too accurately handled, strung together by rhetorical questions and garnished with burlesque humour.[43] In his excursions into 'Scotch history' he is very unkind to himself. But then, as Christopher Hill (who does understand seventeenth-century Scottish history) has pointed out in another context, it is difficult to discuss seriously Trevor-Roper's protean arguments.[44] Less ingenious, though not so conducive to daring speculation or resounding rhetoric, is the older and more laborious but also more rewarding way of establishing and then assessing the facts.

The most important and most revealing items of all are totally ignored by Trevor-Roper—namely, the aims of the covenanters in Scotland and the precise nature of the concessions that Charles I was forced to grant them in 1641. Missing this, he contrives to miss the lot, and not all his very considerable rhetorical powers can make good the loss. For the covenanters brought about a revolution not just in the government of the church but in that of the state as well. Only ignoring the evidence reduces them to the level of blind fanaticism where Trevor-Roper's anachronistic 'Enlightenment rationalism' would place them. The covenants and what flowed from them are, after all, crucial to the understanding of these times. And the true history of the National Covenant lies in its pedigree —by Prayer Book out of Revocation. So, with the Act of Revocation, we are forced to turn yet again to the central issue of the disposition of the old kirklands.

The folly of Charles I's preposterous, so-called 'Act of Revocation' is impossible to exaggerate. As initiated in July 1625 it apparently concerned only the principality lands, which Charles as Prince of Scotland did not personally administer until 1620. What was originally proposed, then, seemed of minor importance, and the king at first did nothing to dispel this comforting illusion. But in the meantime he had secretly drawn up an extraordinarily sweeping measure which was carefully kept from the Privy Council until it had passed the Privy Seal on 12 October 1625. Curiously, no record of this remains, and it is important to point out that to date no authentic copy of the act at this stage in its involved career has been discovered.[45] The Privy Council naturally took alarm at all this, and protested about the rumoured Revocation and the under-hand methods used to introduce it; but the Council's remonstrance went un-heeded, and it was latterly obliged to countenance a wild measure that aimed at annexing to the crown all the old kirklands and revenues alienated since 1540.[46] True, the king promised to deal justly with those who surrendered rights or claims without fuss; but the promise was vague and of dubious worth, the more so as Charles was at the same time rigging the Court of Session and giving the impression that property rights were to be entirely subjected to the royal will. The madness of allowing such an impression to gain ground is manifest; and yet the king blundered on steadily undermining his own credibility. Why?

Charles' primary aim was probably just to raise money, which the English parliament, suspicious of his foreign policy, refused to grant. In addition the crown in Scotland was impoverished, and in spite of increased taxation the expenses of government were hard to meet. The king tried to give some moral flavour to his policy by alleging that it was for the good of the church, which was certainly plagued by poverty; but, far from being welcomed, this alleged means of providing for the church was suspect and bitterly resented. The Revocation was regarded by the nobles as illegal extortion, and by many of the kirkmen the king's brand of Melvillianism was denounced as simply a stratagem for promoting Anglican influence. The money so provided would, it was feared, strengthen the bishops and make possible the pomp and ceremonial that was being advanced in the Church of England under Arminian influences. Thus the proposed Revocation alarmed the Scottish presbyterians, who still formed a considerable faction, as much as it angered and alienated the nobility and lairds.

The Revocation was a veritable Pandora's box. As well as joining together sectarian passion and secular avarice, its legality was dubious and stirred up legal and constitutional controversy. Revocations as such were not unknown; many had been passed from the fourteenth century onwards, the inevitable products of recurring minorities, and of particular interest were the measures projected by Mary in 1555 and by James VI in 1587.[47] These were both wide measures (in stated intention at any rate), but still nothing like as sweeping as that of 1625. That act was unique in two vital respects. First, earlier measures had rarely been enforced and were used largely as a means of raising money through compositions, almost indeed as benevolences. It was suspected, how-ever, that Charles, literal-minded as always, meant business and that the strict letter of the act was to be applied. Secondly, at this very time, title to property was being rigorously defined at law, a good instance of this process being the setting up of the Register of Sasines in 1617. But if Charles had his way, legal title would mean nothing and property rights would stand or fall at his personal whim—an impossible state of affairs.

In fact, the closest analogy to Charles I's Revocation was the Emperor Ferdinand II's Edict of Restitution of 1629 whereby possession of church lands in Germany was to revert to the *status quo ante* of 1552, with a goodly slice of the profits going to the emperor. So large was the claim and so catastrophic the possible consequences to German land-holding and liberties that the Restitution helped to propel the Thirty Years' War into its bitterest and most destructive phase.

Politically, Charles I's Act of Revocation was a dangerous nonsense, and years of bitter wrangling could not make it acceptable. Indeed, if the original Revocation had been applied many of the lairds would have been ruined, which goes far to explain the solid opposition put up by this class to Charles I and his policies in general. In the upshot the Act of Revocation could not be fully implemented and by 1633 had been gradually scaled down to cover Principality lands, and, of curious significance for the future, royal lands and kirklands alienated from the crown in breach of general laws and acts of parliament. In such cases, where the royal revenue had suffered, restitution was to be made: the Revocation Act of 1633 aimed obviously at James VI's alienations.[48] The truly significant feature is that all this was done behind the shelter of existing law and statute. Charles I could evidently be a constitutionalist when it suited his purpose; he failed to see that others might do likewise. All unwittingly, by appealing to existing law and constitutional procedure he was providing the opposition with a powerful weapon. Finally, and almost adventitiously, out of the whole Revocation muddle there emerged a valuable settlement of teinds. But this measure, though much needed and statesmanlike, was unpopular in that it was costly to many landlords.

The main consequence of the attempted Revocation, then, was that Charles I never thereafter enjoyed the unqualified support of the feudal landowners of Scotland, and it was ultimately owing to this fact that his reign terminated so disastrously. In the words of a contemporary observer the policy of Revocation was 'the ground stone of all the mischief that followed after, both to this king's government and family'.[49] Just as in England, protection of property, the primacy of law, and defence of radical protestantism were, by Charles's maladroit policies, forced to go hand in hand.

The king came in time to realise that in his projected Revocation he had overreached himself, and he did his mediocre best to reassure the men of property. But other aspects of his policy had the opposite effect. He disliked heritable jurisdictions and wherever possible annexed them to the crown, a wholly praiseworthy endeavour, for those bastions of feudalism were a drag on sound administration. The nobles, however, could only see in such a policy an attack on their order. Charles also gave offence by introducing the bishops into high offices of state and using them to turn both Privy Council and parliament into mere adjuncts of the Court. This again the nobles bitterly resented; they did not mind bishops having nominal control of the church but they detested prelates who as mere pawns of the Court lorded it over the state and its traditional governing class.

When Charles visited Scotland in 1633, far from trying to allay these growing fears and resentments, he made matters worse by personally brow-beating the parliament and by openly revealing his displeasure at the spiritual and material poverty of the national church. Already in 1629 he had taken up his father's shelved project of liturgical revision; and in 1633 even some of the Scottish bishops were alarmed by the hostile criticisms of their church made by that 'little meddling hocus-pocus', William Laud, who was soon to become Arch-bishop of Canterbury. The nobles for their part feared that if the king could order the church purely by prerogative right then he could do as much in the state. Indeed church and state were simply facets of the same problem of government, grievances on secular matters tending to touch on ecclesiastical affairs, and *vice versa*. Such grievances were embodied in 'A Supplication' which contained mild and deferential reproofs of the king's conduct, but Charles, in his usual tone of bumbling menace, refused to accept it. The Supplication was not published and there the matter should have rested; but, for revising a copy of the 'Supplication', Lord Balmerino, whose father had been ruined for opposing James VI's ecclesiastical policy, was tried for his life.[50]

The charge against Balmerino summarised the real nature of the struggle that was being waged in Scotland: it was simply 'Thorough', a rigorous application of divine right kingship, against existing legal and constitutional practice. The trial dragged on from 3 December 1634 until 20 March 1635, and, though the court was rigged in favour of the crown, only by the narrowest of margins was Balmerino found guilty and sentenced to death. A great outcry then ensued in the country and Charles was forced to pardon him. Balmerino's case had this important result: it seemed to prove that no constitutional means remained for attempting to deter the king from his arbitrary courses, and that to remonstrate with him, however mildly, was to hazard life itself.

Tension mounted again when in 1636 a new Book of Canons was thrust upon the church purely as an exercise of the royal prerogative, neither assembly, parliament nor even Privy Council being consulted. The canons were every whit as disturbing as their provenance; they emphasised the king's supreme power, further exalted the claims of the bishops, threatened to license preachers on the English model, and even raised serious doubts about the continued existence of the lower courts of the church. The Scottish Canons of 1636 were, in fact, Laudian in the fullest sense and anticipated, for good or ill, the Seventeen Canons passed in 1640 by Convocation in England.[51] The new Scottish and English Canons amounted to an uncompromising assertion of divine right monarchy doctrines and endorsement of these by the two national churches. Each set of canons was to play an important part in the politics of the time by goading the opposition to fury, and produced in the long run results fatal for both king and bishops.

By 1637, then, there was widespread alarm in Scotland about the king's aims, and it is ridiculous, though all too common, to ascribe the outbreak of the 'Troubles' solely to the so-called 'Laud's Liturgy' and the violent reaction to it personified by the mythical Jenny Geddes.

The opposition to Charles in Scotland, like that in England, rested on an alliance between the men of property, who felt that their rights were being threatened, and the Calvinists who feared that the king was bent on spreading Arminian and even popish influences. Even before the peremptory introduction of the Prayer Book, which again was done purely through the king's prerogative, an opposition was in existence, eager and ready to turn any such unpopular act to account.[52] The extent of that opposition was the most extraordinary feature of the situation in Scotland; the near-unity of the nation against the king's policies, considering the propensity of the Scots to quarrel among themselves, speaks volumes for Charles' ineptitude. The class in which real power lay, the feudal nobility, showed unusual solidarity against the threats posed by the crown; the folly of the attempt to thrust a thinly disguised Anglican Prayer Book on the Scottish Church in July 1637 gave the nobles the support of the ministers; and the irresistible strength of the allies led in the first instance not to civil war but to a constitutional revolution in both kirk and state. What began as a protest against Laud's Liturgy soon developed into a struggle for 'kirk and kingdom'.

This is in no way to deny the genuineness of the religious reaction to Laud's Liturgy, a reaction which expressed not only the predominant Calvinism of Scotland but also the exaggerated fears of resurgent popery that haunted international protestantism at that time. Nonetheless, those ingrained prejudices and attitudes were used by the opposition to spearhead a strong movement against the king's arbitrary government; and in the space of a few brief months Charles I's authority in Scotland collapsed, leaving the way open for reform of both church and state. By October 1637 the conflict had sharpened. The Privy Council, which was weak and divided (the lay lords blaming all on the clerical), helplessly watched as its decrees were being flouted; and before the end of the year, a revolutionary executive, the 'Tables', had virtually assumed real direction of affairs. By February 1638 deadlock had been reached. The Council could not go forward, and the opposition (or to be more precise the revolutionary government) dared not go back. The opposition's great need was for some kind of constitutional justification, and that was supplied by the National Covenant, which was enthusiastically introduced in Greyfriars Kirk, Edinburgh, on 28 February 1638.

It is again eloquent of Charles' failure that this remarkable document benefited from the advice of the Lord Advocate (then known, even more revealingly, as the King's Advocate), Sir Thomas Hope. But the National Covenant was mainly the work of another lawyer, the devout (and latterly fanatical) Archibald Johnston of Wariston, who was aided in his labours by one of the ablest of the ministers, Alexander Henderson of Leuchars. The result of the joint labours of these men has been variously assessed: 'Some have lauded it as the off-spring of piety and patriotism; others have denounced it as the off-spring of fanaticism and rebellion'.[53] To Scottish presbyterians the National Covenant was, and to some still is, almost an addition to the Ten Commandments; while to Roman catholics and episcopalians it reeked, and probably still does, of the pit. On a first reading the National Covenant does indeed exhale the stench of bigotry; but there was more to it than that. Closer examination shows that this covenant was really a subtle constitutional device which cleverly availed itself of popular discontents. Taking as its basis the Negative Confession (or Covenant as some called it) of 1581, and particularly its swingeing denunciations of popery, the National Covenant of 1638 went on to list the numerous statutes that had established 'the true protestant faith' in Scotland. Here it spoke with the authentic voice of early seventeenth-century puritanism, which was obsessed by the threats posed, or supposedly posed, by the Counter-Reformation, and obsessed too by the need to mount a protestant crusade to ward off these threats. In this attitude there was nothing that was peculiarly Scottish, any more than there was anything peculiarly Scottish about the concept of a covenant. Both Hope and Wariston subscribed whole-heartedly to these beliefs, and Wariston in time was possessed by them virtually to the exclusion of all else. But in 1638 both knew that the really powerful elements in Scottish society were moved by other considerations and that the problem was how to harness up ecclesiastical and political unrest—a common problem in that day and age, as John Pym too was to discover. In Scotland the National Covenant provided an effective means of welding together radicalism secular and ecclesiastical, so much so that it came to be widely known as 'The Noble-man's Covenant' to distinguish it from Charles' abortive riposte, 'The King's Covenant'.[54]

The main contention of the National Covenant is that the king cannot innovate in matters of worship without first obtaining the assent of free General Assemblies and of parliaments presumably no less free. Nor is the inhibition restricted to ecclesiastical affairs. According to the Covenant the king is bound by the fundamental laws of the kingdom, which preserve its 'true Religion, Lawes, and Liberties'.[55] Here Charles was hipped by his own doctrine. In his Act of Revocation of 1633 he had conceded the primacy of law, and in 1638 the opposition adroitly turned this self-same weapon against the king. But as well as sheltering behind the law the National Covenant also made profuse professions of loyalty to the crown, thereby appealing to many who would have shrunk from a more radical approach. Initially, this gave the covenanters the enormous advantage of a unity that was almost nation-wide and probably unprecedented. It has to be borne in mind, for example, that Montrose began his political career as a fervent covenanter; also that most of the great men in the Highlands as well as the Lowlands subscribed to the National Covenant, and that to begin with the dissidents, such as the famous Aberdeen Doctors, were a small and impotent minority.

The cracks that developed in this impressive unity came later over issues very different from those that produced the Covenant in February 1638, and the importance of that initial unity is not to be overlooked. It foiled the king in two vital respects. It meant not only that Charles could not, in spite of the threats he freely uttered during the Bishops' Wars, overawe the opposition in Scotland; and also, and more seriously for him, it meant that active opposition to prerogative rule could not be restricted to Scotland. Successful defiance of 'Thorough' where least anticipated led to its speedy collapse in both England and Ireland as well.

Detailed examination of the measures pushed through by the covenanters cannot be attempted here, but these measures have to be understood if Anglo-Scottish relations in this crucial period are to be properly appreciated. Too late, Charles tried to conciliate the covenanters by promising to withdraw the canons and the Prayer Book, and by allowing an Assembly to meet. In spite of these concessions the General Assembly that met in Glasgow in November 1638 (the first for thirty years) went over to the offensive. The extremists, joined by the Earl of Argyll who soon became their recognised leader, seized the key position and took the opportunity to 'mak siccar' by sweeping away Prayer Book, Canons, Five Articles and bishops as well. These radical moves were aided rather than impeded by the fatuous manoeuvrings of the king's chief agent in Scotland, the Commissioner to the Assembly, the Marquis of Hamilton. This stunning success fused the revolutionary alliance of church and state, with momentous and far-reaching effects. It cut the ground from under the feet of the moderates, and the further concessions later wrung from the king, which would have satisfied the original leaders of the covenanters (the Earls of Rothes and Montrose), could not satisfy Argyll, who had a chronic, and perfectly justified, distrust of Charles I. Nor did the revolution stop with the purging of the kirk. The covenanters were well aware that Charles aimed to reduce them by force, and it was no secret that an Irish army that was to take part in this scheme was to harry the Campbell lands and stir up opposition to Argyll's dominant position in the West Highlands, an easy matter in view of long-standing clan feuds and rivalries. In fact, from 1637 onwards Argyll (then Lord Lorn) had been nervous about his position, well aware as he was that the king had granted Kintyre to Randall MacDonnell, Earl of Antrim.[56]

For Argyll, then, there could be no drawing back, and no real accommodation with the king. Indeed of contemporary politicians—English as well as Scots—Argyll had the clearest insight into the problems of the period and the most consistent approach to them. From the outset he disliked and distrusted Charles I; but he understood that the real issues, while undoubtedly affected by the personalities of the principals involved, far transcended them. For Argyll, the only solution lay in a covenanted king—that is, in limited monarchy but limited not only, as has been suggested, by God's law, but also by the law of the land.[57] For once, Charles took a realistic view of matters: 'So long as this Covenant is in force,' he wrote to Hamilton, 'I have no more Power in Scotland than as a Duke of Venice, which I will rather die than suffer.'[58] Compromise evidently there could be none.

In fact, a revolution had been initiated in Scotland which had many novel features. It was not just a return to primitive baronial turbulence, though it had some tincture of this, but had a strong constitutional motivation, and it could not have been carried out without powerful support from England. There is paradox here, for in a sense the covenanting movement was a nationalist reaction to rule from the south, but not, initially at any rate, anti-English; and the revolt against Charles I in England and Scotland helped, in spite of the intolerable strains and stresses that developed, to cast Anglo-Scottish relations into a firmer mould.

7

The Civil Wars and Cromwellian Union

THE unexpected resistance to Charles I in Scotland had powerful repercussions in England. It speeded on the formation of a numerous, if far from homogeneous, opposition to the king, and by 1639 that opposition, cleverly marshalled by John Pym, was openly praying for the success of the resisters in Scotland. Pym and his allies were also actively preparing to emulate the covenanters by wresting the initiative from the king once he bowed to the inevitable and ended the years of so-called tyranny from 1629 by summoning a parliament. Throughout the crucial years from 1639 until Pym's death in 1644, he and Argyll carefully co-ordinated their measures. And these measures were decisive. Charles lost the initiative in both kingdoms and all the desperate floundering of which he was capable could not recover it for him. His attempts to browbeat his rebellious Scottish subjects into submission failed, and the First Bishops' War ended in a humiliating and dangerous fiasco for the king. Charles lacked the resources and the money necessary to overcome the covenanters who had, in a surprisingly brief space of time, got together a formidable army that was stiffened by seasoned veterans from the Thirty Years' War. The king was forced to make peace in June 1639 by the Pacification of Berwick which effectively deprived him of real power in Scotland. That much was evident when a General Assembly that met in Edinburgh in August confirmed the work of the Glasgow Assembly; and the shift of power became even more obvious when the Scottish parliament also proved to be beyond the king's control and had to be prorogued. In the following spring the king's situation further deteriorated when the English 'Short Parliament' of April–May 1640 supported the covenanters and refused to grant supply without redress of grievances. In spite of this Charles again tried to subdue the covenanters by force but the Second Bishops' War had an even more disastrous issue for him than the first, leaving a Scots covenanting army in possession of Newcastle and London's coal supply. Charles was forced to summon the English parliament again in November 1640, and the Long Parliament, as it became known, from the first sided with the covenanters against the king.

Throughout, developments in Scotland played a crucial role. Encouraged by their success in the First Bishops' War, the Scottish estates, which met in June 1640 in defiance of the king's will, ratified the National Covenant, confirmed the work of the two recent General Assemblies, and then proceeded to pass several acts the effects of which were to free parliament from royal control and to make it the real engine of government. The lever here was the deposition of the bishops who could thus no longer constitute the first estate in parliament. This in turn raised the question of the constitution of the Committee of the Articles, and the opportunity was seized to remodel it. The Articles were not abolished, but an act was passed restoring the old practice whereby each estate freely elected its own representatives; and of equal importance here was the whittling down of the powers of the committee which could no longer engross the work of the legislature. This in itself was revolutionary, but the revolution did not halt there; a Triennial Act was passed, and subsequent acts gave parliament the right to approve or veto nominations to Privy Council and judiciary. Thus, before the Second Bishops' War of 1640 and the invasion of England, which forced Charles to call the Long Parliament, the covenanters had carried out a constitutional revolution in Scotland which ended prerogative and established responsible government.

The programme was revolutionary in more senses than one; not only did it fetter the prerogative, it was carried in defiance of the crown. The policy of the covenanters thus entailed other revolutionary actions, and, most notably, lack of faith in the king led them to resort to force in order to impose their will on the country. The draconian methods employed, however, were products of fear and suspicion, means rather than ends, though it is fashionable today to argue that the covenanting movement was founded on fraud and force. The use of coercion was implicit in the situation, and almost exactly the same pattern repeated itself in England where the revolt against what was regarded as monarchical tyranny soon also adopted arbitrary methods. Indeed, such developments are the staple products of revolutionary situations, familiar enough to students of, for example, the French Revolution or the Bolshevik Revolution.

Failure to grasp the nature of the reforms passed by the covenanters hopelessly obscures the real issues. Professor Trevor-Roper, for one, apparently has no knowledge of these events or their significance; but, then, in his celebrated essay on 'Scotland and the Puritan Revolution', he shows the same tendency to be wrong that he unfairly ascribes to Robert Baillie, who, unlike Trevor-Roper, was, as a mere hapless contemporary, denied the advantage of hindsight. Nor can it be said that knowledge of the covenanting programme is locked up in recondite or difficult sources. The main evidence has long been accessible in the printed records of parliament and Privy Council; and for those who are unable to consult the record sources, they have recently been conveniently summarised by Dickinson and Donaldson in their admirable *Source Book*.[1] So, as far as this vital matter is concerned, it is really hard to understand why Professor Trevor-Roper's 'Scotch history' should rest on such flimsy grounds. To be sure, one vital point he does note—only to fail to recognise its significance. He mentions how the king, alarmed by the intransigence of the Long Parliament, went up to Scotland in August 1641 in an attempt to gain the support of the covenanters— a fact so well known that it could hardly be overlooked. Yet, curiously, Trevor-Roper fails to mention that, to placate the covenanters, Charles actually accepted the new constitution and so gave it complete legal sanction! Instead the professor 'analyses' the situation, using Buckle's hackneyed and grossly oversimplified view of a Scotland dominated, at every turn and in every conceivable way, by crack-brained religious fanatics. In this view, one would almost think that the Scottish presbyterians had a monopoly of unlovely qualities and that intolerance and savage repression flourished only under the regime of the covenants. This was far from being the case, and it is unfortunate for Trevor-Roper that the most recent research emphasises, what needed no proving, that fundamentalist religious beliefs were a common feature of the early and mid-seventeenth century. Such beliefs were basic to the thinking of people as diverse as James VI and I, Argyll, Cromwell, Milton, Rutherford and a host of other notables, down to Lodowick Muggleton and Praise-God Barebones.[2] They cannot all just be dismissed as lunatics. On the other hand, it would be a mistake to lean too far the other way and to ascribe everything to the potency of fundamentalist or millenarian beliefs to the exclusion of more mundane matters. The sacred and the secular were not then sharply separated, as they are for most people nowadays, but interpenetrated each other to form a distinctive politico-ecclesiastical ethos.[3]

To sweep all this aside (the actual work of the politicians, such tangibles as acts of parliament and such intangibles as the thought of the age) simply to provide a crude rationalist analysis based on misapplication of Enlightenment concepts is surely a perverse view of the historian's function. And to touch lightly on a delicate matter, more extraordinary still were the paeans of praise with which leading English historians greeted Trevor-Roper's extraordinary essay in 'analytical history'. What is analysed is surely of first importance, and the most learned analysis of chalk can hardly yield cheese. With his information so limited and his method of argument so defective, it is to be feared that Trevor-Roper's celebrated essay on 'Scotland and the Puritan Revolution' contains more to admire at than to admire.

Yet far from being swathed in impenetrable Scotch Calvinist mist, as so many English and American students of the period are too prone to assume, developments in Scotland between 1638 and 1642 were clear, sharp and decisive.[4] Nor, as we have seen, is there all that much doubt about the motive forces that helped to shape events. One point of importance, however, remains to be stressed. As well as general hostility to bishops and fears of the king's intentions, the need for national unity was strongly felt, and particularly in the Lowlands. In Tudor times England had been welded into a nation-state; but in Scotland that process, though it was being advanced, was not complete. James VI had seen the problems clearly, and it was one that the covenanters could not ignore. What particularly exercised them was that in much of the Highlands and Islands there were 'dark corners of the land' where the established church was feebly organised and others where it was virtually non-existent. James VI had tackled the problem (in fact, the problems of government in the Highlands as a whole) but with very limited success. When effective power passed to the covenanters they accepted the challenge posed by this state of affairs, and they tried to remedy the defects of the national church in those areas.[5] That their efforts made them unpopular

over the greater part of the Highlands and Islands, and actually helped to produce serious tensions between Highlanders and Lowlanders, does not invalidate
the basic soundness of their assessment of the situation. The Highland problem
was real and persistent. It had to be tackled by successive governments, of which
the Cromwellian, admittedly for a very brief space, succeeded best. That problem
troubled the Restoration and Revolution regimes, and it had to be faced once
more in the eighteenth century by the presbyterians.[6]

Another factor that initially promoted unity was the strength of kinship in
mid seventeenth-century Scotland. So, in Lowlands as well as Highlands, if the
great men could agree, their dependents more or less willingly followed. In
marked contrast to England, the upper classes in Scotland had no dread of their
underlings, and so the magnates could openly challenge the king's authority free
from the fear that this might unleash anarchy. Jacqueries, virtually unknown in
Scotland, were therefore undreaded, and the great lords could blandly assume
that, controlled by the magnates and ministers of religion, 'Jock-o'-the Common-
weal' would do just as he was told. By and large he did, but not without in some
quarters evolving notions of his own. But this new spirit of independence did not
become a factor of prime importance until the Restoration period; it existed
during the Civil Wars but was hidden by the divisions of the covenanters. Class
tensions were not prominent in this development, though by the late 1640s
ideological differences were undermining the claims of kinship and feudal
dependence in the Lowlands. In particular, friction arose between kirkmen and
magnates as the latter tried to control the church through lay representation.
The rise of the ruling elder seemed to threaten a form of erastianism that was
distasteful to Wariston, the presbyterian clergy and their supporters.[7]

It is when we turn to examine developments in England that we find ourselves
enveloped in mystery, groping in the darkness visible of a topsy-turvy world of
'hawks' and 'doves' who seemed to be undergoing perpetual metamorphosis, of
'parties' that were not parties in any recognisable sense, of 'episcopalians' who
cared nothing for bishops, of 'presbyterians' who were remarkably vague about
presbytery, 'independents' who were not sectaries, 'levellers' who were not
democrats—and so on *ad nauseam*, if not quite *ad infinitum*. In short, the sociological historians have worked to such bewildering purpose that it is at the
moment extremely difficult to make any sense of English politics from the
summoning of the Short Parliament onwards. What does seem to emerge, however, is that opposition to the king in England was nothing like as widespread,
united, or as ideologically cohesive as was once believed. True, when the Long
Parliament met, the king had virtually no support in it; but whenever actual
issues were raised parliament became hopelessly divided. Then, too, unlike
Scotland, England had a long tradition of popular revolts, and fear of anarchy
drove social conservatives over to the king. The matter was neatly summed up
by Lord Savile in 1643: 'I would not have the King trample on the Parliament,
nor the Parliament lessen him so much as to make a way for the people to rule
us all'.[8] For many the core of the problem in England was how to reform the
church and limit the monarchy without subverting the social structure. Many
so-called puritans who hated the Laudians yet shrank from emulating the

covenanters and suppressing the bishops; and many of the nobility and men of property who feared royal assaults on their rights still saw in monarchy a necessary safeguard of property and social rank.

The English presbyterians sought an answer on the lines laid down in Scotland; but outside London and Lancashire, presbytery in England was not a popular force. Certainly, generally speaking, and not just with reference to the ecclesiastical question, the example of the Scots had an undoubted influence; but Pym, who from the outset was determined to make a common front with the covenanters, could not push through the Commons (never mind the Lords) a programme as logical and well-defined as that already implemented by Argyll and his associates. For one thing, Pym himself had no deep-rooted objection to bishops and for another he was well aware that genuine presbyterianism had little appeal in England at large. Nonetheless, popular sentiment against the bishops was strong, especially in London, where, as the second canto of *Hudibras* jeers:

> No sow-gelder did blow his horn
> To geld a cat, but cried Reform.
> The oyster-women locked their fish up
> And trudg'd away to cry 'No Bishop'.

But if the episcopal regime was to go, what was to be put in its place? There was no easy answer to that question.

These ambiguities and uncertainties were apparent in the fall of the hated Strafford. All factions agreed on his impeachment, but Strafford ably defended himself, arguing that he had always acted with the concurrence of the Council and could not therefore be guilty of treason. The difficulty encountered by Pym and his motley band was that they were really attacking the king and his policies but did not see how this could be done constitutionally. Only an Act of Attainder of dubious legality secured the condemnation of 'Black Tom Tyrant', and even then his quasi-judicial murder was largely a consequence of Charles' hopeless shuffling. The result, as Strafford foresaw, was fatal to the traditional monarchy, but this the king could not be brought to understand. By deserting Strafford, Charles undermined his own position, and it was folly in him thereafter to refuse the accommodation proffered by Pym. Over a year was spent in futile attempts to achieve a workable compromise. Edward Hyde, for example, hoped that if parliament secured the right to approve appointments to the Privy Council, the old constitution would continue to operate; but nothing came of the plan, though to the end of his career the Earl of Clarendon (as Hyde later became) pinned his faith on a return to conciliar government.

Events in Scotland and Ireland really doomed efforts at compromise in England. Charles' concessions to the Scots in August 1641 worsened his position by encouraging the English parliament to hold out for a similar settlement, though even then Pym's demands were rejected as too extreme by a majority of the House of Commons. His hand was strengthened by the sudden and violent collapse of 'Thorough' in Ireland. Nearly every body of opinion in England and Scotland agreed that the Irish catholic rebellion had to be suppressed, and there can be no doubt that the horrors of that rebellion, real and imagined, drew parliament and covenanters even closer together; but few felt that control of the forces needed to suppress the Irish rebellion could be entrusted to the king. Making skilful play with this fear, Pym won reluctant support for his programme. On 5 November 1641 he proposed that parliament should make support for the king in Ireland conditional on Charles employing councillors and officers of whom parliament approved. By a narrow majority the measure passed the Commons, only to be rejected by the Lords. Then came the appeal to the populace at large via the Grand Remonstrance, which came within an ace of failing to pass the Commons. And England came within an ace, for good or ill, of never seeing Oliver Cromwell again—or so he said. The king's position, on the other hand, was visibly being strengthened by a notable shift of conservative opinion, and if he had been a better politician the conflict in England might still have been settled by compromise. But the growing distrust between king and Commons culminated in Charles' mad attempt to arrest the Five Members, the only effect of which was to stiffen the opposition. Even then the Nineteen Propositions offered a reasonable compromise, but Charles rejected them and instead issued commissions of array. England completed the drift into civil war when the king raised his standard at Nottingham on 22 August 1642.

Far from clarifying the issues, the outbreak of hostilities further confused them. Neither side was in a position to wage effective warfare, and the first year of the Great Civil War had a rather Gilbertian flavour. The king, as ever, lacked money, but though his antagonists controlled the greater part of the material resources of the kingdom, they too had difficulty in raising the necessary supplies and only after exhausting sessions in the Commons did Pym manage to remedy this defect. The king also had an initial advantage in that his aims were clear and carried more conviction at the time than they did much later to Whig historians. According to Charles, his object was simply to maintain the ancient constitution, a programme that had an undoubted appeal in an age that set great store by tradition and precedent. But what was parliament striving for? That was by no means clear; and Pym, superb politician though he was, had difficulty in commanding the support of the Commons where a strong body of opinion headed by Denzil Holles argued for conciliation with the king—in the innocent hope that such a thing was possible. The raw parliamentary levies were equally hesitant and bemused, and laid themselves wide open to defeat. After Edgehill on 23 October 1642, when Charles narrowly failed in his awkward lunge at London, the clamour for a compromise peace increased and Pym was hard-driven to maintain his position. His answer was to prepare the way for a military alliance with the covenanters. The mechanics of the protracted negotiations that followed have not received anything like the attention they deserve. The essential fact is that the policy that finally gave rise to the Solemn League and Covenant was the work, not of the Scottish covenanters, but of John Pym.

In the panic before the king's narrow repulse at Edgehill, Pym suggested to parliament an English anti-popish covenant with which the Scottish covenanters should be associated. But while the Commons enthusiastically fulminated against popery, the amorphous jostling groups could not be brought to implement Pym's full policy. He still pushed it, however, and managed to tack to the resolution for a covenant a clause praying that 'our brethren of Scotland . . . will help and assist us in defence of this cause'.[9] Pym then had John Pickering sent up to Edinburgh to argue the case there; but the majority of the House of Commons, pinning its hopes on the negotiations then proceeding with the king, lost interest and the project hung fire.[10] It was not revived until the summer of 1643 by which time the overall situation had changed. The talks with Charles had broken down, and the parliamentarians were petrified by the military successes scored by the royalists, particularly that of 30 June at Adwalton Moor in Yorkshire. Parliament's position was indeed serious, for if the royalists secured a firm hold on the North of England the hope of succour from Scotland would be very much diminished. As it was put at the time, 'All their last hope seemed to be in their blessed brethren the Scots'; and Baillie a little later likewise noted that, 'All things are expected from God and the Scots'.[11] After Adwalton an alliance with the covenanters became top priority; and since Argyll was also alarmed at the prospect of the king emerging victorious from the Civil War the basis for such an alliance existed. But in making the League it was the English parliamentarians and not the Scottish covenanters who really made the running.

So far from forcing the issue on the parliamentarians, as Trevor-Roper implies, the Scots were divided in their response to the growing volume of pleas for help from the English parliamentarians. A considerable party of the covenanters hoped to arbitrate between king and parliament in the expectation that the honest broker would have his reward through the setting up of presbyterian church government in all three kingdoms.[12] To the discomfiture of the neutralists, Charles could not be brought to accept such terms. The king, for his part, could wrest no advantage from the situation, for he too was the prisoner of his own wishful thinking. Convinced by the vacillating Hamiltons that Scotland was at heart loyal and would never actively support his enemies, Charles discouraged a small but growing royalist faction that was gathering round Montrose, who had become alarmed at the policies pursued by the extreme covenanters and was jealously uneasy at the meteoric rise of Argyll.

Montrose always claimed to stand by the National Covenant, and he remained a presbyterian; but he gradually concluded that the ideal of a balanced constitution that was implicit in the National Covenant was being perverted in order to deprive the crown of all power, and that Argyll and his henchmen were working to impose an oligarchical tyranny on the country. It is not easy to deal just measure to these two great antagonists. The conflict between them was undoubtedly sparked off by personal antipathy, for they were like Caesar and Pompey—one could not bear an equal and the other could brook no superior. Each plunged boldly into the dangerous politics of the times; each, at bottom, was probably swayed by honest devotion to principle; and each was ambitious, yet realistic enough to know that the prize was 'to win or lose it all'. Argyll is too readily caricatured as a savage fanatic, a ruthless intriguer and a craven coward—there was much more to him than that. Montrose, on the other hand, is too often depicted as a figure of romance, the Bayard of the north—but this again represents only part of the man. Their situations explain these partial assessments. Argyll wielded the powers of state that Montrose coveted but never held, and while Argyll governed harshly it is not possible to say how Montrose would have behaved if he had achieved his heart's desire and become viceroy in Scotland. But perhaps their most fundamental difference was that Argyll distrusted the Stewarts while Montrose was more loyal than realistic. It made no difference in the end, for the same treacherous hand laid them low.

Some historians have argued that, in view of those growing dissensions, the path of wisdom for Scotland would indeed have lain in neutrality. But such a policy was hardly possible. The covenanters realised that their fate depended on the outcome of the English Civil War, and, failing to gain the assurances they needed from the king, they had perforce to seek them elsewhere. In short, the position of the covenanters, though it looked strong, was fundamentally weak. Far from leading the English parliamentarians by the nose, the Scots from the outbreak of the Great Civil War were dragged along in the wake of events in England; but this crucial point has tended to be obscured by the urgency of the requests for help that reached Edinburgh from London. The reputation of the Scottish army was high, and in order to get use of it, the parliamentarians wooed the covenanters in the most flattering terms. The weakness of Scotland, however, both in material resources and in diplomatic weight, was not hidden from Argyll, who saw only too clearly that if the king triumphed in England the covenanters could not possibly maintain their position. How to secure that position, and himself with it, was Argyll's great problem. Indeed, the secret of the tortuous acts and policies of the covenanters lay in an unending, and ultimately unsuccessful, quest for security.

Between them, seizing the advantages of the moment, Pym and Argyll steadily outflanked their own moderates, helped by the inescapable fact that throughout 1643 the confused amateurish scuffling in England went decidedly in favour of the royalists. In June, after the discovery of a plot to render up London to the king, Pym managed to convince parliament of the absolute necessity of an alliance with the covenanters. Alarmed by the general trend of events, and especially disturbed by evidence of the king's plan to use an Irish army in Scotland, many of the covenanters had come reluctantly to similar conclusions. And so in July a proposal for a formal alliance—the fine fruits of Pickering's diplomacy—was dispatched from Edinburgh to Westminster. Again it is entirely characteristic that Charles, warned of these moves by Montrose, chose instead to believe the Hamiltons who continued to assure him of the loyalty of Scotland. Meanwhile Sir Harry Vane the younger headed a team of English parliamentary negotiators in Edinburgh, the result of whose joint labours with representatives of the covenanters was the Solemn League and Covenant.

Few episodes in the history of Anglo-Scottish relations have been so persistently misrepresented. By generations of devoted presbyterians the Solemn League was regarded as the ark of the covenant, changeless and binding to all eternity, and indeed well into the nineteenth century dwindling numbers of extremists reverenced it uncritically as Britain's pact with God, the more zealously to be defended because so wantonly betrayed. Needless to say, the object of this excessive veneration was not exactly the agreement concluded in

1643. As a reaction to this unrealistic assessment, recent opinion has tended to dismiss the Solemn League as a monumental piece of bigoted folly, the entire blame for which is usually cast on the fanatical Scottish covenanters.[13] Neither view has much to commend it, mainly because both ignore the full circumstances that led to the signing of the League. As we have seen, the alliance had been long in the making and its presiding genius was undoubtedly Pym. Nor were the Scottish covenanters unanimous about it. At the talks in Edinburgh Vane found that a considerable party in Scotland, quite apart from the small and weak royalist group, were still opposed to an alliance. Many still wished to arbitrate between the contending parties in England, and were only with difficulty overridden by Wariston and the extremists.[14]

The talks also soon revealed that the covenanters and the English parliamentarians were not at one on policy and that their main bond was fear of a royalist victory. The situation was a common enough one. After all, most alliances are of convenience; and, as usually happens, in this case each side strove to gain as much as it could while yielding as little as possible. The covenanters insisted on a guarantee for the system of church government and discipline on which their whole programme turned, and thus the Article of the Solemn League and Covenant which undertook to maintain presbyterianism in Scotland was obvious and unexceptionable. But was it not megalomaniacal bigotry to attempt to enforce this church discipline on the entire British Isles? To an age that accepts religious toleration, such a policy stands self-condemned; but the immediate circumstances of 1643 cast a very different light on the matter.

It is a grave mistake to ignore the diplomatic side of the League and to over-concentrate on its religious aspects. In practical terms, the covenanters erred in believing that the presbyterians were a major force in English politics but did not err in fearing the rise of the independents. Besides, they were misled by the Grand Remonstrance into believing that parliament was bound to reform the Church of England and that something like presbyterianism was projected. Hence the Scottish General Assembly's petition to the Privy Council for bringing England and Ireland into conformity with Scotland.[15] But it is not quite the case that the covenanters regarded their own system as perfect and attempted to foist it on the other two kingdoms. This view, widely enough propagated these days, is no more than a misleading half-truth. As early as 1641 Alexander Henderson had made it clear that the covenanters had no such fixed intention; he went further and roundly condemned chauvinist bigotry.[16] In April of the following year he told Baillie that the Scots and English must agree upon a new polity and discipline, 'for we are not to conceive that they will embrace our form. A new form must be set down for us all, and, in my opinion, some men set apart some time for that work'.[17] When part of that vision, the Westminster Assembly, came into being Henderson still called for the elaboration of a new system agreeable to both parties.[18] That the Scottish covenanters were serious about this is proved by their adoption of the Westminster Standards, which were mainly English in provenance. To these standards Scottish presbyterianism, in all its subsequent divisions, adhered. All told, this is hardly the action of people with closed minds.

At bottom, in fact, the League was the inevitable outcome of the covenanting quest for security and aimed hopefully at committing the English parliament to a more or less presbyterian programme. In the light of contemporary realities, then, the attempt to bring the two national churches into line was not in the least surprising. The real surprise would have been if no such effort had been made. But the phrase in the Solemn League and Covenant, that England and Ireland should be reformed 'according to the Word of God, and the example of the best reformed churches', is not simply a veiled exercise in Scottish *amour propre*: all were to contribute to the elaboration of an acceptable ecclesiastical regime.

As for the thrusting of a presbyterian system on Ireland, the whole point of post-Reformation Irish history has been precisely the imposition on the native Irish Roman catholics of alien and detested religious forms. Misconceived and indefensible as that policy appears today, nonetheless it was applied; and the Church of Ireland on the model of the Church of England survived the age of religious bigotry and lurched on in all its mischievous torpor into the age of liberal reform in the nineteenth century. In 1643 the question, then, was not whether it was morally right to force a hated religious settlement on the bulk of the population of Ireland, but simply which form of protestantism was to be so imposed. And here a most curious, and frequently missed, point arises. Certainly the Irish problem was of great concern to the Scottish covenanters; they obviously suffered from endemic anti-popish hysteria, were worried about the fate of their countrymen in Ulster, and at the same time feared that a free, Roman catholic and Gaelic Ireland would have explosive repercussions in the Highlands and Islands. Events were soon to show that these fears were not altogether idle. Nonetheless, bigoted and intolerant though the covenanters were, they did not have a monopoly of these unlovely qualities. The cold matter of fact is that it was the English parliamentarians, and not the Scots, who extended the programme of the Solemn League to cover Ireland.[19] Nor is there anything odd about that, for whichever English party conquered Ireland would inevitably impose an unpopular religious settlement on the Irish. So the attempt was not quite the unaccountable monument to bigotry, Scots or English, that it is often made out to be. It was simply the way of the Ascendancy, no more and no less.

To conclude this brief survey of a great and involved matter, anyone who takes the trouble to read the Solemn League and Covenant, and to relate it to its times, will find it a less repulsive document than it is usually made out to be.[20] It attempted to set the seal on an alliance born of necessity, and it rested on wary compromise. Baillie put the matter in a nutshell: the English wanted a civil league but the Scots contended for a religious covenant with strong civil backing. Vane did not wish to bind the parliament to a rigid presbyterian programme, which he knew enjoyed little popularity in England and would be fiercely opposed by the independents. Finally a compromise formula was worked out and accepted by both parties in September 1643: military aid furnished by the covenanters was to be paid for by the English parliament, and in return Vane accepted, probably without devising, a vaguely worded promise that parliament would endeavour to carry out 'the reformation of religion in the Kingdom of

England [Ireland was later included without consulting the covenanters, some-what to their annoyance] in doctrine, worship and government, according to the Word of God, and the example of the best reformed Churches'. The commitment was vague, and presbyterians and independents could gloss it as they liked; yet some on this basis hoped to build up a 'reformed international', which indeed excited some interest on the continent.

The making of the Solemn League, in fact, is a matter that needs deeper research than has so far gone into it, for this accommodatingly loose phrase-ology, usually attributed to Vane, may well have been the work of the Scottish minister Alexander Henderson, whose views it echoes and who indeed drafted the document. On the political level the covenanters seem to have hoped that their army would produce speedy and total victory for the allies, leaving the presbyterians firmly in power to work out the exact terms of the settlement.[21] In September 1643 that seemed a realistic enough forecast; but in war, and particularly perhaps in Civil War, even the most reasonable calculations have a way of deceiving.

But curious and unforeseen as the effects of the Solemn League and Covenant were to be, it undoubtedly marked a very important phase in Anglo-Scottish relations. Far more than the Reformation, the League involved the *peoples* of England and Scotland, and in giving rise to the Committee of Both Kingdoms, apparently at the instigation of the Scots, it furnished the first real institutional tie between them.[22] The most prominent Scot on this powerful executive com-mittee was Lord Maitland who later as Duke of Lauderdale was again to straddle both kingdoms. The Committee of Both Kingdoms as well as co-ordinating the war effort against Charles I also helped to popularise the idea of union, but in a form that has misled some. In the Solemn League itself occurs the following passage: 'And whereas the happiness of a blessed peace between these Kingdoms, denied in former times to our progenitors, is by the good providence of God granted to us, and hath been lately concluded and settled by both Parliaments: we shall each one of us, according to our places and interest, endeavour that they may remain conjoined in a firm peace and union to all posterity'. That looks plain enough, but is all too easily misinterpreted. The context of this passage shows that 'union' here means simply 'accord', a sense in which the word was then often used; if the sense 'organic union' is substituted then the whole document becomes nonsensical.

Whatever the hopes raised by the Solemn League, they were not to be realised. It did not lay the foundation for a protestant crusade in the tradition of Gustavus Adolphus, and it did not even lead to lasting accord between the contracting parties, let alone to ecclesiastical uniformity between their two countries. Nevertheless, the alliance did play an important, possibly even decisive, part in determining the outcome of the English Civil War; but its contribution was unspectacular and can easily go unremarked. The Army of the Covenant disappointed its ally by failing to produce instant victory, while for their part the covenanters could legitimately complain that they did not receive the promised aid necessary to keep their army in the field.[23] The Bishops' Wars had exhausted the limited resources of Scotland. Even before the Solemn League was signed, lack of money, which the English parliament had undertaken to provide, was already impeding the operations of the Scots in Ulster, and only loans from rich subjects like Argyll enabled the Ulster army to keep going.[24] Then, too, the Army of the Covenant was essentially a feudal host, and its organisation was cumbrous. It really relied for its efficiency on a hard core of professionals, many of whom had served in the Thirty Years' War, and shortage of cash led to difficulties in maintaining a steady supply of experienced soldiers. All things considered, the covenanting army's performance was good, certainly much better than Cromwell's propaganda machine later made out; and beyond dispute its intervention in the English Civil War was strategically decisive. By threatening to break the royalist hold on the north the Scottish covenanters obliged the king to divert his forces from the south, so relieving the pressure on London and forcing on the campaign that culminated at Marston Moor (2 July 1644), where the Army of the Covenant helped to win this much-needed parliamentary victory.

Others, however, hogged the limelight of Marston, to the chagrin of the Scottish commissioners in London, who, dismayed at the growing strength of the independents, caballed with Essex in the vain hope of destroying Cromwell. But Cromwell was too adroit a politician to be caught napping and 'acted with so much dexterity that the project of impeaching him became daily more hopeless'.[25] Instead he caught his adversaries in the meshes of the Self-Denying Ordinance; and increasingly the New Model Army bore the main burden of the fight. Its great victory at Naseby (14 June 1645) confirmed the drift of real power towards the independents, leaving the English and Scottish presbyterians little more than the trappings. All this the covenanters saw and bewailed but could not prevent. By the end of the Great Civil War their stock had slumped, partly because of their army in England's lacklustre reputation (much of which was attributable to its commander Leven's natural desire to safeguard Scotland rather than co-operate in the south against the king), and partly because they were suspected on this account of being half-hearted in the cause and keen to make a treaty with the king leaving their English allies in the lurch.

But the really deadly blow to the reputation of the covenanters sprang from one source—their inability to hold down their own country.[26] Montrose's dazzling campaign from August 1644 to September 1645 is, nonetheless, too often treated as a pointless, if romantic, adventure, whereas even the slightest consideration of its causes and its effects exposes the folly of such facile conclusions.[27]

Much the greater part of the explanation of Montrose's brilliant campaign lies deep in Highland history, which was never as remote and unimportant as the general run of historians, Scottish as well as English, are apt to make out. The key, as we have seen, lies in the age-old link between Irish and Scottish Gaeldom, a problem that Tudor statesmen would readily have appreciated. For, until almost the end of the sixteenth century, Hebridean and West Highland gallowglasses had helped to keep Ireland turbulent and unresponsive to English rule; and even after the Tudor settlement of Ireland and the Plantation of Ulster the MacDonalds remained in Antrim. They maintained their connection with their Scottish kinsmen, and to them for shelter fled those driven from the West Highlands by the Campbells, Macleans as well as MacDonalds. Thus Highland hostility to Argyll furnished the royalist cause in Scotland with an armed following that would have made James VI turn in his grave. James had sought to impose on the Highlands the Tudor policy pursued in Ireland: expropriation of the native landowners, colonisation, and attempts to destroy not only the clans but the old Gaelic culture and way of life. He had tried to colonise Lewis with Lowlanders as Ulster a little later was to be colonised; and he had tried to suppress Gaelic and to force the English language on the Highlanders. The policy had failed; but the Gaels knew that they had merely won a respite.[28] Thus in the period of the Civil War it was obvious and sensible policy for the Highlanders so threatened to serve the crown for once and try to bring down their arch-enemy Argyll. All they lacked was a leader until they found in Montrose the unusual combination of qualities needed to marshal the clans.

Montrose turned to the Highlanders as a last resort, well knowing the fury that such an action would bring down on him from his Lowland compatriots. But it was the Gaels or none; for the Lowland royalists, overawed by the covenanters and suspecting that Montrose was a mere opportunist, would not rise. The nucleus of a force was provided when young Alistair MacDonald (Young Colkitto) crossed from Ireland to regain his patrimony from Argyll, and initial success brought in many Highland recruits to whom Argyll was equally hateful. Argyll was also Montrose's main target, and twice (at Inveraray and Inverlochy) Montrose acted with foolhardy daring to inflict humiliating defeats on the Campbells, on each occasion forcing the great Argyll himself to flee rather than personally lead his clan in battle. As Montrose reported to King Charles after his victory at Inverlochy (2 February 1645): in spite of the great risks incurred, 'I was willing to let the world see that Argyll was not the man his Highlanders believed him to be, and that it was possible to beat him in his own Highlands'.[29]

Argyll's great reputation began to sag—not only among his own clansmen but with the covenanters and their English allies as well. Even more significant, Montrose's last shattering victory at Kilsyth (15 August 1645) broke the covenanting cause in Scotland; but it came too late to be of any service to the king. The struggle in England was in its closing stages; and the experienced David Leslie was able to lead a force of light horse into Scotland, and on 13 September 1645 surprise and crush Montrose's depleted army at Philiphaugh. The hideous massacre that followed was largely an index of the damage that Montrose had inflicted on the covenanters. But in the long run the real significance of his wonderful campaign was its effect on the Highlanders. These astonishing victories put fresh heart into them; and this is apparent in the work of the Gaelic poet Iain Lom,[30] who, however, is more concerned to sing the praises of Clan Donald and the prowess of Colkitto.

Alasdair, son of handsome Coll, expert at breaking
castles asunder, you routed the sallow-skinned Lowlanders,
and if they had drunk kail you knocked it out of them.

Were you familiar with the Goirtean Odhar? Well was
it manured, not by the dung of sheep or goats, but by the
blood of Campbells after it had congealed.

Not Montrose alone but also developments in England were sowing
dissensions among the allies. In the Westminster Assembly of divines the
independents had from the beginning challenged the presbyterians, who in
return excoriated the sectaries as erastians and fomenters of discord. By early
1646 the strife had become rancorous with the publication in February of
Thomas Edwards' *Gangraena*, a virulent presbyterian blast against the sects.
From being a bond of union, religion had become a fundamental cause of
disagreement. The king, following his usual practice, tried to benefit from the
situation, but his inept intrigues were as futile as ever. By April the breach
among the allies had widened. Parliament, in which the independents were
gaining strength, was at odds with the covenanters, haggling over money as
well as ecclesiastical matters. Even the English presbyterians longed to see the
backs of the Scots army (partly because of its disappointing military record,
and partly because of the ruthless foraging in which it had been forced to
indulge), but they found themselves in a quandary. If the Scots were dismissed,
the last real support of the English presbyterians would vanish; but to
retain the Scots was dangerous, not only because that would antagonise the
independents but also because the covenanters were known to be negotiating
with the king—as in fact was nearly every other interested party.

And that indeed was the heart of the problem. Where could the covenanters,
now dividing into extremist and moderate wings, hope to find the security they
so desperately needed? Argyll and the extremists clung desperately to the letter
of the Solemn League and Covenant, while the moderates believed that an
accommodation with the king would yield better prospects. Surely a beaten king
would accept compromises and be forced to keep them in order to retain the
support of the Scots. This looked like a reasonable policy, but again it was
wrecked by Charles' chronic inability to face reality. The discomfiture of the
Scots was completed when the king, at the end of his resources, surrendered
himself to them on 6 May 1646 rather than be captured by the parliamentary
forces. But Charles refused to accept the covenants and soon became a dangerous
embarrassment to his hosts. They could not convert him; to fight for him without
adequate safeguards would have been sheer stupidity; and they could not retain
him without precipitating war with their allies, which, indeed, for a time looked
imminent. And so in the end, in January 1647, after making stipulations for his
safety, they were glad to hand him over to parliament in return for part payment
of the money due to them. It looked like a sell-out: 'Traitor Scot sold his king
for a groat' soon ran the taunt. Malice has a way of spicing histories, usually
gingered up by gross over-simplification. So it is here. There was only one
alternative course of action—a treaty between King Charles and the covenanters
—but this he himself had ruled out. Still the 'Traitor Scot' canard is repeated,
though it rests on no good grounds whatsoever.[31]

Charles I continued dangerous to the end. He tried to make a deal with parliament but failed, mainly because the war-time alliance against him had not yet outlived its usefulness. John Bull's other island still had to be pacified, and the need to subjugate Ireland helped at this time of conflict and confusion to preserve the alliance between the predominant parties in England and Scotland. The defeat of the Scottish army in Ulster at Benburb (5 June 1646) had driven home the lesson. With this very much in mind (not forgetting that Montrose, though in exile, might yet receive aid from the Irish Confederates) Argyll made a conciliatory speech to a committee of parliament on 25 June in which he strongly pleaded for the continuation of the alliance, even hinting at the desirability of a complete union between England and Scotland: 'let us hold fast that union which is happily established between us; and let nothing make us again two, who are in so many ways one; all of one language, in one island, all under one King, one in Religion, yea, one in Covenant, so that in effect we differ in nothing but in name—as brethren do—which I wish were also removed that we might be altogether one, if the two kingdoms shall think fit'.[32]

Though the terms of this speech were later repeated, phrase for phrase, by the Cromwellians, it raised little interest at the time of delivery, and was in all likelihood regarded as purely tactical, which it very probably was. Argyll at this late date can hardly have expected the full implementation of the Solemn League and Covenant, far less an incorporating union; but he needed to hold hard to the English alliance which was his best safeguard against the moderate covenanters. The secret negotiations then proceeding with the king could only spell danger for Argyll; better for him an agreement with the English parliament, even if at worst this meant with the independents, though if the English presbyterians won out so much the better. And so, in spite of growing tensions, covenanters and parliament still talked about joint terms to be offered to the king, the more urgently as by the summer of 1647 there were ominous signs that parliament was in danger of being outflanked. The Scots disliked certain erastian aspects of the proposed church settlement in England, but now the settlement itself was threatened by stirrings both inside and outside the New Model Army.

In England an astonishing variety of radical ideas was beginning to ferment. As Milton put it: 'Liberty, which is the nurse of all great wits; this is that which hath rarefied and enlightened our spirits like the influence of heaven; this is that which hath enfranchised, enlarged and lifted up our apprehensions degrees above themselves'.[33] The tremendous upheaval in England led to the questioning of authority in both church and state; and soon the rule of parliament came to be criticised as tyrannical and corrupt, as in many aspects it undoubtedly was. Thus 'Free-born John' Lilburne, who had suffered for his dissent under Charles I, fared little better at the hands of parliament and Cromwell. As for corruption, it was as rife under the Long Parliament as during the Eleven Years' Tyranny; and particularly galling to the sectaries in arms was the way in which leading M.P.s enriched themselves while the army was bilked of its pay. Salt was rubbed in the army's wounds by the fact that the Scots had received much of the money due to them while the New Model was kept in penury.

The selfishness of parliament (which proposed to withhold the full payment due to the soldiers and disband the New Model and recruit a fresh force for the conquest of Ireland), forced on a crisis. The revolt was led by the rank and file of the army, particularly by the cavalry regiments, and Cromwell (a conservative revolutionary if ever there was one) was driven reluctantly along by the popular agitations. It was the democratic army agitators, headed by Cornet Joyce, who seized the king, hoping to make a deal with him whereby democracy (based on manhood suffrage and government by consent), toleration, and limited monarchy could all co-exist. It is thus well to remember that 'the rule of the sword' was originally intended to be 'the rule of the people'. Thus when the army marched on London (15 June 1647) Cromwell and the other senior officers, soon to be known as the 'grandees', were placed in a quandary. No one saw more clearly than Cromwell the need for a settled peace, but Charles' disingenuous diplomacy kept that at as great a distance as ever. The immediate problem for the grandees was how to deal with this new monster—stranger and more threatening than presbytery—the people, and especially the people in arms? The New Model's Solemn Engagement was a challenge not only to the covenanters and their English allies but to the grandees as well. Cromwell plumped for the army, only to make use of it; but in the process he was forced to adopt some radical courses that were alien to his nature.[34]

The ideas discussed in the unprecedented 'Army Debates' at Putney (October-November 1647) were drawn from many sources.[35] Some were simple and timeless levelling doctrines reminiscent of those of John Ball, others were anabaptist religious views transferred to civil themes, and many were simply denunciations of current social and legal wrongs. Their origins are of interest, but far more important was their durability. Most subsequent political theories in Britain have turned on some aspect or another of these engrossing and at times impassioned talks. Burke on the French Revolution is little more than Commissary-general Ireton on the English Revolution; and though Lord Braxfield in the notorious sedition trials in Scotland in 1793 was probably not aware of it, in refuting Thomas Muir he too used virtually the very words of Ireton, while Muir as strongly echoed Colonel Rainsborough and 'Buff-coat', the gruffly eloquent unknown soldier spokesman. The parallels are astonishing and exact—and possibly not accidental, for a tentative line of descent can be traced.[36]

Cromwell dreaded anarchy and sided with Ireton, a proto-Lockean, whose chief concern was for the sanctity of property. Though the Putney Debates came to nothing, significantly the grandees took care in future to avoid such awkward confrontations. The real victims of the leveller agitations were the parliament and the king; but insofar as Cromwell was the victor, it was one victory he was never able to exploit properly. And again it was King Charles who accommodated his enemies by his escape to Carisbrooke. The consequent upsurge of royalism led the army to close its ranks, and Cromwell took the opportunity this provided to crush the agitators.

The difficulty of achieving a settlement in England increased the existing dissensions in Scotland, and from this point onwards Anglo-Scottish relations no longer consisted of exchanges between two governments (however *de facto*) but degenerated into a tangle of conflicting interests. The essence of the situation was that in each country the constitutional revolution wrought by the traditional ruling classes was being challenged and was ultimately overturned. True, in Scotland there emerged nothing comparable to the popular programme drawn up by the army and the levellers. Nevertheless, there are some striking similarities, for in each country the extremists seized power with the help of the swordsmen; and in the end it was the same sword that hung over all. How did this unexpected revolution arise?

The English presbyterians, shaken by the revolt of the army and the prospect of popular anarchy, turned yet again in desperation to the Scots. But on both sides the old trust was gone. Alarmed by the revolt of the New Model, opinion in Scotland steadily swung towards the king. Argyll opposed this trend, but it was too strong to be halted; and in December 1647 Charles I concluded a secret treaty, the Engagement, with the moderate covenanters. The word 'Engagement' was widely used at that time, and this particular agreement was not exclusively Scottish, for though the terms of the agreement were between the Scots and the king, the Engagement did not solely rely on Scottish support but hoped to draw strength from royalist elements in England as well. Charles was to guarantee presbyterianism in Scotland, give it a trial run for three years in England, and, intriguingly, he was to attempt to bring about a more complete union of the two kingdoms 'according to the intention of his father'. Scottish Engagers, for their part, were to invade England on the king's behalf, uphold the rights of the crown over militia, honours and offices, and secure the royal veto over legislation.[37]

The tables were neatly turned on Argyll, even to the extent of pre-empting his union gambit. Indeed it is noteworthy that, amid the twists and turns of the tortuous situation that developed after 1646, something like James VI and I's concept of union began to commend itself to certain parties. But in every case it was used as a pawn in the political struggle. In other words, political union of the two kingdoms was not prized for its own sake, but as a weapon in the strife of parties (and this, indeed, largely remained the case right up until 1707). Thus Argyll had hinted at a closer union in June 1646 as a possible means of pre-serving his increasingly threatened hegemony in Scotland, and the Engagers in their accommodation with the king looked for a prop in their struggle with the extremists and were well aware that nothing could more effectively bind the king to them than a union of the two kingdoms. The difficulties in the way were recognised: if, by the Engagement, union could not be speedily achieved, then Scotland was to have the benefit of free trade with England and there was to be complete mutual privilege of subjects in the two kingdoms.

Argyll was thereafter obliged to make common cause with the theocratic ministers, who hated the Engagement. On this issue church and state again clashed; a majority of the parliament accepted the treaty but the extreme presbyterians rejected it, and, by winning over Leven and Leslie with most of the army commanders, the minority pretty well doomed the enterprise. England was invaded, but too late and not by the Leslies and their seasoned veterans. For the covenanters the split was final, irrevocable and, ultimately, fatal.

With a makeshift and ill-equipped army commanded by the incompetent

Duke of Hamilton, the Engagers invaded England hoping for reinforcements from the English royalists. In the crucial breathing space gifted to him by the dissensions of the Scots and by Hamilton's chronic incapacity, Cromwell rallied the army, beating the half-hearted English royalists piecemeal before crushing at Preston (17 August 1648) the most formidable of them and their straggling ill-led Scots allies. He then, as usual, took the obvious line, and executed it with brilliant dispatch by supporting Argyll's faction in Scotland, which seized power by the 'Whiggamore Raid' on Edinburgh. Thanks to Cromwell's support, Argyll managed to maintain himself but was thereafter shackled by the dead-weight of the party of the Old Testament. But here again some important points arise that have been smothered under a heavy veneer of myth. First, it was Cromwell who insisted on the exclusion of malignants from office, though his allies heartily endorsed the policy; and second, the rule of the high theocratic party, far from being a constant theme of post-Reformation Scottish history, endured, and even then intermittently, only for three brief troubled years—from 1648 to 1651.[38] That the General Assembly was stronger than parliament is true only of this brief interlude, and the explanation of the rule of the prophets lies in the shifting sands of a revolutionary period.

Still, the short-lived theocratic phase made a deep and lasting impression. It completed the disruption of the alliance that had made the National Covenant possible. Even convinced covenanters came to detest theocratic rule, and undoubtedly much of this revulsion stemmed from class antagonisms. The nobles and lairds despised the upstart extremist ministers, most of whom were of humble origin, and fiercely resented the impartial way in which the severe discipline of the Kirk of the Covenant was administered. As Sir Ewen Cameron bitterly noted: 'Every parish had a tyrant who made the greatest Lord in his district stoop to his authority. The Kirk was the place where he keept his court; the pulpit his throne or tribunall from whence he issued out his terrible decrees; and 12 or 14 soure, ignorant enthusiasts, under the title of elders, composed his councill. If any, of what quality so ever, had the assurance to dissobey his edicts, the dreadful sentence of excommunication was immediately thundred out against him, his goods and chattels confiscated and seazed . . .'.[39] In other ways the acquisitive unco-guid also flourished in these times; such were 'the usurious cormorants', so detested by Sir Thomas Urquhart of Cromartie, who battened on the estates of malignants.

Here, if anywhere, lay the equivalent in Scotland of the English levelling movement, and by the great and the rich it was as heartily abominated. The distaste of the nobles for this theocratic monster they had helped to create long out-lived the brief spell of power wielded by the godly, and that distaste was to become a significant force in Scottish history. All this is true; but equally true is its obverse. The brief experience of theocratic rule became the Zion of future generations of extreme presbyterians.

What undermined the regime of the theocrats in Scotland, however, was not their growing unpopularity but their failure to maintain their alliance with the English sectaries. That alliance had been dictated by circumstances, and each side remained deeply repugnant to the other. The extreme covenanters were never done condemning the heresies of the sects and the horrors of toleration; and the sects for their part regarded the Scottish presbyterians as repressive bigots of almost Laudian dimensions. But at bottom it was political and not religious differences that disrupted the uneasy alliance. The curiosity is that the covenanters of all factions were, after their fashion, ardent royalists, and had claimed to act ever since 1638 in support of the true rights of the crown. Of republicanism they showed no trace; only the eccentric Johnston of Wariston was, ultimately, prepared to accept a republic.

Thus, to all classes and factions in Scotland, the execution of Charles I in January 1649 came as a genuine shock. The king's execution also posed hard and unavoidable questions. If England were to become a commonwealth, or a republic, what was to become of Scotland? Could she continue as a monarchy without falling foul of the Commonwealth? Or would Scotland have to become a republic as well? In short, the regal union was broken, and what was to be put in its place? Not even the resourceful Argyll or the brilliant, if fanatically erratic, Johnston of Wariston could resolve these problems, the more so as the reaction in favour of monarchy in Scotland was too strong to be disregarded even by the most extreme. But the adhesion of the extremists to the royalist cause was grudging, and at best a dubious asset. The Protesters, as the extremists came to be called, were the minority party but in vigour proved more than a match for the majority, who were to become known as Resolutioners.

The Commonwealth could not disregard the threats posed by the royalist reaction in Scotland, especially as it became clear that Argyll was now keen to reach an understanding with the Engagers. He hoped to make of Charles II a covenanted king, and possibly even a son-in-law. Thus within a week of the death of his father the Scottish estates proclaimed Charles II not just as king of Scots but of Great Britain, France and Ireland. The challenge to the Commonwealth of England was deliberate, obvious and perhaps unavoidable; and the challenge from Scotland continued in spite of Charles II's attempts to win more accommodating allies. None such were to be found, for Ireland was being reduced to submission, and no help was forthcoming from that or any other quarter. So in the end Charles was forced to accept the covenants and come to terms with the de facto government in Scotland, in the process callously sending Montrose to his doom. Montrose was to invade Scotland through Orkney with a small force of Danish and German mercenaries; but he found few recruits and his last campaign ended in his capture. On 21 May 1650 he was executed in Edinburgh.

The intransigence of the high theocratic party, however, ruined any prospects the new alliance between king and covenanters might have had. And these were real enough and bright enough. David Leslie, knowing Cromwell's strength but also his weakness, employed fabian tactics so skilfully that the invading English army was on the brink of failure which in view of the relative weakness of Cromwell's position in England might well have proved fatal to his career and possibly even to the Commonwealth. But Leslie's brilliant manoeuvring was denied success, mainly because of the interference of the fanatical ministers who, in the face of the weary and dispirited Roundhead host, insisted on purging the

Scottish ranks of the ungodly, and insisted also on giving battle to prevent Cromwell's army from being evacuated by sea. The result was the rout of the Scots at Dunbar on 3 September 1650.

Scotland never really recovered from that disaster. In vain, Argyll sought to reconcile the contending Scottish factions, but the extreme Remonstrant (or Protester) group continued refractory. To them Dunbar was a divine judgment for co-operating, in however limited a way, with malignants, and they continued to oppose repeal of the discriminatory Act of Classes. In the meantime Cromwell had difficulty finishing off Leslie, who, more evasive than ever, could not be brought to battle. Finally, Charles, leaving Leslie in Scotland to confront Cromwell, slipped past the invaders into England in the hope, delusive as ever, of gaining support there. Little came, for neither a Scots army nor a covenanted king appealed to the English cavaliers, and Charles II and his Scottish supporters were crushed at Worcester on 3 September 1651.

Worcester fight pretty well ended the Civil Wars. The resources of Scotland were exhausted and the country was soon occupied; indeed, within eighteen months of Worcester the Cromwellians, having dismissed the Rump oligarchy in April 1653, were left in firm control of all three 'kingdoms'. For Scotland the débâcle had grave repercussions: its government was defunct, its king in exile, its church bitterly divided and the nation in no better case. Indeed the country's plight was 'such as she had not known since Edward I struck her down'.[40] Immediately after Worcester, direct annexation by the Commonwealth of England seemed to be the only possible result, and in fact the original intention of the English parliament was to treat Scotland as a conquered province.[41] Though in a sense this policy was never really given up, the outcome was otherwise; and the Cromwellian interlude has thus provided one of the most intriguing episodes in the long and checkered relations between England and Scotland.

The British Solomon's visionary ideas at last found strange application, for the Council of State gradually forced parliament to change its policy from outright annexation to political incorporation whereby Scotland was to be 'one Commonwealth with this of England'. The idea of a complete union had slowly become attractive to the party in power, mainly as a means of retaining power. As we have seen, in 1646 Argyll himself had toyed with the notion; but in the making of the Cromwellian union he played no part, and indeed Argyll stood out against it longer than most.[42] That union was a *diktat*, though every effort was made by the Cromwellians to give an appearance of free negotiation. Nonetheless, the 'Tender of Union' was not well received in Scotland; and when the English commissioners, Sir Harry Vane prominent among them, arrived they found 'The Scotch people know not what to say to them now that they are comed'.[43] True, the irrepressible Wariston was suspected of advocating that Scotland should become a separate Commonwealth in close alliance with that of England; but, if so, his plan won no support from either Scots or English. In fact, the kirkmen, in all their divisions, were in great perplexity. The majority of each party was bewildered, but leading members of each were again jostling for position, Protesters and Resolutioners alike trying to win marks of favour from a detested regime. Only a reluctant assent to union was wrung from the 'representatives' of shires and burghs, though who exactly they represented is a bit of a mystery to this day. 'Malignants' were rigorously excluded; and, since they formed most of the traditional ruling class and a fair proportion of the population as a whole, the representation must have been nominal. The negotiations, then, were largely a sham, the more so as the Scottish representatives at first were not treated as plenipotentiaries but only as consultants, and later, when they were allowed a voice in the proceedings, little heed was paid to their views. Difficulty was also experienced in obtaining legislative sanction for a union, which, in fact, was legalised by an ordinance of 12 April 1654 and failed to be ratified by parliament, in spite of strenuous efforts to that end, until April 1657. Quite clearly, the Cromwellian union, whatever its merits, was not attributable to the theory of natural evolution—except possibly in the sense referred to by an embittered Scot, 'as when the poor bird is embodied into the hawk that hath eaten it up'.[44] The Cromwellian union was an unforeseen consequence of the Civil Wars, and the leading motive behind it was to provide security for a regime that enjoyed little popularity or stability.

The constitutional details of the Cromwellian union were never properly worked out, or satisfactorily implemented. Representation is a case in point. After some wrangling, on the basis of taxable capacity Scotland was granted thirty seats in parliament (instead of the sixty demanded by the Scottish deputies), and twenty of these went to the shires and ten to the royal burghs, so necessitating a grouping system of representation in the burghs. The representative system, however, was limited in more ways than one. Indeed, it is questionable if it was representative at all in any real sense of the term. Recently an attempt has been made to argue the contrary case, but it rests on defective data and quite disingenuous special pleading:[45] for example, the extremely limited nature of the franchise is passed over, though the paucity of the electorate could lead to startling results. Thus in August 1654 all the 'electors' of Aberdeenshire came to the conclusion that they were, for various malignant acts, disfranchised, and so no member was returned.[46] The case was not peculiar to Aberdeenshire. Again, most of the elections were rigged in favour of the Court, a fact that became so notorious that the representation from Scotland was attacked in Richard Cromwell's parliament. As Sir Harry Vane bitterly put it: 'A greater imposition never was [placed] by a single person [i.e. a sovereign] upon a Parliament, to put sixty votes [from Ireland and Scotland] upon you. By this means it shall be brought upon you insensibly, to vote by Scotch and Irish members to enforce all your votes hereafter'.[47] The great majority of the Scottish people were no better pleased with the arrangement. True, the representatives from Scotland (both nominated and elected, both Scots and English) could, and sometimes did, speak up for Scottish interests. But there was no getting away from the fact that even by the limited notions of representation then current the parliamentary side of the Cromwellian union was a hollow sham; and anyway Oliver's parliaments were not in themselves howling successes—a fact that is hardly surprising in view of the times, and not to be ascribed simply to Cromwell's alleged lack of ability for political management.

But such criticism of the Cromwellian union as has been made here does not condemn it completely but rather merely emphasises its most basic weakness, a weakness equally obvious in England, where the Cromwellian regime depended just as much on the sword and as little on the consent of the governed as it did in Scotland and Ireland.

Seen in other aspects, however, the Cromwellian union was remarkable for its vision and its idealism, though again these qualities were to some extent obscured by the harsh realities of the times. Still, there is justification for the view recently advanced by Professor Roots that the Cromwellian experiment was in many respects more promising than the union finally achieved in 1707. The Cromwellians aimed at a complete union, or rather fusion, of the two nations which would in the end have obliterated all distinctions—legal, ecclesiastical and so on. The ultimate aim in fact, as with the original vision of James VI and I, was one unified nation, an enlarged England.[48] Scottish opinion could hardly be expected to relish such a prospect, and the main opposition to the union in Scotland was on nationalist grounds reinforced by selfish interests.

At the same time the concern for social justice shown by the Cromwellians appealed to many of 'the meaner sort' in Scotland. This concern was not just a politic pose, nor was it confined only to the top administrators; it ran through the whole regime. As Colonel John Jones (republican regicide and latterly Cromwell's brother-in-law and trusted agent) put it: 'It is the interest of the Commonwealth of England to break the interest of the great men in Scotland, and to settle the interest of the common people upon a different foot from the interests of their lords and masters'.[49] Oliver himself frequently referred to the need to advance the interests of 'the meaner sort' in Scotland;[50] and certainly the nobility were the inevitable victims of the Cromwellians, for only by depriving them of heritable jurisdictions and feudal powers was just government made possible. No steps were taken, however, to assimilate the laws of England and Scotland, the practical difficulties proving insuperable. The regime was intelligent enough to retain as much of traditional Scottish ways as was compatible with security, eking them out with adaptations of English usages. The result was an admirable system of executive government, and of firm and impartial administration, of which only the nobles had any real cause to complain. This is all in marked contrast to what happened in 1707, when concern for social justice was nowhere apparent. Indeed in many respects the Treaty and Act of Union of 1707 was demonstrably a triumph for reaction, granting as it did a fresh lease of life to the sinister heritable jurisdictions and oppressive feudal superiorities in Scotland. In the making of the Treaty of Union of 1707 'the meaner sort' were not considered.

The Cromwellian Union also conferred on Scotland the benefit of complete freedom of trade with England and her possessions, a concession that had earlier been sought by the Engagers and for which there had been a small but growing demand ever since 1603. To concede free trade was generous and far-sighted policy on the part of the Cromwellians; but it was hated by English merchant interests and only grudgingly accepted by parliament—a significant pointer to the future. In any case Scotland was in poor economic shape and unable to profit much from the Union. It has been argued by Professor Lythe, more confidently than the facts warrant, that up until the end of James VI's reign, the economy of Scotland was showing marked improvements.[51] The golden age then apparently vanished in the years of turmoil and stress; but, like any other golden age, it was probably something of a mirage. Some economic advance there was in the early decades of the seventeenth century but limited mainly to coal-mining and salt-panning. Agriculture, the principal source of livelihood, continued on the old wasteful run-rig lines with little evidence of widespread efforts at improvement. Attempts to revolutionise fishing and clothmaking by monopolies failed before the outbreak of the troubles, and foreign trade continued to follow the old medieval pattern at the very time when that pattern was being disrupted. It is not surprising, therefore, that the high taxation and quarterings of the years of Civil War, followed by the wars of the Commonwealth, virtually ruined the rickety economy of Scotland. For all this the evidence is more than adequate, ranging not just from the lamentations of the pious Robert Baillie, the tittle-tattle of the diarist Nicoll, and the traditional groans of the royal burghs, but also to the testimony of Cromwellian officials such as Thomas Tucker in his well-known report in 1656.[52]

Even more revealing than Tucker's impressionistic account of Scotland's economic state was the financial problem that Scotland posed to the Commonwealth. In 1651 Major-general Monk, who was left by Cromwell in command of the English army of occupation, was ordered to levy a monthly assessment of £10,000, which he found impossible to raise. The royalist rising in the Highlands under Glencairn and Middleton in 1653–4 made matters even more difficult for the administration, and at times the money collected fell as low as £4,000 per month. Monk then argued that the original assessment was beyond the country's means and could not be raised, partly 'because of the great destruction and waste made by the enemy, and of what we found necessary to destroy that they might be deprived of sustenance, and the great decay of trade in all parts of Scotland'.[53] In 1657 Monk and the members of parliament from Scotland, many of whom were Englishmen, pleaded in the same strain for lower taxation. Said Captain Thomas Lilburne: 'It is a very poor country, and unless near the south side they make little of their grounds, being only mosses and sheep rakes'.[54] As a result of these representations, from June 1657 the assessment was reduced to £6,000 per month, and it remained at that figure till the Restoration. Nonetheless, even with this relief, Scotland continued to complain. Oliver summed it all up in January 1658 when he declared to his parliament, 'I do think truly they [the Scots] are a very ruined nation', though he felt they had some hope for the future.[55] The sombre part of the conclusion was indeed hard to avoid, for the annual deficit between revenues raised in Scotland and the cost of the administration was in the region of £130,000 a year.[56] Scotland, in fact, was a decided burden to the Commonwealth and Protectorate.

In England the Protectorate also laboured under great difficulties, mainly political and constitutional but also financial and economic. Sword-rule was expensive and unpopular, but Oliver's repeated attempts to return to constitutional government were thwarted by the intransigence of his parliaments. Professor Trevor-Roper blames Cromwell's lack of skill at political management for his failure, but Christopher Hill convincingly dismisses this view as a perversion of Namierite theory.[57] And certainly it is odd, if Oliver was as much a mediocrity as Trevor-Roper suggests, that following his death on 3 September 1658 the Protectorate itself soon failed, his son and heir proving totally unequal to the burdens of office. The republic was restored and the selfish survivors of the Rump, the Bourbons of republicanism, tried to regain complete power by reverting to their old practice of fusing legislature and executive. This was too much for a strong element in the army which, headed by Major-general John Lambert, hoped to restore a military dictatorship. The inscrutable Monk solved the problem with his usual silent address. Like Oliver he was a constitutionalist and hated military government; and so when Lambert made his bid for power in England, Monk, having purged his army of unreliable elements and sounded out support in Scotland, began his famous march south on 1 January 1660. He had already been in touch with Fairfax, who evidently expected him to declare for Charles II;[58] but Monk, in fact, turned to Charles only as a last resort. The king was restored because he seemed to be the best guarantee of stable and constitutional government, and he was restored not by the Cavaliers (who were cowed enough) but by his ex-enemies. This remarkable providence explains why, in Richard Baxter's words, the Restoration was achieved 'without one bloody nose'.[59]

The Cromwellian Union expired with the regime that had created it, though its merits did not go entirely unappreciated at the time. Monk was petitioned by commissioners of Scottish shires and burghs to maintain the union; but again it is hard to say how representative these commissioners were. In parts of Scotland, however, the English seem to have been, considering the circumstances, surprisingly popular, and Monk himself was regarded as a just ruler who had the welfare of the country at heart. He was once even described as 'a very good kindly Scotchman and beloved by all'.[60] Possibly there was an element of flattery in this, but clearly such a description could not have been applied to an out-and-out tyrant; nor was Monk the only popular figure, for Lord Broghill, for a time President of the Scottish Council of State, 'was much beloved of all this natioun for his singular witt and justice for this tyme'.[61] Even the way-going of the garrisons was mourned by some, possibly because they had brought much needed money into the towns and because the burghers appreciated good order. But in some places the garrison had clearly put down local roots. Thus the lament by a local minister for the departure of the English garrison from Inverness in 1662 has a sincere ring about it: 'never people left a place with such reluctancy. It was even sad to see and heare sighes and teares, pale faces and embraces, at their parting farewell from that town. And no wonder; they had peace and plenty for ten yeares in it. They made that place happy, and it made them so'.[62] The minister, it should be added, was no friend of the Protectorate and had thus no reason to invent lies in praise of it. Doubtless, too, Inverness, so frequently plagued in the past by disorder in the Highlands, especially appreciated firm and just administration. But there is surely further significance in the fact that the garrison at Inverlochy also seems to have got on good terms with the neighbouring clans, to police whom was its main charge.

At the Restoration these things weighed little in the balance when the traditional ruling class in Scotland reasserted itself. The feudal nobility detested the Commonwealth and all its works, and implicit in the return of Charles II was the restoration of the oppressive feudal regime in Scotland. To bring back this disruptive anachronism was incompatible with the policy of union pursued by Cromwell; so union, in spite of its intrinsic qualities, found few defenders and was allowed to lapse. Clarendon, indeed, appreciated its merits. But, he concluded, Charles II 'would not build according to Cromwell's models, and had many reasons to continue Scotland within its own limits and bounds, and sole dependence upon himself, rather than unite it to England with so many hazards and dangers as would inevitably have accompanied it, under any government less tyrannical than that of Cromwell'.[63]

Then, too, the Scottish presbyterians in all their divisions had hated the rule of the sects, and rejoiced at their downfall. In July 1653 the General Assembly had been forcibly dispersed and forbidden to meet again, and the church in Scotland, like that in England, had been governed by a unique erastianism which used the authority of the state not for enforcing conformity but for compelling toleration. Nonetheless, the two church parties continued to bicker and quarrel. Each sought the countenance of the Protector but neither was admitted into full favour; the Protesters pleased Cromwell by abjuring Charles Stewart but displeased him by their furious diatribes against erastianism and the hated toleration, while the Resolutioners, who were more disposed to co-operate with the civil power, hankered after King Charles. In the event the Protector found the Resolutioners the better allies; but at best they were lukewarm and, as the astute Monk perceived, at heart loyal monarchists. So to the Scottish churchmen of all parties, as to the Scottish nobles, the undoing of the union was regarded as a condition precedent for the restoration of their former powers.

Curiously, Clarendon apart, no English voice seems to have been raised in favour of maintaining the union. It was manifestly unpopular in England, where the financial burden it entailed was resented and where the merchant interests deplored Scottish competition. For their part, the Scots seem to have imagined that free trade would continue even though the union was to be undone, and it came as a shock to them when it proved otherwise. Free trade, which had seemed of limited value to the Scots during the Cromwellian union, was soon missed when it lapsed at the Restoration.

And so for all its promise (perhaps even in some ways because of its promise), the Cromwellian union was silently given up and doomed to be no more than an intriguing historical episode. But it was not simply a tantalising enigma and left behind something more substantial than a memory. It had brought the peoples of England and Scotland into closer contact; and that closer contact endured. For example, the later covenanters showed something of the contempt for mere prescriptive right that had animated the New Model, and political ideas no longer found a barrier at the Borders. Above all, London and its politics were thereafter to figure more and more prominently in the politics of Edinburgh, but only rarely did the converse apply.

8

Restoration and Reaction: 1660–88

IN the spring of 1660 Charles II gave little thought to Anglo-Scottish relations. His first priority was a smooth restoration in England and the Declaration of Breda was directed to that end. But it has to be recalled that an earlier negotiation at Breda had worked out the terms of Charles' succession in Scotland and led to his coronation at Scone in January 1651; his subsequent reverses, culminating in the Cromwellian conquest of Scotland and the forced union, were not held to have invalidated his treaty with the Scots. In 1660 Charles was already king of Scots and well aware that the overwhelming majority of his Scottish subjects strongly favoured the restoration. As to the nexus between England and Scotland, in 1660 majority opinion in both countries was against the maintenance of the Cromwellian union: Scotland was keen to revert to her former status, and England, conscious that Scotland had been a financial burden, cared little what happened to her northern neighbour as long as her own interests were safe-guarded.[1]

The Restoration, therefore, casts further doubt on the theory of an ineluctable drift towards union after 1603—a century of conversion, as it were, to James VI and I's vision. If there had been such a trend, then the Cromwellian union, work of usurpers though it was, could hardly have been so lightly jettisoned. The evidence of 1660, however, records no pleas for union and clearly demonstrates that all that was then aimed at was restitution of the regal union.[2] The point has perhaps been a little blurred by the union negotiations of the next decade, but these had a logic of their own and one that also tends to run counter to the theory of inevitable drift. Admittedly, on a superficial plane there may well be a temptation to lump together the various attempts at Anglo-Scottish union in the seventeenth century in such a way as to suggest a Grand Design that was finally achieved in 1707. But such an easy road out should be avoided. Like the Europo-centric propaganda of our own day (which would imply that only the Plantagenets had a sound foreign policy and that British colonial and imperial ventures were eccentric aberrations), the notion of a Grand Design for a united Britain, constantly striven for by the far-seeing on both sides of the Border, is fantasy masquerading as history. The only antidote to this slick determinism is to examine each specific attempt at union and to establish exactly what it involved. When this is done, each such attempt is revealed as a phenomenon dominated by its own immediate and usually far from simple circumstances.

Indeed, in the Restoration period the problem of Anglo-Scottish relations, far from easing, was becoming even more complex. Thus, for long enough, the idea of union was contaminated by the experience of it. Yet contemporaries were well aware that the Great Rebellion had been made possible by an alliance between Charles I's English and Scottish subjects. How, then, could the regal union be operated in the best interests of the crown? There was no easy answer to that difficult question. In other respects, too, the Restoration period was crucial to Anglo-Scottish relations. It was then that the England and Scotland that entered into union in 1707 were being formed. Such an observation is neither determinist nor speculative, but a statement of mere fact and one that has profound implications. Union must not be treated as a mystical or metaphysical concept; it has to be assessed in the light of hard realities, and if sometimes the obvious gets played down then the only answer is to insist upon it. For example, if an enduring union of the two kingdoms had been achieved in the time of Edward I or Henry VIII or James VI and I, or even Cromwell, then in each case the end-product must have differed greatly from that of the union negotiated in 1707 because completely different conditioning factors—social, economic and political—would have been involved.

In any consideration of Anglo-Scottish relations, therefore, the late Stewart period has a unique importance. It was then, for example, that the final seal was put on the law of Scotland as a distinctive system, symbolised by the publication in 1681 of Sir James Dalrymple of Stair's epoch-making *Institutions of the Law of Scotland*. Then, too, Anglicanism and non-conformity in their modern forms really date from the Restoration; and so does the most influential phase of the presbyterian tradition in Scotland. England was then also serving her apprenticeship as a great commercial nation and her sea-borne trade was expanding. At the same time the economy of Scotland, denied such development, stagnated unwillingly in the old traditional mould. Thus, in many important respects, in spite of increasing cultural contacts, the two countries were actually diverging.

All appearances to the contrary notwithstanding, this was even true of church matters. The assumption that the Church of Scotland governed by bishops after 1660 was simply a northern extension of the Church of England finds no warrant in the facts. That episcopacy prevailed in both countries was then, indeed, in many ways of political rather than ecclesiastical significance. Yet in 1660 religion was still of primary concern, easily overriding economic considerations, and in each country the basic problem was that of church government. It was a problem that had wide ramifications in both countries, and could in many ways be seen as simply a reflection of the problem of civil government. The social and political rôle of the aristocracy, for example, was affected by the form of church government. But apart from its own intrinsic importance, the church question also had a strong political bearing on Anglo-Scottish relations, since it was in the interests of the restored monarchy to achieve as close a conformity as possible between the two established churches. About that there was nothing new—in spite of political ups and downs, it had been a pretty consistent theme since 1603. In the opening phase of the Restoration, therefore, the problem was still how best to harmonise the two establishments. The utility to the crown of such harmonisation was evident but difficult to achieve, for in both England and Scotland ecclesiastical problems at that point were of extraordinary complexity and delicacy, and, if roughly handled, might well prove explosive. Charles II understood this and was hesitant in his approach to the ecclesiastical problems that had to be faced in 1660. In particular, he took the claims of the presbyterians and the independents more seriously than some modern historians do, if only because none knew better than Charles himself that it was the presbyterians, English as well as Scottish, who had made the Restoration possible.

The Scottish presbyterians, as they saw it, had fought to the bitter end for their covenanted king and, naïvely perhaps, believed that at his Restoration they would receive their just reward. Others entertained similar hopes, and as the presbyterian historian Kirkton remarked, 'All believed it would be the golden age when the king returned in peace'.[3] Charles was in no hurry to disillusion anyone. In England he faced similar difficulties and in particular could hardly overlook the fact that strong efforts had been made in the Convention parliament on behalf of the presbyterian discipline. Personally, Charles detested presbyterianism, which was not, he opined, 'a religion for gentlemen', and his experience in Scotland led him to believe that presbyterianism as well as being socially destructive was politically subversive. But the king's personal likes and dislikes did not dictate his policies, which were governed by his determination not to have to resume his travels. Thus, with so much potential opposition in England and a powerful puritan army only recently disbanded, the restored monarchy could not immediately discountenance the presbyterians or puritans in general, some of whom, in England at any rate, were really moderate episcopalians and thus, it was hoped, capable of being coaxed into a reformed episcopal establishment.[4] Charles, therefore, adopted a cautious policy, hinting at concessions and taking refuge in the vague promise made at Breda that the settlement of the church should be left to parliament. To his credit, he disliked coercion, and even, in a limited way, believed in toleration; but he was unable to oppose the powerful High Church reaction that followed the Restoration. And Chancellor Hyde (soon to be created Earl of Clarendon) was determined from the outset to restore episcopacy and to reconstruct the English church not merely on Anglican but on Laudian lines.

Laud's ecclesiastical policy did not disappear like a mirage, as Professor Trevor-Roper has too confidently asserted.[5] The Laudian party did not die out, and during the Interregnum, both at home and in exile, it retained and even strengthened the archbishop's views, though giving up his extravagant claims to jurisdiction. Taking as their motto 'Nothing can secure the Crown that destroys the Mitre',[6] the Laudians declared all-out war on 'that accursed Genevan tyranny' and tutored a new generation of squires who grew up detesting puritanism and everything it stood for. To the Laudians restoration of the monarchy without restoration of the episcopal regime was inconceivable, and they regarded the talks about accommodation at the Savoy Conference in London in 1661 as little more than a tactical diversion. By March 1661, aided by the general unpopularity of sword-rule and by the bitter divisions in the ranks of their opponents, the Laudians were gaining control of the church. The next two years sealed their triumph, mainly because the preponderance of High Churchmen in the Cavalier parliament made the Laudians irresistible. Clarendon finally aided the process by laying diplomacy aside and launching a bitter attack on the puritans, thus paving the way for the return of the full episcopal regime. It was a blunder of the first magnitude. Clarendon, himself High Church, believed that the power of the crown could restrain the Laudians and keep their persecuting spirit under; but he had overestimated the power of the crown and underestimated that of parliament. Soon he was alarmed by the maelstrom of bigotry that was unleashed; and the king, too, was dismayed when parliament, not content with the restoration of episcopacy, boldly embarked on a repressive ecclesiastical policy.

The Act of Uniformity required that all the clergy of the Church of England should subscribe to the liturgy and doctrines of the church and be in episcopal orders by St. Bartholomew's Day 1662 (a day of ill-omen, this 24th day of August, as good protestants could hardly fail to notice[7]) and that all who did not conform should be ejected. Upwards of a thousand, possibly more, fell under the ban and were 'outed'. Clarendon did not so much disapprove of the penal code to which his name was later attached, and of which this act was to be the cornerstone, as fear its possible consequences—namely, the likelihood of political repercussions. As for the king, he openly detested this repressive legislation and, whether to relieve Roman catholics or not, would have liked to grant indulgences. Their combined efforts, however, to soften the harsh so-called 'Clarendon Code' were easily thwarted by the House of Commons, in itself a pointed reminder that the exalted views of parliament deriving from the Civil War period did not vanish from the face of the earth in 1660. And here it is pertinent to recall that the Cavalier Parliament came to be known as the 'Long Parliament of the Restoration'—a title at once ironical and replete with paradoxical truth, for before it was dissolved in December 1678 this parliament was to strike again some of the attitudes of its more famous namesake.

On ecclesiastical policy the restored bishops, ardent royalists though they were, sided with the parliament. Archbishop Gilbert Sheldon openly condemned the royal policy of indulgence because he believed that only by enforcing conformity could the Church of England be preserved; and Sheldon, unlike Archbishop Burnet of Glasgow in a similar situation, was not censured—a clear indication of the strength and popularity of episcopacy in England. The result was that nonconformity took on a new significance as ecclesiastical divisions enforced by law acquired political and social implications that were to influence English life for centuries to come. To ecumenically minded churchmen of the late twentieth century the policy adopted seems brutal and unchristian, but when assessed against the circumstances of the time it appears not so much reprehensible as realistic.[8] A mixed polity which combined moderate episcopacy with some presbyterian features simply did not work—as the Scottish experience had shown and was to show again. Besides, the Laudians lumped moderate episcopalians like Richard Baxter, who believed in Archbishop Usher's famous 'Reduction'[9], with the presbyterians, while the genuine presbyterians clung to the covenants and would have no truck with bishops however defined. In the prevailing climate of opinion a basis for compromise did not exist. The Clarendon Code, therefore, repressive though it was, saved the Anglican church. The nonconformists, unable to co-operate among themselves, rapidly declined in strength. Thus an inquiry carried out in 1676 at the instigation of the Earl of Danby revealed an over-whelming preponderance of Anglicans in the province of Canterbury, which, almost certainly, was also the case in the province of York.[10] And so, in spite of its dangerous alliance with divine right monarchy, the Church of England in its historic form, strengthened and re-invigorated, weathered the Revolution virtually unscathed mainly because the Laudian theory of the church as a divine institution independent of the royal will survived. It has indeed recently been emphasised by Dr. Lamont that this view of the church was central to Anglican thinking throughout the seventeenth century and provided a hidden reserve of strength that could be used in times of crisis whether under Cromwell or James II.[11] The importance of this for the history of England hardly needs stressing, and the same goes for its impact on Anglo-Scottish relations.

So far as Anglo-Scottish relations are concerned, the main point is that the Restoration Church Settlement in Scotland, in form so like that achieved in England, suffered shipwreck. Nor is the reason far to seek. The ecclesiastical situation in Scotland, though on the surface similar to the English, differed in certain vital respects, and these differences were not sufficiently taken into account. In Scotland, for example, the sects were so weak as to count for nothing. Nor was there, as in England, a centre party. Thus the confrontation between episcopalians and presbyterians in Scotland was of the stark sort that allows little room for manoeuvre, and such compromise as was attempted merely deepened the strife. Recently efforts have been made to controvert this view by asserting that many of the presbyterians were ready to accept moderate episco-pacy.[12] Only by equating the pliable James Sharp with the Resolutioner party as a whole could this case be substantiated, but such a course is firmly ruled out by the evidence. In the *Life of Blair* we are told unequivocally that the presbyterians expected the continuance of their system by a covenanted king;[13] unimpeachable witness to the same effect is provided by *The Letters and Journals of Robert Baillie*, a prominent Resolutioner;[14] and, most conclusive of all, the correspon-dence of Sharp with the leading Resolutioners reveals, again and again, their dread of episcopacy.[15] It is not easy to see how such a mass of clear and un-ambiguous evidence, of which the sources cited are mere examples, can be so blithely ignored.

The notion, then, that the majority of the Scottish presbyterians were really moderate episcopalians can safely be rejected; and the explanation of the restoration of episcopacy in Scotland must be sought elsewhere. Certainly, the bitter divisions between Protesters and Resolutioners seriously weakened the presbyterian case; apart from this, Blair's biographer went to the heart of the matter when he ruefully admitted that the presbyterians, particularly those of the Resolutioner party, were politically simple and 'knew not the mysteries and intrigues of court and estate policy'.[16] In the end it was the Court that decided, not without some hesitation, the form of the ecclesiastical settlement in Scotland

and not, as in England, the parliament. The Resolutioners, too, had a misplaced faith in their spokesman, James Sharp, whom they really ought to have known better. Years before, Oliver had quickly seen through the wily Master James, wittily dubbing him Sharp of that Ilk. In his devious way Sharp had actually submitted to the usurpers to a greater extent even than the leading Protester Patrick Gillespie, and consciousness of his guilt may well have contributed to his remarkable metamorphosis from minister of Crail to primate. At any rate, when the Restoration was clearly pending, this was the man who was sent to London to represent the Resolutioners and who actually crossed to Breda ostensibly to urge their cause. Even this early Sharp may have betrayed them, and certainly from the actual Restoration itself he readily fell in with Clarendon's views. Personally, Sharp does not seem to have had any very strong convictions but simply obeyed the dictates of his nature and went with the tide, though characteristically to the end he assured his dupes that he was striving with might and main to preserve Scottish presbyterianism. Sharp's letters to them have survived, and in these masterpieces of perfidy he stands self-condemned. The only real mystery is about the timing of the decision to restore an episcopal regime in Scotland.

It was delayed mainly by the king's doubts. Charles found himself in a quandary. Much as he loathed presbyterianism and hated to recall his experience of it in Scotland a decade earlier, he was shrewdly aware of its strength in that country, and he for one never really regarded men like Robert Douglas or Robert Baillie as moderate episcopalians. His doubts were fanned by the arguments of his other principal adviser, John Maitland, Earl (and later Duke) of Lauderdale, who was supported by the Earl of Crawford and the Duke of Hamilton. Lauderdale no longer had any brief for presbyterianism; a complete politique, like Lethington, his arguments turned on *raison d'état*. He desired power above all and put nothing before office. At the same time, he was a realist and tried to persuade Charles to adopt a safe policy in Scotland, which he knew still differed in many essentials from England and was not, therefore, amenable to the same policies. The gist of Lauderdale's advice to the king was that trouble had to be avoided, or at least minimised, and with this view the king concurred. Conflict, however, arose between Lauderdale and his rival for the king's favour, Clarendon. Clarendon felt that a presbyterian establishment in Scotland would weaken the position of the Church of England; he never forgot, too, that the Civil Wars had really begun in Scotland, and this he attributed to neglect of that country in London. The same mistake should not be made twice, and in Clarendon's view it was imperative to subordinate Scotland to England. At bottom, Lauderdale and Clarendon were really striving for the same ends but differed as to means; each wanted to strengthen the restored monarchy, and while to a large extent their quarrels were personal they were also about tactics. Clarendon was right to think that in England the best ecclesiastical settlement from the crown's standpoint was a restoration of episcopacy; but Lauderdale was not wrong in concluding that this was the worst prescription for Scotland.

The channels of information open to Charles favoured Clarendon and Sharp. The Scottish nobles, on the whole, were hostile to presbytery, and many of them were eager to prove their loyalty and purge past transgressions against the crown by harsh treatment of their old allies, the kirkmen. Lauderdale thus found himself dangerously isolated (for he especially had much in his past that did not bear recalling), but with courage and skill he continued to stress the dangers of imposing episcopacy on a country in which it did not enjoy much popular support. He pointed out, desperately and inaccurately, that this was the policy that had lured the king's father to destruction, and prophesied that it could only lead to further troubles. His arguments were unavailing, and, after long and frequently bitter debates, Clarendon and the High Church party, aided by the renegade Sharp, prevailed.

In July–August 1661, just about the same time as Anglican preponderance was becoming clear in England, the decision was reached at a Scottish Council in London.[17] An episcopal regime superimposed on presbytery was to be restored; General Assemblies were not to meet, but the controversial canons and prayer book were also to be allowed to lapse. The news was bitterly received by the Scottish presbyterians, the more so as Sharp's duplicity was by then clear and he was thereafter hated as a Judas. Able though he was, the Court probably made a mistake in making him Archbishop of St. Andrews, for as primate he enjoyed wide jurisdictional powers which he was totally unfit to wield fairly or wisely. Yet for this Clarendon and his party cannot be blamed overmuch. They had little choice. The Scottish episcopate had virtually died out and there were few candidates for the bishoprics. The choice of the able but odious Sharp, then, while open to obvious criticism, is perhaps understandable.

The repressive machinery fashioned to root out nonconformity in England was all too faithfully adapted for similar use in Scotland. This again proved to be a mistake. Resistance was feared in England but in the event it proved trifling compared to the troubles that arose in Scotland. The origin of these troubles, however, is largely attributable to the maladroit politicians, like Middleton, who carried out the Restoration Settlement. Difficult though the situation was they had certain advantages: episcopacy was acceptable in the Highlands and North East Lowlands, the polity adopted had some presbyterian features ministerial order was not in question, and prelacy was not flaunted. But the government squandered these assets and seems almost to have revelled in creating unrest, whereas the correct policy would have been to leave well alone and not to harry the presbyterian ministers. Inside the establishment the harm they could have done must have been limited, but outside it they could wreak irreparable damage. Instead of enlisting time as an ally, however, the government rashly emulated the St. Bartholomew carried out in England in the belief that by forcing ministers who had not been presented by patrons or collated by bishops to undergo these processes, and so in the most unequivocal manner accept the new regime, the church would be purged of twenty or thirty extremists. Instead about 270 ministers, many of whom were Protesters and concentrated mainly in the covenanting south-west, refused to comply and, in spite of an extended time limit, had to be driven from their charges early in 1663.

The purge was an act of folly that increased conventicling and in other ways posed difficult problems. Where were 270 adequate replacements to be found?

They could not, and, in spite of recent efforts to present the 'curates' in a kindly light,[18] the evidence as to their poor quality is too strong. Bishop Robert Leighton of Dunblane, for example, described them as 'owls and satyrs'; and he, the most charitable of men, spoke from personal knowledge, for as acting Archbishop of Glasgow between 1670 and 1674 Leighton had to oversee their activities.[19] Many of them were unfit for the ministry, and not a few were loathed by their nominal congregations as government spies.

The stupid way in which the corrupt politicians raised this thorny problem was roundly condemned at the time even by devoted espiscopalians. Indeed, that arch-royalist and later scourge of the conventiclers, 'the Bluidy Advocate' Mackenzie, attributed to the purge most of the discontents that became endemic in the West Lowlands.[20] Proof is not far to seek. The presbyterian risings of 1666 and 1679 both derived from this rash policy and the increasingly severe measures that had to be used to counter its effects. As a result, after the experience of the Restoration period Scottish presbyterianism could have no truck with prelacy; and, since the rôle of the English High Church party in Scotland was known and resented, Scottish presbyterians acquired deep-rooted suspicions of England. The historical significance of this phobia long outlived the House of Stewart: for three centuries it has played a changing but throughout significant part in Anglo-Scottish relations, and to this day a residue of that bitter legacy from the past remains.

But it was not only in ecclesiastical affairs that the Restoration ran a different course in the two countries. Constitutional differences were even more marked and were in the short term even more important. The decision to leave the settlement of outstanding problems in England to parliament rather than impose terms at Breda really inaugurated parliamentary monarchy. The king could wriggle thereafter but was unable to assert full divine right. In England, then, there could be no simple return to the old constitution. The important reforms carried by the Long Parliament between 1640 and 1642 were retained—the conciliar courts did not re-appear, the common law courts reigned supreme in the legal sphere and subsequent attempts to use them in favour of the prerogative enjoyed little success, feudalism was abolished, and control of finance by the House of Commons was reluctantly conceded.[21] Then, too, the Commons could no longer be manipulated by the crown, and gradually this led to the rise of a system of influence of which Danby seems to have been the grand originator.[22] True, the prerogative powers of the crown were still great, but they were ill-defined and poorly adapted for the everyday tasks of government. Charles II, an intelligent if indolent politician, understood that any overt attempt at arbitrary prerogative rule was dangerous, and his strategy (particularly marked in foreign policy) was to by-pass parliament rather than make a hazardous frontal assault upon it. The king's chief weapon was his right, as yet undisputed, to choose his own ministers, which is why the opening years of the Restoration, years of intense selfish intrigue at court, 'take much of their political character from the fact that the obvious passport to political advancement was the favour of the King'.[23] Another advantage enjoyed by the crown was the right to summon parliament at will, as the lax Triennial Act of 1664 allowed. The financial stringency of the crown, however, which was exacerbated by Charles' prodigal nature, reduced these advantages, and before the reign ended the point had twice been driven home (in the cases of Clarendon and Danby) that not even the king's favour could save a minister if parliament would have none of him.

Scotland fared otherwise. There the prerogative triumphed. In 1660 Charles II as king of Scots was limited only by his subscription to the covenants, and when these were swept aside the constitutional reforms which they had helped to buttress were doomed. Nothing was salvaged from the constitution of 1641. The sweeping Act Rescissory of 1661, which even astonished the king, annulled all legislation since 1633 and thus paved the way for the return of the bishops, the Lords of the Articles, and tight royal control of church, parliament, Privy Council and judiciary. There were a few individual protests at these steps but no organised opposition, largely because the administration deliberately created an atmosphere of menace. Few people of consequence had not at some stage in the late troubles actively opposed the king or his father or to some extent countenanced the usurpers; with the removal of the supposed legal cover under which they had acted and the calculated delay over a general indemnity, most found it expedient to stay silent. The new government seized its opportunity to push the prerogative to unprecedented lengths and at the same time voted Charles a large supply for life, thus dealing a further crippling blow to the parliament.

All this was deliberate policy, for the so-called Cavaliers in Scotland were a motley crew consisting mainly of Engagers uneasily mindful of their own spotted careers. The Commissioner Middleton himself had served in the Great Civil War as David Leslie's lieutenant, though later, particularly during Glencairn's rising in 1653–54, he had fought his way into royal favour. He had also at one stage fallen foul of the kirk, been excommunicated and only received back into the fold after a humiliating repentance. Middleton, a good soldier but no politician, was therefore intent on paying off old scores as a means of demonstrating his loyalty and advancing his interest. Round him there gathered a clique of like-minded opportunists, and soon the corruption of Middleton's regime was notorious.[24]

Up to a point, as in England, 'compensation' for losses incurred in the Civil Wars explains the growth of corruption—but only up to a point. The extent of corruption in Scotland sprang partly from lax supervision by the king; partly from the marked poverty of the Scots nobles and lairds for whom, now that they were being brought into closer contact with their much wealthier English counterparts, office became an essential source of income; and partly from their inexperience and ignorance of administration. They were of mediocre abilities at best and little statesmanship appeared in their acts. Mad policies were pursued, including the passing of laws that could not be enforced, simply to provide pin-money for corrupt administrators. Indemnities could be bought and so could judges, provided the government had not pre-empted their decisions. All in all, possibly the worst aspect of the Restoration regime in Scotland was the way in which exaltation of the royal prerogative and venality combined to rot away nearly every vestige of public morality. This may seem a strong statement, but it is fully borne out by the evidence. And it is an important matter. The Restoration regime in

Scotland left behind it a destructive legacy which strangled responsible constitutional government and gave a fresh lease of life to the most reactionary elements in the country, where, in contrast to what happened in England, feudalism was not given its congé. Worse still, the corrupt time-serving tradition survived the Revolution and was visibly at work right up to, and far beyond, the making of the Treaty of Union of 1707. The significance of this, however, has evidently escaped most writers on the subject of the union.[25]

Behind Middleton stood Clarendon who, though personally honest, must bear part of the responsibility for these unhealthy developments in Scotland. At bottom, Clarendon would have liked to maintain the Cromwellian union; this proving impracticable, he tried to keep ultimate control of Scotland in London but not entirely in the hands of the king and his Scottish secretary. Thus, Clarendon persuaded the king to set up a Scottish Council at Whitehall which contained a solid core of English members, so minimising the powers of the Scottish secretary, Lauderdale, and in effect placing the government of Scotland in safe English hands.[26] Shortlived though the experiment was (it was ended at Lauderdale's insistence in 1667), it had some significance. It was this council that allowed Middleton to embark on a policy of 'thorough' in Scotland, in spite of Lauderdale's jeremiads and Charles' doubts.[27] Lauderdale was equally strong for the prerogative, but in the hope of damping down opposition he advocated a gradualist approach. He also feared English domination and constantly urged the king to maintain a separate Scottish administration. He went further and even recommended Charles not to attempt to unite the two kingdoms but rather to foster discord between them. By flattering the national pride of the Scots it was hoped that they might be induced to aid the king should serious disturbances break out again in England.[28] Middleton, on the other hand, had no strategic objectives. He was little more than Clarendon's tool and went to dangerous, and even fatuous, lengths to please his master.

In 1663 Middleton over-reached himself when, with transparent finesse, he got the obsequious parliament to black-ball from office Lauderdale and some of his friends. The so-called 'Billeting Act', however, misfired, owing to Lauderdale's timely appeal to the king. Charles was furious, and it was Middleton who fell. Still his rival failed to achieve real power in Scotland. Not until after the rebellion of the covenanters in November 1666 (the Pentland Rising, which seemed to vindicate long-standing criticisms of Middleton and his fuddled successor Rothes), and not, significantly enough, until the fall of Clarendon was impending in 1667, did Lauderdale attain the supreme direction of Scottish affairs.

The result was a resounding anti-climax. The usual view of Lauderdale is that thereafter he bestrode both kingdoms like a colossus, a veritable satrap in Scotland and, as a member of the famous Cabal, a statesman of the first rank in England.[29] That view needs considerable qualification; in particular, as far as Scotland is concerned, it lacks perspective. If Lauderdale's policies had been applied from the outset in 1660 they might arguably have enjoyed some success, but by 1667 too many intransigent positions had been taken up not only by the government but by the feuding kirkmen as well. By 1667 too Lauderdale was past his best and thereafter deteriorated, latterly to an alarming degree. Nor can the Cabal itself any longer be regarded in the old light; it was not a united ministry, indeed not a ministry at all but simply a group of courtiers entrusted with high office who intrigued endlessly against each other. And this was no accident, for the real mastermind, though not as brilliant as some of his biographers have made out, was the king himself.

Between 1667 and 1674 Charles was trying to circumvent parliament and in particular to control foreign policy. He admired Louis XIV and would have liked to copy his absolutist system. To this end he used members of the Cabal either to further this policy or, where he sensed disapproval, to divert attention from it. Of them all Lauderdale was the most subservient, a yes-man pure and simple of whom it has been well said that 'Never was Eastern despot blessed with a minister of his will more obedient, docile, and sedulous'.[30] That is why he retained office longer than any other of Charles' servants; realising as he did that office depended on the king's favour, Lauderdale saw that the king's every whim had to be catered for. Only one thing prevented him from being the perfect lackey, his almost insane hatred of popery, but that too Charles could turn to advantage. Thus, apparently supreme in Scotland, Lauderdale took care to write triumphantly to Charles that 'Never was king so absolute as you are in poor old Scotland'.[31] Lauderdale, then, gratified Charles II by building up a regime in Scotland that had all the appearance of an absolutism 'à la mode de France'. Yet in spite of his increasingly bad temper and his rough and arbitrary ways, to the end he had a certain popularity with his countrymen, mainly because his outlook, in spite of his subservience to the crown, remained markedly nationalist.

Contrary to his vaunts, however, Lauderdale's career as governor of Scotland was far from brilliant. He failed to settle the church question but managed to advance the prerogative. The policy of indulgence, which he really believed in and tried repeatedly, had little success, and in fact sharpened the existing strife by alarming both presbyterian and episcopalian extremists. The sweeping Act of Supremacy of 1669 offended even the bishops, and for his opposition to the indulgence and to this act Archbishop Burnet of Glasgow, an honest bigot, was deprived of his see. The indulgence also failed to placate the presbyterian dissidents, whom Lauderdale then tried to crush by some fierce legislation, particularly the notorious 'Clanking Act' of 1670 which threatened field preachers with capital punishment. On the credit side, to begin with he saw the need for honest administration and tried to provide it; but again he failed and was soon operating a system every whit as corrupt as those of his predecessors.

All this forms part of the tricky background to one of the most curious incidents in the long history of Anglo-Scottish relations—an attempt at union so mysterious that it has to date defied explanation. There are, it may be suggested, two master clues to the reading of its riddle—first, the economic developments of the Restoration period, and second, Lauderdale's complete subservience to Charles II.

Before the Civil Wars trade and commerce had largely been regulated by the crown and care was usually taken to safeguard the interests of both kingdoms. At the Restoration the Scots fondly imagined either that free trade would be retained or that the older system would be brought back. But things worked out differently, mainly because one of the most durable legacies of the Interregnum proved to be the political influence of commercial interests in England. It was in response to the pressures exerted by such interests that the English Navigation Act of 1660 treated Scotland virtually like any other foreign country on the grounds that concessions to the Scots would strengthen their main trading partner Holland, which happened to be England's greatest maritime rival.[32] Professor Smout, in his book on *Scottish Trade*, minimises the effects of the Navigation Act on Scotland, asserting that the Scottish economy was buoyant.[33] But he conducts his case in the most extraordinary and unaccountable way. Smout ignores the evidence even to the extent of failing to notice the talks about economic union in 1668 and the attempt at incorporating union in 1670; his whole thesis is nullified by this fundamental failure to close with the evidence.

That evidence is varied and plentiful. From 1661 the Scots complained bitterly and in ever-increasing volume about the ill effects on their economy of the new set-up intoduced by the English Navigation Act of 1660. Thus as early as 1661 Lauderdale attempted to have the Navigation Act as it applied to Scotland either suspended or at least relaxed. Foiled in this endeavour, the Scottish parliament then retaliated with a Navigation Act of its own which would give England a dose of its own medicine. But this too failed to produce the desired effect. And so, even before the outbreak of the Dutch war in 1664, there was widespread discontent in Scotland with the new arrangements. The economic depression caused by the Dutch war produced exasperation and protests multiplied. In May 1665, for instance, the Scottish Privy Council begged the king to remove the restrictions which had led to 'so many addresses made to us for representing the sufferings of this Kingdome by the want of trade occasioned by the late Act of your Parliament of England imposing so great customes upon our native Commodities that our whole trade with that Kingdome is totally destroyed'.[34] No doubt, in a bid to attract the king's attention, the Privy Council pitched matters rather high; but in spite of Professor Smout's assertions Scottish grievances over the Navigation Act were substantial and they were real. Indeed, representations against the Navigation Act as it affected Anglo-Scottish trade did not come only from the Scottish side; the English woollen trade also felt injured by the act's restrictions and vainly appealed to the king to have them removed.

Clearly, the Dutch war worsened an already bad situation, and Charles II at length took alarm. Many Scots sympathised with the Dutch, and it seemed likely that the United Provinces might make capital out of the situation by encouraging Scottish Anglophobia or by supporting the covenanters with arms and supplies. The fear was not altogether idle, for, although the Pentland Rising seems to have been a spontaneous outbreak, there was some evidence of plotting between the Dutch and representatives of the more extreme of the Scottish presbyterians.[35] Charles, therefore, had compelling reasons for listening to the pleas of the Scots and attempting to secure a fairer economic relationship between England and Scotland. He seems to have seen the dangerous impasse towards which the two countries were drifting. Overseas trade turned largely on foreign policy, but foreign policy was a luxury Scotland no longer enjoyed; and if England denied economic privileges to the Scots and at the same time strangled their trade through her own wars, then the long-term prospects for Anglo-Scottish amity must be bleak. Scotland would be forced to acquiesce in her own suicide, or else either contrive to break the English stranglehold somehow or accept a closer union—if such could be obtained. The *a posteriori* logic of this reasoning seems impeccable; but pure logic did little to bring about a closer and more equitable union. The evidence proves that the economic crisis sharpened the problem but equally clearly could not produce a political solution.

In 1667, mainly at the king's instance, commissioners from both kingdoms were appointed by the two parliaments to explore the possibility of economic union. Talks began in January 1668 but were deadlocked almost from the start. The English commission was not subservient to the Court and reflected the intransigent attitudes of parliament, while in a different way the Scottish commission, dominated by Lauderdale, was equally difficult and openly strove for a return to the old system, demanding concessions from king and Privy Council, thus by-passing the English parliament and its recently arrogated powers in the economic sphere. The Scots, therefore, bitterly assailed the English Navigation Act, which they stigmatised as 'that first and greatest obstruction of the freedome of trade between the two kingdomes'.[36] It is also noteworthy that they were concerned almost entirely with trade with England and showed scant interest in the colonial trade, which, even as far as England itself was concerned, was then still in its infancy. But all that the English were prepared to concede was a mere sop—to throw open limited trade for six years. The offer was rejected, since it would have seriously impaired Scottish fiscal policy for minimal, and possibly ephemeral, gains. The talks then ground to a standstill largely because of the pressures exerted by the English coal and salt industries, which had suffered from Scottish competition in the past and feared its effects again if free trade were once more conceded. Though some English merchant interests (notably the woollen industry) wanted freer trade with Scotland, they were too slow and hesitant in countering the Newcastle hostmen; and so it fared, too, with the representations of the farmers of the Customs. They had pressed for the act in 1660 only to discover that while it eased collection it diminished the possible yield, and in 1668 they recommended that the Navigation Act should be relaxed in favour of the Scots. Parliament, it seems, did not really determine economic policy but rather responded to the most powerful pressure groups, and on this occasion the restrictionists won. The *status quo* was maintained.

The outcome of the commercial negotiations was highly unsatisfactory; but it need not be concluded that this fact alone dictated the attempt at complete union in 1670 (which also, incidentally, finds no place in Smout's book on trade). An attempt at complete union as a corrective to the failure of 1668 seems logical, and is the traditional explanation; but in reality it fails to take stock of the entire situation. Obscure as the origins of these talks are, certainly it looks very much as if Charles was the main agent in promoting them, though his purpose in doing so remains debatable. He had evidently accepted Lauderdale's view that the two kingdoms should be kept apart and was delighted at the way in which Lauderdale had exalted the prerogative in Scotland. Neither Charles nor Lauderdale can have seriously believed that an incorporating union in 1670 could have maintained absolute rule in Scotland or enforced it on England. The reverse was much more likely; and on the whole it is extremely doubtful if Charles either expected or desired an incorporating union.

At this point Charles II was playing a very deep game. He was secretly negotiating an agreement with Louis XIV and had to divert his leading ministers with all sorts of red herrings. A proposed commercial treaty with France served as one such diversion, an attempt to renew the Triple Alliance another, and even Lord Roos' divorce case preoccupied Shaftesbury, who was gulled into believing it might set a precedent for the king and enable Charles to remarry in the hope of begetting a legitimate and protestant heir. Lauderdale, a notorious protestant bigot, knew nothing of the secret negotiations with Louis XIV and was kept pre-occupied with the project for Anglo-Scottish union, in which, personally, he did not believe, nor act as if he did. The latest writer on this topic, Professor Lee, thinks Lauderdale sincerely desired union, but Lee's argument is strained and in places self-contradictory;[37] and the older view, that Lauderdale showed little enthusiasm for the project seems substantially correct.[38] Lauderdale, however, believed in carrying out royal directives, or, at least, in giving the appearance of doing so; and there is every reason to suspect that these negotiations were a sham designed to divert attention from Charles' foreign policy. So far the case for this interpretation is circumstantial; but it is strengthened by an examination of the actual negotiations.

Lauderdale's henchman Tweeddale was keen on a union and may indeed have introduced the idea to the king; and certainly it is suggestive that the estrangement between Lauderdale and Tweeddale dates from the middle of the subsequent negotiations. At any rate, on the failure of the commercial talks Charles told the Scottish Privy Council in June 1669 that he intended to promote a closer union and to call a parliament for that end. Lord Keeper Bridgeman was left to broach the new line to the English parliament in October, when he declared that the late negotiations had 'produced no effect, unless it were a Conviction of the Difficulty if not impossibility of settling it any other way than by a nearer and more complete union of the two Kingdoms'.[39]

But all too obviously opinion in neither country favoured the scheme. England, conscious that Ireland was a heavy financial burden and knowing from recent experience that Scotland would be the same, put her own interests first;[40] while in Scotland the memory of the Cromwellian union still rankled, causing the new project to be greeted with frank incredulity.[41] Thus the king's letter of 15 September 1669 recommending it to the parliament was not received with any real enthusiasm in spite of the fawning language it evoked. The Scots parliament was completely gagged and there was little or no debate on the issue; only Sir George Mackenzie and a few others spoke out against the proposal—or rather pleaded for full and mature deliberation before embarking on such a momentous venture.[42] Mackenzie's speech was not well received, but even Lauderdale was obliged to admit to the king that there was a deep-rooted and general aversion to the proposal in Scotland.[43] The nobles showed little enthusiasm, but were quick enough to try and profit from the design by demanding payment of past salaries and grossly inflated expenses for serving on the commission, which seems to have become a standard ploy of theirs. In reality, as Rosehaugh put it, the union project was not at all to the liking of the Scots nobles, who hoped to subdue parliament and bishops alike so as 'to get all power devolv'd upon the Council; hoping thereby to make Parliaments unnecessary, and to enhance all the government to themselves, who had the Council at their devotion'.[44] Such a scheme, for which there is some evidence, could not possibly be furthered by union with England. As for the English parliament, it showed even less enthusiasm and was dilatory in the whole business. But finally the parliaments agreed to proceed, and, after some wrangling, decided to waive the precedent of 1604 and leave nomination of commissioners to the crown.

Behind the scenes soundings had been taken by the king's ministers. Lauderdale had already outlined a scheme of union to the English Privy Council, which endorsed it on 10 June 1669. In general its terms largely anticipated those of 1707: the projected union was to be an incorporating one with a united parliament and a full communication of trade; but, possibly at the prompting of the famous Scots lawyer Sir James Dalrymple, the two legal systems were to remain separate, and, significantly, so were the two church establishments. Following the Cromwellian precedent 30 seats were to be granted to Scotland in the House of Commons, and 10 peers and 2 bishops were to be elected by their fellows to sit in the House of Lords.[45] Professor Lee, in reviewing this evidence, concludes that it furnishes clear proof that Lauderdale was wholeheartedly backing the project; but this fails to take proper stock of the startling discrepancy between Lauderdale's recommendations to the English Council in June 1669 and Lauderdale's extraordinary proposals to the English commissioners in November 1670.

In the midst of the actual negotiations in October–November 1670 Lauderdale, who was by then openly quarrelling with Tweeddale, suddenly changed course. Using as his excuse that the Scots members of parliament would never accept a union that would so drastically reduce their numbers, he introduced impossible demands.[46] In a flurry of non-sequiturs he contended that the two parliaments should be kept, that 'a certain number of Englishmen might be appointed to sit in the Scottish Parliament', and that in special emergencies a joint session of the two parliaments might be held in London.[47] These demands were totally at variance with the original scheme put by Lauderdale to the English Privy Council, and he must have known they would be rejected out of hand—as they were, thus terminating the negotiations. Besides, Lauderdale's solicitous concern for the Scottish members was suspiciously out of character.

What, then, caused Lauderdale to make such an obvious *volte face*? In all probability Charles had no further use for the charade. In May 1670 the Secret Treaty of Dover had been signed, and subsequent to this Lauderdale must have been instructed by the king to wreck the negotiations. Otherwise, if Charles had really been keen on union, how could Lauderdale possibly have retained the king's favour? Proof absolute will probably never be forthcoming, since any instructions from the king to Lauderdale would most likely have been verbal; but viewing the matter in the round it looks as if Lauderdale remained in favour because he had faithfully carried out the king's orders. It may well be significant, too, that when the English parliament asked the king to overrule Lauderdale's impossible demands all the answer they received was that Charles, immersed in other affairs, could do nothing.

In any event the trade of Scotland improved after 1670, as, for that matter, did that of England.[48] But still all was far from well in the economic relations of the two countries. The English Navigation Laws continued to hamper Scotland by forcing her to adopt restrictive policies which culminated in 1681 with a system of complete protection designed to shelter her fledgling industries. The policy did more harm than good, for Scotland simply did not have the strength to wage anything like an equal struggle with not only England but France and Holland as well. The age of mercantilism and fierce economic nationalism exposed the weakness of a country unable to develop its resources and not free to gear up its foreign policy to its commercial needs. Long before the Revolution and the devastating wars with France that followed it, the Scottish economy was labouring. In spite of much enlightened legislation industry was making little real headway. Far too many of the numerous ventures set up after 1681 were short-lived or unremunerative, and though there was some evidence of an inclination towards improvement in agriculture it did not amount to much in practice and the rural economy remained largely at the subsistence level. Still, the fact remains that the economic problem did not really become acute in the Restoration period, though it was steadily building up as mercantilist ideas became increasingly accepted and open markets became fewer and fewer. For a country in Scotland's situation this came to pose intractable problems.

More immediately pressing, however, in the relations of England and Scotland in the second half of the Restoration period was the problem of government. The importance of this to Scotland is, and was, obvious, but what tends to be forgotten is the ominous significance that many Englishmen in these troubled times read into Scottish developments. Both Lauderdale and his system of arbitrary government in Scotland were detested in England not just for their intrinsically bad qualities but also as threats to English liberties. Thus as early as 1673 Shaftesbury broke with Lauderdale, his old ally against Clarendon, and co-operated with the opposition to him in the Scottish parliament.[49] As suspicions about the Secret Treaty of Dover hardened and the catholicism of the Duke of York became blatant, Lauderdale's unpopularity in England increased. With the failure of Danby's attempt to placate Anglican opinion and implement a protestant foreign policy, so creating an accommodation between crown and parliament, there came a crisis of confidence. Anti-catholic feeling was running high before Titus Oates appeared with his tall tales about a plot to restore popery and erect an absolutist system of government. Absolutism apparently existed in one of Charles II's kingdoms, and this known fact lent credibility to Oates' lying stories. Thus it was not in the least strange that in the midst of the Popish Plot-Exclusionist agitations Shaftesbury should bitterly denounce Lauderdale's repressive regime in Scotland: 'In England,' he declared in a famous speech, 'popery was to have brought in slavery; in Scotland, slavery went before, and popery was to follow.'[50]

It should be stressed, however, that active resistance to Lauderdale's arbitrary, and latterly inane, regime came not from the political opposition headed by disgruntled grandees like the Duke of Hamilton, with whom Shaftesbury held some correspondence, but from presbyterian dissidents. Shaftesbury and his Scottish correspondents had nothing to do with the rebellion of the covenanters in May–June 1679. The ends aimed at by the rebels, even over the wide spectrum of their differences, were quite other than those of Shaftesbury. This tends to be obscured by the very different connotations given to the word 'whig' which was then entering the political vocabulary of England. In origin it was a Scottish term and meant simply an adherent of the covenants, while in England it denoted those who opposed the Court. It is a tricky term, because in Scotland right up until the union period the original usage held its ground and vied with the English version. The Scottish Whigs, in the older sense of the term, aimed at a godly monarchy limited by God's law, and their political theories derived obviously from Knox and Buchanan. Shaftesbury's political theory, on the other hand, seems to have aimed at a monarchy tightly limited by a parliament dominated by a narrow landed oligarchy. In 1679 the two groups had nothing in common except fear of popery and detestation of Lauderdale.

Nonetheless, the Bothwell Brig rising had a considerable effect on the crisis in England and would have had more if it had been more successfully conducted. The rebellion derived solely from the repressive regime in Scotland, where conventicling had continued and actually increased in spite of ever-more severe counter-measures. And, as in 1666, it was unpremeditated. It was sparked off by an act of atrocious piety, the murder of the hated apostate, Archbishop Sharp, by a handful of fanatics on 3 May. Disorder, however, was not confined to religious dissidence in the Lowlands, for at the very same time, and for quite different reasons, the West Highlands were in a turmoil as MacDonalds, MacLeans and Camerons fought another bitter round in their long struggle with the expansionist House of Argyll.[51] Ironically, therefore, Lauderdale's vaunted absolutism, which raised such clamours in England, was, in reality, a hollow sham. Its wild ranting and corrupt dealing took with the bulk of the subservient and grasping nobility but did nothing to solve the country's problems, and indeed by its crude acts (such as the mad expedient of quartering a Highland militia on the disaffected areas of the south-west in the winter of 1678) actually intensified them.

Shaftesbury was possibly not deceived, but the troubles in Scotland furnished him with a propaganda weapon too good to be ignored. Unfortunately for him, however, and fortunately for the king, the rebellion of the covenanters was easily suppressed. From it Charles even managed to snatch some tactical advantages in the struggle then raging in England; he got his much loved illegitimate and overly ambitious son the Duke of Monmouth out of harm's way by sending him north to suppress the rising and then, this accomplished, dispatched him to Holland and replaced him in Scotland by James, Duke of York. In effect Lauderdale was superseded, but still the cry against him, wooden shoes and popery, was kept up in England. The real target of abuse, however, was the popish Duke of York. Thus the satire of 1680, possibly by Andrew Marvell, lost none of its sting with the way-going of its subject, the decrepit and by then generally discredited Lauderdale:

This haughty Monster with his ugly claws
First temper'd Poison to destroy our Lawes
Declares the Council Edicts are beyond
The most authentick Statutes of the Land,
Sets up in Scotland alamode de France,
Taxes Excise and Armyes dos advance.
This Saracen his Countryes freedom broke
To bring upon our Necks the heavier yoke.[52]

England was not trouble-free either. A new generation of squires had grown suspicious of the aims of Charles II and alarmed by the religious beliefs of his brother. Over all hung the shadow of King Louis. Thus Titus Oates' well-primed bombshell detonated a tremendous explosion. Soon demands were being made for the exclusion of James from the succession; but the issues were complex, and the new parliament that met in May 1679 introduced the first Exclusion Bill as a platform for wider grievances rather than as a complete programme in its own right.[53] Shaftesbury tried to dominate the opposition but the extent of his control over it has until recently been exaggerated, and it now seems clear that, in spite of their triumphs in the elections of August–September 1679 and 1681, the anti-court factions could scarcely be said to constitute a party.[54] Charles, too, unlike his father in a not dissimilar situation, fought back skilfully. To gain time he obtained further financial help from Louis and made some concessions to the opposition. When the moment was ripe he struck hard, and his masterly handling of the Oxford parliament in 1681 broke the opposition. The dissolution shattered the fragile unity of the Whigs, for in the absence of a parliament the opposition elements could not co-operate, and the king was able to step up his devastating counter-attack, driving Shaftesbury into exile. The so-called Rye House plot to murder the king, which was probably as spurious as anything that sprang from the fertile imaginations of Oates and his colleagues, completed the rout of the Whigs. By 1683 the old ruling alliance between crown and High Church Tories had apparently been restored, and it looked as if the Court's triumph would be perpetuated by adroit gerrymandering.

Yet the Exclusion crisis was of crucial importance. At the most obvious level it directed current anti-popish hysteria against the Duke of York. It tried to prevent him from succeeding to the throne, and, in spite of its failure, it underlined the difficulties of his succession, raising grave doubts even in the mind of such a stalwart Tory as Danby. But the crisis was also about the deeper problems of government opened up by Charles II's controversial rule. Shaftesbury's real aims seem to have been to force an oligarchy upon the king (headed, of course, by himself), and to secure real power to the landed interest with concessions to the mercantile. To these ends, anti-popish feeling and alarm for the Anglican settlement were little more than useful propaganda weapons. The actual succession, to begin with, was left undefined—an interesting precedent for the Scots to follow in 1703–4, as was, for some at any rate, Halifax's suggestion that 'limitations' should be imposed on James. Only latterly, and reluctantly, did Shaftesbury endorse the claims of Monmouth; and throughout he was suspicious of the good faith of William of Orange, who seemed too subservient to his royal uncles whose fears of 'republicanism' he shared. William, it should be noted, was as strong for the prerogative and for the mystique of kingship as either Charles or James, and the Exclusion crisis placed him in a dilemma. How best could he safeguard his own interests? He could not do that by standing aloof, nor yet by throwing in with the opposition, and still less, of course, by espousing the cause of Monmouth. Fortunately for him the opposition collapsed before he became too embroiled; but thereafter his English game was more complicated than ever, a factor of the utmost importance in any consideration of the brief reign of James II.[55]

In the last years of Charles II, as Cavalier sentiment revived and rallied round the throne, it looked as if absolutism was to triumph throughout the British Isles. Again the pace was set in the northern kingdom. There the Duke of York had gained a clear ascendancy by ingratiating himself with the nobles and gentry, who were glad to escape from the fierce clutches of the impossible Lauderdale.[56] James at this point was on his best behaviour, out to make friends and influence people; and, except for the implacable presbyterian extremists, the Cameronians, he succeeded to a remarkable degree. Indeed, so favourably was he received that at one critical juncture just before the Oxford parliament he seems to have thought of setting himself up independently in Scotland, safe from Exclusion Bills and supported by Louis XIV; but Shaftesbury got wind of the scheme and his fierce polemics destroyed any slender prospects it might ever have had.[57] James had to content himself with building up a powerful interest in Scotland, which was headed by Queensberry, Gordon of Haddo (later Earl of Aberdeen), the Earl of Perth, Perth's brother Melfort, and the Earl of Moray.

The tame Scottish parliament of 1681 underwrote James' triumph with some extraordinary legislation. James wanted to guarantee the protestant religion in the vaguest possible terms, but Sir James Dalrymple of Stair, the Lord President of the Court of Session, managed to insert the Confession of 1567 into the body of the act. Then came an act defining the indefeasible hereditary succession to the throne which neither religion nor statute could infringe. Based on these acts, a test oath was to be tendered to all office-holders.[58] It was an odd gallimaufry, and well described as 'a medley of popery, erastianism and self-contradiction'. On the surface the Succession Act made sense; James was the undoubted heir by descent and the act was an obvious repudiation of exclusionism. But even though a Roman catholic, James would as king, by virtue of the Act of Supremacy of 1669, have supreme ecclesiastical authority. What then would the acts against popery be worth, and what the laws maintaining the protestant religion? Many confirmed royalists were unable to solve this riddle, including the brilliant but politically inept Stair and some 40 episcopalian ministers, all of whom were deprived. It was like a trial run for James' short inglorious reign, down even to the sacrificial goat in the shape of the Earl of Argyll who for refusing to take the oath without qualification was condemned to death. He escaped to Holland, only to be executed four years later, as was that other luckless venturer, Monmouth.

But, whatever the discontent in Scotland, it was masked, and no open opposition arose. Only the Cameronians, the die-hard remnants of the extreme covenanters, resisted authority. In their famous Apologetical Declaration of 1684 they openly renounced the rule of the perjured Charles Stewart and virtually declared war on the state. Against them the regime unleashed a ferocious form of legalised terrorism similar to the dragonnades of Louis XIV that were in-flaming protestant tempers all over Europe. The resistance of the Cameronians was important mainly because it was later worked into the heroic part of the presbyterian tradition; but in the 1680s most presbyterians condemned the Cameronians as wild fanatics. The bulk of the presbyterians were then either sullenly conforming or at least lying low, and the active religious dissidents, Cameronians mostly, posed no real threat to constituted authority and are accurately described in their own words as 'the poor, suffering, bleeding remnant'.

Thus even before the death of Charles II in February 1685, James, Duke of York, was master of Scotland, which he ruled through his favourites, the com-pliant Drummond brothers, Perth and Melfort, who were soon to be converted to catholicism. More ominous still, in England too as Charles' health gave way James became chief manager of affairs, and his success in Scotland may well have encouraged him to embark on a policy of 'thorough' in England as well.

The controversies produced by the brief reign of James VII and II have continued down to our own time—eloquent testimony to the crucial importance of the issues they raised. At the heart of all the controversies is the mystery of the man himself. After 1689 the triumphant Whig and protestant propaganda machine depicted him as a power-crazed psychopath and priest-ridden fanatic—mean, vicious and implacable in his attempts to demolish the constitution in church and state and to erect on its ruins popery and absolutism. Macaulay in his emphatic way gave classical expression to this thesis, the better to sing the praises of the Glorious Revolution (if not the Reform Bill of 1832) and, of course, 'the eminent personal qualities of William'. No other party line has triumphed so completely or for so long. Defying revolutions in historical tech-nique and impervious to argument, it continued in its essentials down to our own day in G. M. Trevelyan's somewhat fly-blown Whig rhetoric. But in many vital respects the facts are considerably at variance with Whig tradition, and at long last historians can take stock of them without being summarily impaled.[59]

James was no Caliban; his supplanter had better claim to that nickname. Nor did James admire Louis XIV this side idolatry. Indeed his English chauvinism was a large part of his undoing, though some consider, on superficial evidence, that in his youth he had been dangerously Frenchified. However that may be, as a king he gloried in England's standing in the world; and in the end he ruined himself to prove it, for in his critical hour he could have had Louis' support for the asking and would not take it. James was a hard worker of limited intelligence, a compulsive but mournful womaniser whose very amours were woefully mis-managed according to that amusing tattler Anthony Hamilton,[60] and latterly a devout catholic with a tortured conscience. He was convinced that the throne was being threatened and that only strong kingship could save it. His critics dismiss this belief as evidence of paranoia, conveniently forgetting the Exclusion Bill crisis and the campaign of vilification against James that had accompanied it.

King James also seems to have genuinely believed in religious toleration and to have been shocked by the ruthlessness of Louis XIV's dragonnades which began, ominously for public opinion in Britain, in the very year that a catholic king succeeded in England and Scotland. Anti-popish hysteria could draw only one conclusion. But that James wished to emulate Louis, to extirpate all heresy and restore the catholic faith, must be regarded as not proven. Certainly, however, some colour was given to the case against him by two of James' outstanding weaknesses: a certain naïve honesty and a dangerous consistency. In the opening years of the Restoration Charles II had striven for toleration but wisely refused to allow it to lead to a head-on clash with parliament. His brother made no concessions to circumstances but continued to pursue this policy even through the dangerous '70s when more than once he tried to make an alliance with the protestant dissenters. Nor was James ever unaware that the real enemies to toleration were the High Church Tories who formed the core of the royalist party.

James' policy, then, was consistent but foolhardy. In wiser hands much of his programme for Roman catholic emancipation and for toleration all round might have been peaceably achieved, to the immense advantage of the country. But James, who lacked wisdom, had unfortunately a complete faith not only in his own rectitude but also in his own abilities. He could not, therefore, take up a cause without damaging it, partly because of his arrogance but mainly because of his ineptitude and his feeble grasp of reality. In many ways he resembled his father (the best answer to the theory that he was Frenchified), and his father's fate preyed on his mind. He was convinced that only firm policies could prevent a repetition of past troubles. Thus, he blamed his brother for being too easy-going, and he drew the wrong conclusion from Charles' ultimate victory over the Exclusionists. James believed that firmness at the outset would have obviated the whole dangerous imbroglio—a highly debatable proposition. Worse, the new king concluded that he had only to continue the strong policies latterly pursued by his brother and all opposition would melt away.

In sum, James was a decidedly poor politician—indeed, just about the worst possible, for he could not take advice. Only those who told him what he wished to hear could bask in his favour; so only obsequious sycophants and cynical opportunists could serve him—men like the able but unprincipled Sunderland in England or the pliable, if sincere, Perth and his ambitious mischief-making brother Melfort in Scotland. All in all, James' greatest mistake was to drive from his service the limited number of experienced men (like Halifax, Godolphin and Nottingham) who might have been able to introduce his policies in more acceptable form and in a more flexible and less provocative way. James' failure was thus largely personal; but it was also a political failure, not to be explained in terms of new economic forces or groupings of which James was unaware or uncomprehending. James did not lack experience. After all, he had an interest in colonisation; he knew the value of sea-power and maritime trade, and had indeed himself engaged in it with some success. Shaftesbury had no monopoly there. In short, the usual caricature of James does not stand up to analysis.[61]

Nor does the stereotyped account of his reign, which sees it, from beginning to end, in terms of the Glorious Revolution. But, in fact, nothing could have been more peaceful than James' accession. In an extempore and moving speech he assured the English Privy Council that he had been misrepresented and mis-understood, that he did not seek arbitrary power and would preserve the constitution in church and state. The speech was highly acclaimed, though perhaps an oversight was made in not noting the stress that James laid on 'the just rights and prerogative of the Crown'. Opposition there was none, for the Whigs were shattered and the Tories fell over themselves to serve 'Squire James'. The elections too were tightly managed so as to exclude known Exclusionists, and the resulting parliament was accordingly ultra-royalist. Yet James provoked dissension by trying to hector the parliament into repealing the catholic penal laws. News of Monmouth's and Argyll's expeditions, however, stilled resentment and the parliament rallied solidly behind the king.

The ease with which the rebellions were suppressed shows that James not only still had the goodwill of the ruling class in both kingdoms but was indeed popular. Nor did he forfeit his popularity by the harsh treatment meted out to the rebels. The standards of the age expected no less, and it was not until after the Revolution that the Bloody Assizes in England and the severe punishments inflicted on Argyll and his supporters in Scotland were used as propaganda weapons against James and his regime. But in other ways the easy suppression of the rebellions affected matters. The loyalty shown for the king went to his head, and he drove his policies on at a reckless pace. The English parliament, however, which still stubbornly refused to co-operate, was prorogued in November 1685, and thereafter the king turned to the judiciary to justify his prerogative acts. Warnings there were in plenty but they went unheeded. Anyone of average perceptiveness should, for example, have been alerted by the refusal of the servile Scottish parliament in May 1686 to repeal the laws against popery even when offered the bait of free trade;[62] but the rebuff merely served to annoy the befuddled James, who in a dudgeon turned to the Scottish Privy Council, which he purged until it was willing to undertake the task of rescinding the anti-catholic laws. (Incidentally, the rejection of the offer of free trade suggests that economic considerations did not have quite the over-riding importance that some modern economic historians have assumed.)

For two and a half years all seemed to go quietly enough; but James, in persistently, and none too scrupulously, advancing his policy of toleration, was slowly but surely undermining his main supports. Some dim apprehension of this gave a dangerous twist to his activities. In order to offset the loss of episco-palian support, he felt that he must have catholic officers and councillors, but in neither England nor Scotland did the so-called 'catholicising' policy amount to much. Conversion seemed to fare better in Scotland, but even there it was largely illusory. Perth and Melfort went over to Rome, but in spite of their brags few followed their examples. The only perceptible effect was to make the endemic anti-popery of the country even more violent, as a prominent Scots catholic, Thomas Nicholson, later a bishop and first Vicar Apostolic, noted on 8 February 1688 on his return from a sojourn abroad: 'I found things as to the advancement of the Catholic faith far short of my expectations, for instead of finding good inclination of the people and many converts, to our grief we perceived that there were but few converts in this place, and a greater aversion in the people than there was five or six years ago when I left Scotland'.[63] Five days earlier, on 3 February, Lord Perth, himself a zealous convert, was forced to send the cardinal of Norfolk an identical report: 'There have been very few conversions of late. Some few ministers, exemplary men, have come in, many of the ordinary sort, but few in towns. The ministers and university men are so wild and furious . . . that the people take their assertation for full proof of their veracity . . . Others here would have us believe they are our friends, who really are our most dangerous enemies, especially some in the army, the hundredth man in which is not a Catholic, and we have scarce any officers of that persuasion'.[64]

Much the same could have been said of England. And even in Ireland James' policies did not prosper. He disliked and distrusted the native Irish catholics, and he feared that in Ireland a 'catholicising' policy would threaten the English ascendancy. That one important fact alone proves that James was by no means the religious maniac he is often made out to be. If the interests of the catholic church alone had moved him, then Ireland would have been an ideal field for him to labour in; but James put the interests of England before those of his faith. Nor did the Irish catholics miss the point, for in dealing with King James they were hard bargainers. But James, beguiled into it by Sunderland, made the bad mistake of appointing Richard Talbot, Earl of Tyrconnel, an old crony from his rakish ducal days, as Lord-Deputy. It was an irretrievable blunder, for Tyrconnel had for years been struggling to have the Irish Act of Settlement repealed and dispossessed catholic proprietors restored. This was his policy as Lord-Deputy. To implement it he began to build up a catholic army in Ireland, which if it did not alarm James as much as it alarmed his English subjects still rendered him uneasy. An English popish king found Ireland almost as much of a problem as did a protestant king.

Throughout, William of Orange was a keen and increasingly disturbed on-looker. His great preoccupation was to foil the territorial aims of Louis XIV, and for William England's goodwill was vital. The prospect of England becoming paralysed by internal dissensions, or, worse, slipping into the orbit of King Louis, appalled William. But he had other reasons as well for his keen interest in English affairs. William of Orange, who was of Stewart descent, stood next in the succession after James' daughters, and his marriage to Mary, the elder of these, was well-calculated to strengthen his expectations. He had dallied with the Exclusionists, partly to maintain his own interest, partly in an attempt to fore-stall the growth of republicanism, and but for the rivalry of Monmouth he would probably have gone more deeply into the designs of the Whigs. With the execution of Monmouth, William's position was enhanced, and by June 1687 he was in communication with the gathering opposition to James that was headed by such prominent figures as Halifax and Danby.

Much learned ink has been spilled on the problem of when William decided to enter into a conspiracy against his father-in-law, but the controversy is pretty pointless. From his youth William may have dreamed of the throne of England;

but in this matter he was a passive rather than an active agent. Not his desires but shifting and unpredictable circumstances made the realisation of his dream possible. But though he could not by himself create the necessary conditions he was remarkably adept at biding his time and seizing his opportunity. It was really James' folly that made the realisation of William's dream seem possible. Such rash actions as James' wild tampering with the universities, and above all the trial of the seven bishops, alienated public opinion in England. Even High Churchmen flinched and desperately glossed their most cherished convictions: after all, 'Nothing can secure the Crown that destroys the Mitre' can be read in two senses. Bishop William Lloyd of St. Asaph later managed to square the circle: 'For the people's union with their prince; though it cannot be dissolved but by a sentence from God; yet by the prince's own act it may be so loosened, that it may be next to dissolution.'[65] With the aid of such casuistry most Anglicans were willing to preserve their doctrines of passive obedience, especially as the decision could be taken in easy instalments. In the summer of 1688 Whigs and Tories invited William to come over and restrain, not displace, the king. This time the Prince of Orange responded to the feelers from England, which he had hitherto treated with diplomatic caution. The birth of the Prince of Wales on 10 June 1688 had given urgency to the project by depriving William of his strongest ally—time. He could not thereafter afford to wait for James' death, for Mary now stood not first but second in the succession.

It would scarcely be too much to claim that James himself was the real architect of the Revolution. His folly precipitated it; his dithering incompetence, in marked contrast to William's cold efficiency, fostered it; and his panic-stricken flight to France in December 1688 consummated it. On the other side, it is by no means clear that William landed with the fixed intention of deposing his father-in-law; and even if he had entertained such a hope, it is again by no means clear that Danby and the others who had aided and abetted his enterprise would have stood for it. To put James under restraint, not to depose him, seems to have been the prime objective of the plotters. James' flight carried the plot to its logical, if undesired, conclusion, and enabled the Tories to salve their conscience with the sophistry that he had, constructively at any rate, abdicated and that the legitimist heirs succeeded. The absurd fiction that the Prince of Wales was a changeling served its purpose by preserving the theory of indefeasible hereditary right in the desired direction.

The Revolution was made in England, and that was how it turned out in England; but in Scotland the Revolution ran a very different course, and one that was to affect profoundly the relations between the two kingdoms.

9

The Revolution and Anglo-Scottish Relations

COMPLIMENTARY titles have been showered on the Revolution of 1688. It has, at different times, been variously described as 'Glorious', 'Happy', 'Bloodless', 'Respectable', 'Sensible', 'Moral'—and, best of all, if the least complimentary, 'Unexpected'. Label-slapping is not much of an aid to history; and all that can be said for such a multiplicity of different posters is that, perhaps unconsciously, it indicates the complex realities that underlay, and arose from, an apparently simple event. The fall of King James was simple indeed; but the changes ushered in by the Revolution were to have profound effects, both in the short and long terms, and were to be particularly evident in Anglo-Scottish relations. The relationship between the two countries was subtly altered because, although the Revolution was made in England, the Scots did not slavishly follow the English Revolution Settlement. In sum, after the Revolution English ministers came to wield influence over Scotland, a development that was particularly marked in Queen Anne's reign; but the Scottish parliament, once freed from the shackles of the Committee of the Articles, was no longer inclined meekly to rubber-stamp directives from London. In spite, therefore, of growing English influence over Scottish ministers, Scotland's rôle was changed from a relatively passive to a more active one. And from the friction caused by this more abrasive relationship came the crisis that ultimately led to the Treaty and the Acts of Union of 1707.

Again it is futile to rationalise these developments as parts, albeit unconscious, of a Grand Design for union pursued by the enlightened through the ages. Some hard and well-known facts ground such *ballons d'essai*, notably that in 1689 (as even Professor Smout is forced to concede[1]) England cared nothing for a complete union with Scotland. That matter will be examined in its proper place; at the moment the fundamental point is that the so-called union question did not figure in the Revolution Settlements. Instead, at the Revolution each country consulted its own interests and concentrated on its own problems. And by so doing they virtually destroyed the *raison d'être* of the Union of the Crowns.

In this negative way the Revolution Settlements are indeed of prime importance to the union question. Quite simply, the union of 1707 cannot be explained unless the circumstances that gave rise to the crisis in the early years of Anne's reign are understood, and that cannot be done unless the importance of the Revolution

Settlements is appreciated and their implications fully grasped. Here hindsight (a fashionable weapon in the historian's armoury at present) is of no avail whatsoever. Worse, it is an impediment. The great need is not to simplify by making timeless and abstract theoretical models (as Professor Smout and, somewhat more guardedly, Mrs. Mitchison do[2]), but rather to recreate, with every regard to chronology and to accuracy of statement, the complexities that baffled contemporaries and finally drove them, for diverse reasons, into the courses of action that culminated, almost through a series of accidents and desperate shifts, on Mayday 1707 when the Treaty and Act of Union came into force. That Treaty was the resultant of these forces and cannot be understood except in their context; what the union of 1707 subsequently became depends on other contexts.

The complexities extend further. For example, in considering the Revolution Settlements it would be a grave error to fasten only on those aspects that seem to have a bearing on the attainment of union, however tangential. Though union was not in the thoughts of the English Convention and the succeeding parliament that elaborated the Revolution Settlement, what they achieved and what they initiated were of prime importance to the operation of union later. For one thing, the English Revolution Settlement, apparently so tame and so bland in itself, led by slow degrees and through unforeseen circumstances to the system of government that has until recently characterised the United Kingdom and its former overseas dependencies. It is from 1689 that the sovereignty of parliament dates its real origin, though aspects of it had been foreshadowed in the past. But in practice these earlier claims furnished few pointers for the Convention of 1689. The Long Parliament of Charles I, for example, buffeted by revolutionary gales of a very different order from those of 1689, had ended in the rule of the sword and of a single person—an experiment that the English people, with few dissentient voices, was unwilling to repeat. Fear of anarchy was perhaps the main determinant of the Revolution Settlement in England. Nor did the struggle against the Restoration monarchy dictate the terms of the Revolution Settlement, the nature of which was not determined by Shaftesbury's theories.

The Revolution Settlement in England was a compromise and not the Whig triumph hallowed by tradition. The Declaration of Rights, which retained most of the prerogative powers of the crown, went only part of the way towards the Whig theory of contract, and the Bill of Rights was even less Whiggish.[3] The fictions that James II had 'abdicated the government' and that the Prince of Wales was spurious were maintained to ensure that the crown then descended to the next legitimate heir, Mary. All this was in deference to Tory and High Church opinion, which was deeply entrenched in the House of Lords, and possibly even as a sop to Jacobitism. But William's early refusal to act as regent for the Prince of Wales, or latterly to rank simply as Mary's consort, gave a dash to such disingenuous exercises in legitimism. The Prince of Orange's accession to the throne was an obvious breach of indefeasible hereditary right, and it troubled many who had no particular hankering after James. Then, again, there were many in England (and Scotland too) like the historian Edward Gibbon's haberdasher grandfather whose opinions were subordinated to his interest, and who was to be found later in Flanders 'clothing King William's troops, while he would have contracted with more pleasure, though not perhaps at a cheaper rate, for the service of King James'.[4] Such prudential considerations apart, Dutch William's Calvinism, coldness and European outlook all contributed to his unpopularity.

The basic problem of attitudes to the Revolution at the time has been bedevilled by chronic failure to examine Jacobitism, which was not just an addled sentiment. The philosophy of Jacobitism went to the core of the matters at issue, and the Jacobites cannot be dismissed as mere divine right dotards at long last dispatched by 'progress'. In fact most Jacobites had little truck with the moth-eaten *iure divino* notions of such canonical works as the *Basilikon Doron* or Filmer's *Patriarcha*. Thus, to represent the grand debate at the Revolution as between followers of Locke and supporters of Filmer is quite misleading. Instead, the Jacobites came dangerously close to stealing the Revolutionist thunder by appealing to constitutional and legal arguments which showed that the only compact known to the laws of England was that of King, Lords, and Commons, and that strict hereditary succession was an essential feature of the constitution.[5] The last apart, James II never really understood or accepted these views; but his son and heir did. Incidentally, two generations later the great English lawyer Sir William Blackstone (though intent on justifying the Revolution) shared some of these views—notably that government was vested in King, Lords and Commons.[6]

Faced by all these difficulties, the Revolutionists made only minor amendments to the constitution. The Bill of Rights asserted the primacy of law and condemned not only the suspending power but also, if more ambiguously, the dispensing power—'as it hath been assumed and exercised of late'. The rest of the prerogative powers of the crown remained intact, though in practice henceforth treated simply as a branch of law. Papists were debarred from the succession, and the Test Act and the Anglican establishment were upheld.[7] Protestant dissenters were given a grudging measure of toleration, nothing like as generous as that accorded to them by King James, and with this they had to be content. Partial toleration became the solution to the religious problem in England; and, in a way, it extended even to Roman catholics whom William, to please his ally Pope Innocent XI, went out of his way to protect from the full rigours of the law. In short, the grand aim of the English 'Sensible Revolution' in both matters ecclesiastical and secular was to minimise friction, and it was, therefore, cautious in all respects. The English Revolution Settlement, intensely conservative and largely concerned to safeguard property rights and privileges, thus had little or no radical content. No effort was made to reform an electoral system whose defects were already notorious;[8] nor was any attempt made to tackle social problems such as poor relief or education. In short, the English Revolution, which was restricted mainly to law and custom, catered almost exclusively for the 'political nation', whose charter it became; and the really important changes evolved over a period of time in the custom rather than in the law of the constitution. Indeed, the Revolution has been something of a historical mirage; or, to vary the image, a premature Victorian magic lantern show, the quality of the illusion depending on the necessity for belief as well as on expert manipulation.

The development of parliament is very much a case in point. After 1689 parliament met annually not because it was required to do so by law but for practical reasons, the chief of which was not just to pass an annual Mutiny Act but the need to finance a great European war. Indeed, it would be hard to overstress the consequences of the changes in government finance that began in the 1690s in order to wage war on an unprecedented scale against France.[9] In this way parliament gradually consolidated its control of finance and thus obliquely gained a voice over policy, for only on such terms could massive supplies be voted. In time this led to a new relationship between executive and legislature whereby the king's ministers became in practice more responsible to parliament, not simply in the final (and in the past sometimes fatal) resort, but as part of their everyday work. The triennial act of 1694 also led to more frequent elections, which meant more frantic electioneering and the extension of party distinctions from Westminster to the constituencies. But the precise nature and function of political parties in England during William's reign still awaits investigation in depth, though it is significant that, much as Gilbert Burnet disliked the terms 'Whig' and 'Tory', he found them necessary for any meaningful discussion of post-Revolution politics.[10] In William's reign, however, the real political conflict seems to have lain between Court and Country, with the Country Party composed of dissident Whig as well as Tory elements.

Such matters are far from irrelevant to our theme, because not the least of the consequences of post-Revolution political developments was the impact of party on Anglo-Scottish relations. Hitherto the crown had been the main link between the two countries, but, after the Revolution, parliament and the attitudes of the political parties gradually grew in importance. The English Revolution had introduced limited monarchy, and this came to mean that 'Limited monarchy in conjunction with the Union of the Crowns gave to the king's English ministers the indirect rule of Scotland, and the means to sacrifice Scottish interests to English prosperity'.[11] It also meant, as we shall see, the introduction of a new factor—the growing influence of English and Scottish political parties over Anglo-Scottish relations.

So far we have been discussing developments in England; but it was not these alone that changed the nature of Anglo-Scottish relations. Indeed, the effects of the Revolution in Scotland were even more decisive in undermining the *status quo ante*. The settlement in Scotland, in spite of superficial resemblances to its English counterpart, ran its own course. For example, in form the Scottish Claim of Right follows the Bill of Rights, but crucial differences lie in the small print. They arose because in Scotland the Revolution produced a storm which released all sorts of pent-up frustrations for which hitherto no constitutional means of redress had existed. Thus the 'Unexpected Revolution', as Bishop Burnet rightly called it, was eagerly seized upon by many disgruntled groups that hoped to profit from the situation. These groups aimed at different ends, a point that is often obscured because of frequent temporising and the formation of strange tactical alliances in a situation that long remained fluid and uncertain. The ends envisaged ranged from Jacobite desires to undo the Revolution and free Scotland from covert English control, to widespread demands for reforms in both church and state. Among the active politicians the main emphasis was on reform of the state; but the church question was one of the main battlegrounds, partly because of popular pressures which the parliamentarians could barely control and therefore could not ignore.

Here then was one great point of difference—in England the Established Church survived the Revolution not only unscathed but strengthened, and regarded indeed as an essential part of the constitution. After the Revolution the phrase 'the constitution in church and state' reflected existing realities. In Scotland no such easy solution was possible. There the church question was more vexed than ever. The mass of the presbyterians, who a few months earlier had been fulsomely thanking King James for his indulgence, rallied to William in the confident expectation that their system of church government would be restored by law. But they suffered from serious weaknesses. Most of the presbyteries were notional and those that had an existence in fact were weak and feebly organised, while the establishment was manned by episcopalians whose goodwill William was keen to secure. He did not wish the Scottish Church to diverge from the Church of England, knowing as he did that this would tend to cause friction between the two kingdoms. William also believed in toleration and hoped for comprehension, his preference for which was reinforced after he learnt that episcopacy in Scotland was not just 'tulchanism' imposed by authority, as the presbyterian exiles in Holland had assured him, but had in fact won acceptance in wide areas of the country north of Tay and did not altogether lack support south of Tay.[12] But any chance of maintaining episcopacy or securing comprehension was dashed by the intransigence of the Scottish bishops, who, unlike most of their English brethren, were over-dependent on the crown. James remained 'the darling of heaven' to the Scottish bishops, who clung desperately to the doctrine of non-resistance. This fixation gave the church question a new lease of life in Jacobitism, and, though no longer the public force it had been, religion managed to entangle itself in post-Revolution politics.

But one of the really significant features of the Revolution in Scotland was that the most powerful body of opinion in the Convention of Estates of 1689 aimed at reforming the state rather than the church. The Club, however, as the constitutional reformers soon came to be called, did not have matters all its own way.[13] Nor did the main resistance to the Club come from the Jacobites. At the opening of the Convention the Jacobites were numerous, mustering almost half the total membership; but, obviously shell-shocked by events, ill organised and feebly led they were soon outmanoeuvred. By the end of March 1689 William's supporters dominated the Convention, from which the one resolute Jacobite leader, though an indifferent politician, Viscount Dundee (the former John Graham of Claverhouse), had withdrawn in disgust, determined to support King James in other ways. Even then the reformers did not have a clear field in which to work, but were strongly opposed by a reactionary court party headed by the President of the Convention, the Duke of Hamilton, which, among other diversions, advocated union with England.

Much is often made of the efforts made to promote a union at the Revolution, but even when every scrap of evidence is carefully examined the project cannot be said to have amounted to much.[14] The first suggestion for a union seems to have come from William's Scottish supporters at their meeting with him in

London in January 1689. William saw its obvious utility, so far as his own problems were concerned, and accordingly recommended it to the Convention of Estates. Clearly a union would help to establish the Revolution and safeguard the Revolutionists. Certainly it is significant that those who really pushed the idea of union were ministerialists like Sir John Dalrymple and Lord Melville, who hoped that, in addition to any other merits it might have, it would abort demands for radical reform. For a time other groups with other purposes backed, or in some cases seemed to back, the union proposal. The Jacobites saw it as a useful delaying tactic, while others were genuinely willing to countenance it, but for reasons very different fron those urged by the Court. In a letter of 8 January 1689, for example, Andrew Fletcher of Saltoun supported the idea, giving it as his opinion that 'we can never come to any trew setelment but by uniting with England in Parliaments and Trade'. Professor Smout is obviously fascinated by this letter, which he seems to have been the first to uncover, and concludes that it illustrates the strength of pro-union sentiment in Scotland in 1689. This assumes that there was such an indivisible entity as 'pro-union sentiment'; but, even if such a dubious proposition could be demonstrated, the letter is too cryptic in its terms to support such an assertion.[15]

Fletcher's views, and his subsequent change of front, were largely peculiar to himself and can readily enough be explained. The clue lies in the date of the letter, a salutary reminder that chronology is, after all, of the basic stuff of history. The date is given in Scots style. The year it refers to is 1689, and thus the letter was written just before the English Convention Parliament met. At the time of writing that letter Fletcher thought that the English constitution was about to be radically overhauled and the monarchy subjected to stringent limitations—exactly the programme that he later urged in Scotland. Fletcher then believed that his programme could best be achieved by union with a like-minded England; and in a pamphlet published in March 1689 he made it clear that he advocated union to safeguard the still-imperilled Revolution. Whatever happened, says Fletcher, James and arbitrary government must not be restored: another danger loomed in Scotland where authoritarians were conspiring to abort the reforms the country so badly needed: in these circumstances, Fletcher concludes, a union with England 'would redound to all sorts of people, and would be the only means to support an impoverished and sinking nation'.[16] But, faster than the compositors could work, events demolished Fletcher's hopes.

Andrew Fletcher's great concern was for constitutional government on an extreme Whig, and largely idiosyncratic, model, and when the Revolution Settlement in England failed to develop as he had hoped it would he changed his mind about the desirability of a union which could only render radical reform in Scotland more difficult if not indeed impossible. Great patriot though Fletcher was, he was no narrow nationalist; and, as we shall see, there was every reason why from the standpoint of his own political philosophy he should have hated the union of 1707, which preserved so many of the reactionary institutions of Scotland while killing off its most progressive one, the parliament.

As it was, the union project of 1689 got nowhere. True, on 23 April an act nominating commissioners to treat for a union was passed by the Convention of

Estates, which was by then safely in William's hands, and as a consequence those nominated were all firm Revolutionists.[17] But the act proved to be a dead letter, for in England the project met with blank indifference. In practice nothing was done at the Revolution about a union of the two kingdoms.

Anyway, the problems that faced Scotland were too numerous, and too important, to be postponed indefinitely by vague talk of union. William soon realised this and pinned his hopes on Scotland doing as England had done—that is, offering the crown to himself and Mary with only trifling amendment of the constitution. But it could not be. In Scotland the master problem opened up by the Revolution concerned the extent to which constitutional reform should be carried.

The early deliberations of the Convention of Estates set the pace. A majority refused to accept the fiction that James VII had abdicated and instead resolved, with only five dissentients, that through his misdemeanours he had forfeited the crown. The resolution strongly implied a contractual monarchy, an idea that was further elaborated in the Claim of Right which, though modelled on the English Bill of Rights, pressed on to very different conclusions. Some of the Claim of Right's radical features had indeed been raised in the early discussions in England but, attracting little support, had soon been dropped. The Claim of Right retained these radical features and was thereafter accepted by many as the basis of the Scottish constitution. As well as asserting that James had forfeited the crown, it laid down that no papist could be sovereign or hold office; that the royal prerogative could not override law; that the consent of parliament was necessary for the raising of supply; that parliament should meet frequently and debate freely; and that prelacy was 'a great and insupportable grievance and trouble to this nation'.[18] It should be stressed, however, that the Claim of Right was also very much a propaganda weapon, and that its numerous and tediously repetitive charges against James should not all be taken at their face value. The truth is that it was not just James VII but the whole conception of divine right monarchy that was under attack, and the unfortunate James was made the scapegoat.

Ideally, what the extreme reformers aimed at was a return to the constitution of 1641, but this neither William nor his ministers were prepared to accept, so confirming Fletcher of Saltoun's fears. Thus Sir James Dalrymple wrote to the Scots secretary Melville on 9 April 1689 fulminating against a scheme to resurrect the act of 1641 whereby parliament would nominate to offices of state, Privy Council and judicatures: 'that,' warned Sir James 'was to leave nothing to the king but an empty name'.[19] The autocratic William would not have it, and on these issues a fierce struggle was joined. By June, Hamilton, the President of the Convention, was informing William of a widespread discontent 'lest the Government return to the old channels so often complained of'.[20] Among other radical measures a bill to exclude from office any who had served in James' administration was aimed pointedly at the Dalrymples. The 'prerogative men', who realised that a genuine parliamentary regime was dangerous for them, fought back and the bill was lost. But the Club refused to desist from its efforts at reform and was particularly adamant in its demand for the abolition of the Committee of the Articles.

The constitutional opposition was not the sole difficulty with which the government had to contend. It was also hamstrung by Dundee's rising and did not begin to gain confidence until after the battle of Killiecrankie on 27 July 1689. There Dundee's Highland levies scored a victory which if properly exploited might have placed Scotland as well as Ireland in the hands of King James; but Dundee's death in that same battle robbed the Jacobites of their advantage, and thereafter the rebellion languished. This did not, however, end the tale of the government's woes. It was further weakened by religious dissensions in the country at large, and it did nothing to help itself by vacillating weakly between presbyterians and episcopalians. Thus when the government was at its weakest point, in July 1689, episcopacy was abolished by act of parliament. This was done to placate the presbyterians, whose support was then essential, but, with seeming illogicality, presbyterianism was not restored and for almost a year the kirk lurched on as best it could. To some extent this was again owing to the machinations of the Club, which refused to allow a settlement of the church before constitutional reforms had been carried out.

The first session of William's parliament, therefore, failed to settle the kingdom. Not until 1690 was an accommodation reached, for only then did compromise become possible as William's needs pressed even more and, providentially, the strength of the Club declined. The Revolution was at a crucial point, and for William, preparing for his campaign in Ireland, a settlement in Scotland was imperative. It was made possible by the weakening of the Club owing to the complicity of some of its leaders in a Jacobite plot (the details of which, incidentally, prove that constitutionalism and Jacobitism were not incompatibles). The Club, its strength further sapped by skilled government management and the adroit use of influence, put up little resistance in the parliament of 1690. The mournful epitaph on the Club, and on the equally distracted Jacobites, by a simple soul who passed as one of the leaders of the latter, was that 'never men made a more miserable figure in any assembly than your friends did in this'.[21] As a result the basis of a deal was soon reached between government and parliament —presbyterianism in return for moderate constitutional reform. The Lords of the Articles were abolished and presbyterianism was restored, but presbyterianism based on the safe act of 1592 and not on the covenanting model. A more controversial measure abolished lay patronage in the church, a move that could be justified in that most of the patrons were anti-presbyterian and of episcopalian, and even Jacobite, sympathies; but William disliked this measure, partly because it infuriated the most powerful social and political class in the country—the landowners—whose support he sorely needed. Calvinist though he was by upbringing, William was a natural erastian; indeed he was more deeply read in Machiavelli than in the Bible, and his relations with the kirk were never cordial and were at times strained.

The Revolution Settlement in Scotland, then, was a compromise one, but unlike its English counterpart this gave it no emollient effects. In England the extremists were neutralised by a powerful combination of moderates drawn from both Whigs and Tories. In Scotland, however, there was no powerful centre coalition to hold the ring, and the extremists, Whig as well as Jacobite, continued to harass the government and even, from time to time, to co-operate against the Revolution Settlement. The country also remained seriously divided, with support for King James widespread, particularly in the Highlands and North East Lowlands. Nor was that support based purely on sentiment. James had befriended the Highlanders and protected them from the worst excesses of which Campbells and Edinburgh administrations were capable. The same could not be said for King William, as the atrocious blunder of the Massacre of Glencoe in February 1692 made abundantly plain.[22] Even among convinced Whigs William's reputation never quite recovered from that mad act. Jacobitism also derived much of its support from disgruntled episcopalians—the non-jurors who refused to swear allegiance to William and Mary. William tried hard to placate them, but they proved to be as stubborn as their old enemies, the Cameronians. As a body the non-jurors were not to be won over, and all that William achieved by his efforts at toleration was the souring of the presbyterians, his natural allies.

All things considered, William of Orange enjoyed little success or popularity in Scotland. His subsequent canonisation in protestant folklore derives largely from Irish elements which filtered into Scotland in the nineteenth century. William regarded Scotland as a nuisance, a country whose meagre resources contributed little to his epic struggle against Louis XIV but whose problems might, if not firmly handled, jeopardise his task. His attitude to Scotland was therefore ambivalent, a mixture of distaste and apprehension, and his policies were offhand and intermittent according to which feeling prevailed. Matters were rendered more difficult by the fact that throughout the 1690s the political situation in Scotland was in a state of flux, and at no time did William manage to secure stable government. True, in England he found a similar state of affairs, but there, by applying himself to the problem, he found a reasonably effective answer.

For his failure in Scotland, William himself was largely to blame. Cold and untrusting, he did not have the personal gifts that inspire devotion and loyalty; and this lack of charisma was a serious defect. Kingcraft was still an essential part of government; but to the autocratic William, who was determined to be a king in the mystical Stewart mould, kingcraft was a sealed book. He differed from James in being intelligent, but mistakenly he equated kingcraft with power and self-interest; he never suspected that it had to be worked at just as hard as diplomacy. And so he lacked popular appeal. Brave, intelligent, persevering—he was all of these things. But as a king he fell far short of the first class.

In fairness to William, however, it must be stressed that in Scotland he faced an extremely difficult situation. Not only was half the nation Jacobite at heart (though inevitably the activists were much fewer) but also the Scottish statesmen of this period were extremely corrupt and self-seeking. This had long been the case, but the Revolution gave freer rein to these dangerous qualities. Formerly, corrupt and self-seeking though Scottish politicians undoubtedly were, in the last resort they had been amenable to royal control; but after the Revolution William's lack of interest encouraged faction and intrigue. He also tried to play safe by seldom giving his ministers precise instructions, and it is curiously significant how most of his Scottish ministers bitterly complained of his negligence. In short, they wanted firm directives and could not get them. Worse, William too readily dropped those who had the intelligence to formulate policies and the nerve to pursue them. Unadmirable though they were in some respects, both Hamilton and the Master of Stair had legitimate complaints against William on this score; and later, over the affair of the Company of Scotland, Tweeddale and Secretary Johnstone were even more shabbily treated. In such an atmosphere the Scots nobles and lairds fought furiously for office and even more viciously to retain it, feverishly undermining each other and desperately currying favour with court favourites. Of the favourites, the principal 'undertakers' were William Carstares, the prominent presbyterian churchman who was one of William's few intimates, and the Dutchman, Hans Willem Bentinck, Earl of Portland.

The conferment of such powers on a parvenu presbyterian minister and a foreign favourite galled such grandees as Hamilton, Atholl, Argyll and others who jostled fiercely for position. But, as William well knew, the loyalty of the Scottish nobles to the Revolution regime was a shifting commodity. Two examples culled from many must here suffice. In December 1688 the Duke of Hamilton had advised King James to flee, not to France but to Scotland where, Hamilton assured him, he would be able to defend himself until help came from France;[23] yet in the crucial year of 1689 the self-same duke acted as William's chief agent in Scotland. A similar consistency was shown by Hamilton's rival Atholl, who would willingly have served William but in pique at being passed over in favour of Hamilton turned to the Jacobites, and them he as readily deserted when he saw that the Convention would declare for William. The second Duke of Queensberry's career looks more consistent since he was a Revolutionist throughout; but his later conduct suggests that his consistency lay rather in relentless pushing of the family fortunes. Argyll was restored by the Revolution and was more or less committed to it; but his real motive was self-interest, since his restoration revived in the Highlands all the old animosities against his House. And most of these magnates still wielded feudal powers over their dependents, real and formidable powers that were enforceable through heritable jurisdictions and private courts, powers that heavily reinforced the still strong ties of kinship. Indeed, these very powers were shored up by the Revolution, for James VII and II, who had his moments of unblinkered vision, seems to have been ready to demolish these hoary feudal anachronisms which he saw did much to keep the Highlands in disorder and more generally to weaken the central administration.[24]

In the end in both England and Scotland William, who was distrustful of party and was frequently absent on the continent, operated a system of management in which he relied increasingly on individuals who had no strong political beliefs or party ties and to whom statesmanship differed little from estate administration. They were 'managers' pure and simple whose main business was to act as intermediaries between crown and parliament. In England the renegade Sunderland exemplified once more his famous quip, 'What matter who serves His Majesty so long as His Majesty is served?', and guided William from 'behind the curtain'.[25] In Scotland the king found an equally able and unscrupulous manipulator of opinions and consciences—James Ogilvie, subsequently Viscount Seafield and later still Earl of Findlater. Like Sunderland, Seafield too was an ex-Jacobite; but in that age of chronic double-dealing their known past transgressions were actually security clearances.

There was need for such calculating and unpatriotic heads, for in the new set of circumstances created after 1689 the relations between the two countries steadily deteriorated. The strength of each country's parliament increased after the Revolution, though in Scotland skilful management still enabled the ministry to retain a grip on the legislature. Nonetheless, Scottish ministries were now between the upper and the nether millstones, caught between the Court, which reflected English interests, and the Country which resented English interference. And in both theory and fact the Scottish parliament was a fully sovereign body, able to pass laws without reference to England or her needs, and able too if it felt strongly enough about them to force their acceptance on the executive.

William's foreign wars speeded on the process of alienation between the two kingdoms, for again Scotland's trade was sacrificed on the altar of a foreign policy that was really English. Scotland had gradually lost her most-favoured nation status with France, partly as a consequence of growing economic nationalism but partly too because of her political connection with France's enemy England. Yet a large part of Scotland's trade still lay with France, and that trade was severely hampered by the War of the League of Augsburg in which French privateers wreaked havoc on Scottish shipping which the English navy refused to protect and actually prevented from trading with France.[26] For all this sacrifice the Scots won nothing at the Peace of Ryswick in 1697, a point that was bitterly noted. Fletcher of Saltoun was not one of those Scots, common enough in our own day, who affect to regard economic growth as a political or social evil, and he acidly commented: 'notwithstanding the great and unproportionable numbers of sea and land soldiers that we were obliged to furnish for the support of the war, yet not one tittle of advantage was procured to us by the peace'.[27]

And still no concessions could be wrung from the English, who stringently applied their Navigation Laws and used war-time conditions to clamp down on illegal trading by the Scots with the English colonies. The position, bad since the Restoration, was becoming impossible, and there can be no doubt that economic affairs were causing much jealousy and ill-will between England and Scotland. This appeared in heightened form over the activities of the Company of Scotland that was established in 1695.

It is difficult to give a brief, accurate and just account of the Company of Scotland. The matter is complex and moved through various stages, to every one of which due attention needs to be paid. On the whole, encapsulating historians tend to take the easy way out and misrepresent the whole matter as a piece of sublime lunacy destined from the beginning to end 'silent upon a peak in Darien'.[28] True, such historians usually seek to cover themselves by stating that the matter is complex and letting it go at that; as a method, this is as useless as that which pivots on rhetorical questions and masquerades as analysis. The factual data have to be not only mentioned but examined and evaluated, and when this is done the Company of Scotland appears in a rather different light—not better, not worse, but significantly different. The greatest difference is that it acquires perspective and cannot be viewed simply as a catastrophic eccentricity. That is the all-important point; the act of the Scots parliament of 1695 which established the Company and gave it extremely favourable privileges did not come like a bolt from the blue.[29] It was indeed part of a programme designed to free Scotland from the economic restrictions imposed on her by English policy. The need for a Scottish colony to expand markets had long been canvassed, and as long before as 1681 a Memorial to the Privy Council advocated several possible locations, including part of Jamaica which was possessed by England but still claimed by Spain.[30] In pursuance of this policy Scots settled part of New Jersey, and a small Scottish colony at Stuart's Town in South Carolina was established only to be destroyed by the Spaniards in 1686. Some Glasgow merchants who traded extensively if illegally with the American colonies then urged the royal burghs to press for further colonisation under purely Scottish aegis. Incidentally, it will be noted that the situation in the colonial territories was more fluid than is generally supposed—claims to sovereignty over vast tracts of territories abounded but actual possession was much more limited. Indeed, in this period the scramble for America was becoming one of the major sources of international disturbance. That the Scots could operate in any large way here was obviously impossible; but what the Danes and Brandenburgers could do they might reasonably hope to emulate. At any rate, the idea caught on, and in 1693 the Scottish parliament passed an act to enable the formation of joint-stock companies to trade with countries not at war with the King of England or Scotland. This act seems to have been sponsored by English and Anglo-Scottish interests keen to utilise the new-found power of the parliament of Scotland. Its terms were vague and may, or may not, have empowered companies set up under the act to combine colonising with their commercial operations.

Other points bearing on the formation of the Company of Scotland need to be taken into account. William sanctioned the act of 1695, well apprised of its contents, in order to divert public attention from a murkier matter, that of Glencoe. Nor, to begin with, was William Paterson's Darien Scheme taken up by the projectors of the Company. The Company of Scotland really began as an Anglo-Scottish venture, with English merchants and financiers eager to partici-pate and so overcome their exclusion from the most lucrative parts of overseas trade which were monopolised by the great chartered companies. These politic heads would have nothing to do with Paterson's scheme, even though Paterson was their intermediary with the Scottish directors.

Lack of space precludes any detailed consideration of the Company's activities; the main facts, however, are well known and need not be recited here. No serious student should have any difficulty in discovering how the English chartered companies, alarmed by the extensive privileges granted to the Company of Scotland, raised an outcry in the English parliament and forced the English subscribers to withdraw from the venture; how the Directors of the Company tried to obtain help in Amsterdam and Hamburg, only to be thwarted in Amsterdam by the jealousy of the Dutch East India Company and in Hamburg by William's resident; how, left to their own devices, the Company determined to carry on and, foolishly, decided to stake everything on Paterson's glowing vision of a great entrepot on Darien; and how, as much through mismanagement as through the opposition of Spain and England's continuing harassment, the enterprise failed miserably. By March 1700 the last Scottish attempt at settlement in Darien ended in disaster and capitulation to the Spaniards.

The set-back was shattering, draining the country as it did of a dangerously high proportion of its liquidity. The Disaster of Darien, too, came at a bad time —the so-called Seven Ill Years when harvest after harvest failed, rents fell, trade declined, and thousands starved. The Calvinism of Scotland did not set all to the account of the Almighty. Fairly in some respects, and most unfairly in others, the blame was heaped on King William and the English. The Jacobites, indeed, with perverse glee, even referred to the Seven Ill Years as 'King William's Years'. The really important consequence of the Disaster of Darien and the depressed state of the Scottish economy was that it gave rise to criticism of the Union of the Crowns. The matter has been well summarised: 'Contemporary writers are unanimous in charging the political system established in 1603, as the main cause of the national depression, that culminated in the poverty and misery of the last decade of the seventeenth, and the opening years of the eighteenth centuries'.[31]

Fletcher of Saltoun was the most vehement and outspoken of these critics. He held that, 'partly through our own fault, and partly through the removal of our kings into another country, this nation, of all those that possess good ports and lie conveniently for trade and fishing, has been the only part of Europe which did not apply itself to commerce; and possessing a barren country, in less than an age we are sunk to so low a condition as to be despised of all our neighbours, and made uncapable to repel an injury, if any should be offered'.[32] And even the unionist-inclined Seton of Pitmedden, as well as censuring want of enterprise by the Scots, also stigmatised the Union of the Crowns as a serious obstacle to progress and concluded that if England would not grant commercial concessions to Scotland then the existing connection between the two countries should be severed.[33] It was not, moreover, simply a war of pamphlets. There was also resentment against France, and in the session of parliament of 1700 the opposition forced through an act prohibiting importation of brandy and wine until France granted Scotland fairer conditions of trade.[34]

As the affairs of the Company of Scotland worsened only rigorous management, involving bribery and the use of influence, enabled the Scottish ministry to survive. In the session of parliament of 1698 there was strong opposition which William did nothing to placate by his refusal to look at the issues and by his leaving his ministers to shift for themselves. Only narrowly was deadlock avoided. William feared further troubles in the parliament of May 1700 which, however, was necessary to raise supply. The Commissioner Queensberry shuffled desperately, even availing himself of a diplomatic cold, but to no effect. William had again pinned his hopes on a closer union and persuaded the House of Lords to make such a proposal. It was spurned by a House of Commons which, to begin with, welcomed the ructions in Scotland: the Commons were eager to embarrass William and if possible prevent him from entangling England in yet another European war. William, then, had his troubles with both parliaments;

and in an interesting letter of June 1700 to the Dutch Pensionary Heinsius he revealed his true thoughts about Scotland: 'I am sorry to be obliged to tell you that affairs go on very badly in the Scotch Parliament . . . What vexes me in particular is that this affair retards my departure for Holland, for which I long more than ever'.[35]

Thanks mainly to the able and indefatigable Seafield the Scottish administration, helped by judicious bribery, muddled through. The evident ill temper of the Scots could not be harnessed up to specific courses largely because the nation was so divided in both politics and religion. The Jacobites naturally exploited the situation to suit their own ends; but the Whigs, in both the secular and religious connotations of that term, though they were infuriated by William's callous disregard of Scotland's plight, had no wish to recall the catholic exiled Stewarts. These divisions enabled the ministry to save face, and after prolonged debate the immediate crisis was passed in January 1701.

William saw that the respite might be merely temporary and that resentment in Scotland could still easily boil over. As an acute observer of the Scottish scene remarked: 'The Lord pity the nation, for this parliament hath parted in an ill humour'.[36] But the king's thoughts were by then fully occupied with the likely repudiation of the second Partition Treaty by Louis XIV, who was under a strong temptation to secure the entire Spanish inheritance which the will of Charles II of Spain had mischievously dangled before the Bourbons. The matter was extremely complex and Louis can no longer be simply dismissed as an inveterate warmonger, for, whatever he did (stand by the Partition Treaty or accept the will), the risk of war over the Spanish succession was grave.[37] In these circumstances William, for several reasons, knew that it was essential for him to secure Scotland. As Fletcher had pointed out, that country was an important recruiting area for William's armies, Dutch as well as British, and any disaffection there might seriously reduce his manpower; and also even the remotest possibility of Scotland defecting to France had to be forestalled. Already Louis XIV was supporting the Jacobite opposition in Scotland with money and lavish promises of military aid. William, therefore, was more convinced than ever that only a complete union of England and Scotland would solve these problems. In a message to the House of Lords in February 1700 he had already urged a closer union of the two kingdoms. The death of the young Duke of Gloucester, which sharpened the problem of the succession, deepened the king's anxieties, and in his last message to the House of Commons he again urged the need for union. On 8 March 1702, within eight days of sending that message, William was dead. And in the opening years of his successor's reign it looked for a time as if his worst forebodings about Anglo-Scottish relations might be realised.

10

The Background to the Union of 1707

NORTH of Tweed the reign of the last Stewart monarch tends to be equated with the Union of 1707, but south of Tweed it elicits other responses—Marlborough's war, the struggles of Whigs and Tories, or perhaps the glittering society and brilliant literature of the Augustan Age. In English history, therefore, the union figures as little more than an incident, whereas in Scottish history its significance, for good or ill, tends to be writ large. As far as the making of the union itself is concerned English tradition furnishes the better guide, for to assess developments in Anne's reign with 1707 as the pre-determined pivot is simply to evade the real issues; and to assume further that powerful parties in both kingdoms throughout strove consistently, and with rare statesmanship, for incorporating union is to fly in the face of the facts. The evidence mocks any such easy assumptions, but in this matter the evidence has long been subjected to cavalier treatment.

The present writer has elsewhere observed that 'few matters in Scottish history have been so abused by subjectivist and determinist interpretations as the Treaty of Union of 1707', and that most writers on the subject have eloquently explained why a thing so desirable in itself emerged *naturally* and, of course, with a stainless quality curiously at odds with the political morality of the early eighteenth century. It was further contended that the existing literature was marred by far too much lofty generalisation, 'the fruits of a tendency to philosophise on events rather than analyse their causes', and that such philosophical exercises rested in too many cases on wilful refusal to close with the evidence, coupled with a marked ability to avoid awkward or 'sordid' issues.[1] The paper here summarised, which was printed in 1964, ended by predicting that the last had not been seen of such bad practices, desirable though it would be, in the interests of historical thinking, to consign them to limbo and to grapple with the brute facts of the case.

The wish has foundered, and the prediction, unfortunately, has proved all too accurate. Fresh tares of controversy have sprouted since 1964. In face of the upsurge of political Scottish nationalism the union has acquired new paladins who are unable to view the early eighteenth century except from the standpoint of present needs (in itself a fashionable, but dubious, postulate à la Collingwood in the philosophy of history). In the process they have produced some odd history. Professor Smout, for example, arguing by instalments on ever-shifting grounds, does his best to maintain the old economic determinist position and, latterly and incongruously, the imponderables of the human heart. Most specifically, Smout feels called upon to rebut the contention that influence and bribery played a major part in the making of the treaty and in securing its passage through the Scottish parliament. To him, such a view places 'upon the evidence an interpretation that it is logically unable to bear'[2]—but just why, he does not make very clear. Logic, in any event, cannot be divorced from premises, and Smout's premises are weak. On point after point his work can be faulted on the score of factual accuracy; and even more disquieting are the things that he fails to notice. His real failure is of historical grasp, of apprehending and of comprehending; and these fundamental weaknesses in Professor Smout's equipment are highlighted rather than concealed by his olympian style.

The most striking instance of muddling in the grand manner, and of passing resounding judgments on dimly apprehended problems, concerns the crucial session of the Scottish parliament in 1704. Given the basic, if veiled, premise of the present day champions of union that in the crisis between England and Scotland the only real solution lay in incorporating union, one can readily enough appreciate why at their hands the session of 1704 gets short shrift. Largely because of the attitude of the Court, Tweeddale's ministry is a real stumbling-block for the determinists, because the Court, the English ministry and the Scottish ministry then concurred in trying to carry the Hanoverian succession and not a union, incorporating or federal. In the interests of the bold over-arching theory, therefore, which scorns such idle details, the New Party ministry and the peculiar circumstances of 1704 have to be glossed over or even consigned to oblivion. Thus Mrs. Mitchison calmly disposes of the problem altogether when she holds that, 'Again in 1704 Parliament put forward the Act of Security in a modified form; this time the need for money made Queensberry give in'.[3] History is here turned on its head with a vengeance. Not only was Queensberry out of office in 1704 but also by factious opposition he helped to ruin the New Party's policy and so forced the Court to accept the dreaded Act of Security. But of that more in its place. The point to note here is that Smout also deals loosely with this whole matter. In one of his essays[4] he speaks of 'the session 1703–4' as if he were referring to a single prolonged session instead of two separate ones; and nowhere does he really examine the New Party ministry. True, in a later essay[5] he finally notices Tweeddale's ministry only to ascribe to it the wrong policy. Indeed, so confused and confusing are Professor Smout's various accounts that it is difficult to see what he is driving at.

Nor is Smout any more convincing on English politics, as the following passage indicates: 'The English ministers decided after the session of 1703–4 [sic] that there was no solution possible to the dangers from Scotland except an Incorporating Union through which the Westminster Parliament could absorb the Scottish malcontents and render them tame'.[6] Dr. Riley has recently demonstrated, in a thoroughly researched article, just how superficial and mis-leading is this view.[7]

In taking this extraordinary course over the session of 1704 Professor Smout and Mrs. Mitchison may have been unduly influenced by Daniel Defoe. But in his *History of the Union* Defoe deals very sketchily with events between 1703 and 1705, barely mentioning Tweeddale and his ministry.[8] Today, however, there is no excuse for such skimped treatment, for the main facts about Tweeddale's ministry have long been available in secondary works.[9] Besides, any serious student of the union should readily perceive that Defoe is far from being definitive as a recorder of events or as an interpreter of them. There are too many gaps in his knowledge, and he is too prone, moved by an obvious bias, to make snap judgments on little or no evidence. The book certainly has literary merit and an importance of its own, but not as history; rather it is an early example of political reporting designed to mould public opinion. Defoe's *History* is at its best in reporting the actual union debate in the Scots parliament of 1706–7, and at its weakest in dealing with the origin and course of the crisis that led to that debate.

Smout and Mitchison also go astray by failing to grasp the full implications of the crucial point that a system of 'political management' operated in Scotland in the reign of William and continued in the reign of Anne. The great Henry Dundas himself could have taught Seafield and Mar nothing of the arts of management—indeed in many ways those bold pioneers of the greasy craft could have given Dundas lessons. Contemporary evidence demonstrates that in Scotland in Anne's reign a 'spoils system' flourished and that the use of 'influence' was indispensable to government. Professor Smout seems to think that by dismissing as Namierite cynics those who disagree with him he disposes of the problem. But the answer cannot be as simple as that, for much contemporary evidence would also have to be disposed of, and that cannot be done either by turning a Nelson eye on it or bowdlerising it.

Management, in any case, did not arise just to accommodate the Treaty of Union and facilitate its passage through the Scottish parliament. The evidence for its existence, particularly in the last three years of William's reign, is irrefutable. All that can be cited here are a few examples culled from a source that has been available in print ever since 1774, namely the *Carstares State Papers*. From this source there emerges a clear picture of management at work but labouring under unwonted strains. Thus in August 1699 we find Seafield busy fixing the parliament-men in his native North-East and committing to paper his views on the problems he encountered. He writes, for example, that 'Culloden has been with me; and I think, if his pension be continued to him, we will have his assistance'. Forbes of Culloden had been one of the pillars of the Club of Revolution days but had subsequently been bought off by the Court, and rather than see him join his old friends in the Country Party further expenditure would be justified. Even more revealingly Seafield continues, 'I think also that Bracco [i.e. Alexander Duff, commissioner for Banffshire] will be assisting: I have agreed with him for £200 a-year'.[10] The value of Seafield's essays in management was recognised by the king; for similar work in 1698 he had been created a viscount, and the following year he was granted a pension of £1,000.[11]

Nor was it only Seafield who was active in this way. Commissioner Queensberry was also hard at it but in difficulties for lack of ready money. In July 1700 he pressed numerous claims on the Court, including one for a gratuity of £100 for William Paterson, who was then helping the government to ride the storm raised by his ill-starred Darien Scheme. As well, Queensberry stated that the Earl Marischal (a notorious Jacobite) might be detached from the opposition for a pension of £300.* The only difficulty stemmed from the meagreness of resources at his disposal; as Queensberry openly admitted: 'In short, if money could be had, I would not doubt of success in the King's business here; but the low condition of our treasury keeps many things out of my power, which otherwise I could easily compass'.[12]

This was no novice bragging, but a skilled and practised operator speaking from a plenitude of experience. Nor was this a rarefied game of political chess that could only be played by a few pastmasters. Such an indifferent politician as Argyll (not the union duke but his father) would also have bought off the opposition. His words are just as plain as Queensberry's, though accidence was evidently not Argyll's forte: 'When I come to speak, even with those I am best with, of making a model to carry the King's business, by buying some, purchasing others, and making places void for others, tho' these be but of the smaller sort, nor is it yet advisable; many other I meet with, this tutor has this friend to protect, the other has another, which does confound affairs . . . However . . . I will send for you, for your satisfaction and mine, a schedule, by which I'd carry thirty members of parliament off, and so carry the affair'.[13] Argyll's younger son, Archibald, later Earl of Islay and a famous eighteenth-century political manager, evidently owed as much to nature as to nurture.

The Earl of Mar, too, was at the same game, and, characteristically, was most intent on pushing his own fortunes. But he could only bring himself to such squalid things, he tells Carstares, after a struggle with his natural modesty, for, as he puts it, great as his services were, 'There is nothing I like worse than for one to overvalue himself'.[14] Still, his natural modesty would be satisfied with office and sundry other trifles.

Other sources confirm and amplify the picture of management at work provided by the *Carstares State Papers*, notably the *Seafield Correspondence*, the *Jerviswood Correspondence*, and the *Mar and Kellie Papers*. The system, however, did not begin or end in William's reign. That public morality had been at a low ebb in Scotland since the Restoration needs no demonstration; that the abolition of the Committee of the Articles in 1690 extended management because new means had to be found to enable the King's ministers to keep a hold on parliament has also long been common knowledge; and that after William's death the system was labouring under heavy strain is equally well known.[15]

The problem of management continued to be crucial so far as Anglo-Scottish relations were concerned. Indeed, the strain on the system intensified in the opening years of Anne's reign, and this in part explains the unprecedented failure of successive ministries between 1702 and 1705. It is this failure that really needs to be explained, and it cannot be explained by hauls of red-herrings. The crisis entailed defective management, and no explanation that leaves management out of the reckoning can hope to convince. But we need to be clear about

* The references here are to Scots pounds = 1/12 Sterling.

management and the conditions in which it can operate. For, as Christopher Hill has pointed out in refuting Trevor-Roper's opinion that Oliver Cromwell failed because of his ignorance of the arts of management, management only works where fundamental issues do not divide the political nation. Hill's words cannot be bettered: 'Management enables good Parliamentarians to obtain collaboration in working for agreed objectives, or in sharing spoils where objectives are not in dispute; it does not enable the best politicians in the world to square circles'.[16] In Scotland between 1702 and early 1705 management squared no circles because the divisions among the Scots were too many and ran too deep.

Yet in the end improved management helped to make the achievement of union possible. This is proved by another revealing piece of evidence that has contrived to avoid the limelight. In 1705 the second Duke of Argyll was a somewhat reluctant Commissioner faced by many problems, including a parliament that was hard to control. Though he was not a great political manager Argyll, following family tradition, in June 1705 saw where a large part of the solution must lie. He wrote to Godolphin: 'Your Lordship may remember that I told you in a note of this nature before that ten or twelve thousand pounds given to pay arrears of pensions would have been much for the Queen's service; and as then I thought, I now find the not granting of it has lost the Queen above twenty votes: this I only tell your Lordship to convince you that I do not presume to offer any advice without having solid ground for it'.[17] Later, in 1706, the plea did not go unheeded, and neither the Court nor the treaty lost thereby.

On this whole question of management and the use of influence, therefore, it is difficult to see by what 'logic' Professor Smout can transmute incontrovertible evidence into something else. Why he should even try is just as hard to follow, for Sir Lewis Namier did not, as Smout seems to imply, invent the politics of interests or the devices of management. Earlier historians understood the nature of Scottish politics in Anne's reign, though they failed to grasp the full implications of management. Hume Brown, for instance, who saw that the political system turned on management based on small electorates, says, rightly, that 'The freeholders who elected the Commissioners for the Shires, being so few in number, were easily accessible to the blandishments of the existing government, and by the bestowal of pensions and offices they could be induced to return acceptable representatives'.[18] That is management defined in a nutshell. And others as well as Hume Brown have noted that the period of the union was corrupt as well as complicated. R. H. Story summarised it as follows: 'That passionate and tortuous strife was beginning which was to end in the Union; and Jacobite stratagems, Episcopal pretensions, Presbyterian jealousies, personal dishonesties, and political corruptions, weltered together in illimitable babble and confusion'.[19] The language is a bit extravagant for present-day taste, but anyone who has studied the primary sources will appreciate the truth of Story's contention.

The conclusion that the union period was characterised by a corrupt system of management in Scotland is, therefore, neither novel nor unwarranted. But on this score another misconception furnishes a last ditch for austere moralists. They seem to believe that ritual obeisances to 'management' will somehow solve all problems, for to them management appears as a morally respectable device, free from any imputations of bribery or corruption. This is latter-day cant. It is naïve in the extreme to regard management merely as a mechanism, and, as such, as innocent as a fly-wheel. Contemporaries knew better, as when one anonymous critic of the regime in Scotland correctly and succinctly described management as 'the operative influence of men'.

Nor does the fact that politics in England was conducted more along party lines and probably in less venal fashion obscure the issue.[20] Scotland and England differed in many vital respects, notably in their constitutions and election laws, and in their social and political frameworks.[21] These differences intensified the problems that had arisen between the two kingdoms, and it is, to say the least, unrealistic to leave them out of account.

Indeed, the problem of the union and its making bristles with far more complexities than Professor Smout's social-scientific approach can well comprehend. The whole complex issue cannot be elucidated unless the essential points made above are thoroughly grasped. They are not new but old and valid points that cannot be lightly discarded. To them would have to be added: resentment over Darien and bitterness at England's veiled hostility and disregard of Scotland's economic plight; the prospect of another European war in which Scotland had little direct interest but which would seriously injure her trade; and the open interference of the queen's English ministers in Scottish affairs and not, as in William's time, through the mediation of 'undertakers'. All these things roused fury in the great majority of Scots. That fury erupted in parliament, but it did not begin or end there. Parliament was certainly the focus of interest; its proceedings were eagerly followed by the public, and virtually for the first time speeches made there flooded from the presses. But it is a cardinal error to believe that only the parliament was involved, for, diverse though the weight of public opinion was, it influenced the parliamentarians.

The Court was saved in the end by several mutable factors: by clarification of its own objectives; by the inability of the opposition groups to maintain a common front; and by improved management drawing on augmented resources, which came, however, not from the Scottish but the English treasury. Not a little luck produced this happy outcome for the Court. The opposition was formidable in numbers and at times seemed invincible, but in reality it was made up of too many disparate groups to ensure ultimate success. Indeed, at its most powerful the opposition was negative rather than positive. The great bond among its fluctuating constituent groups was detestation of the regal union and the way in which it operated against the interests of Scotland. George Lockhart of Carnwath was a bitter Jacobite propagandist but he often merely articulated views that were generally held in the Scotland of Queen Anne's day. This was certainly the case when he wrote: 'For the Union of the two Crowns may be reckoned the fatal aera from whence we are to commence Scotland's ruin'.[22]

In 1702 there were few in Scotland who retained much faith in the regal union or in the way it worked. All thinking Scots had by the end of William's reign more or less concluded that the existing connection between the two kingdoms was unsatisfactory and that it was slowly strangling the weaker partner. But what to do about it was the problem. There agreement ended and argument began, for, though it was possible for Jacobites and Countrymen to unite against a Scots ministry dominated by the Court and the English ministers, it was difficult for such an alliance of incompatibles to agree on final objectives. There is no escaping the conclusion that the matters that divided the Scottish nation added greatly to the complexities of the period. Thus Smout's habitual blanket references to 'Scots' are meaningless in this context. The Scottish nation was deeply divided, and unless its divisions are clearly understood political activities in Anne's reign, and not just up to 1707, become virtually inexplicable. These divisions, then, have to be elucidated, with reference both to parliament and country.

As is well known, at Anne's accession the Scottish parliament was polarised into two main groupings, the Court Party and the Country Party. They were not parties in the English sense, largely because general elections in Scotland were infrequent (the last had been held in 1689) and as a consequence there was minimal party organisation in the constituencies. The terms Court and Country were in common use from 1698 onwards, although of course the distinction is originally English and found in an earlier period. The Court Party, which, as its name suggests, engrossed office, existed simply to carry out orders from London, and since it controlled patronage it could usually manage parliament. In yet another respect, however, the applicability of the term 'party' is again suspect, for the Courtiers were really a loose alliance of interests and great personal followings. The magnates all had their dependants and these could usually be trusted to follow their leader. Such political ideology as existed was in fact striated by claims of kinship or old feudal ties. But, however loosely held, political ideologies were waxing, so adding to the complexity of Scottish politics, and 'cousins' and souteneurs were no longer quite the pawns they had once been.

Most members of the Court Party passed for Whigs and Revolutioners, but prominent figures in it, such as Seafield and Cromartie, could not be so described. The Old Court Party, therefore, was something of a contradiction. Though not in theory strong for the royal prerogative, the predominantly Whig Court Party in practice jealously guarded it, since only the claims of the prerogative and insistence on allegiance to the sovereign could justify the anomaly of a supposedly independent Scottish government following external directives. The prevailing Court Party line, therefore, was that government was the sovereign's preserve and that ministers merely tried to implement the policies of the Court. For this view a good case existed in law and tradition, but it did not altogether square with the existing realities. The Court Party had scant respect for parliament, and this was obviously at odds with their vaunted Revolution principles and dangerously at odds with post-Revolution developments. As an instance of this, in 1701 a leading Courtier, Viscount Stair, sneered that an act of parliament was simply a decreet of the king's baron court; but the incensed House immediately forced him to retract.[23] In spite of its professed 'Revolution Principles', therefore, the Court Party was intensely conservative and opposed to constitutional reform. Its basic attitude differed little from that of Lauderdale in the time of Charles II: office was the great thing, and tenure of office could only be secured by unswerving obedience to the Court in London.

The Court Party, voicing one part and acting the other, frequently found itself in a dilemma. Though in practice tender to the prerogative, it was also widely regarded as the Revolution Party and as such supposed to be strong for presbytery, the Claim of Right and the liberties of good protestants (which included the right to trample on papists and even recalcitrant non-juring episcopalians). In reality, the Court Party had no firmer ideological motivation than that of supporting the status quo. Its leader, the Duke of Queensberry, was a great feudal magnate with large estates in the south of Scotland whose prestige was heightened by the fact that he led the numerous Douglas connection, though not head of the house by lineage. And, as already noted, kinship, though no longer as powerful as it had been, was still of some importance in a system of politics in which the aristocracy played the leading rôle. At the most obvious level family connections helped to decide the distribution of offices, patronage and honours. Here Queensberry was in his element. Numerous factors told in his favour: the influence of the Court, his key position as commissioner, his great territorial interest, the claims of kinship among the Douglases, and his personal qualities, conspicuous among which were an ingratiating manner and a certain hard bold cunning. These advantages combined to secure for him a large following in a parliament that liked butter with its bread. It was alleged, for example, that fully half of the yield of the customs went to the collectors, who were all parliament-men and devoted followers of Queensberry.[24]

Since the status quo was so profitable Queensberry's faction would have stood by it, as long, of course, as they were in power and enjoying the fruits of the system; but when the status quo showed ominous signs of collapsing their chief concern was to save themselves and salvage as much as possible from the wreck. In these circumstances incorporating union with England had its attractions for Queensberry's group—but only, however, if they could bring it about and continue to dominate the political scene in Scotland and retain patronage in their own hands. To hold up Queensberry and his group as disinterested and statesmanlike unionists throughout the prolonged crisis in Anglo-Scottish relations is, in the light of the evidence, impossible. Of contemporary accounts only the somewhat scrappy memoirs of Clerk of Penicuik suggest such a view, and Clerk, as he honestly if naïvely explains, was one of Queensberry's clients and owed his advancement to the duke's favour.[25] No one else harboured any such illusions, and to his contemporaries Queensberry was simply a great unprincipled operator on the make. Equally suspect was the second Duke of Argyll's devotion to incorporating union, for it too was based on personal considerations of profit and advancement.[26]

By 1702 the Court Party was highly unpopular. It had an ugly image, and outside its ranks few would have disputed the truth of Andrew Fletcher of Saltoun's scathing indictment contained in a speech to the parliament in 1703: ' 'Tis nothing but an English interest in this House, that those who wish well to our country, have to struggle with at this time. We may, if we please, dream of other remedies; but so long as Scotsmen must go to the English Court to obtain offices of trust or profit in this kingdom, those offices will always be managed with regard to the Court and interest of England, though to the betraying of the interest of the nation, whenever it comes in competition with that of England. And what less can be expected, unless we resolve to expect miracles, and that greedy, ambitious, and for the most part necessitous men, involved in great debts, burthen'd with great families, and having great titles to support, will lay down their places, rather than comply with an English interest in obedience to the Prince's commands'.[27] Fletcher for one expected no miracles, and he never tired of urging radical remedies.

But the Country Party, to which Fletcher belonged, had nothing like the co-hesiveness of its rival. Essentially an umbrella movement, the opposition attracted dissident elements of all sorts united only by disenchantment with the existing ministry and its corrupt truckling. Thus it was for a time possible for radical constitutional reformers like Fletcher, who derived from the Club of Revolution days, to join in common opposition to the ministry with disappointed place-hunters like Lord Belhaven, with angry investors who had suffered heavy losses in the Darien Disaster, with presbyterians who feared for the future of the kirk or episcopalians who aimed at forcing concessions out of the Court by virtue of the queen's known devotion to episcopacy, and with Jacobites concerned to impair the relations between England and Scotland in the hope of thereby improving the Pretender's prospects. The parrot-cry of all these uneasy allies was patriotism; but although they all felt that Scotland was getting a raw deal, each group tended to be patriotic only in the light of its own interests.

In 1702–3 the most obvious cement binding this amorphous opposition to-gether was detestation of Queensberry and his myrmidons. After the disastrous parliamentary session of 1703 the Court finally realised this and dropped the commissioner, only to discover that Queensberry, hated though he was for his ruthless self-seeking, was also a surrogate target for deep-rooted resentment of a system of government that would reduce a Scottish parliament almost to the level of an Irish one. In their speeches and writings Fletcher and his associates frequently warned that Scotland was slowly but surely being subjected to the same lamentable state of dependence as Ireland.[28] This fear was not the product of overheated imaginations but had considerable justification in reality. Thus, the works of an inveterate English polemicist of some note, William Atwood, placed Scotland in a similar position to Ireland, claiming that the imperial crown of England was sovereign over all.[29] And many in Scotland could see Poynings' Laws lurking behind the easy assumption of the English ministry that the Act of Settlement of 1701 would lead automatically to an identical measure by the parliament of Scotland.

The volatile nature of the Country Party (since we must use that vague but useful portmanteau term) makes it difficult to analyse its varying composition over the five pell-mell years from 1702 to 1707. Its very title was attractive to all sorts of factions opposed to the ministry, for as adherents of the Country opposition they could plume themselves on serving the nation rather than truck-ling to the Court and the English ministry. In consequence the Jacobites some-times figured as Cavaliers and at other times as members of the Country Party. The Country Party proper, however, protean though it was, had two main seg-ments. There were those who were bent simply on redress of grievances, and there were those who advocated radical reform of the constitution. The greater number fell into the first category and their chief grievances derived from the Darien Disaster. A contemporary observer speaks of 'the Country Party, which took its rise from the ill treatment our nation met with in the last reign about the affair of Caledonia'.[30] That is a correct diagnosis. And it is noteworthy that the Duke of Hamilton, Belhaven, the Marquis of Tweeddale and other prominent members of the Country opposition had all lost heavily in the Darien Scheme. They thus had a strong vested interest in recouping their losses, and no settlement with England that did not include compensation for these would have been acceptable to them. True, Queensberry had also lost in that venture, but, able as he was to reimburse himself from the fruits of office, he could afford to make light of his losses. His philosophical deportment, however, naturally did nothing to commend him to his fellow investors who had no such means of repairing their broken fortunes. Indeed, with many the most powerful motivations derived from such human failings as envy and greed.

This was certainly the case with the recognised leader of the Country party, the Duke of Hamilton, of whom little else can be said with certainty. The heart of his mystery has yet to be plucked out largely because he seems to have been driven by a variety of conflicting motives. Jealousy played its part: the Hamilton line had failed and this duke was really a Douglas who bitterly resented Queensberry's assumed control over that still great name.[31] Hamilton, as premier duke, also sulked about being passed over by the Court in favour of his hated, and relatively parvenu, rival. It was, therefore, his ambition to pull down Queensberry, not, however, to reform the state but simply to take Queensberry's place and line his own empty pockets from the existing jobbery. Hamilton had married a wealthy English heiress but he was always short of money, partly because of his extravagance and partly because he never had full control of the Hamilton estates. These belonged to his mother, Duchess Anne, heiress of the first duke, who treated her eldest son generously but in view of his spendthrift ways was forced to retrench. Another awkwardness arose from Hamilton's relations with the Jacobites. He needed their support, and, besides, by posing as a Jacobite he was, like many others at the time, insuring against the outside possibility of a restoration. Something else again drove Hamilton on, something that was rarely mentioned but obviously deeply felt. That something was the dream of a crown if Scotland and England should go their separate ways, for Hamilton had a respectable claim to the crown of Scotland (though none to the crown of England) through descent from Mary Stewart, daughter of James II of Scotland.

Whatever Hamilton's real aim, if indeed he had one, he covered his tracks well. Clearly, though, such contradictory aspirations were apt to get in each other's way if not to cancel each other out, and possibly it was the conflicting nature of his designs that led him to make some astonishing somersaults. Thus he could successfully woo the Jacobites up to a point and even be accepted by them as their leader; but if he entertained hopes of the crown for himself he obviously could not go all the way with them. So he was forced at the same time to lean on the constitutional reformers and the presbyterians because if his dreams of a crown were ever to be realised then the Revolution Settlement must stand. Only the Claim of Right effectively shut out the catholic Pretender; if the Claim of Right were removed and the Act of Succession of 1681 stood operative and unimpeded, then no one could gainsay the right of James Stewart to the throne of his ancestors. Thus Hamilton, by wily manoeuvring, could gain support from the Jacobites; but in no circumstances could he wholeheartedly support them, and in time they realised this. On another plane of policy, Hamilton was a haughty aristocrat who could not really endorse the radical schemes proposed by Fletcher of Saltoun. As duke, never mind dream-king, Hamilton was a great feudatory with large estates in England as well as Scotland, and the weight of property and immense social powers ensured that Scotland's premier duke was a very pale parlour-pink reformer. The result was as obvious as it was predictable. When Fletcher made his astringent speeches denouncing Queensberry and his lickspittle faction he was lionised by the opposition, including its leader, but when he proposed reforms that would have reduced the powers of crown and nobility alike the applause died away and his support dwindled.

These contradictions caused Hamilton to vacillate too much and too long, and by 1706, at the climax of the union crisis, no segment of the opposition trusted him, but an alternative leader failed to materialise and so they were stuck with him. To the end the premier duke remained a mystery. In the last analysis it may be that, after all, he was merely upholding the shifty traditions of his House which had often trembled on the verge of greatness. As a consequence, the Hamiltons had long had a reputation for feverish ambition without the nerve to sustain it in a crisis, and the opposition must have known that traditionally the support of the Hamiltons was the kiss of death. Anyway, whatever it was exactly that lay at the heart of his mystery, Hamilton was the great political Micawber of his time— always waiting hopefully for something to turn up. Nor was this due entirely to the unpredictable circumstances of his time. This devious hesitancy seems to have been part of his nature, for throughout his adult life the fourth Duke of Hamilton displayed the same curious mixture of great ability flawed by egregious folly. Indeed his unbalanced nature did for him in the end, leading in 1712 to the fatal duel with Lord Mohun.

The vital nucleus of the Country Party really consisted of the constitutional reformers headed by Andrew Fletcher, the laird of Saltoun in East Lothian. They were not numerous, possibly mustering no more than a consistent twenty or so in a parliament of about 230. But of the opposition groups this was the most persistent, able and tenacious, and it had influence out of all proportion to its numbers. Unlike the opportunists and fly-by-nights, it was a party of ideas committed to a definite programme that was geared up to the needs of the country; and, as well as its idealism and drive, this group was more skilled at the parliamentary game than any other if only because it was more experienced and drew on a long tradition. It derived from Revolution days, but its basic ideas came from the first covenanting movement and the constitution of 1641. Its chief link with Montgomery's Club was Fletcher himself, and he was easily the most accomplished political thinker of his time, a fact that is usually obscured by his supposed utopianism. The fashion of the time was to slap exaggerated labels on opponents, and Fletcher and his associates were frequently described as utopian republicans. This rested solely on the fact that their aim was to cut down the prerogative powers of the crown and make responsible representative government a reality. Fletcher was the real moving force in this group though its nominal leader, until he broke away to form the New Party in 1704, was the honest and well-meaning Marquis of Tweeddale.

Fletcher's utopianism was a myth. He was an intellectual, a keen student of society who sometimes wrote in theoretical vein but nonetheless practised a starkly realistic brand of politics. Indeed, it was his theoretical explorations of political science that helped him to make realistic, if painful, assessments of Scotland's problems and requirements. Thus, far from being an ineffectual ivory-tower visionary, Fletcher's cosmopolitanism and his rigorously honest thinking strengthened his political practice. Without the deep thought and the firm conclusions it led to, Fletcher would not have cut the figure that he did. True, some of his main contentions were not novel or peculiar to himself, as when he held that the existing regal union had to be undone and a juster connection negotiated with England. Where he and his group stood out from their contemporaries, however, was in their insistence that a programme of radical reform had to be carried out in Scotland. This was Fletcher's real aim, and lacking such reform he could see no good development for Scotland.[32] At this time he resolutely opposed an incorporating union with England because he believed that it could not lead to better relations between the two countries and that it would abort the constitutional, administrative and social reforms that Scotland after half a century of reactionary stagnation so desperately needed. If it were possible to review here the course of two and a half centuries of incorporating union it could easily be demonstrated that Fletcher was not far wrong. The benefits conferred by the union were not constitutional or administrative.

In keeping with this utopian image, Fletcher is also commonly labelled as the great patriot to whom national independence and the honour of his country meant everything. In short, he tends to be dismissed as a latter-day William Wallace. The stereotype no more explains Fletcher than it does Wallace. Each was, undoubtedly, a great patriot, but in each case patriotism did not rest simply on romantic sentiment. The just society and good government were Fletcher's real passions. Thus he detested fag-end feudalism and excoriated the vicious agrarian system which allowed feudal superiors to grind down the poor tenants. In this he agreed with William Seton the younger of Pitmedden, the essayist, both condemning the harsh oppression of tenants by landlords and recommending that feudalism should be either abolished or curtailed.[33] Then on the larger subject of Scotland's economic difficulties Fletcher held that these could only be remedied by honest administration, freedom from external control, and radical social as well as political reforms. He even insisted on reform of the educational system which he thought too pedagogic and ill-adapted to the needs of the country; he would have improved the traditional grammar training and restricted it to the upper classes who, in his view, alone could benefit from it, and for the lower orders he would have introduced vocational training in the belief that skilled craftsmen would be of more use to the country than a surfeit of stickit ministers. It was the right prescription for his time, but Fletcher's ideas had to wait another half century before being tried out.[34] Fletcher, in short, was not so much visionary as hard-headed and far-seeing, and many of his recommendations, social as well as political, have a remarkably modern ring to them.

Corruption he hated. To him it was 'the blackest of crimes; and when I name any guilty of it, I name a very odious criminal'.[35] Unlike his venal contemporaries he recognised the general rotting effect on the body politic of a system based on corruption. He knew that Scotland's most desperate need was for honest, vigorous and enlightened government. Such a government, Fletcher believed, must serve the needs of the nation and not those of a distant and ill-informed Court or the sinister interests of either English ministers or their corrupt tools in Scotland. The immediate requirement, therefore, was to make the independence of the Scottish government real instead of illusory, and he tried to use the crisis in Anglo-Scottish relations to bring in a carefully thought-out programme of constitutional reforms designed to secure that end. Here his thinking was obviously conditioned by the constitution of 1641, but that was to provide a mere base from which to reform Scottish society. The power of the crown was to be reduced almost to nominal proportions, parliament was to choose the executive, which would be responsible to the legislature, and feudalism in both its administrative and social aspects was to be suppressed. The great landlords naturally did not take kindly to such radical schemes, and Fletcher's main support in parliament came from his fellow barons, or commissioners of the shires, and from the burgesses. But on this occasion the *tiers état* was unequal to its mission, and the revolution failed. Fletcher did have an appeal for the commonalty, but he was no democrat and could not associate the canaille with his schemes. In his view real power in the state should devolve upon parliament, which should be dominated by the elected representatives of the most progressive sections of society, the lairds and burgesses. In a way Fletcher anticipated mid-nineteenth century liberalism as practiced in Scotland. His grand aim was simply to rid society peacefully of much of the lumber inherited from the past.

Such a man, possessed by such ideas, could have nothing but loathing for the Treaty of Union passed in 1707. That Treaty took no stock of the administrative and social evils he condemned. Indeed, it actually made good honest administration more difficult of attainment, paving the way for a system even more corrupt than the one it displaced; and it pandered to the magnates by actually guaranteeing the maintenance of feudalism and the heritable jurisdictions.

It is of some importance, too, to note that Fletcher's programme was not just a response to the crisis in Anglo-Scottish relations but had been maturing in his mind ever since the 1680s. Nor were his political views confined to Anglo-Scottish relations, though in the circumstances he was obliged to lay great stress on the problem of relations with England. His real concern was with the problems of government and society both in their theoretical and practical aspects. Consistent with this, in championing the claims of his own country he never became anti-English. It was his contention that a well-ordered and prosperous Scotland was in the real interest of England and that only mercantilist dogmas obscured this axiomatic truth. In urging his case Fletcher's arguments were sharp and pungently expressed but hardly ever rancorous, a fact that was appreciated by his contemporaries. Thus, in spite of his radicalism and his gift of pointed speech, in an age of venomous politics he had and retained the respect of even his bitterest political opponents. Throughout, they cultivated his personal friendship and enjoyed his stimulating talk. As an instance of this, arising from a chance meeting in London in December 1703 with the pro-unionist Earl of Cromartie (an adept and notorious grafter to boot), we have the fascinating rencontre between the peppery English High Tory, Sir Edward Seymour, and the equally hot and outspoken laird of Saltoun.[36] That angry altercation showed the width of Fletcher's political interests and also the regard in which he was held.

Fletcher deserved the respect of his contemporaries, just as he compels respect today, for there is nothing in his record that even remotely suggests that he ever deviated from the high standard of political morality that he preached. On the debit side it can be said that he was opinionated, hot-tempered, quarrelsome and given to duelling; but his outstanding characteristic was a quite unusual and remarkable honesty.

In considering the state of parties and their attitudes the Jacobites also require consideration. No bigger mistake could be made than to fall into the trap of dismissing them as romantic irrelevances left over from an irretrievable past. From 1689 their fortunes had fluctuated, but they rallied to become one of the most important political factions in Anne's troubled reign. In William's last years they were weakly represented in parliament, but the death of the Duke of Gloucester, opening up as it did the question of the succession, revived their hopes, and Anne's accession found them in buoyant mood. The queen, after all, was a Stewart and by legitimist reckoning next in line after the Pretender, for whom in normal circumstances she would have acted as regent. On all these counts she was more acceptable to legitimists than William had been; and the more infatuated Jacobites could never quite free themselves from the notion that in her heart of hearts the sentimental Anne, who had detested 'Caliban' William, shared their beliefs. Such views were inadvertently encouraged by the Act of Indemnity passed in the first year of Anne's reign; and the queen's well-known devotion to the Church of England also appealed to the episcopalians in Scotland, very many of whom had Jacobite sympathies. Jacobite and episcopalian sympathies were then widely diffused in Scotland, much more so than in 1745; but here caution needs to be exercised, for between sympathy for the exiled house and active plotting (never mind open rebellion), there was for many a considerable gulf. Only the small and rigorously persecuted Roman catholic minority, concentrated mainly in parts of the North-East plain and in parts of the West Highlands and Islands,[37] was Jacobite without qualification. The great majority of Jacobite sympathisers were non-juring episcopalians, and few of them desired a restoration without terms. Most, in fact, were in the same perplexed state as the English Compounders —that is, still bedevilled by the old problem of devotion to a protestant church and a catholic king.[38]

The complexities inseparable from Jacobitism did not end there. After the plot to assassinate William in 1696 most Jacobites lay low, and according to the lord advocate they were 'more quiet and tame than if they had been prosecute with the utmost rigour'.[39] This was not quite the case, for, lightly disguised as Cavaliers

or Tories, the Jacobites continued their activities and directed them more towards parliament. But since there were Scottish Tories who were not Jacobites
this move further complicated matters. Like the Jacobites, the Tories were strong
for the royal prerogative and supported episcopacy—but with the Tories the
church came first.[40] Their main demand was for concessions to the episcopalians
and they did not much care which regime provided them. The Tories thus had a
natural leaning towards the *de facto* government. Two prominent and influential
Tories were Seafield and Cromartie, sound ministerialists and unionists both,
who often urged the Court to favour the episcopalians. The Court Party, however, found it impossible to respond to these appeals, not because of bigotry or
devotion to the established church but simply because it knew that such a policy
would infuriate the presbyterians. The government, in short, was in a dilemma.
To have accommodated the episcopalians would have provided the government
with useful allies and yielded other advantages; such a move would have pleased
the High Church Tories in England, who bitterly condemned presbyterian intolerance in Scotland, and it would also have disposed the English Tories to look
more favourably on union. A policy acceptable to the episcopalians must also
have weakened the Jacobites, who made much of episcopalian grievances. But in
spite of all those alluring prospects the policy could not be implemented. The
government simply could not afford to alienate the presbyterians who might then
commit themselves irrevocably to the opposition.

The inveterate enemies of the episcopalians, the presbyterians, feared a sell-
out. Anne's accession filled them with dire forebodings—if Archbishop Laud
had risen from the grave the Scottish presbyterians could not have been more
alarmed. Thus, on receipt of the news of William's death (which, incidentally,
hurriedly called to mind his virtues and sound views on religion), one presbyterian minister, John Turnbull, confided to his diary, 'sad things seem to be
threatened'; which was soon amplified as follows: 'Our parliament sits down
where heats and factions and the sad consequences of these to the church are
feared'.[41] Another, the young Robert Wodrow (the future historian), later
entered into a correspondence with the Whig publicist George Ridpath in which
they exchanged mutual fears about the threats to presbytery from the episcopalian malignants and the dreaded incorporating union with England.[42] These fears
largely derived from the fact that there was no presbyterian party in parliament,
though uncritical reading of contemporary documents has given some the mistaken impression that there was. Opponents of the constitutional reformers often
denounced them as 'the presbyterian party' or 'the party of the rotten fanatics',
but this was partisan rant and no more to be accepted at its face value than the
wild accusations of Jacobitism that were at the same time so freely bandied
about. Those latter, if all were to be believed, would have had the entire Scottish
nation firm adherents of the exiled Stewarts—which the nation never at any time
was.

The presbyterians were, indeed, weakened by their own political theory under
which the church was *not* represented in parliament. The old First Estate
vanished at the Revolution; and, in fact, ministers were debarred from sitting in
parliament. To whom, then, were the presbyterians to turn for political support?

They could never quite make up their minds. Many put a very reluctant faith in the ministry, following the tradition built up by the able 'Cardinal' Carstares; but others, especially of the younger ministers, supported the Country Party and in particular the constitutional reformers. Both presbyterians and constitutional reformers, after all, drew on the traditions of the first covenanting movement, and many presbyterians believed that civil liberty and presbytery would stand or fall together. As Ridpath wrote to Wodrow in 1706, arguing the case against union: ' 'tis in vain for you to think to preserve your religion if your civil liberty is surrendered'.[43]

The real importance of religious cross-currents of this kind, episcopalian as well as presbyterian, is that in certain circumstances they could be harnessed up to the angry, opportunist and essentially destructive politics of the early sessions of Anne's parliament in Scotland. Thus both Court and Country sought to avail themselves of religious dissensions. The hard core of the Country Party, however, would have no truck with episcopacy, and this fact just as much as the obstacle of Jacobitism weakened the alliance between Cavaliers and Country-men. At first the Court also enjoyed little success in its attempts to capitalise on religious issues, but in the end it pulled off a master-stroke by guaranteeing the presbyterian establishment in Scotland as an integral part of the Treaty of Union.

If Scottish politics in the early years of Anne's reign seem chaotic those of England were scarcely less so. The nature of politics in Augustan England was just as complex and the structure of politics almost as baffling. At present the whole subject is in a very controversial phase and any attempt at brief summary must be foredoomed. But the state of English politics was crucial to the union issue and cannot be ignored. Luckily, however, the problem of Anglo-Scottish relations is relatively unaffected by the clash between Namierites and anti-Namierites. Before the 'Namierite Revolution', as it used to be called, the inter-pretation of Augustan politics rested on a somewhat naïve acceptance of a two-party system. This Arcadian world of Will Wimbles and Tory Fox-Hunters was shattered by Robert Walcott's Namierite interpretation which seemed to dismiss the party structure in Anne's time as imaginary and to stress the over-riding importance of influence and interest.[44] It was, Walcott insisted, a spoils system that operated, and the real political divide was between Court and Country rather than between Whig and Tory. Elections, according to Walcott, generally turned not so much on principle as on interest, and, for example, on the death of William, 'The country did not have to await the outcome of a general election to discover who its new governors would be'.[45] Walcott put forward some good, if hardly novel, points, particularly that party did not determine the composition of the ministry and that in a narrow electorate a group system was all but inevit-able. He was also justified in contending that there was little real continuity in the history of either Whigs or Tories, and recent work on the Restoration period confirms this view. Here some of the anti-Namierites content themselves with crude generalisations that do not stand up to examination.

The real trouble with Walcott's thesis is that it is too narrow in concept and was pushed too far on evidence that is sometimes tenuous and strained. The reaction against Namierism has swept Walcott's work aside, but contentiousness may well have led the anti-Namierites to overstate their case. That Whigs and Tories existed has been amply demonstrated; but their exact significance is still far from being crystal clear.[46] And the really important point made by Walcott has not been demolished—namely, that, when all is said and done, party alone did not determine government, though it could make the way of government hard. Not just Queen Anne but Godolphin, Marlborough and Harley himself all dreaded 'party government', a fear that stemmed from the transitional nature of the constitution at that time. The power of parliament, particularly that of the lower house, was growing, and so too was the power of the executive, which was operating a more sophisticated system of administration; but the power of the crown had not waned to anything like the extent formerly supposed, and Queen Anne, though traditionally caricatured as a weak and pitiable figure, was far from being a cipher. Anne, indeed, was the most consistent, if clearly not the ablest, of the politicians. In these circumstances efficient party government was not feasible, and Court and Country were still powerful operative factors.[47] The marked growth of the group known as 'moderates' between 1704 and 1708 is a significant commentary on all this, for in essence the 'moderates' anticipated the 'ministerialists' of the later eighteenth century. We may conclude that the existence of party complicated these issues without playing a consistently dominant rôle in Augustan politics. The truly great issues of the time—the war, the succession, and derivatively and in minor key, the union—were not the products of party politics but the objects of it. Parties, then as now, like to give the impression of being *deus ex machina*, whereas, in fact, they more often have to accommodate themselves to the issues than the other way round. This will emerge clearly from closer consideration of the Scottish question.

All the same, one fundamental point has to be stressed, and that is that the party structure in England was stronger and more durable than in Scotland. For one thing, general elections in England were much more frequent, making the emergence of rudimentary party organisation possible, and in certain phases of the crisis in Anglo-Scottish relations party responses could have an important, and sometimes even decisive, effect.

11

The Crisis in Anglo-Scottish Relations, 1702–3

WHATEVER hindsight might now suggest, at the beginning of Anne's reign an incorporating union was not generally considered to be the only answer to the problems that had arisen between England and Scotland, and, whether we like them or not, contemporary views should not be ignored. Nor can events be dismissed as mere surface embroiderings to some deep cosmic pattern. Their causes, effects and timing (in spite of the wild claims of 'Psycho-History') still constitute the grammar and logic of political history, and those who disregard the causality of events merely babble. Only a firm grasp of complex events, and the equally complex reactions to them, can illuminate the real problems. A pragmatic analysis of the interaction of events and attitudes, which does not primarily concern itself with the merits or demerits of the Treaty of Union, reveals that the treaty was virtually an accidental by-product of the crisis in Anglo-Scottish relations and neither the fruition of an age-old English plot to subdue Scotland nor yet the result of consummate poker-playing by the Scottish parliament. Such an analysis also demonstrates that the key to the problem lay in political instability in both England and Scotland. A stronger and more confident England would not have yielded the concessions necessary for union, and a less volatile and intransigent Scotland would not have made the granting of them imperative. The union was thus the consequence of weakness and uncertainty, not of strength and confidence.

Apart from the ever-growing problems of government in Scotland, two other matters were crucial to the crisis in Anglo-Scottish relations. The first was the dynastic problem, which was re-opened in July 1700 when Anne's last surviving child, the Duke of Gloucester, died. The succession laid down at the Revolution was then destroyed, and clearly the security of both realms called for a speedy answer to this vital question. At the age of 37 Anne was not old in terms of years, but the bearing of 16 children had undermined her health and made it unlikely that she and George of Denmark would have further issue.

The English parliament solved the problem by the Act of Settlement of 1701 which declared that, in default of heirs of Anne's body, on her death the succession should devolve upon the next protestant heir, Sophia, dowager Electress of Hanover, a grand-daughter of James VI and I, and her issue. Like any other act of the English parliament, this act had no force in Scotland where, for a variety of reasons, it was unpopular. It was generally disliked because there had been no prior consultation about the matter, and yet the English parliament tactlessly included Scotland in the limitations it imposed upon the Hanoverian successor. The act stated, for example, that 'no person who shall hereafter come to the possession of the crown shall go out of the Dominions of England, Scotland and Ireland without the consent of parliament'.[1] Such an assumption of power on the part of the English parliament raised great ire in Scotland, not only among the Jacobites (who, of course, were fundamentally opposed to the Hanoverian succession) but also the Country Party, which keenly resented the affront as an attack on the sovereignty of Scotland. In the stormy session of the Scottish parliament of 1703 Fletcher waxed bitter on this score: 'Did they,' he enquired, 'ever require our concurrence? Did they ever desire the late king to cause the parliament of Scotland to meet, in order to take our advice and consent? Was this not to tell us plainly, that we ought to be concluded by their determinations, and were not worthy to be consulted in the matter?'[2] This was near enough the truth, though Fletcher might well have recognised that William was on such bad terms with the Scottish parliament that he could not raise such an important question there without giving hostages to fortune. Still, in law the succession to Scotland could only be regulated by the Scottish parliament, as numerous precedents demonstrated, and until it was so regulated the existing law must stand—that is, the Succession Act of 1681 as modified by the Claim of Right of 1689.

Throughout the entire crisis the problem of the succession was basic. Fletcher's speech was made during discussion of the Act of Security, which was a rebuff to the English Act of Settlement; and here it is worth recalling that the official title of the Act of Settlement was 'An Act for the Further Limitation of the Crown and better securing the Rights and Liberties of the Subject'. The precedent was noted in Scotland and taken up by a strong body of opinion determined to use the succession problem in order to secure radical constitutional reform. The Hanoverian succession might be accepted but only on certain terms, and in this way the dynastic question made possible some redefinition of the existing un-satisfactory connection between the two countries by purely constitutional means. And here it is important to stress yet again, what so many English historians are apparently incapable of understanding, that in law Scotland was an independent and sovereign kingdom and in no way bound to accept the Hanoverian, or indeed any other, succession. The situation, then, was basically very simple—unless the Scottish parliament could be brought to accept the Hanoverian succession, then on Anne's death the regal union would be dissolved. And since many in Scotland wished to see the union of the crowns either ended or amended, it would have been folly on their part to rush into England's measures, for that would have been the surest way of preserving the status quo. Thus, quite apart from the Jacobites, those who wanted a more equitable regal union could not afford to have the Hanoverian succession without prior terms. When the Countrymen referred to a 'treatie' with England this is what they had in mind and not an incorporating union. An 'entire', 'compleat' or incorporating union was indeed generally abominated; and, anyway, even those few who favoured incorporation with England refused to give prior recognition to the Hanoverian succession since acceptance of it would have weakened the case for a complete union. Thus it was the question of the succession that made a large but heterogeneous and loosely co-ordinated opposition possible in the early sessions of Anne's parliament in Scotland.

The second overriding background factor to affect the relationship between the two kingdoms was the War of the Spanish Succession. It was a war on a scale hitherto unknown, and in the end its requirements compelled the English ministry and parliament to pay heed to the growing alienation of Scotland. But the effects of the war went deeper, for its causes and effects were firmly enmeshed with the problems that then bedevilled Anglo-Scottish relations. Louis XIV had reneged on the Treaty of Ryswick and openly acknowledged the Chevalier as King of England, Scotland and Ireland, and thus as Mark Thomson has trenchantly put it: 'For England the War of the Spanish Succession was also the war of the English succession, and that fact was made plain from the first'.[3]

Obviously, too, the outbreak of the war also deepened the resentment that already existed in Scotland over the Union of the Crowns, for once again Scotland was dragged into hostilities that were none of her making and from which she could derive nothing but blighted trade and worsening of an already gloomy economic situation. Views on the succession and on the necessity of the war were divided; but, on the whole, public opinion on these matters reinforced the demand for a reasonable *quid pro quo* from England—namely, free trade. The whole question of trade, and resentment at the English Navigation Laws, was entirely basic. Of the two main strands of opposition, the Country Party worked consistently either for free trade with England or freedom of Scottish trade from English interference, and the Jacobites, who had different fundamental aims, fully recognised the importance of economic grievances and strove to exploit their disrupting influence.

Bearing all these considerations in mind, the course of events needs to be carefully examined.

One of William's last actions had been to recommend a closer union of the two kingdoms, a call that had raised little real enthusiasm. As a policy it could hardly be said to dominate the statesmen of the time. Marlborough, like William, favoured the project, but, again like William, he was preoccupied elsewhere and that preoccupation continued throughout the crisis; Godolphin was indifferent to union; the High Church Tories, especially the Hyde and Finch groups, headed respectively by Rochester and Nottingham, were opposed mainly on ecclesiastical grounds; and the Junto Whigs gave only vague and qualified support to the notion. But these were not fixed attitudes. They varied as expedience dictated and were not determined by conviction of the merits or demerits of union but by tactical considerations. It was here that the party strife in England most obviously affected the problem of Anglo-Scottish relations.

The king's death led to further difficulties. William had made discreet use of favourites to superintend Scottish affairs; but after his death control lay with the queen's English ministers, and it was soon no secret that Lord Treasurer Godolphin openly pulled the strings. When this produced criticism in Scotland

Godolphin made out that his control of Scottish affairs was a burdensome necessity and that the only answer was to resurrect the Scottish Council that had operated in London in Charles II's time; but this he knew was a non-starter. In fact, Godolphin enjoyed the accretion of power that oversight of Scottish affairs gave him; but, unfortunately, he knew little of Scotland and its problems and cared less. Godolphin was not a great statesman or even an outstanding politician. He was a first-rate administrator, whose paramount concern was to finance Marlborough's war, not to resolve constitutional issues, and initially his policy was simply to maintain the existing system in Scotland with the least troublesome means. Indeed, so identified did he become with the defence of the status quo that his later tactical amendments lacked credibility.

Throughout, only Anne herself consistently advocated union. This she did for reasons of state, chief of which was security. She had little sympathy for the Scots and less liking; as a girl of sixteen she had spent some months in Scotland in 1681 when her father was commissioner there, but, like all the later Stewarts, she was completely English and found Scotland dull and its people repellent. Quite apart from the impressions left on her by her brief sojourn in Scotland, Anne never understood her Scottish subjects whom she referred to at one point as 'these strange people' and at another as 'these unreasonable Scotsmen'.[4] She found them only slightly less repugnant than the Irish, who, as she noted, also yearned to be independent but, as she told Lord Cowper, 'they should not'.[5]

Her reign got off to a bad start in Scotland. War had to be declared on France before the parliament, which was known to be in refractory mood, could be summoned, and war was accordingly declared by proclamation of the Scottish Privy Council on 30 May 1702,[6] a full fortnight after England had (with, be it noted, the concurrence of its parliament) made a similar declaration. As well as adding to the general resentment on this matter in Scotland, this action further embittered the opposition in parliament. Anyway, that parliament was out of date and could not be said to represent national opinion; no general election had been held since 1689, and the existing parliament derived from the old Convention of Estates of Revolution days. It is not surprising therefore that by the spring of 1702 clamours for a fresh parliament were being raised and that Hamilton was insistently petitioning the queen on this score.

But the longevity of the Revolution parliament was not the only question mark hanging over the session of 1702. Under the terms of an act of 1696 entitled, significantly enough, 'An Act for the Security of the Kingdom', the existing parliament was supposed to meet within twenty days of the king's death.[7] Its duration was limited to six months and its powers circumscribed to securing Anne's succession without altering the constitution.

After William's death the correct and most politic course would have been to follow the strict letter of the law, convene parliament, secure the succession and then adjourn, or better still, dissolve. Queensberry, however, was afraid to face the electorate, and he persuaded the queen and Godolphin to continue the old parliament.[8] Worse, the parliament did not meet until 9 June, 90 and not 20 days after William's death. The effect of these ill-advised decisions was to increase irritation with the Court and to identify it with the unpopular Queensberry.

Then, too, these manoeuvres raised doubts about the legality of the session, doubts that were even shared by such consistent Courtiers as Seafield and Stair.[9] Using such arguments to denounce the session as illegal, the indignant Hamilton tried to foil the ministry's plans by leading 70 of his followers out of the parliament—a serious tactical error. Queensberry, the commissioner, seized the opportunity for a quick dispatch of business, notably recognition of the queen's authority and an act securing the protestant religion and presbyterian church government.

Then, following the queen's recommendations, Queensberry obtained an act permitting the crown to nominate commissioners to treat for union but reserving the rights of the established church,[10] just as the English parliament had already done. At the same time the parliament, or its rump, unanimously rejected Chancellor Marchmont's notion to abjure the Pretender. In practice such a motion would have meant accepting the Hanoverian succession, and to many, as a leading Courtier, Murray of Philiphaugh, reported, 'such a step would carry us so far into the measures of England about the succession, that they would become careless and indifferent about the Union'.[11] It is essential to note, however, that all the zeal for union displayed at this time came from Queensberry and the Court Party. Indeed, when the truant opposition woke up to what was afoot and threatened to attend once more, Queensberry put an abrupt end to the session on 30 June. A union seemed to be the best, if not the only, answer to the commissioner's troubles, and there can be no question but that the Court Party in Scotland did its best to secure union in 1702. Furthermore, from the ensuing negotiations it is also clear that the Court itself (most notably the queen) was for an incorporating union; but the conduct of the negotiations casts doubts on Godolphin's commitment to union.

Made up as it was of Queensberry's followers, the Scottish commission was pro-union to a man; but not so the English commission. The English Tories were opposed to union and had already made their position plain. In 1700 they had killed a previous attempt by bitter railing against the Scots, Sir Edward Seymour scoffing that Scotland 'was a beggar, and whoever married a beggar could only expect a louse for a portion'.[12] Finally, on Anne's accession some of the leading Tories were given office and the union project got under way; but, as Bishop Burnet noted, 'The indecent form with which Seymour and others treated the Scots were clear indications that the posts they were brought into had not changed their tempers'.[13] On the other hand, being deprived of office had cooled the Whigs to the idea of a union with Scotland. Indeed, general contempt for the Scots was evident in the offhand way that the English commissioners behaved during the negotiations, frequently failing to constitute a quorum of 13 and forcing so many diets to be given up on this account that on 21 January 1703 the necessary quorum was reduced to seven. There was, therefore, a little justification for the view adopted by Turnbull, the Scots diarist, that 'neither side [was] serious in the matter'.[14] Of the English commissioners only Harley showed himself keen for union, and of the Scots its most zealous advocates were Seafield and Viscount Tarbat. The most resolute unionist of all, however, was the queen. At the outset of the negotiations, on 18 November, she sent a message to the commissioners recommending 'an indissoluble union between the two nations which Her Majesty thinks the most likely means under heaven to establish the monarchy, secure the peace and increase the trade, wealth and happiness of both nations'.[15] And later, on 14 December, when the talks were flagging, the queen appeared in person to receive a progress report and repeat her opening admonition.

Abortive though these negotiations were to prove, they are of no little interest and were indeed of some importance in preparing the ground for the treaty of 1707. Only an incorporating union was discussed, which is not surprising considering the queen's views and that nomination of the two commissions had lain with the crown. So both commissions readily accepted that there was to be one united kingdom and one parliament; and, equally naturally, the Hanoverian succession was to be recognised. The Scottish commissioners cannily stipulated, however, that these two basic points were conditional on complete freedom of trade. After some discussion it was agreed that there should be free trade between England and Scotland, but at first the English commissioners demurred at free trade between Scotland and the English colonies on the grounds 'That the plantations are the property of English men; and that this trade is of so great a consequence and so beneficial as not to be communicated, as is proposed, till all other particulars which shall be thought necessary to this Union be adjusted'.[16] This the Scots commissioners rejected; and finally on 2 January 1703 free trade with the plantations was conceded. Thereafter the negotiations ran into difficulties over taxation and whether or not Scotland should receive a compensation, or equivalent, to offset the burdens incident to union. Here deadlock arose, the English commissioners arguing that the economic benefits of union would far outweigh any adverse effects.

Throughout January the patience of both parties was clearly becoming exhausted and the problem of ensuring attendance became critical. The end came on 30 January over the question of the claims of the Company of Scotland, the Scots commissioners insisting upon recognition of the rights of the Company, or, failing this, agreement 'to purchase their right at the public expense'.[17] No agreement could be reached on this vital issue, resolution of which might have made the proposed union more palatable to public opinion in Scotland, and on 3 February the queen adjourned the negotiations. In announcing this decision the Lord President of the Council, the Earl of Pembroke, urged that certain important points not touched upon in the negotiations should be considered during the adjournment so 'that on both sides we may come the better prepared to settle them at our next meeting; such are the constitution of the parliament, the affairs of the church, and the municipal laws and judicatories of Scotland, for security of the properties of the subjects of that kingdom'.[18] The two commissions, thus primed, were supposed to resume their labours on 4 October 1703; but instead, overwhelmed by events, they were destined never to meet again.

In 1703 developments in both England and Scotland militated against union. Queensberry was more unpopular than ever with his countrymen, and those who supported the opposition capitalised on this. They struck back hard, and, on the pretext that the parliamentary session of 1702 was illegal, they refused to pay the taxes it had levied. This was doubly dangerous for the Court; finance was the

Scottish government's most glaring weakness, and also, of course, doubt about the legality of the session played into the hands of the Jacobites, who suddenly acquired a consuming interest in parliamentary politics. Faced with these problems the Court, while maintaining that the session of 1702 was legal and its acts valid, recognised that a fresh session of parliament was inevitable. Supply was badly needed and only parliament could grant it. But the old parliament could no longer be maintained, and so, whatever the problems it might bring in its train, a general election could no longer be staved off.

The ensuing elections were keenly contested. Influence and threats were extensively used by the ministers,[19] but either the passions that had been roused were proof against influence or the patronage at the government's disposal was too little to control a general election; and, of course, the opposition, too, could apply pressure. Whatever the precise reason for it, the Court Party was seriously weakened by the election results; but the Country Party also lost ground, and the most spectacular advance was made by the Jacobites, or Cavaliers as they now found it expedient to describe themselves.

Anne's accession, accompanied as it was by an Act of Indemnity, had already encouraged the Jacobites to play a more active rôle in politics, a rôle that was not only mischievous (in that their aim was to deepen the crisis) but also puzzling, confused and confusing. The politics of the Cavaliers showed all these features at this time mainly because the group was not homogeneous and their aims were divergent. Some, such as their apologist George Lockhart of Carnwath, were outright Jacobites, and their aim was simply to advance the cause of the Pretender in every possible way: but many of the Cavaliers were closer to the English High Church Tories and their prime objective was to improve the lot of the episcopalians in Scotland. This latter was a more sensible and more realistic policy than it is usually made out to be. The Revolution Settlement of the church was by no means regarded as final, and the episcopalians were still numerous and powerful and the presbyterians were still apprehensive. It was not simply a question of numbers but turned on which denomination had most political muscle. On the whole the politically dominant class, the great nobles, had little use for presbyterianism; on this matter even Queensberry was opportunist, willing to befriend the episcopalians but afraid of antagonising the presbyterians. Of the great magnates only Argyll consistently upheld presbyterianism, and that for reasons as much calculating as religious; and only a few leading politicians subscribed, like the Chancellor Marchmont, to the belief that presbytery, the protestant succession and Revolution principles stood or fell together. There was always the possibility, too, that the Pretender might, like Henry IV of France, decide that the form of communion service should not stand in the way of a crown. He never so concluded, but at this point the matter seemed open; so the Pretender's catholicism was not regarded as an insuperable objection and did not deter staunch protestants from flirting with his cause, the more especially as it was made plain that a restoration would entail, not Romanism, but protestant episcopal government. Thus both Hamilton and Atholl, like so many others, had strong connections with the Cavaliers; and Hamilton certainly went further and kept up a close, if characteristically ambiguous, correspondence with the Pretender.

Then, too, the Cavaliers had donned the mantle of patriotism. Being permanently excluded from office, they were able to avail themselves of every grievance, not only to embarrass the Scottish ministry but also to whip up anti-English feeling. They had been brought low in 1696, but the Darien disaster and the outcry against malign English influence had given them a fresh lease of life. As a group they were completely opportunist and their tactics were purely destructive. Not for nothing were they the original recipients of the newly coined slang name for political fly-by-nights:

> The Crosier and Crown to fix *sicut ante*
> Is the noble pretence of *Squadroni volante*
> But whither they'll prove *Bragada Constante*
> He is wiser than I that can tell.[20]

Their nominal leader, the Earl of Home, was a mere puppet whom, at the right time, Hamilton had no difficulty in manipulating.

In the new parliament the Countrymen proper were reduced to a small, but experienced and formidable, group headed by the Marquis of Tweeddale. Their radical wing was led by Andrew Fletcher of Saltoun, one of the commissioners for East Lothian, and he was ably supported by the Earls of Montrose, Roxburghe, Haddington and Rothes, young nobles who were making their début on the political stage. In 1703 Fletcher's influence over them was supreme and they were popularly referred to as his 'cubs'. The Country Party, however, was too weak to go it alone and was forced to accept the leadership of Hamilton and his dependants even though the programme of the constitutionalists differed radically from that of the effervescent premier duke.

Hamilton's astonishing prestige, which far outstripped his abilities, was largely the fortuitous product of disjointed times. Thus in 1703 his position was notably strengthened by the failure of attempts to broaden the base of the administration, attempts that were to some extent offshoots of the party struggle in England.

Nottingham, hoping to break the understanding between Queensberry and the Junto and to secure a bridgehead for the English Tories in Scotland, tried first of all, through the agency of a leading Scots Tory, Viscount Tarbat, to force an accommodation between the more moderate sections of the Country Party and the Court Party. Queensberry was obliged to give a reluctant assent to the proposed changes, which were accepted but not announced before the elections. By them, as a pledge of goodwill the headstrong chancellor (the presbyterian and rabidly Hanoverian Marchmont) was replaced by the more subtle and pliant Seafield.[21] Tweeddale's group showed some interest in the new move, but the project failed mainly because the Countrymen wanted to displace Queensberry's group altogether, and Queensberry, alive to the danger, fought back. He knew that the Country Party, following the example of the English opposition, was about to demand a thorough investigation into the administration, which was suspected of widespread corruption. The regime in Scotland was indeed notoriously corrupt, as later investigation showed, and Queensberry was, almost literally, fighting for his life. And so, in defiance of the Court, he stealthily and deliberately went out of his way to destroy the projected 'broad-bottom'. The result was a weak and divided ministry. Cromartie* and Seafield opposed Queensberry's policies, and the sole important capture from the Country Party, Tullibardine,† openly feuded with Queensberry over his patent for a dukedom and latterly actively undermined the ministry from within.

The attempt to build a broad-bottomed administration from elements that accepted the Revolution Settlement therefore enjoyed scant success. But the election results had increased the Court's difficulties and put a premium on support for the ministry. In the end, the necessary support was sought in an alliance with the Cavaliers. This move, which again was pushed by Nottingham but only reluctantly supported by Queensberry, though it had at first glance an unnatural appearance had nonetheless a deeper logic of its own. It was the fruition of many years of special pleading by the Scottish non-jurors in an effort to enlist the aid of English churchmen for their down-trodden co-religionists, the Scottish episcopalians. At long last it seemed as if the appeal from Scottish Toryism to English Toryism was to be acted upon.

The English High Church Tories were in disgruntled mood, eager to reduce the rights of dissenters in England and bitterly hostile to the presbyterian establishment in Scotland. Many hopes and fears were spawned by the hatred the English Tories felt for Scottish presbyterianism. It was known, for example, that at the time of the recent union negotiations the Archbishop of York had argued at a private meeting of the English commissioners that, as a condition of union, episcopacy should be restored in Scotland.[22] Nottingham, who had initially sympathised with this view, in the end had agreed with Rochester that it was impossible to raise the matter in the actual negotiations.[23] But thereafter Nottingham, on grounds both of political expediency and religious conviction, pushed the claims of the Cavalier Party in Scotland. In all this he was strongly supported by Tarbat (or Cromartie), who for years had championed the cause of the Scottish episcopalians, and by Seafield, who had the shrewdest appreciation of the ministry's desperate need for support.

The effect of this makeshift alliance was to raise inordinately the hopes of the Cavaliers and to the same degree the alarm of the presbyterians. In return for supporting the ministry the episcopalians were to be granted toleration and the restoration of private patronage in the Church of Scotland. These would have been severe blows to the presbyterians who were, in spite of myths past and present, politically weak and extremely apprehensive. They reacted angrily, inside and outside parliament. Rumours of the proposed toleration led the Edinburgh mob to riot, and the presbyterians in general to fulminate against any attempt 'to establish iniquity by a law'.[24] The net effect was to increase distrust of the Court and further inflame the anti-English sentiments then endemic in Scotland.

Early in 1703 a change in the balance of parties in England also told against union. Anne's accession had put new heart into the Tories, who had triumphed

* Sir George Mackenzie of Tarbat, created, 26 February 1685 Viscount Tarbat, and first Earl of Cromartie 1 January 1703.

† John Murray, eldest son of first Marquis of Atholl, created, 27 July 1696, first Earl of Tullibardine; succeeded as second Marquis of Atholl 6 May 1703, and created Duke of Atholl 30 June 1703.

in the general election of 1702. The queen suspected the Junto of aiming at party government, which she feared, and so the Whigs were driven from office even to the extent of being denied places on the Privy Council. Anne, who had yet to learn that the Tories were just as partisan and driven by the same lust for power, despite warnings from Godolphin and Marlborough did not form a broad-bottom and her first ministry had strong Tory leanings. This gave the *coup de grâce* to the union policy, as Tory xenophobia rode high, making the work of government difficult. The war was the government's chief concern, but the Tories, unlike the Junto, gave it only lukewarm support; and so the triumvirate of Godolphin, Marlborough and Harley had perforce to govern with one uneasy eye on the Junto and the other on the High Tories. While this remained the case, such a controversial measure as union with Scotland had little prospect of success; and, besides, most of the leading English politicians showed themselves indifferent to union. In the wake of the recent abortive negotiations that was understandable enough.

The insouciant attitude of English politicians was shaken by the cataclysmic session of the Scottish parliament of 1703. For the Court that session was a disaster, due in part to the commissioner Queensberry's selfish manoeuvrings which wrecked every attempt to strengthen the ministry by broadening its base.[25] Whatever Queensberry's precise motives, they certainly did not spring from far-seeing patriotism, but rather from his lust for office and his ambitions for the future. If Queensberry could not preside over the resolution of the issues that had arisen between the two kingdoms, then none of his rivals should be suffered to have that honour or the favour that would go with it.

And just what were the relations between the two kingdoms? How critical were they? From time to time attempts have been made to minimise the seriousness of the situation. None entirely convinces. Thus Law Mathieson attributed the main trouble to ministerial weakness and procedural difficulties in the Scottish parliament.[26] More recently Dr. Riley has argued along similar lines, contending that the opposition was neither nationalist nor anti-English and that the difficulties encountered by the ministry really stemmed from bad management.[27] There is some substance to this argument, in that management was an important consideration; but Riley's interpretation sweeps aside another vital factor, namely the mood of angry intransigence that dominated this important session.

Contemporary observers all agree that the crisis was real and that it was acute. Burnet says of the Scots, 'A national humour of rendering themselves a free and independent kingdom did so inflame them, they seemed capable of the most extravagant things that could be suggested to them'. There was, he shrewdly continues, such disorder 'that great skill and much secret practice seemed necessary to set matters right there'.[28] And Sir John Clerk, who was present as member for the royal burgh of Whithorn, has recorded that the parliament was frequently out of temper and 'often in the form of a Polish diet, with our swords in our hands, or at least our hands at our swords'.[29] Other evidence confirms that it was a stormy session and one that did not lack a strong nationalist bias. The latter is most strikingly proved by the forthright speeches of Fletcher and

Belhaven, any one of which would in more normal times have led to charges of leasing-making.[30] By the middle of the session, too, Godolphin became alarmed about the situation and warned Seafield of the possible ill-effects of such a bad parliament. 'We are now,' he wrote, 'in so criticall a juncture with respect to other nations, that all Europe must in some measure bee affected by the good or ill-ending of the Parliament of Scotland.'[31] And the phlegmatic Lord Treasurer was hardly the one to get worked up over a meaningless charade.

It is pointless, then, to play down the critical nature of the session of the Scottish parliament of 1703. To do so, indeed, reduces history to an illusory level. Why, then, in the face of the evidence embark on such a futile course? The object of the exercise is to provide an easy explanation for the passing of the Treaty and Act of Union in 1707. How, asks Smout and others, could the intransigent anti-English parliament of 1703 be brought to accept union in 1707? No way; therefore the traditional account of the parliament of 1703 must rest on myth and legend. But, as often happens, the debunkers have missed the real point. Their question is invalid because based on wrong postulates. Their underlying line of argument rashly assumes that the situation in 1706–7 was in every respect exactly what it had been in 1703. But such manifestly was not the case, and only the most blinkered argument can fail to see this. Many matters that were clouded over in 1703 had been clarified by 1706—the Court's policy had become firmer and clearer; the Scottish ministry was more broadly based and, thanks to improved management, enjoyed wider support in parliament; and the weaknesses of the opposition had been exposed and were skilfully exploited. As a result, many parliamentarians who had opposed the ministry in 1703 could, for a variety of reasons, be brought to support the ministry in 1706.

Anyway, to turn the argument on the union question is totally misleading. The salient point is that in 1703 the union policy was a dead duck and could not possibly explain the polarisation of forces in the Scottish parliament. Union was not even discussed. All that emerged under this head in 1703 was the rescinding of the commission's powers and a stipulation that no further negotiations were to proceed without the consent of parliament.[32] The record also shows that anti-English sentiment and distrust of the Court were strong, and that the weakness of the ministry and its maladroit tactics gave these sentiments free rein.

From the opening day of the session on 6 May the ministry was in a tricky situation, facing a hostile House and with little or no visible policy. The queen's letter to the parliament and her instructions to the commissioner said nothing about either union or succession but simply stressed the need for supply in order to prosecute the war.[33] Yet all began quietly enough. On the first day of the session Hamilton moved that the queen's authority, by virtue of her undoubted right to the imperial crown of Scotland, should be recognised. At this early stage the Court-Cavalier alliance still held, and on 19 May Hamilton's motion passed the House. On that same day, however, the ministry's troubles began. Queensberry boldly decided to move for supply, his aim being to raise money and adjourn, leaving the opposition to huff and puff ineffectively outside parliament. The commissioner hoped that the Court-Cavalier alliance might just carry this stratagem, and accordingly the motion for supply came from the leader of the

Cavaliers, the Earl of Home. On such a vital matter, however, the opposition was not to be caught napping and Tweeddale countered with a general resolve that 'before all other business the Parliament might proceed to make such conditions of government and regulations in the constitution of this Kingdom to take place after the decease of her Majestie and the heirs of her body as shall be necessary for the preservation of our religion and liberty'.[34]

A motion of some kind along these lines was inevitable; but issue on it was not joined until 26 May, the interval being taken up with such routine matters as disputed election returns and private petitions. During that week's grace a good deal of dickering went on behind the scenes, Court and Country competing for the support of the Cavaliers. The opposition won because the Cavaliers discovered that they were about to be duped over the promised toleration. On 28 May they deserted the Court and by refusing to vote for supply forced the ministry to accept Tweeddale's motion; and in spite of government attempts to revive the alliance the gulf between Court and Cavaliers widened. Worse ensued for the ministry as Cavaliers and Countrymen entered into an alliance of convenience, whose designs were aided by the devious machinations of the Lord Privy Seal, Atholl, and even, though unintentionally, by the pro-Hanoverian zeal of Marchmont. In the upshot the ministry completely lost control of the House.

The great cause of contention was the Act of Security, which has recently been described as a Court measure that was turned into a triumph for the opposition —a very unsound view.[35] To introduce such a measure was no part of the ministry's policy; policy indeed was to forestall it. Quite simply, an Act of Security was the necessary consequence of the ministry's failure to win supply. Atholl, who introduced the motion, candidly explained as much to Godolphin: rebuffed over supply, the ministry had no alternative but to try to pre-empt Tweeddale's initiative in the hope of getting a mild act that would protect the interests of the Court and at the same time please enough of the opposition to enable supply to be passed.[36] Anyway, measures of some kind for the security of the kingdom were indispensable; with neither union nor a settlement of the succession in prospect, an Act of Security was an absolute necessity, and it mattered little who actually introduced the motion. The real debate came, as anticipated, over the terms of the act. As early as 26 May Hamilton and Fletcher had scathingly denounced Godolphin's covert power over the servile Scottish ministry, arguing that the parliament must protect the liberties of the kingdom from this malign influence. Fletcher asked that 'the House should take into consideration what Acts are necessary to secure our religion, liberty, and trade, in case of the said event, [Anne's demise] before any Act of Supply or other business whatever be brought into consideration'.[37] Thus, to describe the Act of Security as being originally a Court measure that was converted into a triumph for the opposition is wide of the mark. Rather it was an attempt by the Court to steal the opposition's thunder, and one that conspicuously failed.

Further, the Act of Security, which caused so much wrangling in 1703, was neither unprecedented nor inexplicable. A similar but insufficiently strong measure had been passed in 1696, only to be flouted by the Court at Anne's accession. This piece of political chicanery was pure folly, for, together with the farcical session of 1702 and the union fiasco, it created deep and lasting distrust of the Court. Clearly, another and more stringent act was needed; but how stringent should it be? The opposition agreed that it had to be proof against the combined wiles of Court and ministry, but only the hard core of the Country Party argued that it should reduce the power of the crown to next to nothing, as Fletcher's limitations demanded.* Nor was the act brought ready-made into the session; the Act of Security that finally resulted was the product of weeks of bitter wrangling, grudging concessions and forced compromises. Thus Fletcher's scheme was defeated on 7 July by a fleeting resurrection of the Court-Cavalier alliance made possible by the fact that both groups wished to maintain the prerogative. Fear of covert English influence was not so easily disposed of and led to Roxburghe's clause of 16 July, which stipulated that on Anne's death the successor named by the Scottish parliament should not be the same as that of England unless 'in this session of Parliament there be such conditions of government settled and enacted as may secure the honour and independency of the Crown of this kingdom, the freedom, frequency, and the power of the Parliament, and the religion, liberty and trade of the nation from English or any foreign influence'.[38]

The ministry bitterly opposed Roxburghe's clause, which, of course, threatened the Union of the Crowns and would thus widen the rift between the two kingdoms. In desperation the ministry then put forward the bait of free trade, the ministry's alternative to Roxburghe's clause being that after the queen's death the same person should not be sovereign of both England and Scotland unless 'a free communication of trade, the freedom of navigation, and the liberty of the plantations be fully agreed to, and established by the Parliament and kingdom of England'.[39] The ministry's purpose was perhaps to clear the way for union, since not otherwise was England likely to grant free trade, but of this there can be no certainty, for the ministers were divided on the wisdom of this démarche. Nothing in Queensberry's instruction empowered him to go so far, and most of the ministers feared that the English government would resent such a bold initiative. Significantly enough, though, the lure of free trade did not sway the House, which showed little or no interest in the proposal. Roxburghe's clause

* Fletcher's limitations, twelve in all, were as follows: 1. Annual parliaments, which should choose their own president, adjourn at will, and vote by ballot. 2. For every new peer created an additional shire commissioner should be returned to parliament. 3. None should have vote in parliament other than peers or elected members (i.e. Officers of State should not have votes *ex officio*). 4. No royal veto on acts passed by the parliament. 5. When parliament was not in session executive government should be vested in a committee chosen by parliament. 6. The crown should not have the power of making war or peace, or concluding treaties, except with consent of parliament. 7. All offices, civil and military, and all pensions, should be granted by parliament and not by the sovereign. 8. There should be no standing army without consent of parliament. 9. A national militia should be formed. 10. No general pardons to be valid without consent of parliament. 11. No judge to sit in parliament; heads of judiciary to be chosen by parliament. 12. If the sovereign should break any of these conditions parliament was to declare that he (or she) had forfeited the throne and select a successor. This was a very radical programme for the times and was evidently strongly influenced by the constitution of 1641 and the Club's programme in 1689. It would have produced a constitutional limited monarchy, and, though sovereignty would have been vested in the parliament, it cannot really be described, as it so often is, as republican.

stood, and the best the ministry could achieve, after lengthy argument and considerable anxiety, was the conjunction of the two clauses.[40] In this tortuous and piecemeal fashion the Act of Security slowly took shape, finally passing the House by a majority of 59 votes on 13 August 1703.[41]

It cannot be sufficiently stressed that in its final form the Act of Security was not simply the work of the Country Party and so cannot really be represented as that party's programme. Rather it gave the mood of the House and was regarded by all groups as a possible basis on which future policies could be elaborated. The act carefully left the succession open, and this was acceptable to all save a small group of committed Hanoverians headed by Marchmont. Harley's oft-quoted sneer to Carstares that 'the succession is to be kept open for a lame arm to beg by' may simply illustrate the truth of his later remark that he knew 'no more of Scotch business than of Jappan'.[42] The Act of Security was not drawn up in order to blackmail England and it is wrong to dismiss it as bluff.[43] It was a necessary measure to deal with a critical situation that admitted of no easy solution, and it was a fluid measure that left it possible to react in a number of ways to any English initiative. Thus, the pro-unionists might, given favourable circumstances, use it as a lever; but if, on the other hand, the Court or the English parliament were to prove obstructive, then Fletcher and his allies believed that the Act of Security could afford them the means of radical constitutional reform and a return to the constitution of 1641 at least. And for the Jacobites, of course, failure to settle the succession was in itself a clear gain. The act illuminated and clarified the problems implicit in a difficult situation while carefully, in deference to the needs of the various groups that had contributed to its making, keeping all the options open. At that stage more could not be done. And it is noteworthy that the act laid down contingencies for the future (it was not to become operative until Anne's death) and did not propose basic alterations for the present.

What, then, in its final form did the Act of Security entail? It stated that on Anne's death (which, if matters were unresolved, would inevitably bring to a head the conflict between the two kingdoms) parliament should meet within 20 days, and that any successor should be obliged to accept the terms of the Claim of Right before being acknowledged; should there be no heir, either of Anne's body or designated by parliament, then the estates were to choose one, 'being always of the Royal Line of Scotland, and of the true Protestant Religion', but this successor was not to be the same as for England unless the requirements of Roxburghe's clause were met plus those of the clause relating to communication of trade; and, finally, the act had a sting in its tail in the shape of a clause ordering the arming and regular mustering of all protestants capable of bearing arms. The purpose of this last clause could be variously conjectured as either a precaution against French or Jacobite designs or as a means of protecting Scotland from English aggression. Whatever its exact purpose, the clause was seriously intended, for after the act was accepted in 1704 regular musters of fencible men were held.

The ministry was dumbfounded by this unprecedented situation in which an act had passed the House against the wishes of the Court. Before the Revolution the Committee of the Articles automatically prevented such an impasse arising, but the abolition of the Articles in 1690 created the possibility and posed awkward questions. Was there a right of veto? If so, did it lie with the commissioner or with the sovereign? The opposition naturally alleged that there was no right of veto since it was unknown to the law and could shelter behind no precedent; and learned, if not in every respect scholarly, treatises were hastily put together to sustain the thesis that sovereignty lay with the parliament.[44] If the crown disputed this, then there must be a return to the old constitution as it existed before 1603, and specifically in the version popularised by George Buchanan.[45] Quite apart from Buchanan's partisan views, this argument had point in relation to the central problem of the succession, for, after all, difficulties over the succession had arisen before, and, on every such occasion, from 1318 until 1689, the matter had been dealt with by parliament. However involved the politics of such occasions, this was the law; and a peaceful settlement of the succession without the concurrence of parliament simply was not feasible.

The situation of the ministry was fast becoming desperate. Queensberry's colleagues were already ratting on him, and Atholl, Seafield and Cromartie were openly flirting with the Cavaliers, not out of Jacobite sympathies but the better to ingratiate themselves with the English Tories. This was the predictable reaction to Queensberry's successful wrecking of the broad-bottom. Besides, it was well known that Queensberry's stock at Court was slumping, and this knowledge also encouraged defection among the ministers. Queensberry's one remaining hope was somehow or other to obtain supply, for if that could be done, the other difficulties might be left for later rectification. But here again the commissioner ran into trouble. The House would grant supply only if he accepted the Act of Security, and this the Court forbade him to do on the grounds that acceptance of that act would raise a storm in England.[46] Indeed, an angry English reaction was already making itself felt and was soon reinforced by another act passed by the Scottish opposition in the teeth of the ministry. This was the Act anent Peace and War which gave parliament the last word on these important issues. Like the Act of Security it too was predicated on Anne's demise: after that event, if England and Scotland still shared a sovereign, the right to declare war and to conclude peace was to be vested in the Scottish parliament.[47] It was not, therefore, an immediate attack upon the power of the crown in Scotland but rather an attempt to prevent the country from being swept into unwanted hostilities, a grievance as old as the Dutch Wars of the reign of Charles II and one that still had an inescapable current application. Also, in the event that war was acceptable, the parliament was claiming a place at the peace table to ensure that Scotland's interests could be safeguarded. Nonetheless, the act was a bitter pill for the Court. Even though Queensberry's instructions permitted him in the last resort to accept such a measure, Godolphin was so horrified at the prospect that he wrote to Stair arguing for a union;[48] but that policy could not be suddenly resurrected, and the English ministers were reluctantly obliged to allow the Act anent Peace and War to pass, Godolphin lamenting that it would deprive the sovereign of 'one of the chiefest flowers of the Crown'.[49]

A highly significant deduction follows: only the existence of a very serious crisis could have induced the Court to accept such a revolutionary measure.

By August 1703 the ministry's situation was no longer just desperate but hopeless. Forbidden by the queen to pass the Act of Security, it was allowed to accept the only slightly less unpalatable Act anent Peace and War in the vain hope of inducing the House to grant supply. Equally vain for this purpose was the Wine Act that was passed on the ministry's motion. Article 21 of Queensberry's instructions empowered him 'to endeavour to have the prohibition to import French wine taken off, and rescinded, without prejudice of the prohibition to trade with France during the war'.[50] Tweeddale and others strongly opposed this measure, arguing that to permit trade with the enemy was derogatory to Her Majesty's honour and inconsistent with the Grand Alliance![51] The real grounds of opposition, however, were twofold: first, it was known that the act's chief purpose was to raise revenue, and the more money the government raised the weaker would the opposition's position become; and secondly the act was inconsistent with Country Party policy, for it was the Country Party which in 1700, incensed at the failure to represent Scottish interests at the Peace of Ryswick, had riposted by prohibiting the specie-draining wine trade with France.[52] The Wine Act, then, strange though it appears to modern thinking, was neither unpatriotic nor anti-English but simply reflected the government's desperate circumstances. Its passage through the House was also peculiar, secured as it was by a temporary alliance of vested interests. The ministerialists voted for it not just because it was a Court measure but also because it enhanced the prospect of payment of salaries; the Jacobites liked it because it would facilitate contacts with France and the exiled court; the merchant interests eager to expand trade voted for it; and self-interest led some of the Countrymen to support it since the act re-affirmed to the peers and barons the exemption from customs that they had been granted in 1597.[53]

In spite of this belated and rather tawdry success, there was no disguising the fact that the session had been, from the ministry's standpoint, disastrous. Even an act ratifying the rights of the Company of Scotland, a very considerable concession, failed to improve the temper of the parliament.[54] Fletcher was still hotly pressing for his limitations, and a Triennial Act was being demanded. So on 16 September, fearful lest worse should befall and perhaps playing for time before going over to the offensive, the commissioner touched the acts of the session with the sceptre, excluding only the Act of Security, and adjourned until 12 October. His stock at Court had completely slumped, and not only the opposition leaders but also his dissident colleagues were undermining his position with Godolphin and the queen.[55] Queensberry's parting words to the parliament were diplomatic but sombre: deep matters had to be considered, and both queen and parliament needed time to ponder them.[56] Later the commissioner gave the queen a long and specious account of his services, casting the blame for failure on the opposition and on his treacherous associates in the ministry, only to receive the following frigid reply: 'It seems the parliament has conceived a prejudice against you, and that the people slight my authority under your administration: but I will take care for the future, that neither you shall be exposed to their hatred, nor my authority to contempt'.[57]

The session never reconvened, and the parliament of 1703 remained a costly set-back to the Court. Supply, though desperately needed, had been withheld; a constitutional deadlock had been reached over the Act of Security; the central question, the succession, remained unresolved; and the union policy seemed to have vanished into thin air. Such an unwonted outcome of a meeting of the Scottish estates deserves to be regarded not only as critical but almost revolutionary, and was so regarded by Court and ministry. Queensberry, too, was well aware that this bleak tally of failures might well end his political career and that only some quite remarkable stroke could retrieve his fortunes. In fact, even before the adjournment of parliament he was contemplating a coup that would, he hoped, save his own reputation and blast those of his rivals.

12

Continuing Crisis and Attempts at Resolution, 1704–5

FOR obvious enough reasons, the failure of the Scots ministry in 1703 stimulated the Jacobites into fresh plotting on behalf of the Pretender, and in these frantic and ill-conducted activities Queensberry sought his salvation. But to this day his counter-stroke, which had great if unexpected effects, remains something of a puzzle. The prime question is: did an experienced statesman like the commissioner really believe the information about a widespread Jacobite plot that was put so providentially into his hands by a man who was already infamous, Simon Fraser of Beaufort?[1] In Scotland Fraser's villainy had long been notorious, and both his credibility and his allegiance to the Revolution regime were, to say the least, highly suspect. In sober fact, as the law then stood in Scotland, Simon Fraser of Beaufort's word could not have hanged a dog, let alone have indicted a man for treason.

The explanation lies in Fraser's great, and for long enough frustrated, ambition to secure the Lordship of Lovat. If the lordship was, as Simon always maintained, a male fief, then he was the rightful heir; but if it had been converted into a female fief (and at one point this seems to have been the case), then it rightly passed to the daughter of his cousin, the 9th Lord Lovat, who had died in 1696. Foiled at law, young Beaufort ran amok. In an effort to obtain the lordship, male fief or female fief or whatever, he tried to abduct the heiress, and, failing, forced her mother, the dowager Lady Lovat, who was Atholl's daughter, to 'marry' him. Condemned for treason for his numerous misdeeds, Simon then turned Jacobite, but, soon disillusioned with St. Germains, he managed to make his peace with King William and was pardoned. He did not find the Murrays so forgiving, and in 1701 they had him outlawed for the 'rapt' of their kinswoman. Thereafter Beaufort's immediate aim was to gain a pardon, for an outlaw, however great his dubious abilities, could hardly hope to make good his claim to the Lordship of Lovat. With this in mind, early in 1702 Simon offered his services to Anne's government;[2] but, for some reason he could never understand, he was not trusted and the offer was spurned. He then redoubled his efforts to ingratiate himself with the exiled court, only to discover, for some equally unaccountable reason, that there too he was distrusted. Neither the exiled court nor King Louis put much faith in the ugly person or glib talk of the plausible intriguer; but in the end they gave him a chance to prove himself, and in the late summer of 1703 he came over from France, ostensibly to co-ordinate a Jacobite rising but in reality to play his own hand. The tense political situation secured him a hearing where in more normal times he would have been clapped straight into a dungeon.

As a first step towards a full pardon and the coveted title, Simon Fraser informed Queensberry of his mission, giving copious, and incredibly minute and precise, details. If Fraser was to be believed then nearly every politician of note in Scotland, with the pointed exceptions of Queensberry and his henchmen, was deep in this dangerous conspiracy. No real proof accompanied these allegations, however, which had nothing more to support them than vague general probabilities and the word of a man infamous at law. It is, therefore, hardly possible to believe that such a cool calculating politician as Queensberry was taken in; but he was in straits and Fraser's allegations might, if properly handled, come to the commissioner's rescue. True, as sometimes moved on Queensberry's behalf, he had a responsibility for the security of the realm and could not disregard this information; but he must have known that it came from a tainted source, and he could hardly have overlooked the suspicious circumstance that the person chiefly implicated by Simon Fraser was that worthy's inveterate enemy and Queensberry's rival, John, second Marquis and first Duke of Atholl. For Queensberry to make no effort to corroborate Fraser's story and to lay it by stealth before the queen, while the accused were kept in a state of blissful ignorance, smacked of ulterior designs. Almost certainly the commissioner's aim was to bring low Atholl, Hamilton and others, leaving himself to rule the roost undisturbed.

Fraser's vanity foiled Queensberry's ploy. In London the boastful and bibulous Simon, revelling in that 'pride in his villainy' that Horace Walpole noted at his final trial in 1747, allowed himself to be pumped by the plotter to end all plotters, Robert Ferguson, who soon saw that Fraser was simply serving his own ends and that the result could be disastrous for the Jacobite cause. The rebellion that Fraser was trying to foment would be premature, would receive no help from France, and, worse, would be doomed from the start because of Fraser's double dealing with Queensberry. To prevent such a catastrophe, the Jacobite Ferguson warned Atholl of his danger, and Atholl immediately raised a storm. He denounced the story as false and Queensberry as treacherous. Soon, too, the furious outcry against the commissioner was joined by Hamilton and the Jacobites. On reflection, Anne was inclined to agree with them, though, sensibly, she remained convinced that the Jacobites were up to no good. Godolphin too was embarrassed by the whole affair, for, like so many others, he also corresponded discreetly with the Pretender and a thorough witch-hunt into Jacobite activities did not appeal to him. Thus, far from restoring his falling credit, 'Queensberry's Plot', as it was called in Scotland, caused it to slump even further, and soon Godolphin was casting about for another commissioner.

In a different way this intrigue had an equally explosive effect in England, where it received the significant name of the 'Scotch Plot'. In England the late proceedings of the Scottish parliament, misleadingly reported by observers such as William Paterson and William Greg, had aroused great resentment, which was brilliantly epitomised in the homeric encounter between Sir Edward Seymour and Fletcher of Saltoun.[3] Old national animosities were far from dead, and existing English distrust of the Scots was fanned by news of yet another Jacobite plot hatching in Scotland. It seemed to explain much that was otherwise inexplicable, notably the recalcitrance of the Scottish parliament and in particular its refusal to accept the Hanoverian succession. Unwittingly, perhaps, Anne encouraged this strong reaction when in her speech to the English parliament on 17 December 1703 she complained of 'very ill practices and designs carried on in Scotland by emissaries from France'.[4]

The Whigs latched on and were quick to seize the opportunity to condemn Godolphin's Scottish policy, which, they alleged, had contributed to the recent débâcle in the Scots parliament. In fact, the real target of the House of Lords' self-appointed inquiry into the plot was the English administration, and the bumptiousness of the Lords added to the general ferment. To Scots of most persuasions it represented yet another high-handed intrusion into their affairs. In addition the House of Commons, dominated by Tories, complained that the Upper House, driven on by the Junto, were trenching not only on the rights of the crown but also on those of the Lower House. Nor did the conclusions reached by the House of Lords reduce tensions in any way. The peers found that failure to settle the Hanoverian succession had encouraged dangerous plots in Scotland; but once matters in that country were put right and the succession was secured, the Lords promised to support 'an entire and complete union'.[5] So that tattered and patched old kite was aloft again.

Up to a point, these recommendations were acceptable enough to Godolphin. But to carry on with Queensberry as commissioner, as the Junto wished, proved to be impossible, and already as early as October 1703 Godolphin had been sounding out Tweeddale.[6] The repercussions of the plot strengthened this move. As part of the opposition's reaction to Queensberry's allegations, a delegation from the Country Party (consisting of Roxburghe, Rothes and George Baillie of Jerviswood) was sent to London to protest at the commissioner's behaviour and to demand an early meeting of the Scottish parliament to inquire into the plot. Helped by William's ex-secretary James Johnstone (old Wariston's son), Godolphin set to work on this mission, hoping to form from it the nucleus of a new administration in Scotland. The Tweeddale group responded. The chief difficulty lay in the lord treasurer's rigid insistence on a 'broad-bottom'; for, just as Nottingham had tried to strengthen the ministry in Scotland, so Godolphin now hoped to form a broad-bottom by fusion of moderate elements in the Country Party and the old Court Party shorn of Queensberry and his chief lieutenants. By May 1704 an agreement had been reached whereby Tweeddale and his friends, soon to be known as the New Party, were to head a ministry.[7] But it should be stressed that in the beginning it was agreed to form a moderate Country ministry, a revamping, in new circumstances, of the attempt of the previous year.

Policy was the least of the New Party ministry's problems. The queen, Godolphin and Tweeddale all agreed on policy, which was to carry the Hanoverian succession. About this there has never been any mystery, although for some baffling reason Professor Smout believes that Tweeddale's aim was to work for a federal union, a view that finds no warrant in the facts.[8] Anne's instructions to the commissioner and her letter to the Scottish parliament make it crystal clear that the policy of the new ministry was to carry the Hanoverian succession, as the security of the state required. To expedite this, Tweeddale was to give the parliament 'unquestionable proof of our resolutions to maintain the Government both in Church and State as by law established in that our Kingdom, and to consent to such Laws as shall be found wanting for the further security of both, and preventing all incroachments on the same for the future'.[9] As far as the question of Tweeddale's policy in the session of 1704 is concerned, it is obvious that this unequivocal statement precludes any kind of closer union; and, in fact, Tweeddale's policy was simply to patch up and make do with the existing regal union. Given a measure of reform ('such Laws as shall be found wanting'), this aim was not inconsistent with Country Party principles, and the problem of winning over the rank and file of that party was largely a tactical one.

In an attempt to gain Country Party support 'Secretary' Johnstone, as he was familiarly called, recommended that the act of 1641 enabling parliament to approve nominations to offices of trust should be re-enacted in the hope that such a concession would abort the Act of Security, which would then be quietly dropped. Godolphin agreed, and the queen instructed Tweeddale to dangle the bait before the parliament. What the Court wanted was a straight trade—the Hanoverian succession in return for the act of 1641, plus, of course, an adequate supply. Had this programme succeeded, then it is very doubtful if an incorporating union would have ensued. Difficulties in plenty between the two kingdoms would still have remained, but the critical issue, the succession, would have been resolved.

Anne's letter to this parliament recognised in the plainest possible terms the existence of a dangerous crisis between the two kingdoms. But the policy of compromise was a total failure, and the session of the Scottish parliament that opened on 6 July 1704 proved to be the very eye of the storm in the relations between the two kingdoms. The ministry's plan was wrecked by foreseeable circumstances. Tweeddale's policy did not, contrary to expectation, prove attractive to the mass of the Countrymen who feared that once the succession was settled further reform would be unobtainable. Only Belhaven and some ambitious place-hunters of his easy kidney (such as Montrose, Roxburghe and Haddington) joined the New Party, as it soon came to be called, and Tweeddale's ministry could never count on more than 30 votes.[10] Blame for this failure lay with Godolphin rather than with Tweeddale, for the new commissioner wished to make a clean sweep of Queensberry's group, which he distrusted, partly to strengthen the ministry and partly to have offices to dangle before the Countrymen.[11] Tweeddale, who was neither stupid nor naïve, knew that this was how the system worked; and besides he realised that only thus could he hope to convince his old associates of his good faith. Godolphin refused—partly to keep in with the Junto, who were trying to shore up Queensberry, and partly because he believed that the right method was to force on a coalition between the New Party and the Old. The crafty and obsequious chancellor, Seafield, Godolphin's main counsellor on Scottish affairs, acquiesced; but in the circumstances of 1704 Godolphin's policy was quite unworkable. Tweeddale displayed the greater realism, as Queensberry's treacherous conduct soon proved, and early in the session the new commissioner had every cause to write to Godolphin lamenting the numerous defections of office-holders at Queensberry's behest, concluding pointedly: 'By all this your Lordship cannot but perceive that what methods may have been proper for circumstances with you have had the contrare effect with us'—a polite 'I told you so'.[12]

It has become fashionable to represent Tweeddale as honest but incompetent —a suspect characterisation. He was certainly a rarity in that age, an honest politician; but he was also able and clear-sighted. The charge of incompetence lies rather with the ill-informed but dictatorial Godolphin. Even before the opening of the session Tweeddale showed real acumen. Not only did he stress the need for a united ministry, but he also asked the Court to allow him to determine the order of business and give him some latitude in decision-taking, claiming, with some justice, that the débâcle of the previous session had arisen largely because the commissioner had been tied too rigidly to his instructions and that Court policy was too inflexible.[13] This request was also denied, and policy continued to be implemented by remote control, with the compliant Seafield acting as the main intermediary.

Seafield can easily be over-rated as a statesman, but strictly speaking it is doubtful if he should rank as such. He was a very good manager, an able administrator, and a clever intriguer; but his one aim was to please the Court, and he lacked the moral or political courage to embark on bold but necessary courses. True, his judiciously phrased letters to all and sundry have the aura of statesmanship; but not so his acts. Indeed Seafield's wide contacts, clever mind and persuasiveness merely added to the muddle. He was never short of a promising scheme, but left to him the crisis, far from being resolved, would simply have become an infinite series of knowing letters and clever suggestions. In time the truth of Tweeddale's tactical assessments dawned on Godolphin; but the main beneficiary of the English lord treasurer's belated awareness was not Tweeddale but Tweeddale's successor, who had an inimitable way of thrusting reality to the fore.

As it was, Queensberry, secretly supported by the Junto, acted exactly as Tweeddale had predicted, studiously keeping away from the parliament, where his presence could only have provoked disorders, but retaining his grip on his following through his able lieutenant, the Earl of Mar. Queensberry's first thought was for his own safety, and, keen to ensure the failure of the new ministry and anxious to prevent an inquiry into the plot, he made a deal with the opposition in return for their promise not to press that awkward matter.[14] For different reasons the opposition groups were willing to accommodate their erstwhile bête noir: the Jacobites, naturally eager to leave the plot well alone, were in addition glad of any support against the Hanoverian succession; and the Countrymen, much as they hated Queensberry, were also willing to pay the required price for his support in order to thwart such an apostate ministry.

The peculiar situation that resulted has perplexed many historians, especially those who believe that the practice of politics has everything to do with principle and nothing to do with expedience. In particular those who see the Treaty of Union of 1707 as an act of consummate and deliberate statesmanship, unsullied by base considerations of any kind, have found Queensberry's conduct at this point disconcerting. Faced by this poser, G. M. Trevelyan airily verbalised it out of existence with an absurd statement: 'On occasions when the Presbyterians opposed him, he was capable of walking a few Parliamentary yards arm in arm with the moderate Jacobites, so long as they did not lead him out of his path.'[15] On this occasion Queensberry's harmless little saunter destroyed the Court's policy and deepened the crisis. His contemporaries, including Anne and Godolphin, were not as indulgent to Queensberry as generations of Whig historians were to be. Contemporary opinion attributed Queensberry's actions to self-seeking treachery, and nothing in the evidence invalidates that judgment.

Even more dejected by the Scottish imbroglio than Anne and her English ministers was the family of Hanover. In April 1702, on receipt of news of King William's death, the dowager electress wrote to the Earl of Leven, who was indebted to the House of Hanover for help given to him when he was in exile before the Revolution, and who became one of their chief agents in Scotland. Sophia pathetically stressed her claims on Scottish support—'Je compte beaucoup sur l'affection des Escoisois, puis je suis du sang d'Ecosse'. It was the right note to strike; but all too evidently the affections of many Scots went to the senior stem of the royal family, and many others, who cared not a straw for the Stewarts, were unenamoured of the mother of a wee German lairdie. The involved politics of Scotland puzzled the dowager, though her intelligence enabled her to make shrewd appraisals. At one point she inquired anxiously about the Duke of Hamilton, whether he was for the Pretender, 'ou s'il veut estre roy luy mesme'? The setback of 1703 depressed her and she wrote resignedly: 'Mais, my lord, il semble que je ne suis point a la mode en Ecosse, et que dans le dernier parlement on ne ce souvient pas que je suis au monde'. Indeed, pressure from Hanover helped to determine ministerial policy in Scotland in 1704—that is, insistence on the Hanoverian succession. But the good-humoured and redoubtable old lady (against whom nothing can be said, unless that it was her misfortune to be the mother of an awful brood) was to be even more bitterly disappointed at the outcome of the session of the Scottish parliament of 1704.[16]

For the reasons already outlined, in 1704 the ministry never won control of the House, a clear majority stubbornly refusing to consider the succession or to vote supply. Indeed, as early as 13 July Hamilton wrested the initiative from the ministry with the resolve, 'That this Parliament will not proceed to the nomination of a successor until we have had a previous treaty with England in relation to our commerce and other concerns with that nation'.[17] The ministry tried hard to break the deadlock but failed, and so pressing was the need for supply that neither adjournment nor dissolution was practicable. To add insult to injury, Hamilton graciously proposed a two months' supply—just to give the Court time to think things over! All this Tweeddale honestly reported to the Court; but he received no help from London, and the unlikely combination of Country, Cavaliers and renegade Courtiers proved invincible.

Yet supply was essential. The Scots army, none too strong or reliable at best, was on the verge of mutiny for lack of pay and provisions. The war was in its most critical phase, in which everything turned on Marlborough's daring march on the Danube; but news of his great victory at Blenheim came too late to nerve the Court, and anyway could not have solved its difficulties in Scotland. So there was nothing for it but to defer to the opposition, which rejected the act of 1641 as a mere sop and refused to emasculate the Act of Security. Finally in return for six months' supply Tweeddale was allowed by the Court to pass the Act of Security but without the clause relating to free trade,[18] the queen fearing that this clause would further inflame English resentment.[19] Not content with this, the cockahoop opposition pressed for other awkward measures, notably that the parliament should elect commissioners to treat with England. Then, no longer dependent on Queensberry, the opposition exploded over the plot, but not in a way that gave any comfort to the ministry. Its reality was discounted; and instead of on Queensberry, the Scottish parliament's wrath fell on the House of Lords, and this the queen keenly resented. She refused to be moved on the matter, and the session, which had been quietly conducted hitherto, ended in loud recriminations. The only other significant act of the session of 1704 forbade the import and permitted the export of wool, an act that was regarded in England as hostile to her trade and which paved the way for economic sanctions against Scotland.[20] On 28 August, conscious that nothing could be usefully done, Tweeddale closed this doleful session. He did not try to gloss over his failures and instead of excuses offered his resignation. His honesty, however, had commended him to the queen and she refused to allow him to retire. Yet the Court's failure was undeniable and patent to all: the question of the succession remained as open as ever, and policy was in tatters.

Such a bare summary of the main outcome does not bring out the full significance of this intriguing session. Though latterly marred by displays of ill temper, it was, in the main, better conducted than its rowdy predecessor, and it did not get bogged down in interminable debates over detail. Much of its time, indeed, was taken up with a close examination of the report of a parliamentary commission set up in 1703 to audit the public accounts since 1690.[21] The opposition had instituted the inquiry as an attack on Queensberry's corrupt regime and was gratified to find that the duke owed the treasury £42,144 Scots, some of it possibly spent on 'the secret service' of purchasing votes in 1703.[22] Indeed so many abuses were uncovered that an Act anent Misapplying Public Funds was introduced.[23] But if the opposition had known of Godolphin's instructions to Seafield they might not have been so enthusiastic about cleansing the Augean stables of the Scottish administration. On 12 August Godolphin ordered Seafield to move on arrears of salaries and gratifications.[24] This seemed innocence itself—but an idea was sprouting that was to bear fruit later; in short, those who had claims on the Treasury were to be made to understand that payment would ultimately depend on the goodwill of the Court, and it required little imagination to work out how that was to be won.

Management, in other words, was being tightened up, initially to bring Queensberry's minions to heel, but capable of further use. At the same time a large number of peerages was being created to bolster up the Court interest. This alarmed Fletcher who introduced an act for additional compensatory representation for the barons, which, though supported by the burgess members, was deferred after a second reading.[25] And throughout the session, of course, within its limited means the ministry purchased support. The most interesting deal secured them William Seton the younger of Pitmedden. This former Countryman, a supposedly disinterested writer on trade and latterly a powerful and persuasive advocate of incorporating union, approached Seafield through one of the latter's henchmen for a pension of £100 per annum, promising that 'he will be your servant and give you a suitable returne'.[26]

The attitudes and tactics of the opposition were also noteworthy. Throughout the session the House was evidently annoyed by, and latterly incensed at, the plot and the Lords' inquiry into it. The House of Lords was condemned for meddling in Scottish affairs, while at the same time the opposition went out of its way to praise the Commons for its fair-mindedness.[27] Clearly, an effort was being made to capitalise on the differences that had arisen between the English Houses of Parliament. Attitudes to the plot, however, were ginger and forced the opposition into awkward postures. Had it not been for the fears of the Jacobites and the need for a compact with Queensberry, the plot would have provided justification enough for opposition to the ministry's programme, for, after all, if the opposition was intent on filibustering, one excuse was as good as another, and the plot could have been presented as a major grievance; but, since a thorough examination of the plot was not really desired by many of those who made a noise about it, the matter could not be pressed too far. If the succession was to be fobbed off, then it had to be on other grounds, and the Act of Security seemed to offer a way out: a treaty with England should take precedence over settling the succession. This stumped Tweeddale and his colleagues, who had staked everything on carrying the succession, and so they insisted, through Roxburghe, on reform of the Scottish constitution before all other considerations. The New Party was thus impaled on its original policy.

On the surface it seemed like a bedlam situation, but its meaning was clear enough. Tweeddale believed that Hamilton and his associates were not sincere about a treaty but clamouring for one as 'the most popular handle to throw off the succession at this time'.[28] Of some, notably the Jacobites, this was obviously true; and probably, too, as Tweeddale further believed, the more radical members of the Country Party intended to ruin any prospect of union by making the terms 'so extravagant as they cannot be yeelded to by England'.[29] Others, however, were willing to negotiate but not for an incorporating union, hence the insistence that parliament should nominate any commission appointed. Parliamentary nomination would insure against any overweening influence from England via the Court, would abort any attempt at incorporation, and yet, conceivably, might lead to a better relationship with England through communication of trade and reduction of the power of the Court. The Court, however, was well aware of these possibilities and would not hear of a nomination of commissioners by parliament. Tweeddale, therefore, far from working for a federal union, as Smout believes, was hard pushed to prevent any moves that might lead in that direction. The queen, too, had somehow got it into her head that the English parliament would also claim the right to nominate commissioners, and she seems actually to have imagined that there was a joint Anglo-Scottish Whig plot against the crown.[30] The Court, haunted by the 1640s, always dreaded an alliance of powerful English and Scottish political groups; and so, rather than run the risk of such an alliance emerging, the session in Scotland was hurriedly brought to a close. But in moving for a treaty, the triumphant opposition had all unwittingly given the Court an advantage that was in the end to prove decisive. Perhaps, after all, the opposition might have been wiser to have stuck to the plot.

There was strong English reaction to all this. Recently it has been suggested that the union was the almost accidental by-product of party manoeuvrings in England; while there is much to be said for this view, it does rather neglect another potent factor—namely, public feeling. After the fiasco of the Scottish session of 1703 English chauvinism had risen, and it came to the boil with the crown's acceptance of the Act of Security in 1704. All sorts of rumours swept England and found ready credence:—the Scots were arming a large force for the invasion of England, so the northern defences had to be secured; the Scots were Jacobite to a man; the opposition in the parliament was in French pay; Louis XIV was lavishing vast sums on the Pretender's cause, and was ready to land a formidable army in Scotland.[31] A numerous tribe of pamphleteers spread these stories, their shrill jeremiads increasing public unease and stirring up public wrath. The old English sport of Scot-baiting, which had never died out, then enjoyed a vigorous revival. Particularly obnoxious to the Scots was the work of William Atwood, Whig attorney and inveterate polemicist, whose *Superiority and Direct Dominion of the Imperial Crown of England over the Crown and Kingdom of Scotland* was published in 1704. This shapeless hodge-podge raked over ancient controversies and triumphantly concluded that Scotland, as a fief of the English crown, was bound by the English Act of Settlement. Condemned in August 1705 by the Scottish parliament and ordered to be burnt, it was destroyed in a better sense by James Anderson's scholarly refutation of its argument. Undeterred, Atwood continued to flay the Scots and expose what he took to be their pretensions. Thus, in a stinging pamphlet of 1705, *The Scotch Patriot Unmask'd*, he openly stigmatised the opposition in the Scottish parliament as 'the French faction'. For their part the Scots did not suffer in silence, some of their champions proving every whit as provocative as their opponents, and George Ridpath in particular seems to have delighted in stirring up controversy.[32] But demand for this literature of contention did not need to be created. The large number of pamphlets produced, some of them hefty tomes, is indicative of the existence of a keen public interest. So the intensity of public feeling in both countries cannot be ignored. It certainly was not overlooked by the politicians of the time. Nor was it negligible in its effects, as the affair of the *Worcester* clearly showed.

As for the English politicians, both Whigs and Tories were alarmed and infuriated by the work of the Scottish parliament. As an indication of this, in November 1704 the Scottish question was, for the first time, seriously debated in both Houses of Parliament, the Tory peers—Haversham, Rochester and Nottingham—leading the way. The Act of Security was condemned as an exclusion bill cutting off the Hanoverian succession, thus posing a threat to England's safety; and Godolphin was bitterly criticised for sanctioning it, even his allegiance to the queen being called in question.[33] The alarm felt was no doubt genuine, but it is noticeable that the gravamen of the attack was still directed against Godolphin. The Junto at first gleefully joined the hue and cry, but, after extorting concessions from Godolphin, they soon moderated their views, warning against adopting too high a line with the Scots parliament which might, if too bitterly assailed, be huffed into even more dangerous courses. The Whigs gave out that only a complete union would solve the problems that had arisen, and yet another bill recommending union was passed. All the same, the Whigs, who were not really keen on union, would have preferred a settlement of the succession, and hinted that if the Court would support them they would work for such concessions on trade that 'the succession cannot fail to be settled'.[34] The Whig lords, in fact, initiated a strategy that might put pressure on Scotland to accept either union or succession; it was they who outlined the heads of what was to become the Alien Act. Yet they feared that a complete union would strengthen the Court at their expense, since it was believed that Scottish representatives at Westminster would dutifully toe the ministerial line. The Junto's game, therefore, was complicated and not without its dangers.

The reaction in the Tory-dominated Commons was broadly similar (outrage over the Act of Security and determination to probe the ministry's gaping wounds) and resulted on 5 February 1705 in the 'Act for the effectual securing of the Kingdom of England from the apparent dangers that might arise from several Acts lately passed in the Parliament of Scotland'—the so-called Alien Act. Its first clause recommended that the queen should nominate commissioners to treat for a union, but unless such a treaty was in train or the Hanoverian succession had been accepted in Scotland by 25 December 1705 the Scots were to incur penalties: all Scots, except those already domiciled in England or her possessions, should be treated as aliens, and trade with England in cattle, linen and coal (Scotland's principal exports) was to cease. It was, as Defoe states, an impolitic and unjust measure.[35] Probably too it was unconstitutional, since while the Union of the Crowns endured, naturalisation by law must follow on the precedent of Calvin's case.[36] But constitutional or not and just or unjust, the Alien Act was effective, and particularly so was its threat of economic sanctions. Much depended, though, on how the act was wielded. Here the defeat of the Tories in the general election of 1705 proved providential for the ministry, because the Whigs, unlike the Tories, were prepared to use the Alien Act as a lever rather than as a bludgeon.

The first effect of the Alien Act in Scotland, however, was to heighten aversion to England, as the act's menacing tone led to a frenzy of bitter Anglophobia. The Edinburgh mob took to the streets, and the politicians, divided as ever, scarcely knew which way to turn. Tweeddale continued to enjoy the favour of the Court, and indeed by a belated redistribution of offices late in 1704, the object of which was to weed out Queensberry's defectors, the New Party ministry had its position strengthened. Only Court influence, however, and the party strife in England kept it in being. The Junto distrusted the New Party and pressed Godolphin to restore the Old Party to power, but, keen to minimise the influence of the Junto, the lord treasurer tried hard to maintain Tweeddale's ministry, whose interest he identified with his own.[37] Nonetheless, the Alien Act weakened Tweeddale's ministry and drove the New Party almost frantic. How could its members suddenly reverse all their arguments and push a union policy? Queensberry and other magnates could turn and twist, but their great wealth and personal followings enabled them to get away with it. The New Party was differently circumstanced; its members preened themselves as the party of principle and disinterested patriotism, and as such they could not easily doff and don policies. But in this dilemma their vaunted principles were gradually jettisoned, as they tried to make deals with Hamilton, Argyll and even Queensberry. It was all to no purpose. By January 1705 the canny Seafield had sniffed disaster in the air and, though a leading member of Tweeddale's administration, was intriguing with Godolphin to bring down the ministry. Besides, Seafield was peeved at having to give up the chancellorship in favour of Tweeddale whose undoubted talents did not fit him for this particular office.[38] Tweeddale was also too honest for his rank and file, who, keen to retain office, feverishly angled for Argyll as commissioner in the hope that he would reinforce the existing administration.[39] Queensberry tried to wreck this scheme by pressing for Seafield as commissioner with himself pulling the strings, but the Court would have none of him or his plan.[40] As for Hamilton, he continued to be all things to all men. His lack of cash forced him to importune in all quarters, and at this time his agents in London, who were trying to negotiate a deal on his behalf with the Court, went so far as to describe him as 'chambre à louer'.[41]

Godolphin wasted little time on such diversions. By the end of February 1705 he was bargaining with the one real prospect, Argyll, but finding it hard going. Argyll, under no illusions about his value, wanted money and an English peerage, and not until his demands were met would he deign to accept the commissionership. Even then difficulties remained. The Court's wish was that Argyll should effect a coalition of Old and New Parties, leaving Queensberry and the Junto out in the cold; but the Junto fought back and played on Argyll's known dislike of the New Party, urging him to make a clean sweep of it, an idea to which Argyll was already giving serious thought even before he came up to Edinburgh to open the next session of parliament.[42] The *Worcester* incident may merely have confirmed the already imminent fall of the New Party.

That affair had begun on 12 August 1704 when an English merchant vessel, the *Worcester*, was seized in the Firth of Forth, not by the authorities but by the agents of the Company of Scotland. This was in retaliation for the arrest of the Company's last trading ship, the *Annandale*, by English revenue officials at the instigation of the East India Company. The English government had disapproved of the *Annandale*'s seizure but had not interfered, and the law, which apparently favoured the East India Company, was allowed to take its course. When its turn came to be put on the spot, the Scottish government felt obliged, in deference to public opinion, to adopt the same attitude. The need arose when, determined to reimburse themselves by escheating the *Worcester*'s cargo, the stockholders of the Company of Scotland pressed charges of murder and piracy against Captain Green and some of his crew, who on little or no evidence were tried before the High Court of Admiralty. The trial was a travesty of justice, so weak was the evidence that sought to convict the accused of pirating the *Speedy Return*, a vessel belonging to the Company of Scotland that had mysteriously disappeared in the Indian Ocean. The *Speedy Return* had indeed been taken by pirates; not, however, by Captain Green and not off the Malabar coast but in a Madagascar harbour by the notorious pirate John Bowen. Green and his men were guiltless of this or any other criminal act and were simply the innocent victims of bad Anglo-Scottish relations. Ill fortune had brought them at a time of great tension into the supposedly safe haven of the Forth, there to await convoy for London, a normal precaution against the French privateers that were wreaking havoc on English and Scottish shipping.[43]

Anti-English feeling in Scotland was then so bitter that most people believed in the trumped-up charges, and in March 1705 Green and his men were found guilty and sentenced to death. It was now the turn of English public opinion to be outraged and to demand a reprieve from the queen, who was placed in a quandary. For the crown to overturn due legal process in Scotland could only have added to political difficulties there, especially when the case of the *Annandale* was recalled. Anne could do little more than hint at mercy to the Scottish Privy Council, and the Council, terrified by the clamour for blood, lacked the nerve to do anything. Many of its members absented themselves from the crucial meeting on 10 April, and conspicuous among the absentees, on a variety of ludicrous excuses, were those who belonged to the New Party. Seafield, indeed, was present but lacked the moral courage to act; instead he informed Godolphin that the captain, mate and gunner would have to be sacrificed to the mob.[44] Argyll was all for a reprieve, and had he been in Edinburgh he would not have hesitated to defy, and if need be to suppress, the angry mob. But he was still in London, and the queen's good intentions were frustrated by the unheroic Seafield and the shoddy manoeuvres of the New Party. The leaders of that party had lost heavily in the Darien venture and were naturally keen to recover what they could; but they also hoped to profit from the affair politically. They believed that the ill-will it caused in both countries would ruin the union project, and they further believed that truckling to the mob would win for them in Scotland the popularity that they craved and needed so much. As one of their leaders, Baillie of Jerviswood, wrote to Secretary Johnstone on 31 March: 'Go the matter as it will, we shall by it have the country'.[45] Yet little more than a fortnight later, as the public mood took another turn, the shuffling Baillie claimed to be one of the few who had had scruples about the execution of Captain Green and his men.[46]

In attempting to gain the country the leaders of the New Party lost the Court, which, after this miserable display, could not long resist Argyll's demands for their dismissal. Nor did they gain the country. After the execution of Green and two members of his crew on 11 April the hysteria subsided. Blood-lust gave way to shame and remorse. No one liked to be reminded of the execution of Captain

Green, his first mate John Madder and the gunner James Simpson; and, significant of this changed atmosphere, in September the other condemned men were released without fuss. Thus the cheap popularity that the New Party had stooped so low to earn did not materialise, and the advantage of the affair lay with Argyll.

Against all recognisable odds, the stop-gap expedient of the young Duke of Argyll as commissioner was to prove decisive. At the age of 25 a novice of unknown political worth, he was nevertheless no nonentity; his rank and estate gave him not only great social prestige but also a substantial political 'interest'; and as chief of the Campbells he had more men at command than there were regular troops in Scotland, and better fighting men at that. He also turned out to be a persuasive speaker. Yet Argyll's commissionership was a case of *pis aller*: the more experienced political magnates were all, for various reasons, unacceptable either to Court or parliament, and in Queensberry's case to both. But any who believed that Argyll could be used as a cats-paw were soon undeceived. Proud and masterful, he brooked no nonsense from any quarter, not even the Court itself, and he exploded onto the scene to confound experienced politicians English as well as Scottish. Like Tweeddale he was a realist, but whereas Tweeddale sent humble requests to Godolphin Argyll made peremptory demands. His correspondence is like no other. The differences, for example, between Seafield's clever but deferential letters and Argyll's pronunciamentos is startling and significant. Under the guise of being Godolphin's Caledonian grey eminence, Seafield kow-towed to the lord treasurer's every whim, intent only to serve— that is, keep his place and ferret out as many good things as possible.[47] Argyll, on the other hand, wrote to Godolphin, and even to the queen herself, as if he were addressing his chamberlain at Inveraray. In itself his rude forthrightness was a positive contribution to settling the crisis, dispelling as it did the complacent ignorance of the Court on Scottish affairs.

Throughout his commissionership Argyll insisted on a free hand, threatening to resign otherwise. Thus, he was determined to face the parliament with a strong ministry, and he browbeat the Court into accepting his views. He demanded that the New Party should be laid aside; its members were, he claimed, weak and useless, as the *Worcester* incident plainly showed, and, besides, their fixation on the succession would tie the hands of the ministry.[48] Anne trusted the New Party and refused to dispense with its services, whereupon Argyll tendered his resignation and had the audacity to add: 'I hope your Majesty will not think I resign my post of Commissioner in order to persuade you to make the alterations I proposed'.[49] Anne had to give way and consent to the dismissal of Tweeddale and his friends, only to be outraged at Argyll's next demand. She refused pointblank to restore Queensberry to office, 'which', she declared, 'is a thing I can never consent to, his last tricking behaviour having made him more odious to me than ever'. Again Argyll was insistent, and again he stormed the closet. A week later the queen was forced, though with no good grace, to agree to Queensberry's employment. In this matter Anne and not Godolphin was the real obstacle, and only with the greatest reluctance did she give in; as she told Godolphin, who had urged compliance, 'it grates my soul to take a man into my service that has not only betrayed us, but tricked me several times, one that has been obnoxious to his own countrymen these many years and one that I can never be convinced can be of any use'.[50] In private Queensberry continued to mutter against the Court; but he behaved in public, playing himself in quietly as lord privy seal and setting about his task of reducing his old following to obedience.

Thus a strong ministry, drawn mainly from the Old Court Party, was being built up. But what policy was it to pursue? This awkward question was in the end answered by Argyll's extraordinary personality and unorthodox attitudes. The new commissioner was indifferent to politics, and possibly this as much as anything else explains his success. A contemporary says of him that 'his head ran more on the camp than the court'—meaning that he was by vocation a soldier rather than a politician.[51] He was indeed a soldier of real ability, and one who was determined to rise in his profession. 'Red John of the Battles', as he is known in Gaelic tradition, was greedy and covetous; but his great ambition was to further his military career through politics. Already a brigadier general in the Dutch service, he was keen to obtain a similar commission from the queen.

Two consequences followed. First, Argyll's commissionership was conducted on military lines with a heavy emphasis on discipline. Under his command no backsliding was permitted; those who were not for him were treated as hostile; and the opposition was kept under steady harassing pressure. All this was in marked contrast to the two preceding sessions of parliament. Secondly, Argyll was indifferent to the political outcome. Whatever the ultimate result (settlement of the succession, an incorporating union, a federal union, or even continued deadlock), he simply meant to win a personal campaign in parliament, reap the rewards of victory, and move on to where the real glory was, with the army in Flanders. His self-centred attitudes served him well. Instead of getting trapped in personal commitment to one specific policy, as had happened to his predecessors, he made a tactical assessment of the situation to find out which policy had the better prospect of success. To him it was all as obvious as deciding whether to load with grape or canister.

Then, too, the predicament in which the Court found itself gave Argyll unusual latitude. Chastened by the experiences of 1703 and 1704, with the Act of Security fastened round its neck like an albatross and caught between the Junto and the New Party, the Court was in considerable disarray and unable to make up its mind about policy. At heart it favoured union but gave out that its immediate aim was the succession, and this latter was the policy that Argyll himself, and his Whig allies in England, would have preferred. But when the new commissioner came up to Edinburgh late in April 1705, 'attended with a number of Highlanders and swordsmen, in whom he took great delight',[52] a careful reconnaissance indicated that the succession would be the more troublesome programme to carry. The majority of the ministers favoured a treaty, and, apart from the New Party, only two dissidents of note, Cockburn of Ormiston and the Marquis of Annandale, insisted on the succession. The result of these soundings, in fact, completed Argyll's case against the New Party. They could have been relied upon to support the succession but would not have supported a treaty, and so the leaders of the New Party were ignored by the commissioner and shortly thereafter ditched to make way for members of the Old.

But still Argyll proceeded cautiously. He got two addresses from the queen to the parliament, one stressing the need for a settlement of the succession and the other recommending a treaty. Which he was to make use of was left to the commissioner's discretion, and to everyone's surprise it turned out that the arrogant whipper-snapper had no lack of that commodity. He conflated the addresses, recommending both policies to the parliament, with a slight preference for succession, and leaving all parties confused and uncertain.[53] Even after the opening of the session of parliament on 28 June he continued to move warily, alert to seize any opportunity that might arise. Behind the scenes he had prepared for the coming struggle in other ways, notably by demanding £10,000 or £12,000 from the English treasury with which to pay arrears of salaries. This, he calculated, would buy more than 20 votes, and he was annoyed when Godolphin failed to comply.[54] The New Party had also anticipated some such move which they believed would be aimed at securing the succession.[55] As it was, though he did not get the £12,000 he had demanded from Godolphin, Argyll had considerable patronage at his disposal, which he dispensed skilfully and to best advantage.[56]

Nevertheless, on the opening of the session it looked as if the House was again going to thwart the ministry, the majority refusing, with studied nonchalance, to consider the queen's recommendations. This complacent show of strength turned out to be a blunder, as Lockhart of Carnwath later acknowledged. Lockhart gives an accurate assessment of the situation. As was usually, he avers, the case, opposition strength was greatest at the opening of the session but tended to decline as members found other diversions or even returned home to see to their affairs. Then, too, early in this particular session of parliament many of Queensberry's group voted with the opposition in the belief that Queensberry was still allied to the Country Party. A stop was eventually put to this, but it took time; and, concluded Lockhart, 'the Court, who had the purse and the power, were still gaming upon the Country, who has no arguments or persuasives to induce members to stand firm'.[57]

As to the actual proceedings in parliament, on 6 July Annandale, the secretary, moved for strict limitations before settling the succession and that a Committee of the House should be appointed to consider questions of trade. The motion carried ministerial policy much further than Argyll desired, and soon he and Annandale were at loggerheads—very much a case of Greek meeting Greek, for Annandale too was notoriously wilful and quarrelsome. To repair the damage caused by Annandale's attempt to force the commissioner's hand, the Earl of Mar, one of Queensberry's group who had acted with the Cavaliers in 1704, moved for a treaty (ostensibly what the opposition wanted), but obtained such meagre support that he withdrew his motion.[58] Nothing really could be done by the ministry until Queensberry came up and brought his following to heel; so, to begin with, the commissioner was glad enough to give the House its head. For a fortnight, in a few short sederunts, it discussed matters of trade; but Hamilton grew uneasy lest in the absence of confrontation the opposition might disintegrate into squabbling groups, and on 17 July he put forward a curiously worded resolve. He proposed that the parliament should not proceed to the nomination of a successor until a treaty had first been negotiated with England 'in relation to our commerce and other concerns with that nation'; he also proposed that the parliament should make such constitutional changes as were necessary to secure 'the liberty, religion and independence of the nation'.[59] Hamilton was clearly not proposing an incorporating union, but his resolve played into the Court's hands. Mar again introduced his motion for a treaty, the precise objects of which were not defined, but again it stalled as the House resumed considerations of trade and finance. In this indeterminate fencing, one all-important fact was plainly emerging and that was that the opposition had lost its cohesion, some demanding this and others that, while the double-dealing Hamilton twisted and turned to suit his own mysterious ends.

And what were these? The Duke of Hamilton's tortuous political career was in its most complex and enigmatic phase. The Jacobites no longer trusted him, the exiled court complaining bitterly that he did not even answer letters; and through Louis XIV's emissary, Colonel Nathaniel Hooke, Hamilton was trying to negotiate directly with the Grand Monarch. Hamilton met Hooke in August 1705, in conditions of comic opera secrecy at Holyrood House, and tried to obtain money with which to bribe members of the parliament; but parliamentary battles were not what King Louis had in mind and the request went unanswered.[60] The Country Party as a whole was also disillusioned with Hamilton, whose patriotism seemed too closely confined to his own interest. Fletcher had been estranged by the duke's erratic wavering, and was arguing as vehemently as ever for radical reform but finding little consistent backing. There was, in fact, a widespread suspicion that Hamilton had made a secret deal with the Court, and this rumour seems to have had some foundation in fact. On the other hand, the duke's conduct can perhaps be otherwise explained. He may have believed, as many did in both England and Scotland, that the union project was a will-o'-the-wisp, no sooner pursued than lost, and that it could be safely invoked to prevent the settlement of the succession. The Scottish Jacobites certainly took this line, the more so as they believed that they possessed the means of wrecking any serious attempt at a union, either through resistance in parliament or in the last resort by armed rebellion.

The New Party was also in deep trouble, floating in a limbo of its own making. It was infuriated by Argyll's brash ways but was unable to make common cause with old opposition allies who now flirted with a spurious union policy. By that time Tweeddale was little more than a figurehead, as his nominal followers—supposedly disinterested patriots—strove desperately to find a profitable rôle to play. They shifted about so much that they were landed with the nickname that had originally been fastened on the Cavaliers—'Squadrone Volante' or Flying Squadron. With Roxburghe leading the way, the new Squadrone, racking and in the end fracturing their consciences, bitterly came to terms with the present and sought to make provision for the future. They veered between Court and Country, and inevitably the Court benefited from their shuffling.

By 22 August, with the passing of the Triennial Act, the opposition was spent and only feebly resisting the Court's drive for a treaty. True, it could still erupt over limitations, the need for a Council of Trade and such-like matters; but it had no real concerted policy. True again, it could still impede proceedings by demanding repeal of the more obnoxious features of the Alien Act; but the ministry parried this move by persuading the House to address the queen on the threatened loss of naturalisation rights. Then in vain the opposition, with tepid help from the Squadrone, tried to impose restrictions on the 'treaters' by stipulating that they were only to consider a federal union. In beating down this motion, on the plea that the Scottish commissioners must have the same wide terms of reference as the English, the ministers for the first time spoke of an incorporating union. If a union policy were to prove most expedient then undoubtedly the Scots ministry aimed at incorporating union, if only because nothing less would satisfy the Court or the English parliament; but up to this point the ministers were careful to use the elastic and neutral word 'treaty'. Now, however, they defended the possibility of 'ane entire union'.[61] Thus, by sheer calm persistence and adroit trimming the ministry finally won acceptance for a treaty, and by 1 September it had been agreed that a commission to negotiate should be appointed.[62]

For the opposition, however, all was not yet lost by any means. They still insisted that the parliament should elect the commissioners, bitterly opposing the ministry's claim that it was the queen's right to nominate. There was something to be said for both views, but each side carefully slanted the evidence to accommodate its own position. Traditionally, the crown regulated foreign policy, appointing embassies and negotiators, and this right was always observed in England. But since 1603 Anglo-Scottish relations were divorced from foreign policy as such and placed on a peculiar footing. As a result tradition could be said to favour the estates as much as the Court; thus in 1604 and 1689 the naming of a commission had been left to the parliament, but in 1670 and 1702 the right of nomination had been exercised by the crown.[63] The precedent of 1702, a notoriously bad one, was still fresh in memory, and the opposition was determined not to be caught out like that again. Everything turned on this point. If the opposition had won and nomination had been left to the estates, then very likely the resulting negotiations would have been abortive. A commission nominated by the estates would have contained many who would have been bitterly opposed to an incorporating union; and equally certainly the English commissioners would have had no truck with a federal union. Over this crucial matter it looked as if, as the opposition gleefully anticipated, the session would end in stalemate. This would have left the ministry in an impossible position, since the opposition groups could have made out that they had been earnestly striving to carry out Court policy but had been frustrated by unconstitutional conduct on the part of the ministry.

Court and ministry alike were well aware of the danger and had provided against it. As early as mid-July, Godolphin gave out that 'Duke Hamilton will not oppose a treaty'; and others had it that 'Duke Hamilton has positively engaged to bring it about'.[64] Nothing in Hamilton's conduct during the session gave the lie to such rumours, and Lockhart's acid comments on the premier duke's conduct in this instance have every justification.[65] Indeed, on the vital matter of the nomination of the commission Hamilton had through Mar assured Argyll that it would be left to the queen,[66] even though he continued to head the opposition in its struggle against such a move. His conduct was, and remains, inexplicable, and can only be discussed in conjectural terms. Possibly he was alarmed at his failure to be elected by the estates to the recently created Council of Trade, a fact that clearly indicated that his parliamentary strength was declining. Certainly Seafield played on this, in private taunting the duke that if nomination of the treaty commissioners were left to parliament he might incur a similar rebuff.[67] Possibly also, as well as being promised nomination if he helped the ministry, Hamilton was threatened with a charge of treason arising from his dealings with King Louis if he continued his opposition. It was known that Hooke was Louis' emissary, and those who dealt with him were regarded as being more dangerous than the common run of Jacobite intriguers.

Whatever his precise motivation, Hamilton did not blunder but acted deliberately. In Parliament, late on 1 September he assured his followers that the mode of appointing the commission would not be raised that day; but no sooner had many of them gone off to wine and dine than he expressly moved that nomination should be left to the queen.[68] The ministry was prepared for this remarkable change of front and clinched the matter with a hurried vote before the absent members of the opposition could be recalled by their dumb-founded colleagues. The irascible Fletcher nearly burst a blood vessel; but the vote in the ministry's favour, a bare majority of four, stood. 'From this day,' says Lockhart, 'may we date the commencement of Scotland's ruin.'[69] This was a favourite and overworked phrase of Lockhart's; but from his point of view, in this instance, the apothegm was accurate enough.

Indeed, Lockhart, who is commonly dismissed as an inveterate father of lies, was a politician of some stature and considerable acuteness. By the end of the session he must have been ruefully recalling a letter he had written to Hamilton on 12 April about an interview he himself had just had with Chancellor Seafield. The wily Seafield refused to be pumped by Lockhart and would say nothing of the ministry's intentions in the coming session of parliament. His interrogator was not to know that Seafield was as much in the dark about Argyll's intentions as everyone else was, and that the chancellor was playing his favourite game of omniscient sly-boots. Lockhart continues, more prophetically than he can have realised, 'I suppose they find they're engadged to loose so ravelled a knot that they know not att which end to begin, and will do nothing till his High and Mighty Grace [i.e. Argyll] come down, who as far as I can understand knows nor proposes no way to loose such Gordian knots, but like Alexander the Great to cutt them with his sword'.[70] Aided and abetted by Lockhart's correspondent, that, by and large, was precisely what Argyll did.

In what remained of the session of 1705 the opposition failed to recover from Hamilton's remarkable somersault, and the ministry, scenting victory, pressed home its advantage. The grant of supply completed Argyll's triumph and the work of the session, which ended on 21 September 1705.

13

The Making of the Treaty of Union and the Reaction to it

IMPRESSIVE though Argyll's triumph was, it was largely a personal one and by no means ended the constitutional crisis between the two kingdoms. The Treaty and Act of Union of 1707 certainly did not follow as a mere formality but emerged at the end of a long and tortuous struggle, for great difficulties still lay ahead on any one of which the treaty might have foundered. The true significance of Argyll's success in 1705 was that, by breaking the deadlock between ministry and parliament, it created conditions favourable to the Court. But what use the Court could, or would, make of its restored initiative long remained in doubt.

The truth is that the Court was not entirely a free agent, and the outcome of the union policy (whatever its precise details) would largely depend on English party politics, and specifically on whether the Court could contrive to have Whig support without succumbing to Whig domination. That old dread still clouded the issue. More serious still, Whig support at this time was doubtful, so displeased was the Junto at the result of the session of the Scottish parliament in 1705. The Whigs had hoped for a settlement of the Hanoverian succession in Scotland which would leave them free to broach the union question in their own good time with a view to squeezing from it maximum political advantage. So annoyed were they when Argyll ended up with an act for a treaty that they recommended the queen not to accept the work of the session. The immediate reaction of the Whigs to the treaty project was therefore frigid, and this coolness on the part of the supposed champions of union added to the general air of uncertainty that persisted.[1]

Few at the time were optimistic about the chances of a treaty being negotiated, let alone accepted by the two parliaments. Bishop Burnet was a Scot who had long desired a union but despaired of its ever being accomplished, and he believed that the Scottish parliament had voted for negotiations to waste time and stall the issue.[2] Clerk of Penicuik, who was thrust protestingly upon the commission by his patron Queensberry, also felt that nothing would come of it all, and that he, like the rest of the commissioners, would be left whistling for his expenses.[3] The few consistent advocates of union, such as Cromartie and Stair, fervently hoped for a treaty but displayed wishful thinking rather than assurance.

In fact, most politicians, irrespective of their desires on the matter, were content to play a waiting game and see how things would develop.

The waiting game proved more trying for some than for others. Particularly gruelling was the Squadrone's prolonged period of agonising re-appraisal, as their letters reveal. A leading authority has remarked that their correspondence at this time does not make pleasant reading, for it is 'the revelation of the machinations of a party bent on maintaining its separate existence and taking advantage of every turn in the development of events'.[4] Nearly all politicians did just that, but the members of the Squadrone were more awkwardly placed than most. They had posed as incorruptible patriots and were almost taken in by their own propaganda. In fairness to them, they disliked the thought of union; but increasingly they feared that it might pass, leaving them out in the cold. So once more Roxburghe (who had always had a latent hankering for union) served as their mentor if not exactly as their conscience. By late November Roxburghe had reached the conclusion that union might take in the Scottish parliament and that for the following reasons: 'Trade with most, Hanover with some, ease and security with others'.[5] For Roxburghe, however, his party's dilemma had strong personal connotations; he was working hard for a dukedom and knew that he either had to carry the Squadrone into the Court's measures or else kiss his 'dukery' goodbye. He finally managed to persuade his friends that principles must bend to new circumstances; but until the critical hour struck in the session of 1706 the Squadrone dickered and dithered, the great unknown, courted by all and feared and despised by all.

The new circumstances were soon clarified in one important respect when, to the surprise of most Scots, the English parliament did not prove obstructive over the Alien Act. This complaisant attitude probably owed more to the machinations of party politics than to zeal for union as such. To summarise a tangled web: the Tories, who did not care for union with Scotland, believed that the Whigs too no longer favoured it and would not, as a consequence, accommodate either the Scottish parliament or the queen by repealing the act. The Tories therefore pushed for repeal in the expectation that the Whigs would refuse and so ruin the Court's policy; but the Whigs neatly evaded the trap by accepting the motion.[6] On 15 November the clauses of the Alien Act to which the Scots had taken exception were repealed, a telling stroke, which, as well as discomfiting the Tories, had a good effect in Scotland by convincing many that the union project was seriously entertained not only by the Court but also by the English parliament. All this was noted by Mar who was in London at the time and who passed on the news to his associates. He also reported something else: 'I find here that no union but an incorporating relishes'.[7] But that particular news-flash was not to be broadcast; only those in the know among the Court Party discussed incorporation, and of these some, notably Stair and Carstares, felt that the succession was more vital and that union should be attained in easy and gradual stages.[8] The likelihood of a complete union was not openly aired at this time (i.e. in early 1706), and the public in Scotland seems to have been lulled into believing that some form of federal union was to be the subject of the coming negotiations.

By February 1706 the groundwork had been laid for naming the commission. Argyll throughout showed little interest in the matter and nomination was in effect left to Queensberry, who for months had been making deals and lining up suitable people. Not surprisingly, therefore, the commission named on 26 February was composed largely of Queensberry, his clients and his allies. The one glaring exception to this rule was the inclusion of Lockhart of Carnwath, which was done possibly to give an illusion of fairness and possibly in the hope that Lord Wharton, Lockhart's uncle and a notable member of the Junto, could mend his nephew's ways. Yet many at the time, especially in England, were surprised at the list of Scottish commissioners, some of whom were regarded as disaffected,[9] a mistaken view which could only have arisen from limited knowledge of the Scottish political scene. The 31 commissioners were drawn mainly from Queensberry's group with strong elements from Argyll's interest, ministerialists such as Seafield, and some, like the Earl of Sutherland and Seton younger of Pitmedden, whose services had been bought. The Squadrone were pointedly excluded and were not sure whether to be enraged at this or relieved. Hamilton, too, was left out, somewhat to Argyll's disgust, he having assured Hamilton of a place, and Argyll refused to sit on the commission. Thus, Lockhart alone of the commissioners seems to have been implacably opposed to incorporation. The whole matter has been neatly summarised: 'The chief end of the nomination was not to elicit the mind of Scotland on a most momentous question, but to secure a parliamentary majority to the inevitable surrender to the English demand for incorporation, alias "an entire union" '.[10] The English union commission, also 31 in number, was nominated with the same end in view (i.e. to facilitate the passing of a treaty through parliament), and it was dominated by the Whig Lord Somers, who throughout the negotiations worked closely and privately with the Scottish commissioners, in defiance of the agreed mode of procedure. Somers was determined to counteract the Court's influence so that the political benefits of union would as far as possible lie with the Junto, and specifically that the Scottish representatives at Westminster should strengthen the Junto rather than, as Godolphin hoped, the Court.[11]

Even before the negotiations began it was known that the English commission, intent above all to secure England from French and Jacobite threats, would consider nothing but an incorporating union. Quite apart from the overriding considerations of security, federalism was out of favour in England where it was well known that Marlborough had frequent cause to complain about the difficulties raised by conflict of authorities in the United Provinces. And to English politicians in general federalism seemed synonymous with weak government; a federal constitution would not obviate friction in the future, and the retention of a parliament in Scotland might lead to the undoing of any agreement reached. In short, it was felt that a federal solution could not give England the required guarantee of security. All this the Duke of Portland put to Carstares on 11 April 1706: 'an entire union is contemplated . . . I do not comprehend the mutual benefit of a federal union, nor the means of arriving at it'.[12] Mar broached the same topic to Carstares more cautiously: 'You see that what we are to treat of is not in our choice'.[13] But the lack of choice evidently did not worry Mar, who wrote to Marchmont that a complete union was desirable on all counts.[14]

It would be tediously misleading, therefore, to give a detailed account of the ensuing negotiations. The lines of discussion were set even before the commissioners held their first meeting on 16 April in the Council Chamber of the Cockpit at Whitehall. Even the mode of procedure adopted was an elaboration of the methods used in 1702. It was agreed in 1706 that the two commissions should sit separately, normally communicate only in writing, and observe the strictest secrecy. As for the substance of their discussions, the commissioners again worked on the basis laid in 1702–3, and in fact most of their time was taken up with matters outstanding from the previous negotiations—such as taxation, representation and provision for the law of Scotland. One subject, however, that had been recommended for further discussion at the adjournment in February 1703 was excluded by the terms of reference of the new commissions: they were not to discuss the problem of the two national churches, the strong implication being that, in the event of a union, the two countries should retain their separate establishments.

In a bid to impress public opinion at home the Scottish commissioners at the outset made a halting plea for federalism (which few of them either believed in or desired), but did not sustain it in the face of a blank refusal from the English commissioners.[15] By 25 April agreement had been reached on fundamentals: there was to be a union of the two kingdoms as Great Britain under one imperial crown and with one parliament, and as a consequence the Hanoverian succession was to be accepted. Those were the key propositions. The other articles that were subsequently agreed were necessary corollaries either because, like free trade, they followed logically from those basic postulates or else were needed to ease the acceptance of the treaty by the two parliaments. By 22 July 1706 the Articles of the Treaty of Union, 25 in number, had been worked out and accepted by both commissions.[16]

Apart from the cardinal principles of incorporation, the other salient points of the treaty cannot be gone into in detail here. The main provisions, however, can be briefly summarised. Free trade with England and her colonies brought Scotland within the protection of the Navigation Laws. There was to be one coinage, that of England; a uniform system of weights and measures, likewise English; and, with certain relatively minor reservations, one fiscal system. To offset future liability towards the English National Debt, which was growing rapidly because of the European wars, a sum of money known as the Equivalent was to be paid to Scotland, and after involved calculations it was reckoned at £398,085-10s. sterling. From this sum outstanding claims on the Scottish treasury were to be met, such as payment of arrears of salaries to office-holders; and from it also shareholders of the Company of Scotland, which was to go into liquidation, were to be reimbursed at 5% interest. A smaller Equivalent, hypothecated on increased revenue, was to be used to promote industry in Scotland. On the whole the fiscal and financial provisions of the treaty were fair, in some respects generous, and were calculated, in both senses of the word, to recommend the treaty to the Scottish parliament.

From the point of view of winning parliamentary acceptance the most awkward feature of the treaty was its proposed abolition of the Scottish legislature. No amount of argument could disguise the fact that the new British parliament was simply to be an enlarged English parliament. The representation granted to Scotland was therefore crucial. If pitched too low, this would have proved a major stumbling-block for the Scots; if too high, it would not have been acceptable to English opinion. The first proposals by the English commissioners ran the risk of wrecking the entire project. On grounds of taxable capacity, without reference to population (which was not then the accepted criterion for representation), they recommended 38 M.P.s from Scotland, thus improving on the Cromwellian precedent of 30 but not sufficiently to satisfy the Scottish commissioners who demanded 50. The ratio of taxable capacity between the two kingdoms was 38 to 1 in England's favour, and of population about 5 to 1. In the end representation was decided at 12 to 1; after a good deal of haggling, on 21 June a compromise was accepted whereby there were to be 45 M.P.s from Scotland in the House of Commons and 16 elected Scots peers in the House of Lords. The number of constituencies in Scotland was reduced from 157 to 45; and the election of 16 Scottish peers was to prevent the flooding of the Upper House by needy Scottish lordlings who, it was feared, would simply be ministerial cannon fodder. When it is remembered that the representation of England and Wales remained unreformed and that the total of members in the Commons would be 558, then the terms granted to Scotland clearly did not err on the side of generosity. On the fiscal criteria adopted the number could be justified and even regarded as generous; but it is important to note that these novel criteria were applied only to Scotland. They had no application to the representation of England and Wales; so the argument based on taxable capacity cannot be pushed very far. It was simply a device to effect an acceptable compromise. And the English system of representation, already chaotic and in some respects bizarre, remained untouched. Not fiscal criteria but use and wont plus the existence of many rotten boroughs enabled 70 M.P.s from Cornwall (44) and Devon (26) to sit in each parliament—an anomaly that the opposition in Scotland could hardly overlook. In sum, the representation proposed for Scotland in the projected British parliament could not of itself be an attractive prospect either to the Scottish parliament or the Scottish nation.

The problem of parliamentary representation illustrated the difficulties in the way of a complete union. The two countries were too unequal and too different in too many respects for complete integration. With a sound appreciation of the possible, therefore, integration was restricted to parliament, fiscal matters and the domain of public law. Each country was to retain its own system of private law and its own courts and jurisdictions, including, unfortunately, out of political necessity the outdated and harmful Heritable Jurisdiction of Scotland. One important point was passed over in silence. Nothing was said in the treaty about a right of appeal from the supreme civil court in Scotland, the Court of Session, to the House of Lords—a later assumption pregnant with ill consequences for Scots Law. If such an appellate jurisdiction was intended, it should have been discussed. It was not. And the argument subsequently advanced to justify the appellate jurisdiction of the House of Lords, that the British parliament fell heir to all the rights of the parliament of Scotland, is highly suspect, for it was not clear that the Scottish parliament did have an appeal jurisdiction over the Court of Session, that matter having frequently been a subject of debate in the thirty years previous to the union. Quite apart from that, the House of Lords, with no knowledge of Scots Law and the merest nodding acquaintance with Roman Law, was totally unfitted to act as a court of appeal in Scots cases.[17]

Another matter not touched upon in the treaty was that of church government, but by implication each country was to retain its own forms. The same was to happen over a wide range of topics—such as local government, educational provisions and social administration (such as poor relief), though obviously these might all be subject to amending legislation by the British parliament.

In short, if the treaty of union was accepted, the adjective 'British' would have a somewhat chequered career. It would be meaningful in some contexts, of dubious validity in others, and in some it would be quite inapplicable. There would be for the first time a British state, the United Kingdom of Great Britain. There would be a British crown, empire, government, parliament, foreign policy and armed forces. There would be British subjects, but no British nation, though the national concept could have a limited application to governmental activities. But the concept of a British nation, much heralded at the time, was artificial and mainly illusory. This was epitomised in the legal sphere where one could speak in the abstract sense of British justice but not of British law. One could not even speak at all of a British Church or British universities or education or even culture, any more than one could rationally speak of a British language or of British Literature. The plain fact is that the union of 1707 produced a new state and went some way towards creating a new quasi-national consciousness, but at the same time the union preserved two ancient national entities. It was in essence a union of states, not of nations.

As an 'entire and compleat union', therefore, the proposed treaty was in some respects wanting; much of it, indeed, was devoted to safeguarding Scottish institutions from sudden change. Today some see this incompleteness as the chief defect of the Treaty of Union of 1707. They fail to grasp the obvious and all-important point that by the early eighteenth century an integrated Great Britain that was uniform in all respects was not feasible either in theory or in practice, and that any attempt to create one would almost certainly have ruined the union. Any such possibility really perished with Edward I. Thus in 1706 respect for realities dictated that in some vital ways the treaty should be markedly conservative. And the treaty-makers, far from seeing this as a demerit, saw it as a necessary and recommending feature of their work.

The Court believed, correctly as it turned out, that the main obstacle to the treaty would be the Scottish parliament; so it was decided to seek ratification there before raising the matter in the English parliament. The Court's chief miscalculation was to underestimate opposition from the Scottish people, and here initial public reaction among the Scots may have proved misleading, for the first news of the treaty was mildly received, the attitude being one rather of misgiving tempered by curiosity. In fact, the terms of the treaty were not widely or accurately known before Lockhart furnished his allies with full details, but thereafter every effort was made to stir up public opposition both before the parliament met and throughout its session. Except with the Jacobites, some form of federalism would have been acceptable; but the idea of incorporating union (or rather an 'obliterating union' as the opposition would have it), negating centuries of hard struggle for national survival, was hated, and to the popular mind the treaty seemed nothing but a base betrayal and its negotiators 'traitors' —in Scots homophonic with 'treaters'. The hostile reception given to the 'treaters-traitors', says Clerk of Penicuik, hurt the commissioners who fancied that 'they had been doing great service to their country in the matter of the union'.[18] It may be that the ministry's anxiety to spare the country the details of union had in fact played into the hands of the opposition, and that a bolder and more candid approach to public opinion might conceivably have served the ministry better.

As it was, once the contents of the treaty had been leaked, nearly every sector of the Scottish nation found something objectionable in the proposed union. The Jacobites, rightly enough from their standpoint, saw it as a deadly blow to the hopes of the Chevalier. The episcopalians, most of whom favoured the Pretender, were afraid that union would secure presbyterianism. The presbyterians for their part welcomed the protestant succession, but feared that, under the cloven hoof of the union, bishops would again be thrust upon the Church of Scotland. The constitutional reformers saw that the union would preserve some of the worst features of Scottish life, notably the Heritable Jurisdictions, and that the British parliament would be anything but an instrument of radical reform. And, strangely, the offer of free trade roused little enthusiasm in many of the royal burghs, including Glasgow.[19] Nor in England was the treaty greeted with tumultuous applause. There, apart from some inspired products of the press, the treaty was received in perplexed silence. But soon in both countries numerous broadsheets and pamphlets for and against the union appeared. The religious parties also threw themselves into the fray, and in Scotland the pulpits rang with shrill denunciations of the sell-out to prelatical England while the English Tory arch-prelatists continued to show little relish for the presbyterian establishment in Scotland.

The clash of the rival propagandists is one of great interest and would make an engrossing study in its own right, but it cannot be gone into here at any length. The present-day reader, though, can hardly fail to be struck by the surprising modernity, one might almost say topicality, of much of the writing. On point after point the controversy over the union anticipates the Common Market debate of our own time. In particular it shows a government determined to have its way in the teeth of much popular discontent and considerable opposition in parliament. It also shows how difficult it is to maintain an opposition based on heterogeneous views and requirements, and that over a period of lengthy debate it is more difficult to maintain a negative than a positive stance. But the resemblances cannot be pushed too far, since in the early eighteenth century few paid even lip-service to democracy. The impression of topicality is mainly due to the fact that the writers on the union question dealt with fundamental problems of political science. Another modern touch is that the whole controversy furnishes an early example of propaganda designed to influence attitudes to an involved public question. Previous exercises of this kind had concentrated on religious and theological themes to which politics was subordinated. This was evidently true of the struggle waged against Charles I, and still true of the Restoration period. The union debate for the first time gave political considerations priority, and in so doing used surprisingly mature political concepts. Yet this is not really so surprising, for in the works of late seventeenth-century political thinkers (such as Hobbes or Grotius) sovereignty was a key concept; and sovereignty had an obvious and inescapable relevance to the proposed union.

The best known of the writers on the union question, Daniel Defoe, operated in Edinburgh but was not the first English agent to serve there in Anne's reign. Before him, the task of keeping the English ministers informed on Scottish developments had been performed by Anglo-Scots such as William Greg and William Paterson, the Darien projector, who had both reported on the angry session of the Scottish parliament in 1703. Like many Anglo-Scots, past and present, their attitudes to Scotland were ambivalent and their patriotism was of a highly idiosyncratic kind. Their standard of objectivity is summed up in one of Paterson's reports: the Scots parliament of 1703 was, he held, dominated by madmen, and he added by way of explanation, 'I have now a long time been, and am still as sensible as any, of the loose foot, not only that kingdom but likewise all the remote territories belonging to the crown of England are upon'.[20] By such slanted reports, which were clearly designed to curry favour with their masters, Greg and Paterson worsened an already vexed situation. In spite of Paterson's odd views on the constitutional position, the root of the problem in Anglo-Scottish relations was that Scotland did *not* belong to the crown of England, and its parliament was *not* a mere provincial assembly. The myth to that effect was gaining some credence in London with those who failed to distinguish between political management and constitutional realities, but it was never used by the English ministry who saw that it could do no good but might do a great deal of harm. Yet even today this misrendering of fact has cast a hypnotic spell on certain authors, and has appeared recently in a work by N. T. Phillipson.[21] Such erroneous views could, and can, only obscure counsel. On this and other matters, the English ministry in the course of the years 1705 and 1706 came to realise that it was indifferently served by its agents in Edinburgh, and that better intelligence from that quarter was vitally necessary.

The need seems to have been well known. In January 1705 Charles Davenant, an English economist of note who had acted as secretary to the English union commissioners in 1702 and had thereafter made a special study of Scottish affairs, wrote to Godolphin stressing the need for better liaison. He volunteered to go to Edinburgh as an undercover agent not only to supply accurate reports but also to disseminate Court propaganda, proposing, among other things, to write a book that would extol the benefits of union and help to dispel English as well as Scottish prejudices.[22] But instead of being sent to Edinburgh, Davenant was given the post of inspector-general of exports and imports which he held until his death in 1714.[23] Greg, therefore, reported on the Scottish parliament of 1705 in his usual inaccurate fashion, after which he worked as a clerk in the secretary's office. There he came to grief. The spendthrift underpaid Greg succumbed to temptation and availed himself of Harley's notoriously careless handling of papers to sell information to France. He was found out, tried and convicted of high treason, and executed in April 1708.[24]

By 1706, then, with the treaty nearing its moment of truth, there was a clear need for an able agent in Edinburgh, and Harley had just the man on call. Daniel Defoe, one of the earliest and most talented of journalists, had recently been in ill-odour with government. Harley's predecessor, Nottingham, could not abide Defoe and had had him pilloried in 1703 for his stinging satire 'The Shortest Way with Dissenters'. Harley, however, never lost his early sympathy with non-conformists, and Defoe through his friend William Paterson was able to ingratiate himself with the new secretary of state. In September 1706 Defoe left London for Edinburgh, charged with the mission that Davenant had recommended and which he carried out very much on the lines that Davenant had suggested.

From October 1706 until December 1707 Defoe was kept busy in Edinburgh promoting the cause of union, and as well as churning out numerous pamphlets he also composed the *History of the Union*, which was first published in Edinburgh in 1709. As a historical work it has been overrated, but its propaganda value, like that of his other writings on this theme, was considerable. Though Defoe's knowledge of Scotland and of Scottish problems was limited and in many ways defective, he undoubtedly made the greatest contribution of all to pro-union propaganda. His principal work to this end was a series of *Essays at Removing National Prejudices against a Union*, in which, following Davenant's cue, he sought to persuade both English and Scots that their ingrained animosities hurt the true interests of each nation and that these lay in an incorporating union. A prosperous and contented Scotland, argued Defoe, far from impoverishing England, as mercantilist dogma would have it, could only add to England's wealth and security. This was his main theme, though he touched on others as well. Possibly prompted by inside information from Harley, Defoe also suggested that the church question could be settled quite simply by acts of parliament, one English and one Scottish, guaranteeing the existing establishments. He also tried to dispel the charge that the loss of the Scottish parliament was an infringement of the nation's sovereignty, by arguing that the new constitution would safeguard the rights of property and freehold that existed under the old. This was really an evasion of an important question, for sovereignty entails much more than private property rights; but further on that tack Defoe dared not go without damaging the case for union. The weakness of Defoe here, and those who argued in similar strain, was that he could not deny Scotland's loss of sovereignty and was forced instead to ask the Scots to take the new constitution on trust. Such trust could easily be represented as folly on the part of those who gave it and fraud on the part of those who demanded it. Anyway, the treaty itself was quite explicit on this important point. Scotland lost her sovereignty both in theory and in practice; in theory so did England, but not in practice. For the legislative function is inseparable from sovereignty, and English control over the proposed new legislature was assured.

William Paterson and William Seton younger of Pitmedden wrote in much the same strain as Defoe, concentrating mainly on the anticipated economic benefits of union. Paterson, with typical egotism, had reached the conclusion that the failure of his Darien Scheme meant that Scotland was no longer economically viable and that only an incorporating union and free trade with England held out any hope for her future. Pitmedden took the same line; and, like Defoe, he too dismissed the loss of the Scottish parliament as of minor consequence since laws and liberties would be preserved elsewhere.[25]

On the whole, circumstances conspired to give the pro-union authors the best of the economic arguments.[26] The economy of Scotland was undeniably in a generally retarded and feeble condition: the Darien Disaster had seriously depleted capital and lowered liquidity; the 'Ill Years' of bad harvests had impoverished landlords and tenants alike; trade was hard hit by the war and the activities of French privateers; and in December 1704 a financial crisis had led the fledgling Bank of Scotland to suspend payments. In such circumstances it was easy to urge the benefits of free trade with England, and tempting to go further and rhapsodise over the immediate transformation of the Scottish economy that an incorporating union would ensure.

Not in the least impressed by these arguments was James Hodges, one of the chief writers against an incorporating union. He was a presbyterian minister and veteran publicist who, along with James Anderson, had already earned the support of the Scottish parliament for the part he had played in the Homage Controversy.[27] In his *First Treatise on the Rights and Interests of the Two British Monarchies*, Hodges advocated federal union, arguing that incorporating unions inevitably entailed the destruction of the weaker partners. According to Hodges, rights and privileges must necessarily disappear with the loss of sovereignty; and in his view an incorporating union would spell the end for Scotland, which would 'come into the state of a county of England, the furthest remov'd of all the rest from its centre of government, trade, wealth and business'.[28] The benefits of free trade he dismissed as illusory so far as Scotland was concerned, though he held that they would be substantial for England. He argued, cloudily and feebly, that an independent Scotland operating on what, in some sense came, to be regarded as free trade principles would fare better—an interesting partial anticipation of Adam Smith but, in the circumstances, a visionary one.[29] Hodges concludes, on another surprisingly advanced note, that 'Fundamental national rights are above the reach both of the law, and governors for the time, so that they can neither be annulled, dispensed with, nor disposed of by them'.[30]

Indeed, running through all the anti-unionist tracts there is a strong sense of 'Mazzinian' nationalism, which appears most obviously in the contention that the rights of the nation transcend the claims of the state. Most students of the union have dismissed these views as moonshine, arguing that no real sense of nationalism then existed. But the critics are themselves in error. Nationalism is not set in one mould but capable of expressing itself in many ways; and that it existed long before Napoleon and Mazzini is not open to doubt. On this question the evidence from Britain is conclusive; in both England and Scotland an early form of nationalism of surprising maturity can be traced back to the fourteenth century. It is, for example, implicit in the Declaration of Arbroath of 1320, which in 1706–7 furnished useful weapons for the anti-unionists;[31] and outraged nationalism also breathes fire and slaughter in the war-songs of Laurence Minot. Since the rights of the nation were so constantly invoked during the union debate, we may well conclude that the Mazzinian idiom was new, but that nationalism itself was old. The contrary case depends not on the interpretation of historical evidence but on its suppression and the imposition of current shibboleths.

The chief weakness of the anti-unionist tracts lies, not so much in their use of the concept of nationalism, but in the history adduced to support it. Much of Hodges' history, for example, is either highly slanted, garbled or swathed in early myth and legend—all of which, of course, were shortcomings (as they appear to us) then common in historical argument. Only James Anderson sought salvation in the new science of record scholarship. As he expressed his credo: 'histories being overgrown with legends of miracles and visions on the one hand, and larded with many romantick fables and traditions on the other, there was no safe way left to correct what's amiss, to clear what's obscure, and to add what's wanting, but a diligent search into records and ancient muniments'.[32] Hodges clung to the older way. Besides, he was no historian and had neither the interest nor the equipment to branch out as Anderson was doing. But in his political philosophy Hodges tried to be discriminating and systematic, and it is a foolish bias that dismisses his works, with those of other anti-unionists, as mere 'flights of windy rhetoric and enormous lying'.[33] Limited though his abilities were, Hodges too was something of a pioneer, in his case in political science. He tells us that he had long been contemplating a work in a new genre, *A Compleat Body of Politick Learning*, which was to be practical and not theoretical, and would concern itself with government, law, administration of justice, defence, security, taxation, population trends, provision for the poor, trade, currency, credit, public and private economy, and education. 'All which matters,' he concludes, 'are to be inquir'd into, and calculated with a special regard to the particular circumstances of Scotland.'[34]

Unfortunately, owing to lack of funds the grand design never got beyond the project stage; but even so it is one more illustration of the great change that was taking place in the intellectual climate of Scotland. Further evidence for this change can be found in the works of Sir Robert Sibbald, who in the 1680s had attempted to compile a premature 'statistical account'; and new mental horizons also open up in Fletcher's *Discourses* as well as in his political speeches and writings. It is the fashion for some nowadays to adulate eighteenth-century 'Enlightenment' with an uncritical devotion that is the very reverse of enlightened, and their folly to proceed on the assumption that rational thought was virtually unknown before 1 January 1700. Indeed, for some devotees of the cult the intellectual tradition of Scotland dates only from 1 May 1707—a quite extraordinary and utterly incredible case of spontaneous generation. Such contentions are too preposterous for serious examination, let alone refutation. All that need be said here is that Sibbald and Fletcher, and to a lesser degree Hodges, anticipated some of the attitudes and even to a certain extent the methodology of the so-called, and perhaps mis-called, 'Enlightenment' of the eighteenth century.

Hodges' *Third Treatise*, published in 1706, condemns incorporation even more stridently. It was an attack on Defoe and was evidently printed before the exact terms of the treaty had been made public, for it errs in some notable respects. Thus he warns darkly that, notwithstanding whatever safeguards there may be in the treaty, the British parliament would have the power to create one British Church or one British system of law.[35] But in spite of these rather misplaced strictures his conclusion again had some point. The union proposed, says Hodges, is no union at all but a mere 'tacking of a fraction of the Scots government and sovereignty, first dissolved, and lost to them, to the English government and sovereignty, by them conserved entire and compleat in all circumstances, without least either alteration or diminution'.[36] In more ways than one this is a revealing passage, for not only does it display a realistic grasp of the problem but also it illustrates one of the major handicaps under which Hodges, along with other Scottish writers, laboured. With the notable exceptions of Andrew Fletcher and George Ridpath, their use of the English language tended to be clumsy. They showed none of Defoe's panache, and Defoe, indeed, dismissed Hodges as a wild ranter—'a sad instance of the temper of these times'.[37] But though passion often led Hodges into silly postures and incoherent writing, nevertheless he closed with political problems that Defoe's partisan commitments led him to ignore. Hodges is now a forgotten writer (sunk without trace, as the saying goes), whereas Defoe, thanks in no small measure to *Robinson Crusoe*, enjoys as much fame now as he did notoriety in his own day. Yet on the union as a problem in political science Defoe's views are of little value, while those of Hodges have anticipated every subsequent Scottish objection to the union of 1707, down even to the rueful witticism that reduces the ancient kingdom to 'Scotlandshire'. That he, and others like him, were merely 'wild ranters' is an unfounded assumption that has far too long been elevated to the status of dogma.

This judgment is supported by an anonymous pamphlet, *The State of the Controversy betwixt United and Separate Parliaments*, which appeared in 1706, possibly from Andrew Fletcher's pen. Soberly and ably argued, it advocated a union of interests between the two nations, rejecting the proposed incorporating union as potentially lethal for Scotland. It too was evidently published before the terms of the treaty had become known, and is of interest mainly because it warned of the threat to Scottish judicatures from the House of Lords. It also urged some of Hodge's economic arguments whereby, in the event of a rupture with England, Scotland should declare itself a 'free port' and negotiate treaties with powers other than England.

Writers of less ability, some known by name and some not, joined in the fray. On the unionist side a few, like the anonymous author of *The Comical History of the Marriage–Union betwixt Fergusia and Heptarchus*, indulged mainly in the kind of ignorant and scurrilous sarcasm that still passes for history in certain exalted quarters in England. The more serious of the lesser unionist writers, however, contented themselves with repeating the arguments of Defoe and Paterson, while on the anti-unionist side the hacks freely pirated from Fletcher,

Hodges and Ridpath. In the present brief treatment, therefore, it would serve no purpose to inquire further into the pamphlet literature.

But an obvious and perplexing question arises. How influential were the pamphleteers? That, in Scotland, they had considerable influence over the 'mob' can hardly be doubted, though it must be remembered that for the most part the anti-unionist propagandists were largely articulating views long popularly held. The effect of the pro-unionist authors is much more difficult to assess. They probably had some impact in England, and particularly in London. But in Scotland the disorders of the time show that they had little if any influence on the populace, though they may well have helped to persuade some members of parliament that the way of incorporation was the right, if not indeed the only, way. The difficulty here is that the members were also subjected to other and more tangible forms of influence, and it is consequently hard to say how effectively the arguments of Defoe, Pitmedden and the others wrought on the House.

More generally, the problem facing the modern student of the last session of the parliament of Scotland is as much moral as political. In the study of history, of course, such problems are by no means rare, and they are invariably complex; but in this particular case the difficulties are aggravated by special circumstances, some of which are implicit in the union period itself and others of which derive from the myths in which later generations have enveloped it. The best course is to concentrate on the union period itself and set later opinion firmly aside. After all, the union has meant different things at different times. It has, in a word, developed; and it would be as absurd to judge the making of the union from the standpoint of present attitudes to union as it would be to judge the fledgling United States of the founding fathers from the standpoint of today.

Examination of three major contemporary factors takes us nearest to an overall solution of the problem of the making of the union of 1707. The first two factors concern mainly the ministry and the pro-unionist side: these are, first, the part played by management; and, second, and closely related to management, the use of influence or bribery. The third factor is, of course, the performance put up by the opposition.

That since 1704 management had been steadily becoming more efficient has already been demonstrated. By 1706 the ministry, more broadly and strongly based than hitherto, could, as in 1705, count on Queensberry's group and on the Argyll interest, and could also hope for some support from the Squadrone. The Court's strength, however, did not derive from these groups' ideological commitment to union or, for that matter, to anything else. Hard circumstances had driven them together. Queensberry had been made to see that his following, powerful though it was, simply did not have the strength to go it alone. Nor, as we shall see, did either the Argyll faction or the Squadrone act without paying close heed to self-interest. Thus, skilful management was needed to hold the unionist camp together, and to the end the Court managers, Mar and Seafield, were uneasily aware of this. And it is plain from their correspondence that they were by no means confident at the opening of the session that the union would pass. Patronage and influence, therefore, had an indispensable rôle to play; and no one who carefully studies the sources can fail to be struck by the crucial part played by self-interest.

As against that, it has to be recognised that the parliamentarians fully appreciated the importance of the decision that had to be made. In spite of modern interpretations to the contrary, there *was* a genuine and even dangerous crisis in Anglo-Scottish relations to which a union offered a solution. Many who had previously regarded talk of union as a mere device of the English ministry designed, as Queen Elizabeth would have said, 'to drive time', might respond more favourably to a concrete treaty. Then, too, if the treaty failed, what was to be the alternative? Many feared that the two kingdoms might come to blows, or that France would profit from their differences and advance her own interests. From time to time Godolphin had fanned these fears with discreet threats but took care not to do this publicly. He was aided by such as Roxburghe who feared 'conquest upon the first peace'.[38] These covert threats and apprehensions, however, may have been mere diplomatic bluff, as the curious phrase 'upon the first peace' would suggest. The dangers of a civil war would surely have been at their most intolerable, not in times of peace but while the War of the Spanish Succession still raged. Certainly it is significant that Marlborough never indulged in bellicose utterances but throughout steadily supported the union project.[39] Marlborough was not only a great soldier but also a politician of genius who knew that war was a dangerous and uncertain remedy for political problems. A campaign in Scotland, however successful, would necessarily impede his operations in Flanders by depleting his forces there. Worse, it might also dry up the flow of Scottish recruits on which his army largely depended. Ireland and Scotland were his best recruiting grounds and could not easily be replaced. Nor, in spite of his defeat at Ramillies in May 1706, could Louis XIV be regarded as finished. An English invasion of Scotland would almost certainly have led to French support for those Scots who resisted, and Louis, tired of the Jacobites and their asinine plots, actually hoped for such an outcome. If England got bogged down in a Scottish campaign it would matter little to him whether James Stewart or James Hamilton profited from that situation, since the interests of France would be served by the dispersal of England's forces.

One who saw all this, and was apprehensive of its possible consequences, was the indefatigable James Hodges. In 1705 Hodges published a pamphlet entitled *War Betwixt the Two British Kingdoms Considered*, in which he warned that in such a situation Scotland and England might both lose. He feared that France, which, as a strong protestant, he loathed and feared, would reap the advantage of any Anglo-Scottish hostilities. He therefore pleaded for a peaceful resolution of the crisis, pointing out as a further possible ill consequence of failure to do so the likelihood of rebellion in Ireland. There the Scots were numerous and might, if Scotland were attacked, make common cause with the native Irish 'whom the Scots own to be of one original stock and blood with them'.[39] His argument here was strained but should not be dismissed out of hand, for an English invasion of Scotland might easily have had desperate, though seemingly unlikely, repercussions. By these and other arguments Hodges pushed the case for a peaceful constitutional settlement between England and Scotland, while at the same time he rejected incorporation.

Queen Anne, who was far more intelligent than she is usually given credit for, also saw the issue clearly, and, carefully avoiding all talk of war, insisted that everything possible should be done to carry the union. In 1706 her private instructions to Queensberry, whom she was forced reluctantly to appoint as commissioner, stressed that he was to go all out to get the treaty through the Scottish parliament and that no other result would be acceptable; if the parliament became deadlocked on the question of the treaty the commissioner was to adjourn, and on no account was he to entertain proposals for a federal union or for passing the Hanoverian succession in lieu of the treaty.[40] Queensberry doubtless found ways of quietly conveying this ultimatum to the members, and especially to those who hoped to benefit, over or under the counter, from the union.

But in Scotland at large the treaty was not popular and the ministry was hard pushed to drum up support for the coming session. As a contemporary observer noticed, the ministers 'had no confidence or hopes in the affections of the people, knowing that all this whole affair would turn upon the votes and power of the nobles of Scotland'.[41]

In an effort to pre-empt the votes of the nobles, the treaty paid every possible regard to their order. Not otherwise could the barbarous Heritable Jurisdictions have been guaranteed for all time coming, and with them the entire feudal system. Then, too, the right of peerage, apart from the reduction of representation in parliament (inevitable, since otherwise the House of Lords would be inundated with needy Scots lords), was extended in one alluring respect—the English privilege of peerage guaranteed freedom from arrest for civil process, and this boon was to be conferred on the Scottish representative peers. Scots peers, who customarily spent much of their time dodging captions, found this an attractive prospect;[42] all the more so as many of them believed that faithful service to the Court would ultimately be rewarded with British peerages which, it was hoped, would provide hereditary seats in the House of Lords and thus ready access to the new Golconda of patronage. Not until after the passing of the union, in Hamilton's case in 1711, were they disillusioned on this head.

More palpable inducements swayed some. The Earl of Rosebery, who had long coveted the chamberlainship of Fife with a pension of £300, was fobbed off until it was seen how he would perform in the coming vital session of parliament. He served his turn 'very honestly and firmly', as Secretary Mar acknowledged, and deserved his reward.[43] The ever-active Cromartie was strong for union and equally clear that his services should be amply rewarded; but even the ministry was appalled at the scandalous vigour with which he urged his claims.[44] The Earl of Sutherland, honoured by being placed on the union commission, did not rest content with the honour but pressed hard for a place in the treasury.[45] In fact few families of note which supported the ministry did so without pressing claims on behalf of their members.

All this was, as has frequently been argued, normal enough. But to stress its normality does not dispose of the problem. The situation was unique, and to attempt to explain all in terms of normal procedure is really to miss the point. The central issue posed by the union—whether or not Scotland should retain her independence—was not an everyday occurrence and cannot be satisfactorily explained in everyday terms. True, every effort was made by the ministry to reduce this crucial point to a mundane level and to present the treaty as just another item of business that had come before the parliament. Given the situation, the ministry could hardly do other than play it in low key.

But the problem still remains. How far was zeal for union based on conviction that it was a right and/or necessary measure, and how far did it turn on selfish considerations? What, in Scots legal parlance, was the *mens rea* of the legislators? If the 'gratifications' (offices, pensions etc.) or binding promises, or what could plausibly pass muster for such, did not materialise could zeal for union survive the shock of disappointment? Some of the evidence suggests that it could not. Belhaven, an assiduous place-hunter,[46] failed to find a place, and became the Cato of the union debate in 1706. Then, too, those who had promised to support the ministry but failed to do so ran the risk of having their gratifications withheld. Thus on 5 November 1706 Mar wrote to Sir David Nairne that the Earls of Buchan and Glencairn had defected; he recalled that Glencairn 'had not got his letter of pension, and now we must think before it be given'.[47] In an indirect way, the queen also exerted pressure. She showed an active interest in the proceedings of the Scottish parliament and took every opportunity to make her displeasure known to backsliders. All this, assuredly, was management at work, operating more efficiently than in the past and anxious not to repeat past mistakes. But to recognise management at work does not automatically empty the problem of all moral content. The operation of management clearly negates any argument that the issue was assessed solely on its merits and that the treaty passed on the free votes of the House.

Apart from offices and pensions and promises thereof, the 'bygones' or arrears of salary due to office-holders, past and present, put another powerful weapon in the hands of the ministry. In brief, the claimants were bluntly told that payment would depend upon the parts they played in this vital session of parliament. Thus, on 8 October 1706, five days after the session opened, Mar informed Godolphin that he had discussed with Tweeddale the latter's claims for arrears (which, unlike some, were perfectly valid), 'and I assured him of all the assistance in my power, and that much would depend on himself to make it in my power or not'.[48] Mar's correspondence at this time is full of such transactions. Atholl's case was given an unusual twist; if the duke undertook to absent himself from parliament his arrears would be paid. Atholl spurned the offer, bitterly opposed the union in parliament, and in May 1707 was still trying to secure payment of his arrears.[49]

Central to this whole issue is the disbursement of £20,000 sterling that was secretly sent up from the English treasury. This transaction looks suspiciously like a belated, and yet timely, acceptance of Argyll's advice of the previous session. Nor can Lockhart's version of the use made of the £20,000 be lightly brushed aside, for it is based not just on the spleen of an embittered anti-unionist but on the knowledge he later acquired in 1711 as a member of a commission set up to investigate treasury affairs.[50] It is easier to dismiss Lockhart as a bitter partisan (which he undoubtedly was) than to dispose of the evidence uncovered by the commission. That evidence seriously alarmed the Earl of Glasgow who, as Scots treasurer-depute in 1706, had secretly received and as secretly disbursed the money, in the process suppressing the queen's letter of authorisation. No receipts or vouchers accounted for the £20,000, and in 1711 Glasgow flew into a panic and hurriedly implored the protection of the lord treasurer, the Earl of Oxford, as Robert Harley had by then become. In his letter to Oxford, Glasgow admitted the substance of the charge but pleaded that secrecy had been essential since otherwise he 'had been infallibly "De Witted" '—that is, assassinated.[51]

Earlier, Seafield and Glasgow, in a joint letter to Queensberry in July 1707, had also virtually admitted the charge. They acknowledged that Glasgow had received the £20,000 from Godolphin, and hazarded the weak notion that it might have been debited to the Equivalent. But, they went on, the whole issue bristled with danger. Queensberry, as he must well have known, was told that he had got the lion's share, about £12,000, for his expenses and equipage; but as to other payments, 'its impossible to state these sommes without discovering the haill affair to every particular person that received any part of the money, which hath been hitherto kept secret, and its more than probable, that they would refuse to give assignations if they were demanded of them, so the discovering of it would be of no use, unless it were to bring discredit upon the manadgement of that parliament'. The management of that parliament—as Seafield, Glasgow and Queensberry were all well aware—could not stand close scrutiny. That the matter was, to say the least, delicate is implicit in the joint authors' classical, but evidently unheeded, postscript: 'Your Grace may be pleased to burn this letter when you have read it to my Lord Treasurer.'[52]

Incidentally, the Earl of Glasgow himself did well out of the 'mighty affair of the union', as Defoe called it. Glasgow got the Register's Office for life and with it, he tells us, 'a settlement of 1200 l yearly for my service in the Union Parliament'.[53] And, of course, a moritorium on his involved and suspect account of the excise as well as union payments.

On the whole, it is disingenuous to regard these transactions as simply the winding up of the Scots treasury. It was plainly something more than that, for if the claims were sound, then they should have been honoured without the ministry trying to squeeze so much political mileage out of them. The dues were probably in the main just; but the manner in which they were met definitely smacks of bribery and corruption, and one has to be a very determined casuist not to see what Glasgow and Seafield, and the Commissioners of Public Accounts, saw all too clearly. Nor does another standard objection against this interpretation stand up, namely that many of the sums involved were too trifling to be of any import. Most Scots lairds were then chronically hard-up, and what may now look like trifles were not so regarded by them. Among the impecunious was Secretary Johnstone, and in February 1707 he was desperately trying to secure the sums due to him from the Equivalent—'which I need more than I thought I should do; for my house will fall'.[54]

The Equivalent, indeed, had a major part to play in predisposing members to favour the treaty. Not only was it in itself a liberal coating of sugar for an otherwise bitter pill, but the way in which it was disbursed also wrought powerfully on behalf of the Court. Part of it was earmarked to meet arrears of salaries and was later so used, over and above the payments made by Glasgow. It is not really possible to say how much money Queensberry made from the union, so tangled are the accounts, but certainly he obtained much more than the £12,000 sterling Seafield had referred to. The same applies to others—*toties quoties.*

It must also be borne in mind that the sums involved were in sterling. To assess their real value in Scotland in 1706–7 is extremely difficult, but a start can be made by multiplying by twelve to get the reckoning in Scots money. In many cases, too, the sum would have to be doubled because of later disbursements from the Equivalent. Thus, Lord Banff's paltry £11. 2 shillings, which has caused much learned mirth, appears in more sobering guise as 266 1. 8 shillings Scots; for, as anyone who has had cause to examine estate ledgers and accounts of that period must recognise, that was far from being a negligible sum of money. As for Campbell of Cessnock's modest £50, even assuming that it was not paid twice over, it scales up to 600 1. Scots. No Scottish laird of the time would have regarded such a sum as a mere trifle, and for many it represented a good year's rental. Similarly Marchmont's £1,000 becomes 12,000 1. Scots; and so on through the entire account.

Then, too, the Equivalent was politically serviceable in other ways. Thus the Squadrone was gulled into the Court's interest by a tacit promise, later broken, that, as nominees of the directors of the Company of Scotland, they would be allowed to handle that part of the Equivalent intended to recoup the shareholders.[55]

But that self-interest was a prepotent operative factor is most strongly brought out by the attitude of Argyll, who is commonly supposed to have been one of the great architects of union. Early in 1706 he went off to the wars in Flanders, there to make interest and to annoy Marlborough with his incessant demands and complaints. Argyll felt that he was being passed over for promotion and that he had a better claim to a major-generalship than some who had recently been raised to that eminence. Like Achilles he began to sulk in his tent, taking no notice of the ministry and its pressing need for support for the union. For the Court this was a very serious matter because if the Argyll interest had defected, or failed to hold together, then the treaty's chances in the Scottish parliament would have been very slight. In July 1706, therefore, Mar and Godolphin asked Argyll, in humble enough terms, to come over and help out the ministry. Mar received the following answer, couched in Argyll's usual bald style: 'My lord, it is surprising to me that my Lord Treasurer, who is a man of sense, should think of sending me up and down like a footman from one country to another without ever offering me any reward. Thier is indeed a sairtin service due from every subject to his Prince, and that I shall pay the Queen as faithfully as any body can doe; but if her ministers thinks it for her service to imploy me any forder I doe think the proposall should be attended with an offer of a reward'. Argyll then recites his oft-repeated grievance about being passed over in the army promotion list and concludes: 'My Lord, when I have justice dun me here and am told what to expect for going to Scotland, I shall be ready to obey my Lord Treasurer's commands'.[56] Argyll's support and his presence were alike indispensable, and so Marlborough, who detested 'Red John', was given the disagreeable task of winning him over. Not until Argyll was promised a major-generalship did he agree to attend the parliament and 'serve the Queen in the affair of the Union'.[57]

Those who regard the union as sacrosanct are troubled by the curious brand of patriotism that runs through this correspondence. They prefer not to dwell on it, or else dismiss it as a minor eccentricity on Argyll's part. But obviously it was much more than that, and no good historical purpose can be served by playing it down or ignoring it.

Before the session was weeks old the ruthless self-seeking of the House of Argyll again threw the ministry into a panic. Argyll threatened to upset everything unless his every demand was met; this time his object was to strengthen his political interest, which was already substantial, and, with an eye to the post-union future, make it the greatest in Scotland. As an English peer, Earl of Greenwich, he himself expected to have a hereditary seat in the House of Lords; he therefore demanded that his young brother Archibald should be created a Scots peer and thus become eligible to be returned as one of the sixteen representative peers. The ministry was in a quandary; it had a long list of similar supplications and feared to give offence to the patient queue. Expostulation was vain. The Campbell brothers were adamant, and the ministry finally had to give way. All that remained was for Lord Archie, as he was familiarly called, to pick his title, but even this simple operation could not be carried out without a characteristic display of arrogance. He chose the title Earl of Dundee, to the wrath of the Grahams who felt that they had a lien on it. Their chief, the Marquis of Montrose, whom the ministry had just lately won with a grant of office (the presidency of the council),[58] was livid and threatened to throw in with the opposition. A situation developed that could only justly be rendered by the talents of Gilbert and Sullivan, as the great men of the ministry vainly prostrated themselves before Argyll and Montrose. Finally, as a last resort, the Earl of Loudoun, a cadet of the Campbell family, interceded with Argyll and his brother and managed to make them see reason. After a prolonged chrysalis stage Lord Archie finally emerged as the Earl of Islay;[59] in time he was to become the greatest of the eighteenth-century political managers of Scotland.

In short, the evidence which supports the view that many Scottish politicians regarded the union as a political job from which profit could be made is wide, varied and irrefutable. And certainly at the time, and for long enough thereafter, there was a widespread belief in Scotland that naked self-interest had played a large if not dominant rôle in securing the passage of the Treaty of Union through the Scottish parliament. This belief is the *leitmotiv* of a poem attributed to the Gaelic poet John MacDonald, sometimes known as the Bard of Keppoch and sometimes as Iain Lom. The poem bitterly summarises the angry reaction of the Highland Jacobites to the union, as the Bard of Keppoch scathingly denounces Queensberry, Seaforth and even Hamilton as base self-seeking rascals who had only one end in view—'to trade away from us before our very eyes our crown and sovereign rights'. The supposedly Jacobite Seaforth had succumbed to temptation and played a double rôle, and him the Bard roasts with burning words: 'Earl of Seaforth from Brahan, there will be no peace for you as long as you live; there will be a hot hunt at your heels abroad, anywhere within the bounds of Europe; but if I had my way, truly I would melt gold for you, and inject it into the shell of your skull until it would reach your boots'.[60] The aged Iain Lom was Jacobite long before Jacobitism as such existed. He had sung the deeds of Montrose and young Colkitto. His poem on the union is, therefore, in some respects obviously partisan. Nonetheless, it reflects the views of one who evidently knew the politics of the south; and it receives striking confirmation in the records of the time.

In fact, resentment of the union was not confined to the Jacobites, and appears again in the works of Fergusson and Burns, neither of whom had any strong party commitments. Fergusson's laments are couched in serio-comic vein in the form of a colloquy between the ghosts of two notable Edinburgh philanthropists, George Heriot and George Watson, whose benefactions were threatened by a Mortmain Bill in 1773. In spite of the satirical setting and the device of reporting sighs for the good old days, Fergusson was probably serious when he wrote:

> Black be the day that e'er to England's ground
> Scotland was eikit by the UNION's bond.[61]

But the bitterest and most explicit expression of this feeling is in Burns' 'Such a Parcel of Rogues in a Nation':

> What force or guile could not subdue
> Thro' many warlike ages
> Is wrought now by a coward few
> For hireling traitor's wages.
>
> . . . .
>
> 'We're bought and sold for English gold'—
> Such a parcel of rogues in a nation![62]

And this view of the union as the product of corrupt jobbing was by no means confined to emotional types like poets, who might be expected to see things in an impassioned or exaggerated way. That hard-headed Orcadian and notable Whig historian, Malcolm Laing, also accepted that union was the result of bribery and summed up with the terse and caustic comment: 'Never was an union so cheaply purchased'.[63]

The real point to note here is that eighteenth-century writers, and people in general, were familiar with the politics of influence and did not hesitate to call a spade a spade. Not until Victorian historians, steeped in 'Balmorality', imposed completely alien standards on eighteenth-century politics did it become bad form to mention the unmentionable, even if this required that reams of evidence should be either unread or misread. And that evidence is not purely Scottish. In 1707 English observers, like Defoe, were also well aware of the corrupt attitudes of Scottish politicians; but as long as Defoe's main task was to produce pro-union propaganda he carefully kept the more awkward pieces of information to himself. Once the union was safely carried the need for reticence ceased, and in April 1707 Defoe accurately described to Harley the antics of the Scottish peers: 'The great men are posting to London for places and honours, every man full of his own merit and afraid of every one near him: I never saw so much trick, sham, pride, jealousy and cutting of friends' throats as there is among the noble men'. Indeed, Defoe adds that he even had hopes of bribing some members of the General Assembly of the Church of Scotland, and concludes ebulliently, 'In short money will do anything here'.[64]

Now, these 'great men' of whom Defoe complained were precisely the same nobles whose 'disinterested patriotism' had carried the union, as Whig historians to this day are never tired of reminding us. But this union, as Defoe well knew, wrought no terrible Jekyll and Hyde transformations. It did not overnight change high-principled statesmen into greedy and unscrupulous grafters; and Harley and Godolphin could not have been in the least surprised by Defoe's new and more factual style of reporting. Other English politicians who were not so closely involved had no difficulty in working out that the union had been carried by 'unjustifiable means', and many feared that the Scottish members at Westminster would bring their corrupt practices with them.[65] The English ministry, of course, pooh-poohed such fears; but a recent historian, Edward Hughes, has suggested that the blight of a 'spoils system' did indeed spread from Scotland to England just after the union.[66]

Finally, part of the explanation of the passage of the treaty of union through the Scottish parliament is to be found in the state of the opposition. From the outset of the session in 1706 the opposition creaked ominously; its cohesion, badly damaged by Hamilton's flagrant backsliding in 1705, was not restored, and of this the Court Party was well aware. Seafield noted that Hamilton, who still smarted from being excluded from the union commission, was violently opposed to the treaty 'bot knows not how to unite his pairtie'.[67] In view of Hamilton's recent conduct, it was scarcely surprising that both Cavaliers and Countrymen had lost faith in him. The surprise is that he was still regarded as leader. Most likely this was because neither party was able to come up with a satisfactory replacement who was acceptable to the other. The death of the Earl of Home on 20 August 1706 deprived the Cavaliers of a trusted if not particularly able leader. Atholl, who hated the union (especially since Queensberry, restored as commissioner, was backing it), tried to fill Home's shoes and at the same time refurbished his Country image. He was accepted, mainly because he was an able as well as experienced politician, but he was not entirely trusted by either the Cavaliers or the Countrymen. The Hamiltons were uniquely placed in this respect; they could boast a long tradition of loyalty to the crown and respect for the prerogative, and at the same time had a presbyterian and constitutional background that was much more convincing than Atholl's. So, in a sense, the opposition was stuck with Hamilton, no other being able so plausibly to have a foot in both camps. At the same time the jealousy and distrust that existed between Hamilton and Atholl seriously impeded the opposition.

The Jacobites, in fact, placed their main hopes on armed rebellion and assistance from France, but, thanks in no small part to the blustering but essentially prudent Hamilton, neither ploy succeeded. Also, the two main segments of opposition reacted in different ways to the treaty. Certainly, both condemned incorporating union, but they were at odds when it came to considering specific parts of the treaty. The Countrymen found it hard to vote against the Hanoverian succession and free trade; the Jacobites, on the other hand, regarded the Hanoverian succession as the most obnoxious item in the treaty.

The Court also managed to weaken another bulwark of the opposition by placating the presbyterians. It is doubtful if this secured more than a handful of votes in parliament, but it did much to lower the political temperature in many parts of the country. Even before the Act of Security for the church was passed there is evidence that in some areas the outcry of the presbyterians was subsiding. Thus on 4 September 1706 Charles, Lord Selkirk wrote to his brother the Duke of Hamilton, 'I am extremely scandalized with the presbiterean ministers of this place for severall who both prayed and preached against the union are now come over to the measure . . . God deliver us, for I see nothing but absolute ruin to this poor nation and ourselves only to blame for it'.[68] The situation, however, remained tricky, tempers flaring again when the parliament met and the exact terms of the treaty became known. The Commission of the General Assembly at first bridled at the articles of union and was only with difficulty restrained from demanding sweeping and specific safeguards which the government probably could not have conceded. Worse, the Commission in its first violent reaction to the proposed terms of union considered objecting to bishops in the House of Lords, and talked too of the need for defensive measures against such a covert threat. In producing a more restrained clerical attitude to the union King William's old grey eminence Carstares, by then principal of the university of Edinburgh, played an important rôle. Largely at his prompting the Commission of Assembly on 16 October applied to the parliament for reasonable safeguards for the Church of Scotland and guarantees for the maintenance of presbyterian government. As a result, at the height of the storm over the union, on 12 November 1706 an Act of Security for the church was passed by the parliament, and this act was accepted as an integral part of the Treaty of Union.[69] Problems still remained but diplomatic handling of them prevented any serious collision between church and state. Presbyterian dislike of union and fear of its possible consequences by no means disappeared after the passing of the church's Act of Security; but it subsided a good deal. The church courts ceased to fulminate against the union, the extremists were deprived of leadership, and this led to a visible weakening of one of the main supports of the anti-unionists. The nature of presbyterian institutions made this inevitable, since none could speak for the church except through its lawfully constituted courts. The winning over of the Commission of Assembly was the master stroke here, an important reminder that everything did not begin and end in parliament.

14

The Attainment of Union

SO far the treaty's reception in Scotland has been discussed topically without reference to the strict course and interaction of events. Such a treatment, however, while of value in elucidating important background considerations like management, can give misleading impressions. In particular this abstract approach tends to blur the total situation, and above all to minimise its day-to-day uncertainty. To obtain a more balanced view, therefore, the unfolding of events has to be considered. Specifically, the following matters require attention: the progress of the treaty in the Scottish parliament; the impact of the parliamentary debate on the nation at large plus the effect of extra-parliamentary agitations on parliament; and, to round matters off, the fate of the treaty in the English parliament. But at the outset an important question arises, one already touched upon and which, if not carefully handled, can also produce misconceptions. Why was the treaty first submitted to the Scottish parliament; why not first to the English parliament, or to both legislatures simultaneously?

As already stated, the Court, expecting the greatest difficulties over the proposed union to occur in Scotland, presented the treaty to the Scottish parliament before having it brought up at Westminster. This was no accident but a carefully thought out move. Nor was the decision taken because, as some hold, the Scottish politicians counted for nothing, or because acceptance of the treaty was a foregone conclusion. On the contrary, it was clear that success or failure lay with the outcome of the Scottish session of 1706; and, while the Court hoped that it would pass, the possibility of failure still weighed heavily, as Anne's instructions to Commissioner Queensberry testify. If, however, the treaty managed to run the gauntlet in the Scottish parliament, then its prospects at Westminster would be greatly enhanced; but the converse did not necessarily apply. For one thing, if the treaty passed the English parliament before being considered in Scotland, the possibility of amending its clauses would have been diminished, and this would have aided the opposition rather than the ministry. The opposition in Scotland could also have made out that the Scottish parliament, like the Irish parliament, was little more than a rubber-stamp, forced willy-nilly into England's measures. On the other hand, if the treaty were first considered in Scotland and were to fail there, then the Court, the English ministry and parliament would avoid an obvious rebuff and be better placed to devise fresh policy. As to submitting the treaty to both parliaments at the same time, it was impossible. Not only would this have been a lengthy and tortuous procedure but also one that would have added immensely to the Court's difficulties. In such an event the opposition in both parliaments would have been strengthened, and the prospect of collusion between them, which the Court feared, could have become a grim reality. Almost certainly, had this impracticable method been attempted, the treaty would have fizzled out in interminable discussions and procedural wrangles. Worse, if, as seemed likely enough, the two parliaments had become deadlocked on vital aspects of the treaty the invidious task of trying to compose these differences would have fallen to the crown, and this too could only have led to further complications. However regarded, the method of submitting the treaty to both parliaments at the same time had nothing to recommend it, and accordingly it was not even considered. The decision to essay the fate of the treaty in the Scottish parliament was therefore a purely tactical one based on practical considerations, and it carried no implications of subordination or superiority of legislatures. As a pro-unionist wag put it at the time, the Scottish parliament could, if it liked, pride itself on having the first go at the treaty, while the English parliament could flatter itself that it was called upon to have the last word.

The Scottish parliament opened on 3 October 1706 in an Edinburgh which, in spite of atrocious weather, was thronged with people from all parts of the kingdom.[1] Various reasons caused them to congregate in the capital, some concerned about the fate of their country, others drawn by curiosity and possibly the desire to witness what might well be the last ceremonial Riding of the Parliament—the traditional colourful pageant that preceded the formal opening of the session. But it was soon made clear that not all had come simply to spectate. Many, perhaps influenced by the recent example set by the *Worcester* affair, had obviously resorted to the capital in the hope of overawing the ministry and ensuring the rejection of the treaty. The subsequent harassing of the ministry 'out of doors'—that is, outside parliament—was not just the work of the notoriously volatile Edinburgh mob but reflected a widespread general will. There can be no avoiding the conclusion that, whether through ignorant prejudice or not, popular sympathy, and not just in the capital, lay with one segment or other of the opposition. The idea of incorporation was hated, and, in spite of differences in language, creed and politics, the Scottish nation at large was hostile to the treaty.

As much was soon demonstrated in the capital. Hamilton, who had strained his foot, was borne in a litter to and from the Parliament House, and only with difficulty could his bearers make their way through the wildly cheering crowds.[2] 'God bless his grace for defending the country against the Union!' was their battle-cry. Very different were the reception and the benisons bestowed on the commissioner and other leading unionists; as ritually as Hamilton was lionised, Queensberry and his associates were violently barracked and threatened.[3] Indeed, all sources agree that an atmosphere of menace hung over the capital[4]—as Mar wrote on 19 November to a colleague in London, only bad weather prevented a march on Edinburgh, where, as it was, 'everyday here we are in hazard of our lives'.[5] And Defoe later testified to much the same effect.

But, while giving way to the odd tremble, Queensberry's brazen fortitude proved equal to the occasion; and, taking their cue from the commissioner, the ministers for the most part kept their nerve. In holding the ministry steady the presence of Argyll was invaluable; his aloof arrogance and contempt for the mob prevented any repetition of the miserable débâcle of authority occasioned by the affair of the *Worcester*. As a result of good luck and firm management, aided in no small measure by the ineptitude of the opposition in parliament, only relatively minor disorders broke out in the capital, the worst of which occurred on 23 October when the house of a noted unionist, Sir Patrick Johnstone, was rabbled.[6] To the mob of Edinburgh Johnstone was a fallen idol, a former lord provost and sitting member for the city whose popularity failed to survive the fact that he had served as a union commissioner. The assault on his house was entirely the work of the mob, the parliamentary opposition criticising it as futile and premature and likely to give the government a good excuse to tighten up on security. The opposition read the situation correctly, and the government was indeed quick to turn the riot to advantage. The Privy Council, still rocked by the backwash of the *Worcester*, took decisive steps: not only was a strong proclamation issued against tumults but the unusual expedient was also taken of quartering troops in the city and indemnifying them against any slaughters that might occur; and as a further precaution the small standing army of 1,500 men was concentrated near Edinburgh. Even so, its commander-in-chief, the Earl of Leven, who also held Edinburgh Castle, was far from confident of the adequacy of these measures and expressed his fears to Godolphin about the weakness of the forces under his command.[7]

On the last day of October Godolphin assured Leven that strong forces would be stationed in the North of England and Ireland 'to bee in a readiness in case this ferment should continue to give any farther disturbance to the publick peace'.[8] Throughout, Godolphin acted coolly. He was convinced that there was too much talk of rebellion for there to be much substance to it; and, besides, mob riots were then commonplaces of urban existence and not to be equated with armed insurrection. On other grounds, too, the English lord treasurer did not believe that a rebellion was likely, partly because the war was draining France's strength, which would discourage any extensive commitments in Scotland, but mainly because he had come to realise that Hamilton, for all his bluster, was not cut out for desperate enterprises. The duke could not be said to lack courage, but he had much at stake and was unlikely to risk his all to please either the Pretender, Louis XIV, or the plebeian mob of Edinburgh. Whatever his precise game, Hamilton would win or lose it all in the parliament; and, in Godolphin's view, there too would the fate of the treaty be decided.

Anne's letter to the parliament again warmly recommended union, which, the queen declared, 'has long been desired by both nations and we shall esteem it as the greatest glory of our reign to have it now perfected, being fully persuaded that it must prove the greatest happiness of our people'; it would, she continued, be the surest foundation of lasting peace and increasing wealth and prosperity, enabling Britain to 'resist all its enemies, support the protestant interest everywhere and maintain the liberties of Europe'; as to religion the Scottish parliament could take whatever steps it felt were needed to secure the liberties of the established church; and in conclusion the queen guaranteed that the English parliament would be equally zealous for union.[9] These sentiments were dutifully echoed by the commissioner and the chancellor. The opening ritual over, the parliament heard the Articles of Union read, ordered them to be printed along with the record of the negotiations, and adjourned for a week.[10]

The debate on whether the union was to be or not to be really began on 12 October. From the beginning the opposition, aware that influence had been at work and fearing that the government had a majority, resorted to fabian tactics.[11] The anti-unionists, therefore, seized on every opportunity to delay matters in the hope that the ministry's nerve would break as popular clamours mounted now that the details of the treaty were known.[12] Alternatively, the opposition hoped to wreck the treaty by amendments that would make it unacceptable to the English parliament.[13] In spite of their differences and their difficulties, the anti-unionists were strong enough to prevent the ministry from rushing the treaty through the House. Although unable to defer its consideration, the opposition at least managed to secure that each article had to be voted upon and that neither the treaty, nor any part of it, could be ratified until all the Articles had been approved. This was a cumbrous and lengthy process that offered full scope for destructive tactics that could be geared up to the agitations outside parliament.

Throughout the session an appeal to the nation at large remained a basic tactic of the opposition, a point made in the important diet of 12 October when it was contended that parliament alone did not have the right to decide on such a fundamental issue as an incorporating union. Such a union, the opposition argued, would destroy the existing constitution, and this could not be done without a mandate from the country, either by a general election or by constitution at least. The request seemed reasonable but was brushed aside by the ministry on the specious plea that the parliament had been elected to consider union in 1703, which was tantamount to saying that the terms of the treaty negotiated in 1706 did not matter. Certainly, it is no coincidence that after 12 October the opposition to the ministry, inside and outside parliament, hardened. In the face of all this, the pro-unionists argued that parliament was competent to accept or reject the treaty as it saw fit. The opposition then tried to embroil the government with the church by asking parliament to sanction a national fast, which was then the traditional response to a national crisis. The ministry beat down this motion, thus strengthening the suspicions of many presbyterians that Queensberry and his impious crew were ready to betray church as well as nation. A long wrangle on these various points was ended when at last the ministry brought the House to the issue 'proceed or not'. The first important vote of the session revealed the truth of what the opposition had feared, for the motion to proceed with the consideration of the Articles of Union carried by a majority of 66, the Squadrone at last showing its hand by casting its 25 votes for the government.[14]

Strengthened by improved security measures, the ministry became more confident, and in spite of all sorts of ingenious delaying tactics by the opposition the reading of the Articles was completed by the end of October. The opposition then tried to defer detailed consideration of the Articles 'for some considerable time that the sentiments of the Parliament of England thereanent be known and the Members of Parliament may consult those whom they represent'; but these and other objections were repelled, and on 2 November the House accepted Marchmont's motion for detailed consideration of the Articles.[15] The members then began to argue about which Article should be considered first—not as odd a matter as it might appear at first blush. Defoe as usual seized the opportunity to sneer at the opposition, but in this instance his partisanship outran his good sense.[16] Everything, clearly, turned on Article I. To defer its consideration for as long as possible was the obvious tactic for the opposition; and just as obviously the ministry insisted on beginning with Article I. To defer Article I might give the anti-unionists the opportunity to undermine the treaty in the other articles, in which event Article I would either at last be rejected or go by default; but if, on the other hand, Article I were considered first and were to pass then the opposition would be put at a sore disadvantage. To accept the basic principle of incorporation and then carp about details could hardly gain the opposition kudos in its rôle of champion of the independence of the nation.

Defoe did not quite see the significance of this vital vote, but the members of the parliament did. Thus both ministry and opposition exerted themselves to the full on this issue, over which a hot debate raged until 4 November. By then petitions against the union were beginning to be presented to the House and these provided the occasion for repeating the arguments already advanced by the opposition. In answer to all this, for the government side on 2 November William Seton younger of Pitmedden, one of the commissioners for union, justified the treaty on grounds of economic and political necessity. The burden of Seton's speech was that the Union of the Crowns had proved to be unsatisfactory and that only an incorporating union with England could benefit Scotland.[17] It was an able speech, well argued, and without a trace of sentiment. Perhaps Pitmedden's very coolness annoyed the hot Belhaven who then delivered an impassioned, but probably studied, harangue to the effect that the union would destroy and impoverish the nation. It is the comical side of Belhaven's craggy rhetoric that is usually stressed nowadays; but running through his disjointed and highly emotional pleas there was a powerful substratum of sense. It was to the concept of the nation that Belhaven appealed—'our ancient mother Caledonia'. In Belhaven's view the nation of the Scots long antedated parliaments, which in fact came into existence to safeguard the nation's rights and liberties and could not abate them. But the thought nearly drowned in the orator's lachrymose rhetoric.

Belhaven's speech, famous in its day and long thereafter, was what the Victorians described approvingly as 'a crowned masterpiece of eloquence', and as such it long figured in the repertoire of that genre; it is what our own hard-boiled generation scornfully dismisses as a 'tear jerker'. But in any given generation no uniform standards of taste can be said to apply, a considerable gulf yawning between the popular and the sophisticated. Present-day historians (all, as the Americans say, from Missouri) are evidently psychologically much nearer the 'parliament-men' of the union period than they are to the great Victorians, and, like the blasé members of the Scottish parliament, are little moved by the cloying patriotism of Belhaven's speech—except to mirth. For this the orator's histrionic style may have been largely responsible. The speech was, in fact, the work of a highly emotional political maverick and completely different from the deadly rapier thrusts of a Fletcher. But it reads much better than it must have sounded when acted, and this furious speech was indeed of considerable influence. Belhaven was carried away, but well knew where he was going. Seafield felt that the speech was 'contrived to incense the common peopel'; and here it must be remembered that large-scale political meetings were then forbidden and would have been suppressed as seditious. The press, like the pulpit, provided a bridge between parliament and people; and, when rushed into print, Belhaven's speech of 2 November 1706 made an immediate hit with the populace. It reinforced the angry anti-unionist mood outside parliament, which was doubtless a large part of the orator's intention.[18] Here its fire and fury was not held to signify nothing: its 'smeddum' had an irresistible appeal to the hoi-polloi, which, in every age, enjoys pyrotechnics, the noisier the better.

Defoe, in his *History*, printed Belhaven's speech in full but did not comment on it beyond noting that it was quashed in parliament by the laconic Marchmont, who dismissed it, in a few terse sentences, as a nightmare vision. It was unusual for Defoe not to dilate on what he took to be the follies of the opposition, and the reason for his restraint in this instance is curious. Part of the explanation is that at the time he hastily composed an anonymous skit in verse, 'The Vision', which lampooned Belhaven:

> Then the Nation in Sack-cloth appear'd,
> And the Visionist sadly bewail'd her;
> For Mischiefs the like were ne'er heard,
> Her priv'lege of Slavery fail'd her.[19]

Belhaven was stung into replying but mistook his target. He believed that 'The Vision' was from the joint pen of the Earl of Haddington and Dr. Wellwood, and his counter-production was accordingly aimed at the Squadrone. His 'A Scots Answer to a British Vision' was a witty enough piece of its kind, though, as might easily be surmised, the defects of Belhaven's prose were not wanting in his poetry. Defoe enjoyed the fun and kept it going with 'A Reply to the Scots Answer to the British Vision', in which Belhaven was apostrophised as

> Supream in Thought, to Grammar unconfin'd;
> Thy lofty Genius soars above the Wind.

But after the passing of the Treaty of Union, when political ardour had cooled somewhat, Defoe and Belhaven became fast friends. Defoe was forgiven for his banter and after Belhaven's death on 21 June 1708 did his best to rehabilitate his friend's memory. One way of doing this was, in the *History of the Union*, to refrain from adverse comment on Belhaven's febrile anti-union utterances, contenting himself with describing the speech as being 'much talked of in the world', and its author as 'a person of extraordinary parts and capacity'. But it is noticeable that the claims of friendship did not altogether overcome Defoe's diplomatic address or his justly renowned irony.

To return to the scene of those speeches, the debate on Article I raged on.

Just before the matter was put to the vote on 4 November Hamilton made another powerful speech, which resembled Belhaven's in blending hard sense and pathos. In it he stigmatised the treaty as a base betrayal of those 'who assisted the great King Robert Bruce, to restore the constitution and revenge the falsehood of England and the usurpation of Balliol'—and much more to similar effect. But there was nothing sentimental about his peroration: 'Shall we yield up the sovereignty and independency of the nation, when we are commanded by those we represent, to preserve the same, and assured of their assistance to support us?'[20] Hamilton then made a cryptic statement about 'a peculiar concern of his family' that he would not at that moment trouble parliament with if he might be allowed to bring it forward later—a request that was readily enough granted. It is just conceivable, as Mar believed, that this may have been a veiled reference to his claim to the Scottish throne which Article I bade fair to bury forever.[21]

In the same general vein Atholl protested against the treaty as 'contrary to the honour, interests, fundamental laws and the constitution of the kingdom';[22] which complaint was to become a stock prop of opposition. The Marquis of Annandale, who had always hated the idea of incorporation, took the other tack and advocated a federal union.[23] All was to no avail. Brought to the vote at last, Article I was approved by a majority of 30, the Squadrone again supporting the ministry.[24] A crumb of victory went to the opposition, however, and for that the historian can only be grateful. This was that the votes in the House should be recorded, and henceforth voting lists were drawn up so that it was easy to see who voted for what—'an extraordinary method' (meaning unprecedented), as the diarist Hume of Crossrigg noted.[25]

Voting on the other Articles fluctuated a good deal. The opposition again fought desperately over Article II, which required recognition of the Hanoverian succession. Hamilton was particularly exercised over this Article, which, of course, would almost certainly dispel forever his dream of a crown. Basing his pleas on the numerous anti-union petitions that were being presented to the House, the duke asked for a recess in which to acquaint 'the Queen with the general aversion of the nation'.[26] And on that same day, 15 November, Belhaven delivered another speech, briefer and more restrained than his first but still having an eccentric ring to it, though the eccentricity had, as usual, an ulterior purpose that was clearer to his contemporaries than it is today. Belhaven likened the treaty under consideration to 'the first and worst Treaty that ever was set on foot for mankind . . . when the serpent did deceive our mother Eve'. Even so, according to Belhaven, were the nation and its representatives required by the ministry to 'Eat, swallow down this incorporating union, tho it please neither eye nor taste, it must go over: You must believe your physicians, and we shall consider the reasons for it afterwards'. He continued, 'I wish, my Lord, That our loss be not in some small manner proportionable to our first parents, they thought to have been incorporate with the Gods: But in place of that, they were justly expelled Paradise, lost their sovereignty over the creatures, and were forced to earn their bread with the sweat of their brows'. Ludicrous though they appear to modern eyes, these novel commentaries on the Book of Genesis went down well with the presbyterians whose thoughts, secular as well as sacred, were saturated in Old Testament lore. But Belhaven did not dwell overlong on the theme of Paradise Lost, the rest of his speech being a reasoned plea for reform of the Scottish constitution rather than its dissolution. He concluded that 'Limitations of our own making is the best security'.[27]

Fletcher, ever on the watch for an opening, eagerly returned to his favourite theme of limitations, but, as before, his ideas on this head were of slight appeal even to his own party. Then Annandale proposed that the Hanoverian succession should be recognised and the treaty dropped. The queen had expressly warned the commissioner against such a manoeuvre, and the ministry's supporters went all out to repel it. In the end Queensberry's 'led-horses', as Lockhart called them, carried the day and Article II was put to the vote. In spite of its fierce resistance the opposition could muster only 57 votes, the ministry winning by a majority of 58.[28] Quite evidently, therefore, there was wide support for the Hanoverian succession, and some of the Countrymen parted with the Cavaliers on this issue. All the same, prior to the vote being taken, it was cannily moved, and accepted by the House, that approval of the Hanoverian succession as laid down in Article II of the Treaty of Union 'shall not be binding or have any effect unless terms and conditions of an Union of the two Kingdoms be finally adjusted and concluded'.[29]

Of all the Articles of Union, IV, conferring freedom of trade, was the most popular, which is not surprising in view of the economic resentment built up at the English Navigation Laws for nearly half a century. True, Article IV was discussed at length but mainly with a view to amending details; and when it finally came to a vote the opposition dropped to a mere 19, even Lockhart voting for the measure.[30]

In the event, the most keenly contested parts of the treaty after the first two Articles were III, XV and XXII. Article III stipulated that the United Kingdom of Great Britain should be represented by one parliament, the parliament of Great Britain; XV dealt with the Equivalent; and XXII fixed the representation of Scotland in the parliament of Great Britain.

On 18 November a bitter struggle raged over Article III in a bid to preserve the Scottish parliament in some form. At the outset of the debate the opposition argued that this article should be reserved to the end, but their motion was defeated. Annandale made the, by then, ritual protest that loss of the parliament was 'contrair to the honour, interest, fundamental laws, and constitutions of this kingdom; is a giving up of the sovereignty, the birthright of the peers, the rights and privileges of the barons and boroughs'. If all these were lost, he continued, what security did the subjects of Scotland have for their future liberties? It was a good question, and in the absence of a good answer, Annandale concluded: 'And therefore, I do protest, that this shall not prejudge the being of future Scots parliaments and conventions within the kingdom of Scotland, at no time coming'. Here it has to be recalled that Article I, which effectively disposed of the kingdoms of Scotland and England, said nothing about their respective parliaments whose fates turned on Article III. The hard fight put up over Article III, therefore, had two objectives—to preserve the Scottish parliament, and to damage the treaty. If the treaty were subjected to drastic amendment in such an important article, then it would almost certainly fail. Thus, over Article III Hamilton really exerted himself to introduce wrecking amendments, and in particular he moved that if the treaty were implemented the Scots members should have the right of veto over all measures that touched on it and that any infringement of its terms should lead to automatic dissolution of the union. Stair parried Hamilton's motion by arguing that at that stage it was not feasible to consider constitutional safeguards and that this could only be done after all the articles of the treaty had been accepted—a specious answer that showed that the opposition had no monopoly of prevarication or chicanery.[31]

In the best speech delivered in the union parliament the opposition was answered by Seton of Pitmedden the younger.[32] He had once been of the Country faction but had switched sides, either because he had changed his mind or because his personal interest lay with Seafield. Be that as it may, Seton's speech of 18 November on Article III was sensible and clearly phrased, partly, no doubt, because he had already rehearsed its leading ideas in his pamphlets. He pointed out that Scotland, a constitutional monarchy, was not 'a Polish aristo-cracy' (the bad example of Poland seems to have weighed heavily with the Scots unionists),[33] and that it was not lawful for the gentry, in a well-known Polish phrase, to 'explode the diet'—i.e. overturn the chamber by filibustering or even by force. Nor was the government democratic, 'whereby every subject of Scotland may claim a vote in the legislature'. According to Seton the govern-ment of Scotland had long been a limited monarchy, and sovereignty lay with the crown in parliament. He further claimed that 'there are no fundamentals of government in any nation, which are not alterable by its supreme power, where the circumstances of times requires'. Thus, in order to annihilate the Scottish parliament, the unionists were forced to stress its absolute sovereignty and omnicompetence.

Seton's arguments were cogent, but his premises were none of the soundest. His was not the normal view of the constitution, particularly since 1689 when the Claim of Right was held to have laid down fundamental law, something that even the most committed Hanoverians dared not utterly deny. There were, too, serious doubts about the omnicompetence of parliament, which was an English rather than a Scottish concept; and, clearly, the question of the *locus* of ultimate sovereignty, whether it lay with crown or parliament, was still very much *sub judice* in Scotland, as witness the session of the parliament of 1703. Seton seems to have been conscious that he was stretching his argument a bit far, for he carefully acknowledged the existence of natural rights, particularly of liberty and property, but he took care not to examine these metaphysical concepts too closely. On the other main matter of substance on which he touched, the representation granted to Scotland, Seton pointed out that it was calculated on the basis of taxable capacity and on that reckoning was more than fair. In general his arguments throughout were legalistic and drew heavily on a one-sided reading of Grotius; and his theoretical approach to politics was entirely Aristotelian. Strong echoes of Aristotle's *Politics* run all through Seton's work, and he was evidently hostile to any form of Platonism. Nonetheless, his speech was a remarkable *tour de force*, which, delivered dispassionately and persuasively, well deserved the applause it received.[34] But it suffered from a fundamental weakness. Seton could only assert as an article of faith that entrenched safeguards were unnecessary and that the British parliament would deal fairly with Scotland. Here, in a sense, he was hoist with his own petard, for his doctrine of the absolute sovereignty of parliament raised awkward questions that he could not answer. In short, in the important matter of legislation the British parliament would be free to act as it willed.

Article III finally passed with a substantial majority;[35] and a belated attempt after the vote was taken to add a clause to the effect that the parliament of Great Britain 'shall meet and sit once in three years at least in that part of Great Britain now called Scotland' was fobbed off to the Greek Kalends.[36]

The discussion on Article XV was lengthy and disjointed. Much of it was taken up with the disbursement of the Equivalent, and this mouth-watering business brought many powerful interests into conflict. The directors of the Company of Scotland felt that the Company should not be wound up as an act of state and maintained that the views of the shareholders should determine its future. In the light of what Seton had said on rights of property, this was a good point; but the real fears of the directors were lest the reimbursement of the shareholders from the Equivalent should prove illusory. Such fears were not altogether idle, as the sequel showed, and the handling of the Equivalent was to be a bitter disappointment to many besides the directors of the Company of Scotland. As to the proposed liquidation, however, the Scottish government held that the Company operated under statute and that parliament could repeal the relevant act if that was deemed necessary. After much argument on this issue the ministry had its way: the Company of Scotland was to be dissolved. The main trouble, though, concerned the distribution of the Equivalent, which the ministry was determined must be used primarily to pay government arrears of salaries, while the Company of Scotland contended that it had a prior claim. In theory, the ministry failed to win its case, but in practice carried its point, for the arrears of salary were met from the Equivalent long before the tortuous business of paying the shareholders got off the ground. Other interests tried to chisel what they could out of the situation, and the wool producers secured the lesser Equivalent of £2,000 per annum for the promotion of the wool trade. But this scheme, too, hung fire and did not even begin to be implemented until 1727, too late to provide any succour to the moribund wool trade. And throughout the debate on Article XV the anti-unionists condemned the Equivalent as a vast covert bribe, the price of their country's independence; but with politics, as with greatness, consistency has nothing to do, and, illogically, at times the opposition's argument seemed to be that the Equivalent, covert bribe and all, was not great enough. Eventually, on 30 December, Article XV was approved by 121 votes to 54.[37]

By December 1706 the Court was clearly in the ascendant, not only outvoting the opposition in parliament but also dealing firmly with disorders in the country. The opposition, aware of its weakening position, had organised a large meeting of freeholders and lairds in Edinburgh, the object of which was to draw up and forward to the queen a national address against the union—a pale carbon copy of the National Covenant of 1638. Hamilton's vacillation ruined the project.[38] Its only result was that on 27 December the ministry passed yet another proclamation against tumults, which also forbade petitioners to congregate in Edinburgh.[39] Thus, by the time Article XXII, which dealt with parliamentary representation, came to be discussed early in January 1707 the opposition was growing desperate. It had accomplished little. Only minor amendments had been made to the treaty, which were unlikely to prejudice its chances at Westminster. By that late stage, therefore, only a bold stroke could undermine the treaty; so, at Hamilton's instigation, a last-ditch stand on Article XXII was carefully planned.

The members of the opposition aimed to wreck the treaty by withdrawing from the parliament and throwing themselves upon the country. They intended to recognise the Hanoverian succession but to reject incorporation, and then to petition the queen with an elaborate justificatory address which was (shades of 1638!) actually drawn up by Lord Advocate Stewart who hated the idea of union. The object was to advertise the extent of opposition to union in Scotland in the hope that the English parliament would take alarm and drop the treaty. In 1702 Hamilton had, with no great success, employed a similar tactic; but the duke argued, somewhat speciously, that the English commissioners had been half-hearted about the negotiations in 1702 mainly because they knew that Queensberry and his friends represented neither Scottish parliament nor nation. There may have been something in all this, to some extent with reference to 1702 but even more so far as the current situation early in 1707 was concerned. Certainly, if resolutely carried out in January 1707, such a demonstration would not only have embarrassed the Court but also have caused trouble both by encouraging the Tory opposition in England and disconcerting the union's supporters. To have carried the union with little more than half a House would, at best, have been regarded as a half-hearted acceptance, and it would not have been easy to ignore or explain such a well-advertised grandstand display as the withdrawal of so many members.

But again the plan came to nothing because of Hamilton's incurable wavering. At the crucial moment, when the opposition was to state its case in parliament and then ceremoniously withdraw, he called off on the plea of toothache! The duke's health at this time does not seem to have been good, but his exasperated followers were probably correct when they diagnosed his indisposition at this point as being due to an attack of cold feet. In all likelihood the ministry had been informed of Hamilton's plan and managed to intimidate its author with veiled threats—probably a treason charge deriving from his dealings with Colonel Hooke. Hamilton's supporters, however, knew that only some dramatic move could by then damage the treaty, and they literally frog-marched their invalid leader into the Parliament House, hollow tooth and all. There he burked again, refusing to play his assigned rôle, and, to the government's intense relief, the plan flopped. Seafield later stated that if the opposition's plan had been carried out the government was resolved to 'prorogate the Parliament, and give over the prosecution of the union'.[40] Instead, as things turned out, the effect of this débâcle on the opposition was catastrophic. It deepened the general distrust of the Duke of Hamilton, and thereafter the opposition wilted.[41]

The burden of leadership then fell on the disgusted Atholl who was left to advance objections to Article XXII. He hastily put together all his old arguments and condemned the proposed representation as derogatory to the peerage of Scotland and subversive of national rights. The Scottish peers numbered 160 as against 180 in England, and yet, complained Atholl, they were to be reduced to a mere 16 in the House of Lords; the barons and burgesses were to decline in number from 155 to 45; but, Atholl held, since there was to be no reduction of English representation, surely Scotland would be left at the mercy of a predominantly English legislature. Many petitions and addresses, Atholl continued, had been presented to the House against an incorporating union, but not one for it. (In fact, the ministry, belatedly aware of this discrepancy, had tried to get up pro-union addresses but found no support, even their own vassals refusing to sign them. *Faute de mieux*, therefore, the ministry, like Argyll, had to dismiss the anti-union addresses as meaningless scraps of paper, fit only to make kites with).[42] Atholl concluded by demanding a new parliament in order 'to have the immediate sentiments of the nation since these articles have been made public'. A point worth stressing, however, is that, like the addresses to which he had referred, Atholl did not condemn union as such but pleaded for 'honourable, just, and equal terms which may unite them [the two kingdoms] in affection and interest'.[43]

Others spoke to similar purpose; but in spite of noisy opposition the ministry had its majority and Article XXII was approved. Finally, on 16 January 1707, the Treaty of Union, along with the Act of Security for the Church of Scotland, was ratified by 110 votes to 67 as the Scottish Act of Union, a majority of 43 out of 177 votes cast.[44]

Ratification of the union did not quite end the business of the last session of the Scottish parliament. The most important remaining items concerned the disbursement of the Equivalent and the mode whereby Scottish members should be returned to the parliament of the United Kingdom (a term, incidentally, that does not date from 1800 but was frequently used in the Treaty of Union of 1707). Both these matters required immediate attention and this could best be given by the Scottish parliament, which was *au fait* with the details. The intricate problems raised by representation were tackled first. The negotiators of the Treaty had agreed that Scottish electoral law and even procedure should be maintained. This was sensible, for, since the franchises in England and Scotland were completely different and rooted in deep legal as well as social differences, it would have been folly to attempt to enforce uniformity. So it was left to the Scottish parliament to work out the new constituencies and election procedures. Not without numerous protests the 45 M.P.s were allocated on the basis of 30 to the shires and 15 to the royal burghs, the latter necessitating a grouping system. When the relevant acts were passed, a further complication had to be faced. From 20 January on, it had become known that the English ministry intended to continue the existing English parliament, even if the union came into being, until the general election that was due in England in 1708. Quite apart from the revealing light that this decision cast on English attitudes to the union, it posed a practical problem.

How were the first Scottish members of the British parliament to be returned? The Scottish ministry was afraid to leave the matter to the electors, freely conceding that the mood of the country would go against the government. On 12 February the ministry solved the problem by availing itself of its safe majority to allow the parliament to nominate its representatives. The opposition naturally, and correctly, opposed the measure, which made a mockery of any known theory of representation. But the result, after furious wrangling, was a virtual nomination by the ministry. In the process the Squadrone was duped. It had been promised lavish representation in return for supporting the Court, but, with the Treaty safely through the Scottish parliament, the cynical Queensberry, to accommodate the ambitious Argyll, dismissed the Squadrone's claims, thus earning its undying hatred.[45]

The precise means of allocating the Equivalent, a matter of deep concern to many, also caused all sorts of smouldering antagonisms to flare up again. In the upshot the Squadrone were again tricked. Part of the price they had exacted for supporting the Court's measures was that they should have oversight of the disbursement of that part of the Equivalent set aside to compensate the shareholders of the Company of Scotland. This would have given them such powers of patronage that it seems unlikely that the Court ever meant to honour its pledge. However that may be, once the Treaty had been safely converted into an Act of Parliament the Court reneged on the deal and insisted, very plausibly and indeed very properly, on a Commission for the Equivalent that would be answerable to the British parliament.[46]

On 19 March the Treaty of Union and its ancillary acts, as accepted by the English parliament, received final ratification in Scotland, and on 25 March the Scottish parliament, its business completed, was adjourned to 22 April. There, on 25 March, the parliamentary record ends, from which some have concluded that there was no formal dissolution and that for over two and a half centuries the Scottish estates have been deep-frozen in the adjourned state, capable of resuscitation at need to provide 'home rule'. Apart from the patent absurdity of such anachronistic notions, the point of law is that the parliament of Scotland was formally dissolved on 28 April 1707. Private correspondence in the Mar and Kellie muniments refers to a dissolution by proclamation on 28 April;[47] and the proclamation recorded under that date in the Register of the Privy Council could not have been more specific or final: 'whereas by the treatie of Union happily concluded and approven in the parliaments of our Kingdoms of Scotland and England respectively . . . by the third Article of the said Treatie, It is stipulated that the United Kingdom of Great Brittaine be represented by one and the same parliament, to be styled the parliament of Great Brittaine . . . Therefore wee have determined to dissolve our present parliament of Scotland'.[48] The proclamation goes on to do just that.

The passing of the Act of Union in Scotland has been well summarised: 'The Union was, in fact, carried by the Parliament, with the assistance of the Church, against the country'.[49] To that we would only add that management played a large part in securing the parliament. Mar, a manager of considerable ability, well knew how and where to ply his talents to most effect. That the mood of the country, however, was hostile to incorporation is beyond dispute; and equally so is the fact that the parliamentary opposition failed to capitalise on national resentment. The failure to co-ordinate extra-parliamentary resistance to union arose partly because the opposition in parliament, from which a lead was expected, was at odds with itself and feebly led, and partly because the country too was deeply divided. In the country at large the union was clearly detested; but how to concert measures against it was the problem. Many looked for salvation in the return of the legitimist line, some clinging to the hope that James VIII might make a reasonable constitutional monarch. The snag here was that James Edward was still a youth of 18 and an unknown political quantity. Certainly his later career showed that he was open-minded and fair, unlike his obstinate father, but that was not known in 1707. In any event, the presbyterians and constitutionalists, much as they hated the union, wanted no truck with the Pretender, especially as he remained a Roman catholic. These differences ran deep, gave rise to confused attitudes of mind, and made concerted action outside parliament difficult. Nonetheless, the principal defects stemmed from weak leadership. If Hamilton had been capable of decisive action, popular resistance to the union, in spite of divergent interests, would probably still have been feasible; but with what results it would be idle to speculate.

As it was, in November–December 1706, when the treaty still swung in the balance, though gravitating towards the Court, tentative attempts were finally made to harness up the anti-unionism of the Jacobites and that of the extreme presbyterians, the Cameronians. But the plans for a joint rebellion were feeble and ill-managed. In the end, in spite of rumours of risings on every hand, only localised disturbances occurred; and it is just possible that the chief of these, the riots in Glasgow and Dumfries, were spontaneous outbreaks.

The riots that shook Glasgow for three weeks in November and the first fortnight of December were sparked off by the refusal of the magistrates to sign an anti-union address. The local Jacobites then played upon the fears of the mob, in the process managing to demonstrate that it was possible to forge a working alliance between Jacobites and presbyterians. They cunningly whipped up Glasgow's presbyterian traditions, and appeals to patriotism and the 'good old cause' soon produced results. Indeed, it was a fiery sermon on 6 November that gave rise to the first disorders, when a Knoxian minister, James Clark of the Tron, exhorted his flock to put no trust in addresses to parliaments or princes but to follow the good old way and 'up and be valiant for the city of our God!'[50] Whether this was a reference to St. Mungo's 'Dear Green Place', or a call to build the New Jerusalem is not clear; but the day after that sermon was delivered the mob, powered as usual by the students and apprentices, rose and seized control of the city. Provost Aird, in fear of his life, fled to Edinburgh for safety. In his absence the rioters wrung an address from the council, and this address was forwarded to the capital. Glasgow's refugee provost then ventured to return home, only to run into even worse troubles. The mob was again rampant, and, not without considerable danger, the provost and some of the other dignitaries again sought refuge in the capital. By this time the rioters were led by one Finlay, who was an old soldier of Dumbarton's regiment. Finlay was evidently of Jacobite sympathies and he tried to turn rioting into armed insurrection; but, repulsed in an attack on the Tolbooth, the object of which was to obtain arms, he set out for Edinburgh. First, however, he had to increase his small band of followers by 'raising the country', and with this in mind he headed for Kilsyth where he expected to be joined by a band of supporters. They failed to materialise. Worse, at Kilsyth he got word that a force of dragoons had left Edinburgh, bound to restore order in the west. Finlay then made for Hamilton where rumour had it that a large force of anti-unionist dissidents had rallied. The Duke of Hamilton's mother, the redoubtable Duchess Anne, was indeed a strong presbyterian and a great patriot who bitterly opposed the union; but, like her son, she dreaded the thought of civil war and did not encourage musters.[51] Besides, Duchess Anne hated the Jacobites and could not bring herself to make common cause with them; so Finlay found no reinforcements at Hamilton and had to beat a hasty retreat on Glasgow, where, on the arrival of the troops, he and other ringleaders were arrested. On the premature withdrawal of the troops from Glasgow, however, fresh disorders broke out. The Privy Council, whose patience all this while had been sorely tried, then concluded that Glasgow's town council and magistrates were so inefficient as to be of suspect loyalty, and on 9 December the Council threatened to deprive Glasgow and its crafts of their rights and privileges unless order were immediately restored.[52] Coming on top of the fiasco of Finlay's rebellion the threat was effective, and the riots subsided.

Tied up with these outbreaks in Glasgow, in nebulous intention at any rate, were the disorders in the south-west that arose from Cameronian discontent with the union. On 20 November some 300 armed Cameronians entered Dumfries, ceremonially burnt the Articles of Union as 'utterly destructive of the nation's independency, crown rights, and our constitute laws, both civil and sacred', and, in their classical style, bitterly condemned and rejected the work of those in parliament who 'shall presume to carry on the said Union by a supream power, over the belly of the generality of this nation'.[53] They received much popular support, but the strong nationalism of the Westland Whigs was betrayed by their supposed leader, Cunningham of Eckat, who was in Queensberry's pay and who received £100 and a commission over a company of foot for his secret service work. The grand aim of the anti-unionists, in short, was for a concerted rising of dissidents, including Jacobite Highlanders and disgruntled presbyterians. The plan was ruined by the mercurial Duke of Hamilton who at the last moment countermanded the necessary orders.[54]

Some historians have doubted whether such an alliance, whose difficulties are obvious, was ever projected.[55] The evidence for it is considerable if not conclusive. Iain Lom, for example, in his poem on the union, states that he was present at the gathering of the clans and blames the failure on Viscount Dupplin who was supposed to bring the orders from Atholl in Edinburgh but who succumbed to the bribes offered by the ministry.[56] Most decisively of all, however, Hamilton's inactivity and Queensberry's unobtrusive preparations prevented any serious outbreak. By December the English force lying on the

Border had been reinforced with 800 cavalry and was ready to move north at Queensberry's call.[57] On occasion the strain threatened to get the better of the commissioner's nerves, but Godolphin and Marlborough constantly advised determination as a better answer to Queensberry's troubles than the introduction of English troops. The event justified their cool assessment of the situation, for, though Scotland seethed with resentment and disaffection was rife, the union passed without any serious popular uprising.

The last hope of the anti-unionists lay with the English parliament; but, well aware of this, the Court took steps to ensure the treaty an easy passage. In spite of the need for supply and the claims of other pressing business, so determined was the English ministry to carry the treaty that parliament was repeatedly adjourned until 3 December 1706.[58] Not since the Revolution had there been such a long delay in dealing with public affairs; its purpose was obviously to give the Scots ministry as clear a run as possible in dealing with the treaty, for opposition to it in the English parliament could only have aggravated the problems of the Scottish ministry by stiffening the resistance of the anti-unionists in Scotland. By the end of November, however, it looked as if the treaty would succeed in the Scottish parliament; and at the opening of the English parliament on 3 December the queen again took the opportunity to recommend the union. But still the English ministry played safe and carefully managed the parliament so that it did not immediately consider the treaty. Instead the House of Commons went about its routine business, granting supply and so on, waiting really for the Scottish parliament to complete its work and, hopefully, produce an acceptable Act of Union. Not until this was done were the treaty and the Scottish Act brought up for consideration in the House of Commons on 22 January 1707.

They met with an easy reception. The English High Church Tories, who disliked the Scots and scorned the idea of union with them, had pinned their hopes on the rejection of the treaty by the Scottish parliament and were at a loss when it passed there. True, their main leaders, Nottingham and Rochester, still hoped to repeat more successfully the delaying tactics that had been tried in Edinburgh; but the English ministry, profiting from Queensberry's experiences, took care to give the opposition no openings. The Court and the Junto combined to force the necessary measures through the Commons, which on 4 February resolved itself into a Committee of the Whole House to consider the Articles of Union and the Scottish Act of Union. In vain the opposition howled 'Posthaste!' as the Articles were hurriedly read with no time allowed for debate. The government coolly countered protests that the treaty was being rushed through the Commons with the bland retort, 'That deliberation always supposes doubts and difficulties, but no material objections being offered against any of the articles, there was no room for delays'.[59] The ministry maintained its firm grip, and the opposition, soon obliged to recognise that it was powerless, put up a feeble resistance. Throughout, too, the government cleverly presented a low profile, and only a short enabling clause was left as a target for the disheartened opposition. The Court managers in fact drafted the union legislation and drove the all-important bill through the committee stage in one prolonged sitting. Shortly afterwards, on 28 February, the bill received its third reading and passed by a vote of 274–116, a majority of 158 out of 390 cast.[60] (Incidentally, the legislation that took the United Kingdom into the European Economic Community in 1972 followed remarkably similar lines.)

The Lords deliberated in the wake of the Commons, and necessarily at a slower pace that allowed some debate. In general the Tory peers were averse to the proposed union, believing that it would be harmful to the English constitution in church and state. Thus Nottingham objected to the name 'Great Britain' on the grounds that it would subvert the laws and liberties of England. The judges unanimously repelled this objection. Nottingham and Rochester then argued that the union was a threat to the church, but the government met the cry of 'the church in danger' by pointing out that the Archbishop of Canterbury had already been directed to draw up a bill guaranteeing the Church of England, similar to that already conferred on the Scottish establishment. Another Tory peer, Haversham, condemned the proposed union because in the nature of things it could not be entire, and pleaded for a federal union that would, he believed, be more acceptable to public opinion in Scotland. Haversham held that forcing an incorporating union on an unwilling Scotland was asking for trouble and might well provoke rebellions.[61] Federalism, however, was roundly rejected by the Lords not just because it was believed to be a cumbrous and inefficient system of government but also because it could not give the essential guarantee of permanency to the union or, even more important, to the successsion.

The delay in the Lords was contrived by the ministry in order to give the Commons time to complete and send up their union bill.[62] When the bill finally arrived in the upper house it was hurried through all its stages in less than three days, and in spite of the protests of about twenty Tory peers the Act of Union passed both Houses on 4 March, received the royal assent on 6 March, was finally ratified on 19 March and came into operation on 1 May 1707. Godolphin in a letter to Marlborough expressed his relief when he called this 'the best sessions of parliament that England ever saw'.[63]

The treaty's easy passage through the English parliament showed that, quite apart from masterly management, there was no great opposition to it there. Of all the remarkable changes of the time this was the most remarkable. At the beginning of Anne's reign there had been strong aversion in England to the idea of union with Scotland, but by 1707 it was English insistence that made union possible. There is no mystery about what caused this change in attitude—it was brought about by fears for the security of England. A disgruntled Scotland raised the spectre of French intervention and the opening of the old 'Northern postern', which, the Civil Wars apart, had been lockfast for over a century. Nor were these fears and changes in attitude confined to the parliamentarians. They were widespread among all classes. The people of the northern counties of England, for example, were greatly alarmed by the Act of Security and had openly expressed their relief when the negotiations for union got under way.[64] And while the treaty was under consideration by the parliaments there were no anti-union outbursts in England, though Scottophobia did not miraculously vanish in 1707. It was far otherwise in Scotland where the mood of most people in 1707 was sombre if not sullen. On 1 May Harry Maule wrote to Mar, who

was in London, describing the black mood in Scotland which contrasted so
sharply with the jubilation in England.[65] Most Scots evidently felt that there was
little to celebrate at 'the end o' an auld sang', as Chancellor Seafield had drolly
described the winding up of the Scottish parliament.

Clerk of Penicuik, who accompanied Queensberry on his triumphal progress
to London, noticed that south of Tweed there was nothing but joy at the achievement of union. Queensberry, henceforth to be known as the Union Duke and
soon to be created Duke of Dover, 'was complimented and feasted wherever he
went, and when he came within 20 miles of London the whole city turn'd out to
meet him'. Clerk concluded that the citizens of London were as much relieved as
overjoyed, 'for they were terribly apprehensive of confusions from Scotland in
case the union had not taken place'.[66] Anne's various addresses to her parliaments, English and Scottish, testified to the same effect. Their conclusion was
always the same: union was essential for the prosperity and security of both
kingdoms. Her last words to the English parliament on this matter, on 24 April
1707, recommended the members to 'omit no opportunity of making my subjects sensible of the security, and the other great and lasting benefits, they may
reasonably expect from this happy Union'. The next meeting, she continued,
would be of the united parliament, 'when we shall all join our sincere and hearty
endeavours, to promote the welfare and prosperity of Great Britain'.[67]

In England a number of publications eulogised the union pretty much on the
lines laid down by the queen. For example, an interesting Latin oration exulted
that the glories of Anne's reign (Marlborough's victories and the securing of
European liberties) were enhanced by the Britannic union.[68] After the Scottish
parliament had passed the treaty Defoe celebrated the coming union in verse in
strains already made familiar in his pamphlets.[69] On the final passing of the
treaty a Mr. Vernon, possibly King William's old secretary of state, James
Vernon, was so transported that he too burst into poetry—or tried to. But in
spite of his efforts 'to elevate the Turn of it to the Sublime', his verse failed to
take wing:

> What Great, what Godlike William wish'd in vain
> Kind Providence reserv'd for Anna's Reign.[70]

The only sour note came from Jonathan Swift; his Scottophobia could only
prophesy disasters from a

> Blest Revolution, which creates
> Divided Hearts, united States.[71]

Possibly Swift's spleen owed something to what he took to be England's harsh
treatment of Ireland as compared to its seeming generosity to Scotland.

Other interested parties, apart from professional and amateur literati, were
favourably impressed by the union of 1707, and not least the Irish parliament
which in the late 1690s and early 1700s more than once petitioned for a union
with England. William Molyneux's well known pamphlet of 1698, *The Case of
Ireland's being bound by Acts of Parliament in England*, in which he argued that
Ireland was, like Scotland, a separate kingdom with an imperial crown of its own,

hinted at the desirability of union. But, in spite of Molyneux's sophistical arguments, Ireland was a dependency of the imperial crown of England, and as such, being bound by the English Act of Settlement, could make no capital out of the succession question. Nevertheless, in October 1703 the Irish parliament requested the queen to arrange for a union with England, more or less on the lines suggested in the Anglo-Scottish negotiations of 1702, but met with a cold response.[72] The achievement of union between England and Scotland in 1707 gave the Irish parliament another opportunity to press its case, and it petitioned the queen for a similar measure.[73] But England regarded Ireland as little more than a colony, and again the petition was denied.

The situations of Ireland and Scotland, however, were totally different and should not be confused.[74] Constitutional considerations apart, the Irish parliament represented a minority of the population and, in spite of its engrossment of political power, felt itself threatened and looked to union as a solution to its difficulties. It had far less claim to represent the people of Ireland than the Scottish parliament had had to represent the people of Scotland. And even when every allowance is made for the narrow views of representation then prevalent, this difference is a factor of fundamental importance. In brief, a union with Great Britain that would have met the needs of the Anglo-Irish Ascendancy could only have further alienated the native catholic Irish, since, whatever economic benefits such a union might have provided, it could have granted no measure of relief for the persecuted and downtrodden majority. In Scotland there was no persecuted majority to foul the issue. So, although in 1707 the union did not command the consent of the entire nation, there was nothing in it to render impossible its general acceptance in time.

As Anne noted, in 1707 England and Scotland ceased to be distinct political entities, and in the strictest political sense Anglo-Scottish relations terminate in the union. But it is not always wise to confine inquiry to the strict letter, and it is particularly unwise in this case where the union was far from complete. In many respects England and Scotland retained their separate identities, and consequently, in ways too gradual and too complex to be gone into here, the union altered the relationship between the peoples of England and Scotland. It would take another volume to do justice to this great and virtually unexplored theme.[75] Suffice it to say here that the union did not, as some seem to imagine, obliterate everything that had gone before. The reasons for its failure to do so are clear enough, except to those who wear blinkers. Further, it has to be stressed that, unlike the Act of Union with Wales, the union of England and Scotland was not unilaterally decreed. The two Acts of Union of 1707 ratified a treaty between two high contracting parties (a fact that English historians usually clean mislay); and, as we have seen, that treaty built on foundations from the English and Scottish past. What it did was to create a new political framework for development, a framework that made possible responses to changes in society and government that could apply to the whole of Britain. But in most spheres actual change came slowly through other agencies other than the union itself.

The Treaty and Acts of Union of 1707, in short, should not be regarded as a collective totem or deodand, as something beyond logical cause and effect, the work of Heaven or Hell and thus perfect or imperfect, according to taste, but, regardless of taste, static, unchanging and unchangeable. The Treaty of Union was the work of men, and it has had a chequered history. Nor throughout its history has it operated in a uniform way or always been regarded in the same light. It has meant different things to different generations. Indeed at the time the union was passed few politicians seem to have regarded it as permanent, and most unionists were content to welcome it as a peaceful solution to the most pressing problem of all—that of the succession. In consonance with this, within half a dozen years of its coming into existence strenuous efforts were made to repeal it which only narrowly failed. And, significantly, among those who worked hardest to undo the union in 1713 were some of those who had worked hardest to achieve it—notably Seafield (by then Earl of Findlater), Argyll and Mar.

Mar is indeed a sore disappointment to those who see the union as the work of the Almighty. Unable to ingratiate himself with George I and obsessed as ever by his own interest, Mar promptly turned Jacobite and headed the futile rising of 1715, one of the stated aims of which was to undo the union. The Jacobites obviously profited from nationalist resentment in Scotland over the union, and notably its failure in the short term to improve, let alone transform, the Scottish economy. Jacobite strength thus increased noticeably after 1707, particularly in the Lowlands. But following its final shattering defeat at Culloden in 1746, by the second half of the eighteenth century Jacobitism was dead in all but its rich legacy of song and romance. By then, too, Scotland's economy, firmly based on the colonial trade, was entering the take-off phase of the Industrial Revolution. Only the most determined casuistry could then deny that the country's prosperity owed much to the free trade conceded by the union. And so, in the second half of the eighteenth century, the union increasingly won acceptance. English people did not bother about its details and regarded it as the fulfilment of a manifest destiny; the Scots worried more about the details, but they too came to accept the union as part of the natural order of things.

The greatest Scottish philosopher of the eighteenth century, David Hume, ascribed much of human motivation to habit. In Humean terms, by the end of the eighteenth century the union of 1707 had become a habit, and Scotland was apparently content to become North Britain. By then the impact of the union was not only political and economic but social and cultural as well, and no part of its influence was spurned. This acceptance was carried over into the nineteenth century when the glories of empire were felt to rest upon the union. For many Scots, particularly the landed aristocracy, participation in a worldwide empire more than compensated for loss of independence. The Scottish past could then, following Sir Walter Scott, be viewed as antique romance, and the present, when it was considered at all, seen in the whimsical light of the 'kailyaird'. In keeping with this new *Weltanschauung* the Irish union was regarded as the second buttress of this mighty fabric, and Ireland was expected to conform as Scotland had done.

But from about the middle of the nineteenth century doubts began to arise.

Their causes were many and varied, but possibly the most potent was the one that is hardly ever mentioned—the continuing assertion of English nationalism. It is the fashion to believe that such a commodity does not exist, or that, if it does, it never asserts itself. This odd delusion derives from the fact that history has on the whole been kind to the English people, who have rarely in modern times needed to indulge in raucous nationalism. Shouldering the white man's burden, within the British Isles as well as in the four corners of the earth, was seen as something different. Nevertheless, English nationalism has been, in its quiet purposeful way, the most potent in the British Isles: it calmly took over the United Kingdom, as Henry VII had put it, 'the greater drawing the lesser'. The vision of Britain that had entranced such a dedicated unionist as Cromartie in 1706 ('May wee be Brittains, and down goe the old ignominious names of Scotland and England'[76]) rapidly dimmed. Long before the dawn of the nineteenth century 'England' meant 'Britain' and, as occasion rarely required, *vice versa*. But growing uneasiness about the union in Scotland did not spring solely from such semantic abuses, although they were, and still are, often resented.

Far more potent in producing disquiet were changing concepts of government. Throughout the eighteenth century government was limited in scope and lax in operation. As a result, for over a century after union Scottish administration was to a large extent free from dictation from Westminster, or at least held on a remarkably loose rein. Paradoxically, political management made of Scotland virtually a separate satrapy: Henry Dundas had more freedom of movement than had Queensberry or any of Anne's other commissioners, and Godolphin had had far more say in the running of Scotland than had the younger Pitt. But from 1827 onwards management disintegrated as government became steadily more intensive and ever more centralised. Attempts at devolution since have so far done little to disguise this increasingly obvious fact of life. Undoubtedly, too, the vague disquiets first caused by these developments were reinforced by sympathy for the suppressed nationalities of Europe, such as the Poles and Italians. The Risorgimento found many friends in Scotland, notably the Free Church. But even more influential in the long run was Ireland's epic struggle for self-government, and from 1886 onwards home rule as an issue never really died in Scotland. But, to adapt slightly a witty saying that each passing generation confirms, 'home rule' dies at Westminster as soon as Englishmen understand what it means.[77] Yet even when 'home rule' seems to be politically dead, it refuses to lie down. The experiences of the past thirty years (of a United Kingdom in decline, shorn of empire and labouring to overcome chronic and steadily worsening economic problems) have called in question ever more strongly the utility of union.

Today this new and more critical approach to union is confined to Scotland and Wales (Northern Ireland being, on any reckoning, a special case). But quite clearly, in both Wales and Scotland, political nationalism, though growing, cannot at present be said to represent majority opinion; and, indeed, criticism of union has revealed the hidden strength of unionism. This it does by putting the champions of union on their mettle, and evidently more than just a blind defence of the status quo motivates unionists of all parties. Many see in the continuance of the union, and the preservation of Britain as a unitary state, the only hope for progress or even survival, and condemn any moves towards the Balkanisation of the British Isles as atavistic and retrograde. English people in particular regard any attempt to break, or alter, the Anglo-Scottish union as unthinkable. If forced to think about it (which they rarely do) they dismiss any such notion as ludicrous. Their reaction tends to be: if home rule for Scotland, why not for Yorkshire, or *reductio ad absurdum*, why not back to the heptarchy? As persiflage this is quite good, but as serious argument it reeks of ignorance. The mournful truth enshrined in such sayings is that English people know less about Ireland, Scotland and Wales (their vague and meaningless 'Celtic fringe') than they do about almost any foreign country. And, unfortunately, the same appears to be true of most English historians. Some kind of psychological block or inhibition seems to prevent them from understanding 'these curious people', to adapt and extend Queen Anne's phrase. The early reaction in England to the recent troubles in Northern Ireland furnishes bitter proof of that state of blissful, but highly dangerous, ignorance.

With the general English assessment that it is ridiculous to think of altering the union, far less ending it, many Scots would agree. Others, with varying degrees of emphasis, disagree. On this matter, as on so many others, the Scots do not speak with one voice, though most of the inhabitants of Scotland still feel themselves to be Scots, and most react, in some fashion, to the claims of nationalism. Not all, however, believe that nationhood must necessarily entail statehood. Yet all, unionists and anti-unionists alike, claim to have the best interests of Scotland (and of England) at heart: they simply disagree about the means of promoting these interests. And here an odd point arises. Attitudes to the union question do not seem to be dictated by class loyalties or by adherence to political ideologies, which is not a little curious considering the paramountcy pundits ascribe to class and ideology. These factors certainly play upon the issue, but not as decisively as political theorists would expect. A large part of the explanation for this lies in the fact that the Conservative Party and the Labour Party are in total disarray on the question of the government of Scotland.

Fifty years ago unionists were all Conservatives; indeed until very recently the Conservatives in Scotland were called the Unionist Party. Since 1967, however, the Tories in Scotland, prodded by a masterful leader, Mr. Heath, have had to rethink their position. But the leadership obviously outran its rank and file, many of whom remained mutinously opposed to even the most modest measures of devolution. The fall of Mr. Heath and the emergence of a more traditional leader in Mrs. Thatcher has completed the disarray of the Conservatives on this question. The net result is a bewildering chaos of attitudes among Scottish Tory M.P.s, each averring that his own particular fancy is official party policy. What the average Conservative voter, in Scotland and elsewhere in the United Kingdom, is to make of all this is apparently nobody's business; and how the Conservative party's damaged credit in Scotland is to be restored by such incredible manoeuvres is, so far, the best kept secret in the United Kingdom.

Scarcely more comprehensible, and even more farcical, is the present position of the Labour Party. Indeed, most of the confusion that surrounds the whole

Scottish question stems from the fact that the Labour movement (which was once as dedicated to home rule as were, and still are, the Liberals) has since 1948 changed its mind and now, in spite of more recent gyrations of policy, contains the most determined supporters of monolithic centralised bureaucratic government. The Labour Party's late spasmodic conversion (or 'reconversion' as the party faithful would have it) to devolution has not altered the fact that many of the most ardent unionists and centralists in Scotland (and in England and Wales too) are to be found on the left. Their theory is that class 'patriotism', if not class war, should override all other outdated sentiments. The snag is that voters do not necessarily vote by class; many of them remain stubbornly convinced that they are individuals and sometimes even act as such. In two general elections in 1974 the two major political parties discovered to their horror that some sort of mental devolution was already at work and operating through the ballot boxes. The progress made by the Scottish National Party in February 1974 forced on some basic re-thinking on the issue of the government of Scotland, and in the October general election of that year the Labour Party was constrained to pledge itself to a meaningful measure of devolution within the United Kingdom, promising a Scottish Assembly with legislative and certain, though unspecified, economic powers. The resulting White Paper of November 1975 withheld any real economic power, and proposed such a system of Westminster checks and rights of veto on the Assembly, while increasing the already dangerously over-extended powers of the secretary of state, as to give rise to charges of colonialism. The secretary of state, critics alleged, was to be turned into a governor-general, a term of ill omen in view of the contemporary constitutional crisis in Australia. But, in fact, a closer analogy goes further back in time. If the White Paper as it stands becomes law then what will emerge bears a startling resemblance to eighteenth-century political management in Scotland with the secretary of state cast hopefully but unconvincingly in the rôle of Henry Dundas. Devolution as proposed by the Labour government in 1975 will see the apotheosis of Pooh Bah, a suitably Gilbertian answer to the problem.

But the prospects of such a dénouement are less than good. The White Paper pleased few. Predictably, it did not go far enough for some but went far too far for others. Clearly, in view of Conservative attitudes to the question, which are as divided as those of Labour, actual legislation, if any, still lies in the laps of the somewhat dithering gods and their trusty vicegerents on earth at Westminster. It need scarcely be added that the confused attitudes already noted, Tory and Socialist alike, are obviously the result of the upsurge of the Scottish National Party, though it is apparently mandatory for Tory and Labour spokesmen to deny this self-evident fact. It is hard to escape the conclusion that the union deserves better of its champions than the inane statements and at times puerile antics of its more Rip van Winkle paladins.

Pace the antics of the politicians, the union question today is a serious one. It involves many factors, some of which are bewildering in their complexity and unpredictable in their consequences. But there is reason to believe that at bottom attitudes to the union rest on an emotional basis, and this is just as evidently true of those who would maintain the union as it is of those who would end it or amend it. There has recently been a striking illustration of this. Until lately the 'Scotnats' were usually dismissed as pathetic sentimentalists, keening over a dead past and dreaming impossible dreams. How, the hard-headed unionist would inquire, could an independent Scotland maintain a viable economy? No way at all, answered the experts on the dismal science, thus burying the question for all rational people. 'The Black Black Oil' has changed all that. Scotland now has a reasonable opportunity of prosperity, and a continuing decline in her economy would not be easy to justify. As a consequence, the Scottish Nationalists now project a hard-headed image that Wall Street itself might envy; and it is the unionists who now play on the heart-strings, chiefly over the great things achieved in common since 1707. They have every right to do so. The United Kingdom *has* undoubtedly achieved great things and contributed much to the development of the modern world. The snag is that the United Kingdom's great achievements belong to a particular phase of history that has vanished beyond recall, and more than *chansons de geste* are now needed to justify the union.

The problem now really is (as Dean Acheson, a former American Secretary of State, noted some years ago) that Britain has lost an empire and failed to find a rôle in the world. Can the United Kingdom find a new *Staatsidee*, complicated as that must be by membership of the European Economic Community? If not, it is doubtful if the union of England and Scotland can continue unaltered on the old eroded assumptions.

ABBREVIATIONS USED IN THE NOTES

APS *Acts of the Parliaments of Scotland* (Record ed.).

BM British Museum.

DNB *Dictionary of National Biography.*

EHR *English Historical Review.*

HMC Historical Manuscripts Commission.

NLS National Library of Scotland.

PRO Public Record Office.

PSAS *Proceedings of the Society of Antiquaries of Scotland.*

RPC *Register of the Privy Council of Scotland.*

RSCHS *Records of the Scottish Church History Society.*

SHR *Scottish Historical Review.*

SHS Scottish History Society.

SRO Scottish Record Office.

STS Scottish Texts Society.

TRHS *Transactions of the Royal Historical Society.*

Notes

Chapter 1

1. Cyril Fox, *The Personality of Britain: its Influence on Inhabitant and Invader in Prehistoric and Early Historic Times* (4th edn., 1959), 28 *ff.*; for a discussion of the validity of 'Fox's Law', see Glyn Daniel, 'The Personality of Wales', in I. Lloyd and L. Alcock, eds., *Culture and Environment: Essays in Honour of Sir Cyril Fox* (1963), 7–23.

2. H. J. Mackinder, *Britain and the British Seas* (2nd edn., 1907), ch. I; and some perceptive comments in W. Gordon East, *The Geography Behind History* (2nd edn., 1965), ch. III.

3. P. C. Bartrum, ed., *Early Welsh Genealogical Tracts* (1966), 201, *s.v.* Macsen Wledig; Gwyn Jones and Thomas Jones, *The Mabinogion* (Everyman, 1949), 79–88.

4. H. M. Chadwick, *Early Scotland* (1949), 150 *ff.*

5. K. Jackson, 'Edinburgh and the Anglian Occupation of Lothian', in *The Anglo-Saxons: Studies Presented to Bruce Dickens*, ed. P. Clemoes (1959), 35–42; K. Jackson, ed. and tr., *The Gododdin: the Oldest Scottish Poem* (1969), the title of which, presumably, is not to be taken literally; and for the place of the work of Taliesin and Aneirin in Welsh literature, see Thomas Parry, *A History of Welsh Literature*, tr. and ed., H. Idris Bell (2nd imp., 1970), ch. I, 1–22.

6. K. Jackson, *Language and History in Early Britain: a chronological survey of the Brittonic Languages 1st to 12th c. A.D.* (1953), 117. Jackson, *Gododdin*, 65–6, suggests transmission of the poem via the later British kingdom of Strathclyde.

7. Jackson, *Language and History*, 7–10.

8. Jackson, *op. cit.*, 219; W. R. Kermack, 'Early English Settlement in South-West Scotland', *Antiquity*, XV (1941), 83–6; W. F. H. Nicolaisen, 'Scandinavian Personal Names in South East Scotland', *Scottish Studies*, XI (1967), 223–36, which concludes that such names are in fact English; and Nicolaisen, *ibid.*, 75–84, 'Scottish Place-Names: 28, Old English wic'.

9. Sir Walter Scott, *The Antiquary*, ch. VI.

10. F. T. Wainwright, *The Problem of the Picts* (1953), ch. VI, 'The Pictish Language', by Kenneth Jackson.

11. F. M. Stenton, *Anglo-Saxon England* (2nd edn., 1947), 39.

12. *Ibid.*, 25.

13. R. G. Collingwood and J. N. L. Myres, *Roman Britain and the English Settlements* (2nd edn., 1937), 422.

14. For a brief cogent treatment of this involved question, see Gordon Donaldson, *Scotland: Church and Nation through Sixteen Centuries* (1960), ch. I.

15. Kathleen Hughes, *The Church in Early Irish Society* (1966); the same author admirably summarises her work in the Introduction to A. J. Otway-Ruthven, *A History of Medieval Ireland* (1968).

16. There is doubt about the meaning of all 'Cumbraland', most authorities taking it to denote Cumbria south of Solway; but Stenton, *op. cit.*, 355, believes that it meant Strathclyde. If Strathclyde is the correct meaning then Edmund was giving away something that was not his to give and the triumph of the Scots correspondingly empty. Most likely all 'Cumbraland' meant Cumbria south of Solway.

17. G. W. S. Barrow, *The Acts of Malcolm IV, King of Scots 1153–65* (1960), 38.

18. Peter Hunter Blair has produced a good survey, *Roman Britain and Early England* (1963), and also a stimulating topical work, *An Introduction to Anglo-Saxon England* (1967). There is also a concise treatment by D. P. Kirby, *The Making of Early England* (1967).

19. A. O. Anderson, *Scottish Annals from English Chroniclers* (1908), 65–78.

20. For an appraisal of the controversy, see J. O. Prestwich, 'Anglo-Norman Feudalism and the Problem of Continuity', in *Past and Present*, no. 26 (1963), 39–57.

21. J. E. A. Jolliffe, *Constitutional History of Medieval England* (2nd edn., 1947), 75; so too, rather less dogmatically, Stenton, *Anglo-Saxon England*, 672. A contrary view appears in G. O. Sayles, *The Medieval Foundations of England* (1948), ch. XVI.

22. Eric John, *Land Tenure in Early England* (1960), ch. I.

23. R. Allen Brown, *Origins of English Feudalism* (1973), 94.

24. Dorothy Whitelock, *The Beginnings of English Society* (1952), 53.

25. W. P. Ker, *Epic and Romance* (edn., 1931), 40.

26. *Cf.* W. J. Watson, *The History of the Celtic Place-Names of Scotland* (1926).

27. On this vital and often overlooked point, see J. M. Bannerman, 'The Scots of Dalriada', in Gordon Menzies, ed., *Who Are the Scots?* (1971), 72–4.

28. John Cameron, *Celtic Law* (1937), 155.

29. G. W. S. Barrow, *The Kingdom of the Scots* (1973), Pt. I, ch. II.

30. W. F. Skene, *Celtic Scotland: a History of Ancient Alban*, 3 vols. (2nd edn., 1886–90). D. A. Mackenzie, *Scotland: The Ancient Kingdom* (1930) fails to fill the gap; and W. R. Kermack, *The Scottish Highlands: a Short History* (1957), chs. 3–5, is good but very brief.

31. Barrow, *Kingdom*, Pt. I, ch. I.

32. The problem is discussed by David Murison, 'Linguistic Relationships in Medieval Scotland', in G. W. S. Barrow, ed., *The Scottish Tradition: Essays in Honour of Ronald Gordon Cant* (1974), 71–83.

33. For an exposé of Hill Burton's jaundiced view of 'the Scottish Celts', see J. M. Robertson *The Saxon and the Celt* (1897), ch. IV.

34. A. A. M. Duncan, 'The Earliest Scottish Charters', *S.H.R.*, XXXVII (1958), 103–35.

Chapter 2

1. R. L. G. Ritchie, *The Normans in Scotland* (1954), 92.

2. Barrow, *Kingdom of the Scots*, 3, and *passim*.

3. A. A. M. Duncan, *Scotland: the Making of the Kingdom* (1975), 133.

4. G. W. S. Barrow, 'The Beginnings of Feudalism in Scotland', *Bull. Inst. Hist. Research*, XXIX (1956), 1–27; and for a brilliant account of Scotland in transition the same author's introduction to his edition of *The Acts of Malcolm IV*. See, too, Duncan, *op. cit.*, ch. 7.

5. Duncan, *Scotland: the Making of the Kingdom*, 142.

6. Miss M. Morgan, 'The Organisation of the Scottish Church in the Twelfth Century', *T.R.H.S.*, IVth ser., XXIX (1947), 135–49, takes the traditional view that diocesan structure was due mainly to Anglo-Norman influence; but G. Donaldson, 'Scottish Bishops' Sees Before the Reign of David I', *P.S.A.S.*, LXXXVII (1952–3), 106–17, controverts this view, demonstrating that most of the sees are of much earlier origin, though, of course, the important work of reformation carried out under David I and his successors is fully recognised.

7. I. B. Cowan, 'The Parochial System in Medieval Scotland', *S.H.R.*, XL (1961), 42–55; on this topic, see too Morgan, *art. cit.*

8. See Barbara E. Crawford, 'The pawning of Orkney and Shetland: a reconsideration of the events of 1460–9', *S.H.R.*, XLVIII (1969), 35–53; and also Kai Hørby, 'Christian I and the pawning of Orkney: some reflections on Scandinavian foreign policy 1460–8', *ibid.*, 54–63.

9. Text in E. L. G. Stones, ed., *Anglo-Scottish Relations, 1174–1328: Some Selected Documents* (1965), 1–5. G. O. Sayles, *Medieval Foundations of England*, 352, gives an unsatisfactory account, glossing the treaty briefly and failing to notice the Quitclaim of Canterbury, thus leaving the erroneous impression that the Treaty of Falaise was permanent.

10. Margaret Moore, *The Lands of the Scottish Kings in England* (1915).

11. Stones, *Anglo-Scottish Relations*, p. XXIV.

12. Keith Feiling, *A History of England* (1952), 194.

13. Ritchie, *op. cit.*, 49.

14. That it was an adjudication and not an arbitration is proved by George Neilson in a brief but excellent article 'Bruce versus Balliol 1291–1292' in *S.H.R.*, XVI (1919), 1–14.

15. *Annales Angliae et Scotiae, ap Rishanger* (*Rolls Series*, 1865), 371.

16. May McKisack, *The Fourteenth Century, 1307–1399* (1959), 40.

17. R. G. Nicholson, 'A Sequel to Edward Bruce's Invasion of Ireland', *S.H.R.*, XLII (1963), 30–40.

18. Stones, *op. cit.*, 161–70.

19. E. A. Freeman, *Historical Essays* (1871), 'The Relations between the Crowns of England and Scotland', 71.

20. *Ibid.*, 77.

21. T. F. Tout, *Political History of England, 1216–1377* (2nd edn., 1920), 263.

22. Tout, *Edward the First* (edn., 1924), 200–1.

23. F. M. Powicke, *The Thirteenth Century* (1953), chs. XII–XIV.

24. G. W. S. Barrow, *Robert Bruce and the Community of the Realm of Scotland* (1965), *passim*, e.g. 441–3.

25. For an interesting review of the evidence, see R. S. Rait, *Outline of the Relations between England and Scotland, 500–1707* (1901), Introduction, i–xxxviii.

26. H. A. L. Fisher, *History of Europe* (1 vol. edn., 1942), 311.

Chapter 3

1. McKisack, *England in the Fourteenth Century*, 99–100.

2. R. G. Nicholson, *Edward III and the Scots* (1965), 1.

3. E. L. G. Stones, 'The Treaty of Northampton, 1328', in *History* (1953), 54–61.

4. James Campbell, 'England, Scotland and the Hundred Years' War in the Fourteenth Century', in J. R. Hale, *et al.*, eds., *Europe in the Late Middle Ages* (1961), 185.

5. Nicholson, *op. cit.*, 99–102.

6. *Ibid.*, 103.

7. See Kenneth Fowler, *The Age of Plantagenet and Valois: the Struggle for Supremacy, 1328–1498* (1967), 13–14.

8. Quoted W. C. Dickinson, *Scotland to 1603* (2nd edn., 1965), 179–80.

9. For a discussion of the diverse views, see R. G. Nicholson, 'David II, the historians and the chroniclers', in *S.H.R.*, XLV (1966), 59–78. Professor Nicholson exonerates David from most of the charges brought against him; so does B. Webster, 'David II and the Government of Fourteenth Century Scotland', *T.R.H.S.* (5th ser.), XVI (1966), 115–30.

10. Nicholson, *art. cit.*, 67–9.

11. *Ibid.*, 69. But it should be noted that P. Hume Brown, *History of Scotland* (1900), I, 178 *ff.* correctly analysed the sequence of events and came to an opposite conclusion about David II's guilt.

12. For detailed discussion, see Gordon Donaldson, *Scottish Kings* (1967), 34–7, 70, 81.

13. W. R. Kermack, *The Scottish Highlands: a Short History*, ch. 7; Donald Gregory, *History of the Western Highlands and Isles of Scotland* (ed. 1881), *Intro.*, 25–85.

14. For a very interesting summary of the new views, see Jennifer A. Brown, 'Taming the Magnates?', in Gordon Menzies, ed., *The Scottish Nation* (1972), 46–59; it is neatly counterbalanced by Ranald Nicholson, 'Crown in Jeopardy', *ibid.*, 31–45.

15. S. B. Chrimes, *Lancastrians, Yorkists, and Henry VII* (1964), 6.

16. J. R. Lander, *The Wars of the Roses* (1965), 22–3. Lander's view is accepted by G. R. Elton, *England Under the Tudors* (ed. 1967), 1–2, but, somewhat incongruously, is rejected on p. 6, where Elton refers to 'the wild murders and civil wars of the fifteenth century'. J. G.

Dickens, *The English Reformation* (1964), 123–4, rejects revisionist views of the fifteenth century.

17. Quoted Fowler, *op. cit.*, 29.

18. G. O. Sayles and H. G. Richardson, *The Governance of Medieval England* (1963).

19. V. H. H. Green, *The Later Plantagenets* (ed. 1966), 379.

20. Feiling, *History of England*, 220.

21. E. F. Jacob, *The Fifteenth Century, 1399–1485* (1961), 34–7; Stones, *Documents*, 173–82.

22. Chrimes, *op. cit.*, 41.

23. Donaldson, *Scottish Kings*, 63.

24. The best account of the fall of the Black Douglases is Ranald Nicholson, *Scotland: The Later Middle Ages*, ch. 13.

25. The older view is tentatively accepted by Agnes Conway, *Henry VII's Relations with Scotland and Ireland, 1485–1498* (1932), 5–8, but is discounted by J. D. Mackie, *The Earlier Tudors* (1952), 51 and n.

26. R. L. Mackie, *King James IV of Scotland* (1958), 85.

27. R. S. Rait, *Parliaments of Scotland* (1924), the main findings of which are conveniently summarised in a pamphlet by the same author, *The Scottish Parliament* (1925), published by the Scottish Historical Association.

28. In H. C. Darby, ed., *Historical Geography of England before A.D. 1800* (2nd edn., 1948), 231.

29. J. C. Russell, *British Medieval Population* (1948), 146; for criticism, see McKisack, *The Fourteenth Century*, 312–14.

30. T. M. Cooper, 'Population of Medieval Scotland', in *S.H.R.*, XXXVI (1947), 2–9; E. M. Barron, *Scottish War of Independence* (2nd edn., 1934), 430.

31. For Scotland, T. Bedford Franklin's short *History of Scottish Farming* (1951) is strongest on monastic agriculture, most of the surviving records of which are in print; a more compendious work is J. A. Symon, *Scottish Farming: Past and Present* (1959), the obvious counterpart of Lord Ernle's *English Farming: Past and Present* (4th ed., 1927). Many English ecclesiastical estates have been studied in detail: notably R. A. L. Smith, *Canterbury Cathedral Priory* (1943), and R. H. Hilton, *Economic Development of some Leicestershire Estates in the Fourteenth and Fifteenth Centuries* (1946).

32. Slicher van Bath, *Agrarian History of Western Europe, 500–1850* (1963), 18–20.

33. R. Gregory Smith, 'The Scottish Language', in *Cambridge History of English Literature* (1908), II, 88–99, is rather dated. The best brief introduction is in *Chambers' Encyclopaedia* (edn. 1967), XII, 339–40; see, too, D. Murison, *art. cit.*, in Barrow, ed., *The Scottish Tradition*, 71–83.

34. Joseph Hall, ed., *Poems of Laurence Minot* (3rd edn., 1914), 4.

35. See C. S. Lewis, *English Literature in the Sixteenth Century* (1954), Bk. 1, ch. i.

36. W. J. Entwistle, *European Balladry* (2nd edn., 1951), 229–30.

37. Both versions printed in F. J. Child, *English and Scottish Popular Ballads* (ed. 1898), I, 253–4.

38. Kenneth Jackson, 'Common Gaelic: the Evolution of the Goedelic Language' in *Proceedings of the British Academy*, XXXVII, 71–97.

39. W. C. Mackenzie, *The Highlands and Islands of Scotland* (1949), chs. VII–IX; also G. A. Hayes-McCoy, *Scots Mercenary Forces in Ireland (1565–1603)* (1937), 4–37.

40. See W. Mackay Mackenzie's introduction to his edition of *The Poems of William Dunbar* (1932).

41. R. G. Nicholson, 'Domesticated Scots and Wild Scots: the Relationship between Lowlanders and Highlanders in Medieval Scotland', in University of Guelph's *Scottish Colloquium Proceedings*, I (1968), 1–20.

42. Hall, ed., *Minot*, 3.

43. Quoted in Derick Thomson, *An Introduction to Gaelic Poetry* (1974), 31.

44. A. F. Leach, *Schools of Medieval England* (1915); but *cf.* Joan Simon in *British Journal of Educational Studies*, III (1955), 128–43, and IV (1955), 32–48; also W. N. Chaplin, in same, XI (1962), 99–124.

45. John Durkan, 'Education in the Century of the Reformation', in *Innes Review*, X, 84.

46. Kenneth Charlton, *Education in Renaissance England* (1965), ch. i, 'The Medieval Background'; and Joan Simon, *Education and Society in Tudor England* (1965), ch. i, 'The Fifteenth Century Background'. There is a brief but useful conspectus of the subject by John Lawson, *Medieval Education and the Reformation* (1967).

47. *A.P.S.*, II, 238.

48. R. Weiss in *New Cambridge Modern History*, I (1957), ch. V, 110–11.

49. F. M. Powicke and A. B. Emden, eds., Rashdall's *Universities of Europe in the Middle Ages* (1936), II, ch. XI, 'The Universities of Scotland', by R. K. Hannay.

50. David Patrick, ed., *Statutes of the Scottish Church* (S.H.S., 1907), 13–14.

51. J. G. Dickens, *The English Reformation* (3rd. imp., 1966), ch. 3.

52. For numerous instances, see D. Hay Fleming, *The Reformation in Scotland* (1910), ch. IV; and Gordon Donaldson, *The Scottish Reformation* (1960), ch. I.

53. I. B. Cowan, *The Parishes of Medieval Scotland* (1967), *intro*, V.

Chapter 4

1. R. B. Wernham, *Before the Armada: the Growth of English Foreign Policy, 1485–1588* (1966), 19.

2. For John Stewart, son of Alexander, Duke of Albany, see J. Balfour Paul, ed., *Scots Peerage*, I (1904), 154.

3. He is a controversial figure but this is the conclusion of his biographer, Marie W. Stuart, in *The Scot who was a Frenchman* (1940); other scholars have concurred, notably G. Donaldson, *James V to James VII*, ch. 3, and R. G. Eaves, *Henry VIII's Scottish Diplomacy 1513–1542* (1971).

4. E.g., W. L. Mathieson, *Politics and Religion: A Study in Scottish History from the Reformation to the Revolution* (1902), I, 4.

5. Hall's *Chronicle* (ed. 1809), 665.

6. Ed. and tr., A. Constable (*S.H.S.*, 1892).

7. G. Donaldson, *James V to James VII*, 22, and the same author's 'Foundations of Anglo-Scottish Union', in S. T. Bindoff, *et al.*, eds., *Elizabethan Government and Society: Essays Presented to Sir John Neale* (1961), 312.

8. Donaldson, in Bindoff, *op. cit.*, 286.

9. For discussion of this view as applied to Scotland, see J. H. Burton, *History of Scotland* (ed. 1876), III, ch. XXXVI; for England, G. R. Elton, *Tudor England* (ed. 1958), 109–14.

10. For a detailed discussion, see A. G. Dickens, *The English Reformation*.

11. D. Hay, 'The Church of England in the Later Middle Ages', *History*, LIII (1968), 35–50; but for a more qualified view, see Dickens, *op. cit.*, 86–7.

12. Donaldson, *James V to James VII*, ch. 4.

13. C. F. Arrowood, tr. and ed., as *The Powers of the Crown in Scotland* (1949), and a judicious review of the same by J. H. Burns, *S.H.R.*, XXX (1951), 60–8.

14. An important corrective to the journalistic trivia that passes for Border history is T. I. Rae, *The Administration of the Scottish Frontier, 1513–1603* (1966).

15. F. W. Maitland, 'The Anglican Settlement and the Scottish Reformation', in *Cambridge Modern History* (ed. 1934), II, 551. Though much lauded, this is a feeble piece of work—the worst thing this great legal historian ever produced.

16. J. D. Mackie, *The Earlier Tudors* (1952), 406.

17. 'A Proposal for Uniting Scotland and England', in *Miscellany of Bannatyne Club*, I (1827), 3–18.

18. J. H. Burton, *History*, III, 191–3.

19. Arthur Clifford, ed., *Sadler State Papers*, I (1809), 163; for Sadler's career, see A. J. Slavin, *Politics and Profit, a Study of Sir Ralph Sadler 1507–1547* (1966).

20. M. H. Merriman, 'The Assured Scots: Scottish collaborators with England during the Rough Wooing', in *S.H.R.*, XLVI (1968), 10–34.

21. Hester W. Chapman, *The Sisters of Henry VIII* (1969), 111.

22. Well illustrated in A. I. Cameron, ed., *The Scottish Correspondence of Mary of Lorraine* (S.H.S., 1927).

23. J. Bain, ed., *Hamilton Papers*, II (1892), 325–6.

24. For examples of French bribery, or bribery undertaken by the French faction in Scotland, see Donaldson, *James V to James VII*, 72–3.

25. Wernham, *Before the Armada*, 176.

26. Gladys Dickinson, ed., 'Instructions to the French Ambassador, 30 March 1550', in *S.H.R.*, XXVI (1947), 155–6.

27. That such ideas were widely held in France at this time, see J. E. Phillips, *Images of a Queen* (1964), 13–15.

28. Wernham, *op. cit.*, 211.

29. *Source Book of Scottish History* (2nd edn.), II, 162–3.

30. Mortimer Levine, *The Early Elizabethan Succession Question, 1558–1568* (1966), ch. I.

31. T. G. Law, ed., *The Catechism of John Hamilton* (1884).

32. Law, *op. cit.*, intro., p. xii.

33. D. Patrick, ed., *Statutes of the Scottish Church 1225–1559* (S.H.S., 1907), 149–91.

34. On the vexed question of causation, see D. Hay Fleming, *The Reformation in Scotland* (1910), who is strong on the weaknesses of the old church but whose dogmatic protestantism makes his interpretations suspect. A sounder guide is W. L. Mathieson, *Politics and Religion*, I, chs. I and II, who stresses the complexity of the situation and argues, convincingly, that politics played a major rôle. The most up-to-date and thorough treatment is in G. Donaldson, *The Scottish Reformation* (1960), which, however, is mainly concerned with the evolution of the polity of the reformed church and deals lightly with the actual Reformation-Rebellion; but the same author's *Scotland: James V to James VII* furnishes the necessary background.

35. T. Thomson, ed., *Diurnal of Occurrents of Scotland, 1513–75* (Bannatyne Club, 1833), 269.

36. For an interesting, if not very deep, discussion, see J. A. S. MacEwan, *The Faith of John Knox* (1961); and for a more general account J. T. McNeill, *History and Character of Calvinism* (1954).

37. T. M. Parker, 'Protestantism and Confessional Strife: sect. 2, Development and Spread of Calvinism', in *New Cambridge Modern History*, III (1968), 89 *ff.*

38. Donaldson, *James V to James VII*, 88.

39. Quoted in Conyers Read, *Mr. Secretary Cecil and Queen Elizabeth* (1955), 145.

40. D. Laing, ed., *Works of John Knox* (Bannatyne Club, 1848), *History*, II, 16–22; and also in VI, pt. i, 15–21.

41. Read, *op. cit.*, 146.

42. Laing, ed., *Knox*, VI, pt. i, Knox to Queen Elizabeth, 20 July 1559, 47–51.

43. *Miscellany of S.H.S.*, IX (1958), 96.

44. Read, *op. cit.*, 156.

45. The best account of events in Scotland at this time is the contemporary 'Journal of the Siege of Leith, 1560', in *Two Missions of Jacques de la Brosse*, ed., Gladys Dickinson, *Miscellany of S.H.S.* (1942).

46. J. W. Thompson, *The Wars of Religion in France, 1559–1576* (1909), 48.

Chapter 5

1. A. G. Dickens, *The English Reformation*, 305.

2. See in general, Mortimer Levine, *The Early Elizabethan Succession Question 1558–1568*; Helen G. Stafford, *James VI of Scotland and the Throne of England* (1940); and Joel Hurstfield, 'The Succession Struggle in Late Elizabethan England', in Bindoff, ed., *Elizabethan Government and Society*, 369–96.

3. The classical statement of this theory is to be found in R. S. Rait, *The Parliaments of Scotland* (1924), 48–50, 199–200.

4. The text can be found in William Dunlop, *A Collection of Confessions of Faith*, II (1722), 13–98; in Knox, *Works*, ed. Laing, II, 93–120; and in a convenient modern edition with helpful introduction by G. D. Henderson, *The Scots Confession of 1560* (edns. 1937, 1960).

5. Henderson, *op. cit.* (edn. 1960), 32.

6. Laing, *Knox*, II, 103; Henderson, 39.

7. Laing, *Knox*, II, 'The Book of Discipline', 186. There is also a good modern edition with valuable commentaries by J. K. Cameron, *The First Book of Discipline* (1972).

8. This important point is elaborated in Gordon Donaldson, *The Scottish Reformation* (1960), 54–5.

9. Donaldson, *op. cit.*, 74.

10. The social and economic significance of the transfer of kirk-lands is insufficiently recognised by T. C. Smout, *A History of the Scottish People*, ch. III; and S. G. E. Lythe, *The Economy of Scotland in its European Setting 1550–1625* (1960), 24–8, also makes little of it, merely giving some superficial comments on the supposed general economic consequences of the Reformation. The importance of the theme is stressed but inadequately explored by R. K. Hannay, 'On the Church Lands at the Reformation', *S.H.R.*, XVI (1919), 52–72. The pioneer work is being done by Dr M. Sanderson, a specimen of whose work, 'The feuars of kirklands', has appeared in *S.H.R.*, LII (1973), 117–36. A revision article by T. M. Devine and S. G. E. Lythe, 'The Economy of Scotland under James VI', *S.H.R.*, L (1971), 91–106, mentions the topic but makes little of it.

11. Laing, II, 'Book of Discipline', 221–2.

12. Quoted in Peter Chalmers, *Historical and Statistical Account of Dunfermline* (1844), I, 309.

13. C. Hill, *Puritanism and Revolution* (Panther edn., 1968), ch. 2, 46.

14. James Scotland, *A History of Education in Scotland* (1970), I, 44 repeats this hoary old canard.

15. Patrick Collinson, *The Elizabethan Puritan Movement* (1967), 102–3, 179 *ff*; and Norman Sykes, *Old Priest and New Presbyter* (1956), ch. I, esp. 14.

16. Laing, *Knox*, II, 202. For differing view-points, see J. D. Mackie, *John Knox* (Hist. Assocn. Pamphlet, 1951), who argues that the superintendents were temporary expedients; and an adverse review of the same by G. Donaldson, *S.H.R.*, XXXI (1952), 165–7. Mackie, *A History of the Scottish Reformation* (1960), 144–7 and note, 153–7, maintains his position. So does Donaldson, *Scottish Reformation*, ch. V. In *S.H.R.*, XXVII (1948), 57–64, Professor Donaldson suggests that the First Book of Discipline owed much to the example of Denmark. Janet G. Macgregor, *The Scottish Presbyterian Polity* (1926), 42–7, regards the superintendents as temporary travelling preachers, and Duncan Shaw, *The General Assemblies of the Church of Scotland 1560–1600* (1964), 76 *ff.*, also sees them as temporary expedients but concerned more with administration.

17. Laing, *Knox*, II, 128–9.

18. For details, see Gordon Donaldson, *Thirds of Benefices* (S.H.S., 1949).

19. Jasper Ridley, *John Knox* (1968), 528, points this out.

20. Laing, *Knox*, IV, 141–212.

21. Quoted in A. F. Pollard, *The History of England from the Accession of Edward VI to the Death of Elizabeth, 1547–1603* (1910), 198.

22. Collinson, *op. cit.*, ch. 2, esp. 30.

23. Though dated, there is a good treatment in W. H. Frere, *The English Church in the Reigns of Elizabeth and James I (1558–1625)* (1904); more briefly, in Dickens, *op. cit.*, 294–306; J. B. Black, *The Reign of Elizabeth* (2nd. edn., 1959), ch. I; and Collinson, *op. cit.*, Pt. I, ch. 2.

24. Copious details in Frere, *op. cit.*, 25–6, 62–3, 102–9, 191; for some brilliant insights, see Christopher Hill, *Puritanism and Revolution*, ch. 2.

25. Dickens, *op. cit.*, 303.

26. Charles Hardwick, *A History of the Articles of Religion* (edn., 1876), ch. VI, 'The Elizabethan Articles', and Appendix No. III, which gives parallel texts of 'Articles of Religion in the Reigns of King Edward VI and Queen Elizabeth'.

27. Hardwick, *op. cit.*, 123–4.

28. R. B. Wernham, *Before the Armada*, 259 *ff*.

29. M. Levine, *op. cit.*, 30–1.

30. J. H. Pollen, ed., *A Letter from Mary Queen of Scots to the Duke of Guise* (S.H.S., 1904), Appendix of Illustrative Documents, 'Lethington's Account of Negotiations with Elizabeth in September and October 1561', 40. The passage quoted is in Scots: 'set my windiescheit befoir my e'.

31. J. E. Neale, *Queen Elizabeth* (Penguin edn.), 112–13.

32. Wernham, *op. cit.*, 261; but the thought, an old one, occurs in Mandell Creighton's *Queen Elizabeth* (edn. 1899), 37, 56, 77–9, and seems to derive from Sir James Melville's *Memoirs* (Bannatyne Club, 1827), 122, where Sir James informed Elizabeth . . . 'ye may not suffer a commander'.

33. Wernham, *op. cit.*, 270.

34. Levine, *op. cit.*, 121; the letter is in J. P. Collier, ed., *The Egerton Papers* (Camden Soc., 1840), 41–9.

35. Levine, *op. cit.*, 177.

36. That the Marian cause is still hotly urged is proved by Antonia Fraser's *Mary Queen of Scots* (1969), which, apart from reviving the sentimental arguments for Mary at great length, has little to contribute that is new. An extremely useful source book with valuable introduction is I. B. Cowan, *The Enigma of Mary Stuart* (1971).

37. T. F. Henderson, *Mary Queen of Scots* (1905), II, 428.

38. See G. Donaldson, *Scotland: James V to James VII*, ch. 7, which gives the best brief treatment of Mary's reign.

39. Gordon Donaldson, *The First Trial of Mary Queen of Scots* (edn. 1974).

40. R. S. Rait and A. I. Cameron, *King James' Secret* (1927), 102.

41. Patrick Collinson, *op. cit.*, 61.

42. Brian Woodcock, *Medieval Ecclesiastical Courts in the Diocese of Canterbury* (1952), 3; details in Sir Robert Phillimore, *The Ecclesiastical Law of the Church of England*, II (1895), Pt. IV.

43. Donaldson, *Scottish Reformation*, ch. VII, 'Conformity with England'.

44. W. Law Mathieson, *Politics and Religion*, I, ch. VII, 'Church and State, 1560–1586'.

45. Thomas McCrie, *Life of John Knox* (edn., 1839), 328–30.

46. Ridley, *Knox*, 506–9.

47. Collinson, *op. cit.*, 133–4.

48. Donaldson, *Scottish Reformation*, 189–90.

49. Collinson, *op. cit.*, 110.

50. The point is well made in Thomas McCrie's *Life of Andrew Melville* (1st edn. 1819, new edn. 1856), which is a miracle of scholarship for its time. McCrie 'is not a showman . . . but a historian of principles and policy' (*D.N.B.*), and he is only lightly regarded by those who have either failed to read, or comprehend, his works.

51. Collinson, *op. cit.*, 110, 208.

52. The main portions of the Second Book of Discipline are printed in Dickinson and Donaldson, eds., *A Source Book of Scottish History*, III, 22–31.

53. Maurice Lee, 'The Fall of the Regent Morton', in *Journal of Modern History*, XXVIII, 111–29.

54. John Bruce, ed., *Letters of Queen Elizabeth and James VI* (Camden Soc., 1849), 63.

55. Stafford, *op. cit.*, 107–8.

56. *A.P.S.*, III, 541–2.

57. T. G. Law, *Collected Essays and Reviews* (1904), 'The Spanish Blanks and Catholic Earls, 1592–94', 262.

58. Bruce, ed., *Letters of Elizabeth and James VI*.

59. Collinson, *op. cit.*, 407; for James' deceitful rôle, *ib.*, 448 *ff*.

60. Bruce, *op. cit.*, 132–8; Stafford, *op. cit.*, ch. VII.

61. That Cecil was sincere in this, see Hurstfield, in Bindoff, ed., *Elizabethan Government and Society*, 375–9, 391–3.

62. Quoted in Stafford, *op. cit.*, 290.

Chapter 6

1. Sir A. H. Dunbar, *Scottish Kings, 1005–1625* (1906), 262, 271.
2. For the confusion of titles caused by the regal union, see S. T. Bindoff, 'The Stuarts and their Style', *E.H.R.*, LX (1945), 192–216.
3. *Don Quixote*, ch. XIII.
4. G. Donaldson, 'Foundations of Anglo-Scottish Union', in S. T. Bindoff, ed., *Elizabethan Government and Society*, 282–314.
5. W. F. Bolton, ed., *The English Language: Essays by English and American Men of Letters, 1490–1839* (1966), 19–20, excerpts from William Harrison's (1534–93) *Descriptione of Britaine*.
6. *Ibid.*, 24, excerpts from *Camden's Remaines Concerning Britain* (1605).
7. Art., 'Scottish Language' in *Chambers's Encyclopaedia* (edn. 1967), vol. XII, 339–40; and Marjory A. Bald, 'The Pioneers of Anglicised Speech in Scotland', *S.H.R.*, XXIV (1927), 179–93.
8. Sir Thomas Craig, *De Unione Regnorum Britanniae Tractatus*, ed. C. S. Terry (S.H.S., 1909).
9. Craig, *op. cit.*, 242, noted that this was a common belief in England and ascribed it to 'sour grapes' at repeated failure to reduce Scotland by force. He also noted that many people in England denied that any such aggressions had ever occurred!
10. *Abbotsford Miscellany*, I (1837), 'Satire Against Scotland', 297–302. *An Answer* to it is also printed, *ibid.*, 305–17, which observes that 'on madman may make worke for ane hundrethe chirurgeonis'—a timeless truism.
11. *A.P.S.*, IV, 436.
12. For examples, see C. H. Firth, 'Ballads illustrating the Relations of England and Scotland during the Seventeenth Century', in *S.H.R.*, VI (1909), 113–28.
13. For James' character, see Wallace Notestein, *The House of Commons, 1604–1610* (1971), Intro; and David Harris Willson, 'King James I and Anglo-Scottish Unity', in William Appleton Aiken and Basil Duke Henning, eds., *Conflict in Stuart England: Essays in Honour of Wallace Notestein* (1960), 43–55.
14. C. H. McIlwain, ed., *Political Works of James I* (1918), 271–3.
15. Willson, *op. cit.*, 44–5.
16. Brian P. Levack, 'The Proposed Union of English Law and Scots Law in the Seventeenth Century', *Juridical Review* (1975: Pt. 2), 102–5.
17. John Bruce, ed., *Report on the Union of England and Scotland* (1799), II, p. xxii.
18. Quoted Notestein, *House of Commons*, 84–5; Bruce, *op. cit.*, II, p. lvii.
19. Quoted S. R. Gardiner, *History of England from the Accession of King James I* (edn. 1884), I, 328.
20. *A Speech used by Sir Francis Bacon in the Lower House of Parliament, 5 Jacobi concerning the Article of General Naturalization of the Scottish Nation*, in Bacon's *Reasons for the Union* (1706); also in Bruce, *op. cit.*, II, pp. cii–cxxviii.
21. *A.P.S.*, IV, 366–71.
22. *R.P.C.*, VII, 536. *Cf. R.P.C.*, VIII, 34–5, where the Scots Privy Council condemned as 'a noveltie of a dangerous preparative' an attempt to summon certain Scottish Borderers before the English Privy Council to answer charges.
23. Quoted Notestein, *House of Commons*, 211–12.
24. Levine, *Early Elizabethan Succession Question*, 122–4.
25. G. F. Black, *Surnames of Scotland* (edn. 1962), li.
26. Cobbett's *State Trials*, II (1809), 696.
27. *Ibid.*, 611–12.
28. W. S. Holdsworth, *A History of English Law*, IX (2nd. edn., 1938), 80; but the problem continues to present difficulties and is still largely determined in the light of expedience—*cf.* Immigration Acts of 1968 and 1971.
29. Ivan Roots, *The Great Rebellion, 1642–1660* (1966), 25.
30. Cobbett's *Parliamentary History of England*, I (1806), 1110.
31. Notestein, *op. cit.*, 22–3.

32. Clayton Roberts, *The Growth of Responsible Government in Stuart England* (1966), chs. I–IV.

33. *A.P.S.*, III, 431–7.

34. David Masson, ed., *R.P.C.* (2nd. ser.), I (1899), intro., pp. cxxxix–cxlvii.

35. R. S. Rait, *The Parliaments of Scotland* (1929), 7–8, 59–60, 301–3, 367–74.

36. Quoted C. Hill, *Puritanism and Revolution* (Panther edn., 1968), 46.

37. C. V. Wedgwood, 'Anglo-Scottish Relations, 1603–40', in *T.R.H.S.* (4th. ser.), XXXII (1950), 36–8.

38. I. B. Cowan, 'The Five Articles of Perth', in Duncan Shaw, ed., *Reformation and Revolution: Essays presented to Hugh Watt* (1967), 161.

39. *Ibid.*, 177; but *cf.* G. Donaldson, *James V to James VII*, 209–11.

40. C. Hill, *Century of Revolution* (1961), ch. IV, cogently summarises the main causes of discontent.

41. The best recent general treatment is Ivan Roots, *The Great Rebellion*, which adopts the middle position. The notoriously complex aetiology of the Civil War is brilliantly discussed by C. Hill in his paper 'Recent Interpretations of the Civil War', in *Puritanism and Revolution*, 13–40. A useful brief introduction is E. W. Ives, ed., *The English Revolution, 1600–1660* (1968), which consists of essays on various themes by distinguished contributors.

42. On the question of inevitability, see the refreshingly sceptical and skilfully argued paper by G. R. Elton, 'A High Road to Civil War?', in C. H. Carter, ed., *From the Renaissance to the Counter Reformation: Essays in Honour of Garrett Mattingly* (1966), 325–47. The quotation is from 328.

43. This appears to me to be very much the case with his essay, 'Scotland and the Puritan Revolution', which is to be found in H. R. Trevor-Roper, *Religion, the Reformation, and Social Change* (1967), 392–444.

44. Hill, *Puritanism and Revolution*, 21, 32–3.

45. Masson, ed., *R.P.C.* (2nd. ser.), I, intro., pp. xli–ii.

46. *Ibid.*, intro., *passim*; text, 81–2, 193–4, 351–2. As Masson stated, historians have dealt inadequately with this complex matter, a judgment that remains as true now as when it was penned. The best general account is still P. Hume Brown, *History of Scotland* (edn., 1911), II, Bk. VI, ch. III.

47. *A.P.S.*, Index, *s.v.* 'Revocation' for a long list.

48. *A.P.S.*, V, 23–8; for representations made to the king, *ibid.*, 219–20, and *R.P.C.* (2nd. ser.), I, 193 and *passim*; also subsequent volumes, e.g., *R.P.C.* (2nd. ser.), IV, pp. vi–ix.

49. J. Balfour, *Annals of Scotland* (1824), II, 128.

50. *State Trials*, III, 591–711.

51. Godfrey Davies, *The Early Stuarts, 1603–1660* (2nd. edn., 1959), 94.

52. Donaldson, *James V to James VII*, 311.

53. John Cunningham, *Church History of Scotland* (2nd. edn., 1882), I, 529.

54. John Row, *History of the Kirk of Scotland* (1842), II, 281–2.

55. Dickinson and Donaldson, eds., *Source Book of Scottish History*, III, 95–104.

56. C. V. Wedgwood, *The King's Peace* (1955), 224–6.

57. Douglas Nobbs, *England and Scotland 1560–1707* (1952), 91, 110; for a fuller account of Argyll's policy, see E. J. Cowan, 'Montrose and Argyll', in G. Menzies, ed., *The Scottish Nation*, 118–33.

58. Quoted David Stevenson, *The Scottish Revolution 1637–42* (1973), 97.

Chapter 7

1. Dickinson and Donaldson, *Source Book*, III, 238–9, 241–7.

2. See W. M. Lamont, *Godly Rule: Politics and Religion, 1603–1660* (1969); and the stimulating essays in Hill, *Puritanism and Revolution*, chs. 11 and 12.

3. In his interesting article, 'The Apocalyptic Vision of the Covenanters', in *S.H.R.*, XLIII (1964), 1–24, S. A. Burrell rather falls into error by failing to grasp the political background

and over-concentrating on the eschatological writings of the period. A better perspective, and a more balanced appraisal, is afforded by I. B. Cowan, 'The Covenanters: a revision article', in *S.H.R.*, 47 (1968), 35–52.

4. There is a thorough account in David Stevenson, *The Scottish Revolution 1637–44* (1973). Older treatments in the general histories of Hume Brown and Law Mathieson are still of service.

5. D. C. Mactavish, ed., *Minutes of the Synod of Argyll, 1639–1661* (2 vols., S.H.S., 1943–44). For a similar reaction in England, see C. Hill, 'Puritans and the dark corners of the land', in *T.R.H.S.*, 5th ser., XIII (1963), 77–102.

6. W. Ferguson, 'The Problems of the Established Church in the West Highlands and Islands in the Eighteenth Century', in *Records of Scottish Church History Society*, XVII–Pt. 1 (1969), 15–31.

7. Stevenson, *op. cit.*, ch. 3.

8. Quoted C. Hill, 'The Many Headed Monster in Late Tudor and Early Stuart Political Thinking', in Carter, ed., *Renaissance to Counter-Reformation*, 310. For another revealing instance, see Hill, *Puritanism and Revolution*, 27.

9. *Lords' Journal*, V, 22 Oct. 1642, 418–19; *Commons' Journal*, II, 819, 832, 842, 854; Cobbett's *Parliamentary History*, III, 15–17.

10. J. H. Hexter, *The Reign of King Pym* (1941), 29–30.

11. C. V. Wedgwood, *The King's War, 1641–47* (1958), 273; Baillie, *Letters and Journals*, II, 115; and *Parliamentary History*, III, 143, for parliament's decision to seek the help of the Scottish covenanters.

12. *R.P.C.*, 2nd ser., VII, 359–63, 372–80, esp. 375. *Cf. Commons' Journal*, II, 813, for the efforts of the Scots as mediators.

13. As, for example, by Rosalind Mitchison, *A History of Scotland* (1970), 213–14.

14. Baillie, *Letters and Journals*, II, 90.

15. C. V. Wedgwood, 'The Covenanters in the First Civil War', in *S.H.R.*, XXXIX (1960), 2–3. R. L. Orr, *Alexander Henderson, Churchman and Statesman* (1919), 286–9.

16. W. M. Hethrington, *History of the Westminster Assembly* (1843), 124–5, and Appendix.

17. John Aiton, *The Life and Times of Alexander Henderson* (1836), 514.

18. A. F. Mitchell and G. Struthers, ed., *Minutes of Westminster Assembly, 1644–49* (1879), intro. and *passim*.

19. W. Law Mathieson, *Politics and Religion*, II, 61.

20. The Solemn League and Covenant is seriously misrepresented by Trevor-Roper, *op. cit.*, *Religion, Reformation and Social Change*, 404–5. A thorough and judicious general account is given by C. V. Wedgwood in *The King's War*, which brings out clearly the intricate factors involved. Valuable also is a paper by S. W. Carruthers, 'The Solemn League and Covenant: Its Text and Translations', in *Records of Scottish Church History Society*, VI (1938), 232–51, which, however, concentrates on the evolution of the text rather than on the involved politics that underlay it. The text of the Solemn League and Covenant itself should be carefully read; it can be found in Dickinson and Donaldson, *op. cit.*, III, 122–5, or in Gardiner's *Constitutional Documents of the Puritan Revolution* (var. edns.).

21. Wedgwood, *art. cit.*, 9.

22. Gardiner, *History of the Great Civil War* (2nd edn., 1888), I, 359–60, forcefully develops this point, even going so far as to suggest that the Committee of Both Kingdoms contained 'the first germ of the modern Cabinet system'—an intriguing exaggeration.

23. C. S. Terry, ed., *The Army of the Covenant* (S.H.S., 1917), I, lxxv–vi; also H. W. Meikle, ed., *The Correspondence of the Scots Commissioners in London, 1644–1646* (Roxburghe Club, 1917), intro., xv–xviii, xxiv.

24. *R.P.C.* (2nd. ser.), VIII (1908), 5.

25. Aiton, *op. cit.*, 537.

26. C. V. Wedgwood, 'The Covenanters in the First Civil War', in *S.H.R.*, xxxix, 12–15.

27. The best studies, though both rather in romantic vein, are John Buchan's *Montrose* (1928), and the brief life by C. V. Wedgwood (1952). The real source, though highly biased in its subject's favour, is Mark Napier, *Memorials of Montrose*, 2 vols. (1850).

28. *A.P.S.*, IV, 138–9; *R.P.C.*, VI, 8, and VII, 84–90; for discussion of the problems, see W. C. Mackenzie, *The Highlands and Islands of Scotland: a Historical Survey* (new edn., 1949), ch. X, 202–20, and more briefly W. R. Kermack, *The Scottish Highlands: a Short History* (1957), ch. 10, 79–87.

29. Napier, *Memorials*, II, 176.

30. Annie M. Mackenzie, ed., *Orain Iain Luim* (*Scottish Gaelic Texts Society*, 1964), with translations and notes. John MacDonald (c. 1624–c. 1707), known as the Bard of Keppoch or Iain Lom (the Bald, meaning possibly of speech), provides the most important Gaelic source for current events in his time. The passage quoted is on p. 25.

31. R. Mitchison, *History of Scotland*, 223, repeats the charge though it is effectively demolished by C. V. Wedgwood, *The King's War*, 602–11; and indeed by Mrs. Mitchison's subsequent argument.

32. W. L. Mathieson, *Politics and Religion*, II, 147–8; David Masson, *Life of Milton*, III, 419; and C. V. Wedgwood, *The King's War*, 567.

33. John Milton, *Areopagitica*.

34. These points are forcefully developed in H. N. Brailsford's admirable study, *The Levellers and the English Revolution*, ed. C. Hill (1961).

35. Fullest treatment in C. H. Firth, ed., *The Clarke Papers* (3 vols., Camden Soc., 1891); excerpts from the same with useful introduction by A. S. P. Woodhouse, *Puritanism and Liberty* (1938); and helpful commentary in Brailsford, *op. cit.*, ch. XIII.

36. Caroline Robbins, *The Eighteenth-century Commonwealthman* (1959), discusses this intricate problem.

37. Text of the Engagement in Dickinson and Donaldson, eds., *Source Book of Scottish History*, III, 134–9.

38. The myth received its classical imprimatur in A. V. Dicey and R. S. Rait, *Thoughts on the Union between England and Scotland* (1920), 70–8. It has become the stock interpretation with those who prefer glib formulas to wrestling with intricate facts.

39. *Memoirs of Sir Ewen Cameron of Lochiel* (Abbotsford Club, 1842), 87–8.

40. C. S. Terry, *A History of Scotland* (1920), 406.

41. C. S. Terry, ed., *The Cromwellian Union* (S.H.S., 1902), intro., xvii.

42. *Ibid.*, xxxii.

43. *Letters from Roundhead Officers in Scotland* (Bannatyne Club, 1856), 43.

44. T. McCrie, ed., *Life of Mr. Robert Blair* (Wodrow Soc., 1848), 291–2.

45. Paul J. Pinckney, 'The Scottish Representation in the Cromwellian Parliament of 1656', in *S.H.R.*, vol. 46 (1967), 95–114, argues to little purpose in an attempt to controvert Terry, *Cromwellian Union*, which remains the best authority on the subject.

46. *Letters from Roundhead Officers*, 89–91.

47. Terry, *Cromwellian Union*, lxxxiii.

48. I. Roots, *The Great Rebellion*, 175.

49. Quoted by C. Hill, *Reformation to Industrial Revolution* (1969), 166; also in Hill, *God's Englishman: Oliver Cromwell and the English Revolution* (1970), 129.

50. *Cf.* Oliver's speech to parliament 25 January 1658, in W. C. Abbott, *Cromwell's Writings and Speeches*, IV, 718.

51. S. G. E. Lythe, *The Economy of Scotland in its European Setting 1550–1625* (1960), is too slight to sustain its weighty theme.

52. Baillie, *Letters and Journals*, III, 288, 357, 387; John Nicoll, *Diary of Public Transactions, 1650–1667*, ed. D. Laing (Bannatyne Club, 1836), 194, 207, 222; Thomas Tucker, *Upon the Settlement of the Revenues of Excise and Customs in Scotland* (Bannatyne Club, 1825) and also in *Miscellany of Scottish Burgh Records Society* (1881), 1–48.

53. Quoted C. H. Firth, *The Last Years of the Protectorate*, II (1909), 116.

54. *Ibid.*, 116.

55. Abbot, *loc. cit.*

56. M. P. Ashley, *Financial and Commercial Policy under the Cromwellian Protectorate* (2nd edn., 1962), 91. T. Keith, *Commercial Relations of England and Scotland, 1603–1707* (1910), 59, puts the deficit for 1659 at £134,808–4–2.

57. H. R. Trevor-Roper, 'Oliver Cromwell and his Parliaments', in Pares and Taylor, eds., *Essays presented to Sir Lewis Namier* (1956), 1–48; reprinted in Trevor-Roper, *Religion, Reformation and Social Change*, 345–91; for the refutation by C. Hill, *Puritanism and Revolution*, 22–4.

58. W. Ferguson, 'A Note on the Edinburgh University Library MS DK. 5.25. "Brian Fairfax's Account" ', in *The Bibliotheck*, vol. 3, no. 2 (1960), 71–2.

59. J. M. Lloyd Thomas, ed., *The Autobiography of Richard Baxter* (Everyman edn., 1931), 92.

60. Firth, *op. cit.*, 124.

61. Nicoll, *Diary*, 183.

62. W. Mackay, ed., *Chronicles of the Frasers* (S.H.S., 1905), 447.

63. Clarendon, *Life, by Himself* (edn., 1759), II, 93.

Chapter 8

1. These points are well brought out in Professor Andrew Browning's admirable introduction to his invaluable *English Historical Documents, 1660–1714* (1953).

2. The 'inevitability' argument, though considerably toned down, still operates and informs G. Donaldson's brief but stimulating chapter on 'Scotland and England' in his *Scotland: The Shaping of a Nation* (1974); and in a covert way it is to be found in a rather superficial and muddled essay by T. C. Smout, 'The Road to Union', in Geoffrey Holmes, ed., *Britain After the Glorious Revolution, 1689–1714* (1969), 176–96.

3. James Kirkton, ed. C. K. Sharpe, *Secret and True History of the Church of Scotland from the Restoration to the Year 1678* (1817), 60. Sharpe, a poor editor, gives biassed and worthless notes, and a good modern edition of this interesting work is badly needed.

4. J. M. Lloyd-Thomas, ed., *Autobiography of Richard Baxter* (Everyman edn., 1931), 135–41, 171, 180.

5. H. R. Trevor-Roper, *Archbishop Laud* (1940), 429 *ff*. In his carefully researched book *The Making of the Restoration Settlement: the Influence of the Laudians, 1649–1662* (1951) R. S. Bosher has demolished this facile view.

6. Bosher, *op. cit.*, 81.

7. Baxter, *Autobiography*, 175. The Act is in C. G. Robertson, *Select Statutes, Cases and Documents to Illustrate English Constitutional History, 1660–1832* (1904), 12–26.

8. See Anne Whiteman, 'The Re-establishment of the Church of England, 1660–1663', in *T.R.H.S.*, 5th ser., V (1955), 111–32 for some shrewd appraisals on this head, esp. 130–1.

9. Baxter, *op. cit.*, 150, and App. I, 257–66.

10. Andrew Browning, *Danby*, I (1951), 197–8. Professor Browning accepts the authenticity of the inquiry's conclusions even when margins of error are taken into account. For further details, see Browning, *English Historical Documents, 1660–1714* (1953), 411–16.

11. W. M. Lamont, *Godly Rule*, esp. Ch. 3, 56–77.

12. Donaldson, *Scotland Church and Nation through Sixteen Centuries* (1960), 88.

13. T. McCrie, ed., *Life of Robert Blair* (Wodrow Soc., 1848), 353–5.

14. D. Laing, ed., *Letters and Journals of Robert Baillie*, III, 400–1, 405–7, 410, 414–15, 444–5, 458–62, 464, 468, 470–1, 473, 475–7, 484; see too L. W. Sharp, ed., *Early Letters of Robert Wodrow* (S.H.S., 1937), 302.

15. Sharp's letters are printed in O. Airy, ed., *Lauderdale Papers* (1884), I; and in even more convenient form in R. Burns, ed., Wodrow's *History of the Sufferings of the Church of Scotland* (I, 1828), Introduction.

16. *Life of Blair*, 353.

17. Sir George Mackenzie of Rosehaugh, *Memoirs of the Affairs of Scotland* (1821), 52–6; also *Life of Blair*, 381–90.

18. Dickinson and Donaldson, eds., *Source Book of Scottish History*, III, 164; also G. Donaldson, *James V to James VII*, 367–8.

19. D. Butler, *Life and Letters of Robert Leighton* (1903), 436–9, 455; E. A. Knox, *Robert Leighton, Archbishop of Glasgow* (1930), 208, for 'owls and satyrs'.

20. Mackenzie, *Memoirs of Affairs of Scotland*, 77–8. For the discontents, see I. B. Cowan, *The Scottish Covenanters, 1660–1688* (1976).

21. D. L. Keir, *Constitutional History of Modern Britain* (var. edns.), ch. V.

22. Browning, *Danby*, I, ch. X, esp. 191 *ff.*; see, too, A. Browning, 'Parties and Party Organization in the Reign of Charles II', *T.R.H.S.*, 4th ser., XXX (1948), 21–36.

23. K. H. D. Haley, *The First Earl of Shaftesbury* (1968), 184.

24. That Middleton's corruption was common knowledge, see John Nicoll's list of reasons for the commissioner's downfall in 1663, in *Diary of Public Transactions*, 393; also Mackenzie of Rosehaugh, *Memoirs*, 65–6, 82, 97, 112–13.

25. This crucial point is completely overlooked by T. C. Smout, *loc. cit.*, in Holmes, ed. *Britain after the Glorious Revolution*. The omission seriously weakens Smout's argument.

26. G. Burnet, *History of His Own Times* (ed., 1838), I, 76.

27. Clarendon, *Continuation of Life*, II, 101–7.

28. Burnet, I, 74.

29. W. C. Mackenzie's *The Life and Times of John Maitland, Duke of Lauderdale* (1923), an interesting but superficial account, subscribes to this view; there is a more realistic assessment in Maurice Lee, *The Cabal* (1965), ch. 2.

30. John Hill Burton, *History of Scotland*, VII, 184–5.

31. O. Airy, ed., *Lauderdale Papers*, II, 164.

32. L. A. Harper, *The English Navigation Laws* (1939).

33. T. C. Smout, *Scottish Trade on the Eve of Union, 1660–1707* (1963), 240.

34. Theodora Keith, *Commercial Relations of England and Scotland, 1603–1707* (1910), 91. This pioneer study is still the best general account.

35. See C. S. Terry, *The Pentland Rising and Rullion Green* (1905), which proves that it was a spontaneous local rising; but that collusion with the Dutch was feared, P. Hume Brown, *History of Scotland*, II, 310, and A. Lang, *History of Scotland*, III, 306–7.

36. Edward Hughes, 'The Negotiations for a Commercial Union between England and Scotland in 1668', in *S.H.R.*, XXIV (1927), 35. Smout, *Scottish Trade*, overlooks this important paper, and indeed the negotiations of 1668 and 1670 altogether. For the relevant documents, see J. Bruce, *Report on Union* (1799), II, App. XXXI.

37. M. Lee, *The Cabal*, 51 *ff.*, following W. C. Mackenzie, *Lauderdale*, 288 *ff.*, who is not a very good guide.

38. Archibald Robertson, *Life of Sir Robert Moray* (1922), 142–4; Andrew Lang, *Sir George Mackenzie, King's Advocate, of Rosehaugh* (1909), 91.

39. Quoted Keith, *op. cit.*, 93.

40. Haley, *Shaftesbury*, 199, 236–7.

41. Mackenzie, *Memoirs of Affairs of Scotland*, 137–42.

42. *Ibid.*, 149–54.

43. Airy, ed., *Lauderdale Papers*, II, 154.

44. Mackenzie, *Memoirs*, 167. The same author's *A Discourse concerning the Three Unions between Scotland and England* (1714) is more disputatious than informative.

45. Lee, *Cabal*, 53.

46. C. S. Terry, ed., *Cromwellian Union*, 206.

47. Mackenzie, *Memoirs*, 207, from a diary of the negotiations kept by Sir John Baird who was one of the Scottish commissioners; not in Terry.

48. T. C. Smout, *Scottish Trade on the Eve of Union*, 240–1.

49. Robertson, *Moray*, 146–7; Haley, *Shaftesbury*, 340–1.

50. Haley, *op. cit.*, 510–11.

51. *R.P.C.*, 3rd. ser., VI, 203–5.

52. H. M. Margaliouth, ed., *Poems and Letters of Andrew Marvell* (1952), I, 204; quoted Lee, *Cabal*, 28.

53. J. R. Jones, *The First Whigs: The Politics of the Exclusion Crisis* (1961), ch. I, gives the best synopsis of the issues involved.

54. Haley, *Shaftesbury*, chs. XXI–XXVII, puts the whole issue into a new and more convincing perspective.

55. The point is forcefully, at times too forcefully, developed in Lucille Pinkham, *William III and the Respectable Revolution* (1954); her case seems sound but marred by too much special pleading.

56. Burnet, I, 337.

57. F. C. Turner, *James II* (2nd. edn. 1950), 193–4.

58. Dickinson and Donaldson, eds., *Source Book of Scottish History*, III, 185–9.

59. Contrast G. M. Trevelyan's brief and tendentious *English Revolution, 1688–89* (1938), with Maurice Ashley's *The Glorious Revolution of 1688* (1966), an impartial and judicious survey. But as to freedom from being impaled, Professor J. R. Jones' *The Revolution of 1688 in England* (1972) induces wry second thoughts.

60. Count Anthony Hamilton, *Memoirs of the Count de Grammont* (var. eds.). It is only fair to Hamilton to state that many of his stories are confirmed (or at least related) by other contemporary narrators such as Burnet: so that if not true, at least they were current gossip.

61. F. C. Turner, *James II*, is by no means as impartial as its judicial air would imply; on Mr. Turner's own showing much is doubtful about James and his career, but Mr. Turner hardly ever gives his subject the benefit of the doubt.

62. *A.P.S.*, VIII, 579, 581–2.

63. Quoted by M. V. Hay, *The Enigma of James II* (1938), 55–6.

64. *H.M.C.*, *Stuart*, I (1902), 30–1.

65. William Lloyd, 'A Discourse of God's Ways of Disposing of Kingdoms' (1691), in Gerald M. Straka, *The Revolution of 1688: Whig Triumph or Palace Revolution?* (1963), 28. This important theme is explored in greater detail in the same author's *Anglican Reaction to the Revolution of 1688* (1962).

Chapter 9

1. T. C. Smout, 'The Road to Union', in G. Holmes, ed., *op. cit.*, 179.

2. Smout, *op. cit.*; also the same writer's 'The Anglo-Scottish Union of 1707, I. The Economic Background', in *Econ. Hist. Rev.*, 2nd. ser. XVI (1964); both these essays revise somewhat the substance of Smout's earlier views on the union in his *Scottish Trade on the Eve of Union* (1963), ch. XII. Mrs. Mitchison's views are given in her *History of Scotland* (1970), ch. 18.

3. For a penetrating discussion of the problems associated with the English Revolution, see Jennifer Carter, 'The Revolution and the Constitution', in Holmes, *op. cit.*, 39–58.

4. Edward Gibbon, *Life and Letters* (Chandos edn.), 10.

5. George L. Cherry, 'The Legal and Philosophical Position of the Jacobites, 1688–89', *Journal of Modern History*, XXII (1950), 309–21; also Straka, ed., *Revolution of 1688*.

6. Sir William Blackstone, *Commentaries on the Laws of England* (1765–69), I, chs. 2 and 3.

7. For details see D. Ogg, *England in the Reigns of James II and William III* (1955), ch. VIII; and D. L. Keir, *Constitutional History of Modern Britain* (3rd. edn.), 268–88. The main documents are conveniently brought together in Stephenson and Marcham, *Sources of English Constitutional History* (1937), Section XI, 599–612.

8. E. and A. Porritt, *The Unreformed House of Commons* (2 vols, 1903), I, 8–9; II, 90. But, as the Porritts noted, a measure of electoral reform was carried in Scotland.

9. P. G. M. Dickson, *The Financial Revolution: a Study in the Development of Public Credit 1688–1756* (1967), 46–7.

10. Gilbert Burnet, *History of His Own Time* (1838), II, 526–7.

11. Douglas Nobbs, *England and Scotland, 1560–1707* (1952), 162–3.

12. T. Maxwell, 'Presbyterian and Episcopalian in 1688', in *Records of the Scottish Church History Society*, XIII, 25–37.

13. J. Halliday, 'The Club and the Revolution in Scotland 1689–90', in *S.H.R.*, XLV (1966), 143–59.

14. The evidence, such as it is, is fully set out in G. W. T. Omond, *The Early History of the Scottish Union Question* (1897), ch. V.

15. Smout in Holmes, ed., *op. cit.*, 183–4, citing S.R.O., Misc. Papers 260–1: Fletcher to Russell, 8 January 1689.

16. *A Letter to a Member of the Convention of Estates in Scotland* (1689), 7.

17. *A.P.S.*, IX, 60.

18. *A.P.S.*, IX, 37–40. For a good summary of the Revolution Settlement in Scotland and excerpts from the main documents, see *Source Book of Scottish History*, III, 198 *ff.*, 240–1, 254–5.

19. *Leven and Melville Papers* (Bannatyne Club, 1843), 10.

20. H.M.C., *11th Rept.* (1887), Pt. VI, 177.

21. Earl of Balcarres, *Memoirs touching the Revolution in Scotland, 1688–90* (Bannatyne Club, 1841), 59.

22. There is no really good work on the Massacre, which is best studied in the contemporary documents drawn together, but somewhat misleadingly, in *Papers Illustrative of the Political Condition of the Highlands of Scotland, 1689–96* (Maitland Club, 1845). Of secondary works those by John Buchan (1933) and John Prebble (1966) are too melodramatic and unscholarly to inspire confidence. D. J. Macdonald, *Slaughter under Trust* (1965) is better though still in places weak on historical background. S. B. Baxter, *William III* (1966), 273–4, is a woefully inadequate attempt to exculpate William from, as Baxter puts it, 'the wretched affair'.

23. F. C. Turner, *James II*, 436.

24. Audrey Cunningham, *The Loyal Clans* (1932), 11, 227, 294, 351–2, 390.

25. J. P. Kenyon, *Robert Spencer, Earl of Sunderland 1641–1702* (1958), ch. VIII.

26. T. C. Smout, *Scottish Trade on the Eve of Union*, ch. XI; and a more comprehensive and cogent, though briefer, account in Theodora Keith, *Commercial Relations of England and Scotland*, 140–56.

27. A. Fletcher, *Political Works* (1749), 'First Discourse concerning the Affairs of Scotland', 60.

28. Far the best accounts are still Frank Cundall, *The Darien Venture* (1927); F. R. Hart, *The Disaster of Darien* (1929); and G. P. Insh, *The Company of Scotland* (1932).

29. *A.P.S.*, IX, 377–80; *Source Book*, III, 339–41.

30. *R.P.C.*, 3rd. ser., VII, 664–5. For background see G. P. Insh, *Scottish Colonial Schemes 1620–1686* (1922), Ch. IV.

31. James Mackinnon, *The Union of England and Scotland* (1896), 15.

32. A. Fletcher, 'First Discourse', in *Political Works*, 56.

33. William Seton of Pitmedden, *Essays upon the Present State of Scotland* (1700), 110.

34. Sir David Hume of Crossrigg, *A Diary of the Proceedings in the Parliament and Privy Council of Scotland, May 21, MDCC–March 7, MDCC VII* (Bannatyne Club, 1828), 32–7; *A.P.S.*, X, 234.

35. Paul Grimblot, ed., *Letters of William III and Louis XIV, 1697–1700* (1848), II, William to Heinsius, June 7–18, 1700, 415.

36. Hume of Crossrigg, *op. cit.*, 75.

37. Mark A. Thomson, 'Louis XIV and the Origins of the War of the Spanish Succession', in *Essays 1680–1720, by and for Mark A. Thomson*, ed. R. Hatton and J. S. Bromley (1968), 144–5.

Chapter 10

1. W. Ferguson, 'The Making of the Treaty of Union of 1707', *S.H.R.*, XLIII (1964), 89–110; the quotations come from p. 89.

2. T. C. Smout in Holmes, ed., *Britain after the Glorious Revolution*, 194.

3. R. Mitchison, *History of Scotland*, 306.

4. Smout, *op. cit.*, 182.

5. T. C. Smout, 'Union of the Parliaments', in G. Menzies, ed., *The Scottish Nation* (1972), 156–7.

6. Smout in Holmes, *op. cit.*, 182.

7. P. W. J. Riley, 'The Union of 1707 as an episode in English politics', *E.H.R.*, LXXXIV (1969), 498–527.

8. Daniel Defoe, *History of the Union between England and Scotland* (edn. 1786), 78 *ff.*

9. James Mackinnon, *The Union of England and Scotland* (1896), ch. V; W. Law Mathieson, *Scotland and the Union* (1905), ch. II; A. Lang, *History of Scotland* (1907), IV, 97–101; P. Hume Brown, *History of Scotland*, (edn. 1911), III, 73–77; P. Hume Brown, *Legislative Union of England and Scotland* (1914), 68–74; G. S. Pryde, *Treaty of Union of Scotland and England* (1950), 15–16; W. Ferguson, *art. cit.*, 99–102, and W. Ferguson, *Scotland: 1689 to the Present* (1968), 42–5.

10. J. McCormick, ed., *Carstares State Papers* (1774), Seafield to Carstares, 17 August 1699, 492–3.

11. James Grant, ed., *Seafield Correspondence* (S.H.S., 1912), 238, 255.

12. *Carstares State Papers*, Queensberry to Carstares, 31 July 1700, 583–6.

13. *Ibid.*, Argyll to Carstares, 8 August 1700, 598–600.

14. *Ibid.*, Mar to Carstares, 17 August 1700, 618–20.

15. Ferguson, *Scotland: 1689 to Present*, chs. I, II.

16. C. Hill, *Puritanism and Revolution* (Panther, 1968), 22–4.

17. Duke of Argyll, ed., *Intimate Family Letters of the Eighteenth Century* (1910), I, 26.

18. Hume Brown, *Legislative Union*, 33–4; *ibid.*, 50, for Seafield's abilities as a manager and manipulator of electors; and 70 for use of influence in parliament.

19. R. H. Story, *Life of Principal Carstares* (1874), 275–6.

20. Geoffrey Holmes, *Politics in the Age of Anne* (1967) disposes of Professor Walcott's contentions that party meant little and that in effect a spoils system flourished. Unfortunately, Holmes does not attempt to assess the situation in Scotland.

21. W. Ferguson, *Electoral Law and Procedure in Eighteenth and Early Nineteenth Century Scotland* (unpublished Glasgow Ph.D. thesis, 1957), ch. I.

22. George Lockhart, *Memoirs* (1714), 394.

23. Hume of Crossrigg, *Diary*, 14 January 1701, 51–2.

24. George Ridpath, *An Account of the Proceedings of the Parliament of Scotland, which Met at Edinburgh, May 6 1703* (1704), 286, quoting a speech by Fletcher; also Fletcher, *Speeches* (1703), 65, 75. For the latter work I have used the copy in Edinburgh University Library, *EE 9/24.

25. J. M. Gray, ed., *Memoirs of the Life of Sir John Clerk of Penicuik* (S.H.S., 1892), 43–68.

26. Ferguson, *art. cit.*, 102–3, 106–7. Professor Smout sees the significance of this evidence (Holmes, *op. cit.*, 190–1), only to dismiss it.

27. Ridpath, *op. cit.*, 298, quoting Fletcher's speech; also in Fletcher, *Speeches* (1703), 8–9.

28. Andrew Fletcher, *Political Works* (1749), 289–90.

29. For a full discussion see W. Ferguson, 'Imperial Crowns: a Neglected Facet of the Background to the Treaty of Union', *S.H.R.*, LIII (1974), 22–44.

30. Ridpath, *op. cit.*, 2.

31. Balfour Paul, *Scots Peerage* (1907), IV, *s.v.* Hamilton; VII, *s.v.* Selkirk; and VII, *s.v.* Queensberry.

32. For Fletcher's ideas see his *Political Works* (1749); for his career W. C. Mackenzie, *Andrew Fletcher of Saltoun* (1935) is serviceable but mediocre. There is a good brief treatment by G. W. T. Omond, *Fletcher of Saltoun* (1897), especially 69–70 for a summary of his famous limitations.

33. Fletcher, *Political Works*, 118–19; William Seton of Pitmedden, *Essays upon the Present State of Scotland* (1700), 77–80.

34. *Proposals for the Reformation of Schools and Universities* (1704), attributed to Andrew Fletcher of Saltoun. *Cf.* D. J. Withrington, 'Education and Society in the Eighteenth Century', in N. T. Phillipson and R. Mitchison, eds., *Scotland in the Age of Improvement* (1970).

35. Fletcher, *Political Works*, 53.

36. 'An Account of a Conversation concerning A Right Regulation of Governments For the common good of mankind', in *Political Works*, 261–319.

37. Distribution of catholics is covered in 'List of Popish parents and their children in various districts in Scotland, 1701–05', in *Miscellany of Maitland Club*, III (1843), 387–440. See, too, W. Ferguson, 'The Problems of the Established Church in the West Highlands and Islands in the Eighteenth Century', in *Records of Scottish Church History Society*, XVII (1969), 20–3.

38. George Hilton Jones, *The Mainstream of Jacobitism* (1954), ch. I.

39. *Carstares State Papers*, Lord Advocate to Carstares, 14 September 1697, 344.

40. P. Hume Brown, ed., *Lord Seafield's Letters, 1702–1707* (S.H.S., 1915), 123–9, a paper by Viscount Tarbat (later first Earl of Cromartie), 'The Present State of the Scots Divisions'.

41. Rev. Robert Paul, ed., 'The Diary of John Turnbull, Minister of Alloa and Tyninghame, 1657–1704', in *Miscellany of S.H.S.*, I (1893), 413, 416.

42. 'Correspondence between George Ridpath and the Rev. Robert Wodrow', in *Miscellany of the Abbotsford Club*, I (1837), 354 *ff.*; also in L. Sharp, ed., *Early Letters of Robert Wodrow 1698–1709* (S.H.S., 1937). The correspondence began in April 1706.

43. 'Correspondence' (Abbotsford), Ridpath to Wodrow, 23 February 1706, 384.

44. Robert Walcott, *English Politics in the Early Eighteenth Century* (1956).

45. Walcott, *op. cit.*, 96.

46. Holmes, *British Politics in the Age of Anne*, a richly documented work that throws a flood of light on the politics of the period. J. H. Plumb, *The Growth of Political Stability in England, 1675–1725* (1967) is stimulating but in places rather speculative.

47. See the judicious essay by Henry Horwitz, 'The Structure of Parliamentary Politics', in Holmes, ed., *Britain after the Glorious Revolution*, 96–114.

Chapter 11

1. C. Grant Robertson, *Select Statutes, Cases and Documents, 1660–1832*, 90.

2. A. Fletcher, *Speeches*, 30.

3. Hatton and Bromley, eds., *William III and Louis XIV*, 240.

4. David Greene, *Queen Anne* (1970), 132.

5. *Ibid.*, 155.

6. Hume of Crossrigg, *Diary*, 82–3.

7. *A.P.S.*, X, 59–60.

8. Mackinnon, *Union of England and Scotland*, 66.

9. Hume, *Diary*, 86.

10. *A.P.S.*, XI, 26.

11. *Carstares State Papers*, 715.

12. G. P. R. James, ed., *Vernon Letters*, II (1841), 408.

13. G. Burnet, *History of His Own Time*, II, 707.

14. *Miscellany of S.H.S.*, I, 423.

15. *A.P.S.*, XI, 'Proceedings of the Commissioners', App., 148.

16. *Ibid.*, 153.

17. *Ibid.*, 161.

18. *Ibid.*, 161.

19. P.R.O., S.P. 54/1, No. 10.

20. *Ibid.*, 'Lynes upon the Nobility of Scotland, 1703'.

21. See P. W. J. Riley, 'The Formation of the Scottish Ministry of 1703', *S.H.R.*, XLIV (1965), 112–34.

22. Correspondence of George Baillie of Jerviswood 1702–8 (Bannatyne Club, 1841), II.

23. G. M. Trevelyan, *England Under Queen Anne*, II, 231, n.

24. Trevelyan, II, 233.

25. Riley, *art. cit.*; also Riley, 'The Scottish Parliament of 1703', *S.H.R.*, vol. 47 (1968), 129–50.

26. W. Law Mathieson, *Scotland and the Union* (1905), Ch. II.

27. Riley, *art. cit.*, *S.H.R.*, vol. 47.

28. Burnet, *History*, II, 738.

29. J. M. Gray, ed., *Memoirs of the Life of Sir John Clerk of Penicuik* (S.H.S., 1892), 49. Analogies with anarchic Poland were then common—*cf.* Defoe's poem *The Dyet of Poland: A Satyr*, published in March 1705.

30. Copious extracts from these are given in George Ridpath's *Account of the Proceedings of the Parliament of Scotland, which Met at Edinburgh, May 6, 1703*. They were also printed at the time.

31. H.M.C., *Seafield*, Rept. XIV, App., Pt. III, 199.

32. *A.P.S.*, XI, 101.

33. *A.P.S.*, XI, 36–7; B. Curtis Brown, *Letters of Queen Anne* (1935), 'Instructions to the Duke of Queensberry', 119.

34. *A.P.S.*, XI, 41.

35. Riley, *art. cit.*, *S.H.R.*, vol. 47, 139–40.

36. Hume Brown, *Legislative Union*, App. I, Atholl to Godolphin, 30 May 1703, 157–60.

37. Fletcher, *Political Works*, 194.

38. *A.P.S.*, XI, 69.

39. *Ibid.*, 69.

40. *Ibid.*, 70.

41. *Ibid.*, 74; the figure is given by Ridpath, *Proceedings*, 262.

42. H.M.C., *Portland*, IV, 103, for the 'lame arm'; *Jerviswood Corr.*, 27, 21 Dec. 1704, for the other quotation.

43. G. S. Pryde, *Treaty of Union* (1950), 15–16, adopts this view but on very flimsy evidence.

44. *E.g.*, G. Ridpath, *Historical Account of the ancient Rights and Power of the Parliament of Scotland* (1703).

45. George Buchanan, *De Jure Regni apud Scotos*; there is no really good modern translation, the best being by C. F. Arrowood, *The Powers of the Crown in Scotland* (1949).

46. Mackinnon, *Union*, 118, 127.

47. *A.P.S.*, XI, 107.

48. J. M. Graham, ed., *Stair Annals*, I (1875), 380–1.

49. Curtis Brown, *Letters of Queen Anne*, 118–19; H.M.C., *Rept. XIV, 3 Seafield* (1894), 198.

50. Curtis Brown, *op. cit.*, 119.

51. *A.P.S.*, XI, 102.

52. *A.P.S.*, X, 234.

53. *A.P.S.*, XI, 103, 112. For the act conferring this privilege, *A.P.S.*, IV, 136.

54. *A.P.S.*, XI, 109.

55. Alexander Cunningham, *History of Great Britain from the Revolution to the Accession of George I* (1787), I, 360.

56. *A.P.S.*, XI, 112.

57. Cunningham, *op. cit.*, I, 360.

Chapter 12

1. W. C. Mackenzie, *Simon Fraser, Lord Lovat, his Life and Times* (1908), glosses matters in Lovat's favour. Better accounts are: Mackinnon, *Union*, Ch. V; Hume Brown, *Legislative Union*, 64–8; and G. H. Jones, *The Mainstream of Jacobitism* (1954), 66–9.

2. H.M.C., *Rept. XV, App. 9, Johnstone MS.* (1897), 120.

3. Fletcher, *Works*, 261–319.

4. Mackinnon, *Union*, 149.

5. *Lords' Journals*, XVII, 505–6, 554; *Parliamentary History*, VI, 222–3.

6. Cunningham, *op. cit.*, I, 361.

7. N.L.S., MS 7104, No. 32, Marlborough to Tweeddale, 4 April 1704; and MS 7121. Tweeddale to Godolphin, 18 May 1704.

8. T. C. Smout, 'Union of the Parliaments', in G. Menzies, ed., *The Scottish Nation* (1972), 156; and correspondence on this matter in *Scottish International* for December 1972, and January and March 1973.

9. N.L.S., MS 7102, 'Instructions to Marquis of Tweeddale', and 'Additional Instructions'; *A.P.S.*, XI, 125–6, for Anne's letter to the parliament.

10. Lockhart, *Memoirs*, 113–14.

11. N.L.S., MS 7121, *passim*.

12. N.L.S., MS 7121, Tweeddale to Godolphin, 18 July 1704.

13. *Ibid.*, Tweeddale to Godolphin, 3 June 1704.

14. Lockhart, *Memoirs*, 112–13; Burnet, *History*, II, 763.

15. Trevelyan, *op. cit.*, II, 226.

16. Sir William Fraser, ed., *Melville and Leven* (1890), II, 55–9.

17. *A.P.S.*, XI, 127; Hume, *Diary*, 137–9.

18. *A.P.S.*, XI, 136–7.

19. N.L.S., MS 7121, No. 40.

20. *A.P.S.*, XI, 177–8.

21. *A.P.S.*, XI, 43, 47, 76.

22. *A.P.S.*, XI, 161. 'Secret service' work was the explanation put before Godolphin on 20 November 1705—*Mar and Kellie Papers*, I, 238–9.

23. *A.P.S.*, XI, 204.

24. *Seafield Correspondence* (S.H.S., 1912), 379.

25. *A.P.S.*, XI, 174, 187.

26. *Seafield Correspondence*, 382.

27. *A.P.S.*, XI, 152.

28. N.L.S., MS 7121, Tweeddale to Godolphin, 14 July 1704.

29. *Ibid.*, Tweeddale to Godolphin, 6 August 1704.

30. *Seafield Correspondence*, 378–9.

31. Daniel Defoe, *History of the Union*, 84–91; Burnet, *History*, II, 763–4.

32. For this controversy, see William Ferguson, 'Imperial Crowns: a Neglected Facet of the Background to the Treaty of Union of 1707', in *S.H.R.*, LIII, 22–44.

33. *Parliamentary History*, VI, 368–74; *Vernon Letters*, III, 279–82.

34. *Jerviswood Correspondence*, 16.

35. Defoe, *History*, 86.

36. Mackinnon, *Union*, 190.

37. Riley, *art. cit.*, *E.H.R.*, LXXXIV, 508–9; *Jerviswood Correspondence*, 12–13, Roxburghe to Baillie, 30 Nov. 1704.

38. *Jerviswood Correspondence*, 30, 38, 42.

39. *Ibid.*, 31 *ff*.

40. *Ibid.*, 46–7.

41. *Ibid.*, 47.

42. Riley, *art. cit.*, *E.H.R.*, LXXXIV, 508–9.

43. Sir R. Temple, *New Light on the Tragedy of the 'Worcester'* (1930), gives the best account.

44. *Seafield Letters*, 27.

45. *Jerviswood Correspondence*, 66.

46. *Ibid.*, 77–8.

47. *Seafield Letters*, 36–8, 40, 45—and *passim*.

48. See his correspondence in 9th Duke of Argyll, ed., *Intimate Society Letters of the Eighteenth Century*, I, 1–62. The letter referred to is dated 6 April 1705, 11–12.

49. *Ibid.*, 14–15.

50. 'Letters from Queen Anne to Godolphin', ed. G. Davies, *S.H.R.*, XIX (1922), 191–2.

51. Lockhart, *Memoirs*, 133.

52. Cunningham, *History*, I, 419.

53. *A.P.S.*, XI, 213–14.

54. Argyll, ed., *Intimate Society Letters*, I, 25–6.

55. *Jerviswood Correspondence*, 105.

56. Hume Brown, *Legislative Union*, 94–5.

57. Lockhart, *Memoirs*, 142–3.

58. *A.P.S.*, XI, 215.

59. *A.P.S.*, XI, 216.

60. W. D. Macray, ed., *Correspondence of Colonel N. Hooke* (Roxburghe Club, 1870), I, 279–80, 291; Mackinnon, *Union*, 276–9.

61. *Seafield Letters*, 84–5.

62. The full text is in *A.P.S.*, XI, 295.

63. Bruce, *Report on Union*, I, 76 (1604); *ibid.*, 234 (1689); 217 (1670); 248–9 (1702).

64. *Jerviswood Correspondence*, 114.

65. Lockhart, *Memoirs*, 170–7.

66. Cunningham, *History*, I, 426–7.

67. *Seafield Letters*, 71–2.

68. *A.P.S.*, XI, 237; Hume, *Diary*, 171, where 'carried by about 40' is evidently a mistake; Lockhart, *Memoirs*, 169–72.

69. Lockhart, *Memoirs*, 172.

70. H.M.C., *11th Report (1887) Pt. VI, Hamilton Ms.*, 201–2.

Chapter 13

1. Riley, *art. cit.*, *E.H.R.*, 509–12.

2. Burnet, *History*, II, 780; that Burnet quite despaired of union, *ibid.*, 798–9.

3. Clerk, *Memoirs*, 58.

4. Hume Brown, *Legislative Union*, 104.

5. *Jerviswood Correspondence*, 138. *Cf.*, *ibid.*, 28, 44.

6. *Parliamentary History*, VI, 476; Burnet, *History*, II, 786.

7. H.M.C., *Mar and Kellie*, I, 239.

8. *Ibid.*, I, 243, for Stair's views; and 250–1 for Carstares'.

9. Burnet, *History*, II, 792.

10. Mackinnon, *Union*, 219.

11. Riley, *art. cit.*, *E.H.R.*, 514–15.

12. *Carstares State Papers*, 742, 749 (both in French).

13. *Ibid.*, 743–4.

14. H.M.C., *Rept. XIV*, App. III, *Marchmont MS.*, 158.

15. *A.P.S.*, XI, App., 165–6; Clerk, *Memoirs*, 60.

16. The Articles of the Treaty of Union of 1707 are printed in *A.P.S.*, XI, 406–13, and App., 201–5; also the English Act in *Statutes at Large*, IV (1763), 223–34. The Scottish Act is also printed in G. S. Pryde, *The Treaty of Union of 1707* (1950), 83–102; *Source Book of Scottish History*, III, 480–94, and in G. Donaldson, *Scottish Documents* (1970), 268–77. The best account of the proceedings of the commissions is in *A.P.S.*, XI, App., 162–200. The best commentaries are provided by J. H. Burton, *History of Scotland*, VIII, 118–35, and P. Hume Brown, *History of Scotland* (edn., 1911), III, 81–7; and there is a somewhat rambling account in Mackinnon, *Union*, 225–38.

17. A. Dewar Gibb, *Law from over the Border: a short account of a Strange Jurisdiction* (1950).

18. Clerk's *Memoirs*, 64.

19. A. M. Carstairs, 'Some Economic Aspects of the Union of the Parliaments', in *Scottish Journal of Political Economy*, II, 61–72; Theodora Pagan, *The Convention of the Royal Burghs of Scotland* (1926), 196–8; and *A.P.S.*, XI, 325, 'Address of Merchants and Trades of the City of Glasgow'.

20. H.M.C., *Portland*, IV (1897), 68, Paterson to Harley, 25 Sept., 1703. See, too, Ferguson, *art. cit.*, *S.H.R.* (1974).

21. N. T. Phillipson, 'Culture and Society in the 18th Century Province: The Case of

Edinburgh in the Scottish Enlightenment', in Lawrence Stone, ed., *The University in Society* (1974), II, 408–9.

22. D. A. G. Waddell, 'An English Economist's View of the Union', in *S.H.R.*, XXXV (1956), 144–9.

23. *D.N.B.*

24. Howells, *State Trials*, XIV, 1371–95. For some account of Harley's extensive intelligence service, see Angus MacInnes, *Robert Harley: Puritan Politician* (1970).

25. Seton of Pitmedden, *Scotland's Great Advantages by a Union with England*, 11. For a useful discussion of the pamphlet literature, see Mackinnon, *Union*, ch. VIII.

26. The most recent account of the economic arguments is in T. C. Smout, *Scottish Trade on the Eve of Union*, ch. XII.

27. *A.P.S.*, XI, 221, 10 Aug., 1705.

28. James Hodges, *The Rights and Interests of the Two British Monarchies*, Treatise I (1703), 10.

29. *A Letter from Mr Hodges at London to a Member of the Parliament of Scotland* (1703), 4.

30. Hodges, *British Monarchies*, Tr. I, 45.

31. Sir James Fergusson, ed., *Declaration of Arbroath* (1970), 41.

32. James Anderson, *An Historical Essay, showing that the Crown and Kingdom of Scotland is Imperial and Independent* (1705), 15.

33. Law Mathieson, *Scotland and the Union*, 121.

34. Hodges, *A Letter etc.*, 3–4.

35. Hodges, *British Monarchies*, Tr. III (1706), 8.

36. *Ibid.*, 12.

37. Defoe, *History of the Union* (edn., 1786), 223.

38. H.M.C., *Rept. XIV, 3 Seafield*, 198, 17 July 1703; *ibid.*, 13 July 1704, 203, and also 207, 9 Aug., 1705; *Jerviswood Correspondence*, 28.

39. For Marlborough's views, see W. Coxe, *Marlborough*, II, 176–7, and Fraser, ed., *Melville and Leven*, II, 212. The quotation from Hodges is from p. 85 of the pamphlet cited, *War Betwixt the Two British Kingdoms Considered*. For the dependence of Marlborough on Ireland and Scotland for troops, see B. Van 'T Hoff, ed., *Correspondence of Marlborough and Heinsius* (1951), 80.

40. Curtis Brown, *Letters of Queen Anne*, 190–1.

41. Cunningham, *History*, I, 420.

42. J. Hill Burton, *History*, VIII, 130–1.

43. H.M.C., *Mar and Kellie*, I, 369.

44. *Ibid.*, 285. Cromartie was a slippery customer, as even Mar found: *cf.* Fraser, *Cromartie*, II, 'Correspondence of George First Earl of Cromartie', 1–56.

45. H.M.C., *Mar and Kellie*, I, 255.

46. *Seafield Correspondence*, 385, Belhaven to Seafield, 24 February, 1705.

47. H.M.C., *Mar and Kellie* I, 312–14.

48. *Ibid.*, I, 286.

49. John, 7th Duke of Atholl, ed., *Chronicles of Atholl and Tullibardine Families* (1908), II, 57, 58, 73. Riley, *art. cit.*, *E.H.R.*, 525–6, suggests that Atholl may have assigned his dues to his brother Dunmore as payment of a debt, but there is no record of payment of £1,000 to Dunmore.

50. Lockhart, *Memoirs*, App. 405–20. For Lockhart's appointment to the commission, see A. Aufrere, ed., *Lockhart Papers* (1817), I, 324–5; the commissioners found much that was amiss—*Parliamentary History*, VI, 1110–16—but the matter was hushed up.

51. H.M.C., *Portland*, V, 114, Glasgow to Oxford, 22 November 1711.

52. Sir Tresham Lever, *Godolphin* (1952), 180–1, citing *B. M. Add.*, MS 34, 180, f i.

53. H.M.C., *Portland*, V, 100, Glasgow to Mar, 15 October 1711.

54. *Jerviswood Correspondence*, 190.

55. H.M.C., *Mar and Kellie*, I, 379.

56. *Ibid.*, I, 270.

57. *Ibid.*, 279.

58. Lockhart, *Memoirs*, 216.

59. H.M.C., *Mar and Kellie*, I, 288–304; *Seafield Letters*, 96, Seafield to Godolphin, 14 October 1706.

60. Annie M. Mackenzie, ed. and tr., *Orain Iain Luim* (*Scottish Gaelic Texts Society*, 1964), 222–9.

61. M. P. McDiarmid, ed., *The Poems of Robert Fergusson* (S.T.S., 1956), II, 143.

62. Henley and Henderson, eds., *The Poetry of Robert Burns* (1897), III, 128.

63. Malcolm Laing, *History of Scotland* (edn., 1800), II, 374.

64. H.M.C., *Portland*, IV, 398.

65. For this see Bruce, *Report on Union*, I, 362.

66. Edward Hughes, *Studies in Administration and Finance, 1558–1825* (1934), 338.

67. *Seafield Letters*, 94.

68. *National Register of Archives* (*Scotland*), Report 800, Sir William Fraser's MSS., p. 14.

69. *A.P.S.*, XI, 320–2, for the passing of the act; *ibid.*, 402–3, for its terms; and for an excellent commentary on the act and its effects, see R. H. Story, ed., *The Church of Scotland: Past and Present* (1890), IV, 37–8.

Chapter 14

1. Lockhart, *Memoirs*, 218–19.

2. Defoe, *Union*, 236. For the cause of Hamilton's indisposition, see Duke of Argyll, ed., *Intimate Letters*, I, 55, Leven to Godolphin, 26 October 1706.

3. Lockhart, *Memoirs*, 222.

4. Defoe, *Union*, 236–84; Lockhart, *Memoirs*, 215 *ff.*, esp. 218–29.

5. H.M.C., *Mar and Kellie*, I, 329.

6. Defoe, *op. cit.*, 237–8; Lockhart, *op. cit.*, 223–8; *A.P.S.*, XI, 309–10; Hume, *Diary*, 176–7.

7. *Edinburgh Review*, October 1892, 518.

8. Sir William Fraser, ed., *Melville and Leven*, II, 205.

9. *A.P.S.*, XI, 305–6.

10. *Seafield Letters*, 93; Hume, *Diary*, 172–3.

11. Lockhart, *Memoirs*, 221. On the first day of the session the government had a majority in an election dispute, which Seafield took as a good omen—*Seafield Letters*, 93; but Mar was more circumspect—H.M.C., *Mar and Kellie*, I, 283–4.

12. *Seafield Letters*, 94–8.

13. *Ibid.*; Defoe, *Union*, 230.

14. *A.P.S.*, XI, 307; Hume, *Diary*, 173–4; Lockhart, *Memoirs*, 220–2; Defoe, *Union*, 288–90.

15. *A.P.S.*, XI, 311–12; Hume, *Diary*, 178–9.

16. Defoe, *Union*, 308. This work is at its best for the session of 1706, which is given lengthy if rather partisan treatment.

17. *A Speech in the Parliament of Scotland, the Second Day of November, 1706*, by William Seton of Pitmedden, junior (1706).

18. Belhaven's speech is in Defoe, *History*, 317–28; for its effect, *Seafield Letters*, 100. It was printed as *The Lord Beilhaven's Speech in the Scotch Parliament Saturday the Second of November* (1706), and frequently reprinted thereafter.

19. Frank H. Ellis, ed., *Poems on Affairs of State: Augustan Satirical Verse, 1660–1714*, VII (1975), 216.

20. Lockhart, *Memoirs*, 252–3.

21. For the incident, Hume, *Diary*, 179; for Mar's interpretation, H.M.C., *Mar and Kellie*, I, 313.

22. *A.P.S.*, XI, 313.

23. *Ibid.*, 312–13.

24. *Ibid.*, 313–15.

25. Hume, *Diary*, 179.

26. *Ibid.*, 182–3.

27. *The Lord Beilhaven's Second Speech in Parliament, the Fifteenth Day of November, 1706, on the Second Article of the Treaty* (1706).

28. *A.P.S.*, XI, 326–7.

29. *Ibid.*, 322.

30. *Ibid.*, 333–4.

31. *A.P.S.*, XI, 328; Defoe, *Union*, 354–5, for Annandale's speech; Hume, *Diary*, 183–4, for Hamilton's.

32. Defoe, *op. cit.*, 360–3.

33. Clerk, *Memoirs*, 49.

34. Defoe, *Union*, 364.

35. *A.P.S.*, XI, 329–30.

36. *Ibid.*, 332.

37. *Ibid.*, 375–6.

38. Lockhart, *Memoirs*, 285–90.

39. *A.P.S.*, XI, 371–2.

40. Lockhart, *Memoirs*, 325.

41. *Ibid.*, 293–327.

42. *Ibid.*, 235.

43. *A.P.S.*, XI, 386–7.

44. *Ibid.*, 402–14.

45. H.M.C., *Mar and Kellie*, I, 367–9, 370–2; *Jerviswood Correspondence*, 183–9.

46. H.M.C., *Mar and Kellie*, I, 379, for the Squadrone's expectations; Clerk, *Memoirs*, 67–9, for the commission.

47. H.M.C., *Mar and Kellie*, I, 389.

48. Reg. Ho. (S.R.O.), P.C. 1/53, 507–8.

49. Mackinnon, *Union*, 326.

50. George Eyre Todd, *History of Glasgow*, III (1934), 66–71.

51. Rosalind K. Marshall, *The Days of Duchess Anne* (1973), 220.

52. Reg. Ho. (S.R.O.), P.C. 1/53, 492.

53. William McDowall, *History of Dumfries* (1867), 548–54.

54. Lockhart, *Memoirs*, 283.

55. See Andrew Lang in *The Union of 1707* (1907), chs. VII and VIII.

56. Annie A. Mackenzie, ed., *Orain Iain Luim*, 'A Song Against the Union', 225–6.

57. H.M.C., *Mar and Kellie*, I, 353.

58. Defoe, *Union*, 481.

59. Abel Boyer, *History of Reign of Queen Anne, 1706–07* (1707), 439–40.

60. See *Commons Journal*, XV, 272–317 passim; *Parliamentary History*, VI, 543–83.

61. *Parliamentary History*, VI, 563–5.

62. Burnet, *History*, II, 802; *Parliamentary History*, VI, 555–6.

63. Coxe, *Marlborough*, II (1818), 180.

64. *Parliamentary History*, VI, 477; Trevelyan, *Ramillies and the Union*, 247–9.

65. H.M.C., *Mar and Kellie*, I, 389.

66. Clerk, *Memoirs*, 67–8.

67. Bruce, *Union*, II, dxlviii–dxlix.

68. John Cunningham, *Ad . . . Annam . . . De Optatissima nostra cum Scotis Conjunctione et Coalitione ORATIO* (1707).

69. Daniel Defoe, 'A Scots Poem: Or a New-Year's Gift, From a Native of the Universe, to His Fellow-Animals in Albania', in Ellis, *op. cit.*, 238–82.

70. *The Union, A Poem . . . for the Scotch Union. By Mr. Vernon* (1707).

71. H. Williams, ed., *The Poems of Jonathan Swift* (1958), I, 96.

72. J. A. Froude, *The English in Ireland in the Eighteenth Century* (1881), I, Bk. II, Ch. II, 317–39; J. C. Beckett, *The Making of Modern Ireland* (1966), 156–7; and R. Dudley Edwards, *A New History of Ireland* (1972), 138–9.

73. T. F. T. Plucknett, ed., *Taswell-Langmead's English Constitutional History* (10th edn., 1946), 528.

74. On this point see Edith Mary Johnston, *Ireland in the Eighteenth Century* (*Gill History of Ireland*, vol. 8, 1974), ch. 3, and 193–5; Miss Johnston, however, tends to minimise the differences.

75. It is discussed in diffuse fashion by Mackinnon, *Union*, chs. XI–XV; in rather superficial and erratic vein by Sir Reginald Coupland, *Welsh and Scottish Nationalism* (1954); and outlined very sketchily in Pryde, *Union*.

76. Fraser, ed., *Cromartie Correspondence* (1876), II, 1–2.

77. Coupland, *op. cit.*, 330–1, where, however, the reference is to federalism.

Further Reading

SINCE surprisingly little has been written on the specific theme of Anglo-Scottish relations, a short selective guide rather than a swollen and pretentious bibliography seems more appropriate. In general, primary sources and articles in learned journals will not be listed here. Rather, the object is to include the most useful secondary works, and particularly those that have references and good bibliographies that can direct the reader to the primary sources.

There is a notable dearth of wide-ranging surveys. G. W. T. Omond's *Early History of the Scottish Union Question* (1897) and R. S. Rait's *Outline of the Relations between England and Scotland, 500–1707* (1901) are not only slight and outdated but skimped of reference. More reliable information, with references to the primary material, can be found in the relevant volumes of two recent historical series: the *Oxford History of England*, general editor G. N. Clark, and the *Edinburgh History of Scotland*, general editor Gordon Donaldson. Volumes from these series are cited in the appropriate places below, with the former series designated as *O.H.* and the latter as *E.H.*

For earliest times, Cyril Fox, *The Personality of Britain: Its Influence on Inhabitant and Invader in Prehistoric and Early Historic Times* (var. edns.), is a brilliant demonstration of the complex interaction of topography, archaeology and history. Kenneth Jackson, *Language and History in Early Britain: a chronological survey of the Brittonic Languages 1st. to 12th. c. A.D.* (1953), accentuates the importance of the linguistic approach. The importance of language is vindicated in a different way, and much sound information and valuable references provided, by W. J. Watson, *The History of the Celtic Place-Names of Scotland* (1926), a surprisingly fresh and readable book.

On the more purely historical side, R. G. Collingwood and J. N. L. Myres, *Roman Britain and the English Settlements*, *O.H.* (2nd. edn., 1945), has become a classic, though it is now in some respects superseded. Sir F. M. Stenton, *Anglo-Saxon England*, *O.H.* (3rd. edn., 1971), is a brilliant and scholarly synthesis which has so far triumphantly withstood the ravages of time. R. H. Hodgkin, *A History of the Anglo-Saxons*, 2 vols. (1935), is very readable and well illustrated but lacks the authority of Stenton's great book. Peter Hunter Blair has produced an excellent survey, *Roman Britain and Early England* (1963), and a stimulating topical work, *An Introduction to Anglo-Saxon England* (1966).

D. P. Kirby, *The Making of Early England* (1967), may also be mentioned. H. M. Chadwick's *Early Scotland* (1949) does not reveal this distinguished scholar at his best. A. A. M. Duncan, *Scotland: The Making of the Kingdom*, *E.H.* (1975), is a learned and vigorous account from earliest times to 1286, which appeared too late for full advantage to be taken of it in the present work. R. L. G. Ritchie's *The Normans in Scotland* (1954) is scholarly and readable but tends to overstress 'Norman' influence. In miniscule scale compared to Professor Duncan, Gordon Menzies, ed., *Who Are the Scots?* (1971), is a stimulating collection of essays by various hands on Dark Age and early medieval themes.

Some important digests and collections from the early evidence compel inclusion. Two seminal works by A. O. A. Anderson remain essential: *Scottish Annals from English Chronicles* (1908) and *The Early Sources of Scottish History*, 2 vols. (1922). William Croft Dickinson, Gordon Donaldson and Isabel A. Milne, eds., *A Source Book of Scottish History from Earliest Times to 1424* (2nd. edn., 1958), gives a good coverage with valuable introductions and commentaries. E. L. G. Stones, ed., *Anglo-Scottish Relations 1174–1328: Some Selected Documents* (1965), provides impeccably edited texts and good translations.

G. W. S. Barrow has contributed greatly to the study of early medieval Scotland, most notably perhaps in his two volumes in the *Regesta Regum Scottorum*, vol. I, *Malcolm IV* (1960), and vol. II, *William I* (1971), each with an invaluable introduction. Professor Barrow's collected papers, *The Kingdom of the Scots* (1973), and his study of *Robert Bruce and the Community of the Realm of Scotland* (1965) are also essential reading, though some of the conclusions of the latter have been challenged. On the English side of this period Sir Maurice Powicke, *King Henry III and the Lord Edward: The Community of the Realm in the Thirteenth Century*, 2 vols. (1947), and the same author's *The Thirteenth Century*, *O.H.* (2nd. edn., 1962), are works of the highest scholarship but not at their best on Anglo-Scottish relations.

For the period 1286–1513, Ranald G. Nicholson's exhaustive *Scotland: The Later Middle Ages*, *E.H.* (1974), is indispensable alike for its convincing synthesis of this notoriously difficult period and its rich documentation. The same author's *Edward III and the Scots* (1963) is a definitive treatise. Gordon Menzies, ed., *The Scottish Nation* (1972) is another collection of essays, though of variable quality. Three biographies have much to say on the problem of Anglo-Scottish relations: E. W. M. Balfour Melville's thorough but plodding *James I* (1936); A. I. Dunlop's learned but somewhat shapeless *Life and Times of James Kennedy, Bishop of St Andrews* (1950); and R. L. Mackie's lively and scholarly, though in places superficial, *James IV* (1958). May McKisack, *The Fourteenth Century*, *O.H.* (1959), makes little of Anglo-Scottish relations, and while there is much in E. F. Jacob's *The Fifteenth Century*, *O.H.* (1961), it is poorly presented. Of more specialised works, Agnes Conway, *Henry VII's Relations with Scotland and Ireland, 1485–1498* (1932), is a good treatment; less substantial is R. G. Eaves, *Henry VIII's Scottish Diplomacy 1513–1542* (1971); and A. J. Slavin, *Politics and Profit, a Study of Sir Ralph Sadler 1507–1547* (1966) provides more illumination.

The sixteenth century as a whole is well covered by Gordon Donaldson in *Scotland: James V to James VII*, E.H. (1965); and J. D. Mackie, *The Earlier Tudors*, O.H. (1952), and J. B. Black, *The Reign of Elizabeth*, O.H. (2nd. edn., 1959), are very good on the relations between England and Scotland. R. B. Wernham, *Before the Armada—the Growth of English Foreign Policy, 1485–1588* (1966), takes full stock of Anglo-Scottish relations and demonstrates their importance in the tortuous web of sixteenth-century diplomacy. So also do Dickinson, Donaldson and Milne, eds., *A Source Book of Scottish History, vol. II, 1424 to 1567* (2nd. edn., 1958). Conyers Read, *Mr Secretary Cecil and Queen Elizabeth* (1955), is a hard read, but quotes freely from contemporary documents and puts the Reformation-Rebellion in Scotland into a new and more convincing perspective. Two fine books point and counterpoint each other, showing not only the similarities between the Reformation in England and Scotland but also the sharp contrasts: Gordon Donaldson, *The Scottish Reformation* (1960), and A. G. Dickens, *The English Reformation* (1964). In one brief monograph, *The Early Elizabethan Succession Question, 1558–1568* (1966), Mortimer Levine almost does more to elucidate the central problem of the time than does the entire corpus of Mariana, with its virulent charges and heart-rending rebuttals, while the later manifestations of the same problem are ably dealt with in Helen G. Stafford, *James VI of Scotland and the Throne of England* (1940). These matters, as well, of course, as others, are also touched upon in Douglas Nobbs, *England and Scotland, 1560–1707* (1952), which, though slight, contains some acute observations.

Little has been written specifically on the Union of the Crowns, but seventeenth-century English history has occasioned a rich and varied crop of studies centred mainly on the Civil War and Interregnum. In spite of new, largely sociological, approaches older works like S. R. Gardiner's *History of England 1603–42*, 10 vols. (1887, 1884–89), *History of the Great Civil War 1642–49*, 3 vols. (2nd. edn., 1888–91) and C. H. Firth's *Last Years of the Protectorate*, 2 vols. (1909) are still important. More recently numerous works by Christopher Hill have illuminated this period, particularly his *Economic Problems of the Church from Archbishop Whitgift to the Long Parliament* (1956) and *Puritanism and Revolution* (Panther edn., 1968). C. V. Wedgwood, *The King's Peace 1637–1641* (1955) and its sequel, *The King's War 1641–47* (1958) gives a thorough and well-written synthesis which covers not only England but Scotland and Ireland as well. This is a particularly commendable feature of Miss Wedgwood's work, for a marked weakness in the recent literature has been the adoption of a silly and disparaging approach to Scottish history by many English historians, which usually proves either that they cannot bother to do their homework or that their prejudices are invincible. For whatever reason, this defect flaws an otherwise praiseworthy attempt at synthesis by Ivan Roots, *The Great Rebellion 1642–1660* (1966). To some extent this defect is made good by David Stevenson, *The Scottish Revolution 1637–42* (1973), which is, however, thorough on the facts but over-sparing of interpretation. An excellent but strangely neglected work is J. H. Hexter, *The Reign of King Pym* (1941), which emphasises Pym's rôle in promoting an alliance between covenanters and parliamentarians. R. L. Orr, *Alexander Henderson, Churchman and Statesman* (1919), also casts interesting light on that matter, particularly with regard to the making of the Solemn League and Covenant.

Numerous volumes of documents provide essential reading, not just for the documents they contain but also for their valuable introductions. The Scottish History Society has made notable contributions in this way, as, for example: G. M. Paul, ed., *Johnston of Wariston's Diary, 1632–1639* (1911), vol. II, 1650–54, ed. D. H. Fleming, and vol. III, ed. J. D. Ogilvie (1940); C. S. Terry, ed., *The Army of the Covenant 1643–1647*, 2 vols. (1917); S. R. Gardiner, ed., *Charles II and Scotland in 1650* (1894); C. S. Terry, ed., *The Cromwellian Union* (1902); and C. H. Firth, ed., *Scotland and the Commonwealth* (1895) and *Scotland and the Protectorate* (1899). Of importance too are A. F. Mitchell and G. Struthers, eds., *Minutes of the Westminster Assembly 1644–49* (1879), and H. W. Meikle, ed., *The Correspondence of the Scots Commissioners in London, 1644–1646* (Roxburghe Club, 1917). For the Cromwellian union, and indeed all the various attempts at union up to and including 1707, John Bruce, *Report on the Union of England and Scotland*, 2 vols. (1799) remains basic.

For the Restoration and Revolution periods A. Browning, ed., *English Historical Documents 1660–1714* (1953) gives excellent documentary coverage and a typically concise, lucid and penetrating introduction. Still in the documentary vein, Dickinson and Donaldson, eds., *A Source Book of Scottish History, vol. III, 1567 to 1707* (2nd. edn., 1961), is here at its bulkiest and best. Some biographies are helpful, most notably K. D. H. Haley, *The First Earl of Shaftesbury* (1968), a brilliant and thoroughly researched work, far superior to most historical biographies, that clarifies many matters as well as its protean subject. There is no comparable Scottish political biography in this period, those of Lauderdale by W. C. Mackenzie (1923), of Mackenzie of Rosehaugh by Andrew Lang (1909), of Sir Robert Moray by Archibald Robertson (1922), and (best of all but still limited) of Graham of Claverhouse by C. S. Terry (1905), all being unsatisfactory.

The Revolution and the Union are dealt with in W. Ferguson, *Scotland: 1689 to the Present, E.H.* (1968). The Company of Scotland and its activities are best covered in Frank Cundall, *The Darien Venture* (1927); F. R. Hart, *The Disaster of Darien* (1929); and, somewhat melodramatically, by G. P. Insh, *The Company of Scotland* (1932), and, less dramatically, in the same author's edition of *Darien Shipping Papers 1696–1707* (SHS, 1927). On economic developments T. C. Smout, *Scottish Trade on the Eve of Union 1660–1707* (1963) is sprightly but seriously flawed. Theodora Keith, *The Commercial Relations of England and Scotland 1603–1707* (1910) takes more notice of economic friction between the two kingdoms and remains an important pioneer study. L. A. Harper, *The English Navigation Laws* (1939), is an exhaustive examination of these involved matters. On the economic front a wealth of information can be gleaned from W. R. Scott's *The Constitution and Finance of English, Scottish, and Irish Joint Stock Companies to 1720*, 3 vols. (1910–12).

On the union of 1707, Daniel Defoe, *History of the Union* (edn., 1786), is a classical account that requires considerable care in handling. The best comprehensive study is still James Mackinnon, *The Union of England and Scotland* (1896), which, though prolix and badly dated in some ways, strives to be fair to all concerned. P. Hume Brown, *The Legislative Union of England and Scotland* (1914), is also valuable though marred by some unfortunate slips. G. S. Pryde, *The Treaty of Union of Scotland and England 1707* (1950), is a brief, trenchant summary of the Whig interpretation of this particular piece of history, of which G. M. Trevelyan, *Ramillies and the Union with Scotland* (1932) is the full-blown account. Most of the leading politicians involved have so far been lucky enough to escape the attention of biographers, and those who have been tackled have escaped lightly: notably Godolphin by Sir Tresham Lever (1950); Fletcher of Saltoun, in a slight but useful life, by G. W. T. Omond (1897); and Harley by Angus McInnes (1970), which concentrates more on this remarkable statesman's 'intelligence system'.

Index

309